Shared Source CLI Essentials

Shared Source CLI Essentials

David Stutz, Ted Neward,
and Geoff Shilling

O'REILLY®

Beijing · Cambridge · Farnham · Köln · Paris · Sebastopol · Taipei · Tokyo

Shared Source CLI Essentials
by David Stutz, Ted Neward, and Geoff Shilling

Copyright © 2003 O'Reilly & Associates, Inc. All rights reserved.
Printed in the United States of America.

Published by O'Reilly & Associates, Inc., 1005 Gravenstein Highway North, Sebastopol, CA 95472.

O'Reilly & Associates books may be purchased for educational, business, or sales promotional use. Online editions are also available for most titles (*safari.oreilly.com*). For more information, contact our corporate/institutional sales department: (800) 998-9938 or *corporate@oreilly.com*.

Editor:	Brian Jepson
Production Editor:	Sarah Sherman
Cover Designer:	Emma Colby
Interior Designer:	David Futato

Printing History:

March 2003:	First Edition.

ISBN: 0-596-00351-X

[M]

Table of Contents

Preface

Version 1.0 of the Microsoft Shared Source CLI (still affectionately referred to by many as "Rotor," its code name) was released to the programming community at large in November of 2002. It is a portable implementation of the programming tools and libraries that make up the ECMA-335 CLI standard, distributed as source code.

The fascination that source code holds for programmers has long been known at Microsoft, yet it remains an unusual way for Redmond to distribute its software. In the case of Rotor, however, the choice was obvious: for experimentation, learning, and as a teaching vehicle, source code has no peer. There is no finer way to learn about any computer standard than to browse and tinker with an implementation directly.

This book is a companion to Rotor's code. It illustrates the design principles used in the CLI standard, using Rotor's own implementation of that standard. More broadly, this book is about virtual machines, and the illusions, trapdoors, invisible linkages, and hidden levers from which they are built. Complex software systems, and the ways in which they bridge the abstract world of the programmer with the physical world of a computational model frozen in silicon, are invariably a fascinating topic.

The Rotor Distribution

Over five years ago, I wrote a memo outlining how and why Microsoft should invest in building a companion runtime to its then current Component Object Model (COM). This idea was not new, either inside or outside of Microsoft; products were already shipping for this purpose in the form of C++ frameworks and integrated development tools, such as Delphi and Visual Basic. The popularity of these language-specific approaches made it clear that the technical community was ready to accept features in their everyday tools and APIs that had once served to distinguish programming languages from one another, such as direct support for thread-based concurrency, structured exception handling, garbage collection, and the runtime enforcement of typesafety.

The technologies that made up the list of features in the original proposal had been waiting in the wings (for decades, in some cases), and some were already available to programmers as Windows APIs. Augmenting these APIs with a library implementation that could be shared in place of a growing number of subtly incompatible and overlapping component runtimes made obvious sense. A small team was empaneled by David Vaskevitch to flesh out the details and to make an initial technical proposal, which was run through Microsoft's somewhat harrowing consensus-building process. Having been deemed a Good Idea, the proposal became the initial strawman for the product now called the Microsoft .NET Framework.

Very early in the development of the .NET Framework, there was discussion of creating a source-code distribution of the technology for researchers, academics, and experimenters. This discussion was spurred by Microsoft's desire to attract a critical mass of developers, toolmakers, and innovative software products to the new platform. Realizing that having a portable implementation of the CLI was important for both standardization purposes and for the research community, Paul Maritz sponsored the formation of a small team under Geoff Shilling to explore the idea and begin implementation plans. With help from many individuals, both inside Microsoft and out, Geoff's small team developed and built the Shared Source CLI.

In the interim between memo and product, a wonderful thing happened. While the original goal had been to provide a core set of modern services for COM programmers, what emerged five years later was far more useful. The original runtime library, in the hands of Brian Harry, Mike Toutonghi, and a talented cast of thousands, had become a complete, general-purpose virtual execution model. Even better, this model had been carefully refined as it was shepherded through the ECMA specification and standardization process by Jim Miller. The CLI standard had been born.

The CLI, at its heart, is an approach to building software that enables code from many independent sources to coexist and interoperate safely. The intent of its design is not simply to sweep gnarly hardware and device-driver details under the rug in the form of a "universal virtual machine," but rather to build a virtual computational model that can be brought up safely within existing host environments and can expose the native capabilities of these environments directly. The design implications that come along for the ride are profound, and they are explored at length within this book.

To use any or all of Rotor's rich codebase for your own noncommercial purposes, read and abide by the simple, one page shared license that accompanies the code. The code can be found on the CD that accompanies this book, along with additional documentation and related materials. As with any collaborative effort, this CD is only a snapshot in time; go to Rotor's homepage on MSDN (*http://msdn.microsoft.com/net/sscli*) or to *http://www.sscli.net* for details about current versions or other late-breaking information.

Rotor is now in your hands. It is no longer a Microsoft-only endeavor, but rather an ongoing collaboration with all of you who wish to enhance and extend the CLI standard. Because Rotor takes the form of source code, it is easy for interested individuals to offer suggestions, upgrade or patch the implementation, and offer support. This book will help you participate by furnishing context; I hope that you enjoy discovering the fine points of the CLI as much as we have enjoyed writing about them!

—David Stutz
Redmond, Washington
November 24, 2002

Who Should Read This Book

This book is not about the C# language, the Visual Basic .NET language, the Base Class Libraries (BCLs), or any other part of the .NET Framework that has received marketing attention and lots of press coverage. This book is about the one piece of the .NET Framework that makes all of the above possible: the CLI standard. As standardized runtime plumbing, it plays a critical role in Microsoft's .NET strategy. Its technical depth makes it an excellent subject for discourse.

To illustrate the finer points of the CLI standard, this book uses the Shared Source CLI as demonstration material. The book, however, is by no means a complete overview of Rotor. The compiler discussions, the detailed descriptions of its test harnesses, the coverage of BCL implementation details, and countless other subjects are missing. As a complex industrial codebase, Rotor deserves this kind of detailed attention; alas, this book isn't where you'll find it!

The target audience for this book falls mainly into four categories:

The research community
    There has long been tremendous interest in virtual machines, and Rotor's implementation of the CLI should provide many traditional research opportunities in areas, such as security, memory management, and code generation, as well as less traditional opportunities centered on the industrial, "real world" character of the heavily instrumented code.

The teaching community

Many curricula already include managed execution and its capabilities among their subjects, and Rotor should provide a bountiful experimental testbed within which to explore this topic. Compiler, systems, and architectural courses should all find teaching material in Rotor's codebase.

The professional community

Hordes of programmers, familiar with COM and C++, are moving to the .NET Framework with little or no familiarity with managed environments. Architects and team leaders will be asked hard questions, and Rotor's behind-the-scenes look at the .NET execution engine should provide them with excellent resources from which they can extract answers.

The community of CLI implementers

Rotor is intended to serve as a useful baseline when bringing the CLI to other platforms. While this group will undoubtedly be smaller than the other three, it will be this community that provides the most leveraged contribution, whether porting it to new platforms or using it as learning material for its own new implementations.

More informally, if you live and breathe for virtual machine specifications, such as the Java Virtual Machine specification or the Smalltalk "blue book," this book is definitely for you. If you have implemented a Scheme or a Forth compiler just for the heck of it, this book is for you. If you find yourself defending a favorite "misunderstood" programming language from Philistines who don't properly understand its boutique feature set or the intrinsic value of its totally hackable runtime and compiler, then this book is for you. In short, if you care about the internals of programming languages, developer tools, or runtime systems, this book should provide you with enjoyable reading.

How This Book Is Structured

The CLI provides a number of services to programming languages and tools that wish to produce *managed code*, and the runtime mechanisms needed to create and run *managed components* are the focus of this book. After introducing the CLI, its core concepts, and the Rotor implementation, the following topics are covered:

The CLI type system

Unlike some virtual execution environments, the type system is the heart of the CLI. Chapter 3 examines what constitutes a type, how types map into internal data structures and processor-specific values, and how Rotor implements the features found in the ECMA CLI specification.

Component packaging

Assemblies are the construct that the CLI uses to package executable code safely. Chapter 4 covers what assemblies are, how they are built and loaded, and what design goals they were intended to meet.

Type loading and JIT compilation

The ECMA CLI specification specifically states that CIL was designed to be transformed into native CPU instructions before being directly executed. Chapter 5 focuses on the details of how Rotor converts types, expressed as CIL and metadata, into native code, and what triggers this process.

Managed code

Running native code safely under the control of a virtual execution environment is not simple. Chapter 6 details the execution engine and how it uses mechanisms such as threads and exceptions to maintain control while also allowing extensive access to the underlying platform.

Garbage collection

The CLI provides a memory management model that frees programmers from the details and concerns of manually allocating and freeing memory. Chapter 7 explains how Rotor tracks the liveness of object references, how memory is allocated and released, and how finalization is implemented.

The Platform Adaptation Layer (PAL)

The PAL is what makes the Shared Source CLI easy to port, as demonstrated by running Win32, Mac OS X, and FreeBSD implementations. Chapter 9, which discusses the implementation of the PAL, will be especially interesting to anyone interested in porting Rotor to other platforms. It is also of general interest, however, since the PAL enumerates the systems constructs that are assumed to exist within the CLI specification.

In addition, this book contains four appendixes that discusses:

- The contents of the CD
- Where to obtain the Rotor source tree and how to build, install, and troubleshoot it
- How to port Rotor to other platforms
- Rotor macrology

Assumptions This Book Makes

Because this book uses industrial source code as its demonstration material, there are some fairly heavyweight assumptions made about our readers' familiarity with programming languages and systems.

We assume that you have some familiarity with C# or Java, as well as a good understanding of C++, which is what comprises most of the sample code in this book. The C++ used in the Rotor source is very straightforward and does not exercise the "dangerous" features of the language. A few examples use CIL or snippets of assembler. To understand these, a cursory knowledge of any assembly language should help. Because so many of the operating system interactions in Rotor are made via its Win32-based abstraction layer, you should have a basic familiarity with the Win32 API; although, again, this can be quite cursory.

References will be made to particular sections of the Rotor code without reproducing that code directly in the book's text. It is expected that readers will have downloaded the Rotor code (either from the Internet or from the CD), and will have walked through the code from the friendly confines of their favorite text editor, debugger, or development environment.

Rotor's code was originally drawn from the same codebase that is used to build the commercial .NET Framework. Several of its major subsystems were swapped out, and extensive changes were made to make the code approachable and more portable. In addition, numerous parts of the commercial product were removed because their presence would be irrelevant and confusing. Despite these significant changes, the code retains the complexity of a cutdown and transformed version of a larger work. Not all of its sections are pretty or easy to browse. For some, these imperfections will make the code appealing, since large, real-world codebases rarely see the light of day. If you are not one of these masochists, you may be occasionally frustrated as you follow our guided trip through the code. We apologize in advance, but exhort you to make the journey with us despite these minor inconveniences!

Online CLI Resources

Rotor's homepage can be found at *http://msdn.microsoft.com/net/sscli*. Rotor's online community (newly minted at the time this was written) can be found at *http://www.sscli.net*.

The official web home of ECMA and its standards specifications is *http://www.ecma.ch*, although the specifications for ECMA-334 and ECMA-335 are also widely mirrored.

OnDotNet (*http://www.ondotnet.com*) and its umbrella site, the O'Reilly Network (*http://www.oreillynet.com*) often have CLI and Rotor-related articles and weblog entries.

The University of Pisa hosts a .NET web site (*http://dotnet.di.unipi.it*) and Rotor-related mailing lists, as well as indexed source code and other resources. DevelopMentor hosts several CLI-related mailing lists, which are archived at *http://discuss.develop.com*. There is an active newsgroup at *nntp://microsoft.public.shared_source.cli*.

There are two significant open source projects built around the CLI specification: the Mono project (*http://www.go-mono.org*) and the DotGNU Portable .NET project (*http://www.southern-storm.com.au/portable_net.html*). Look to these sites for yet more interesting source code.

Conventions Used in This Book

The following font conventions appear in this book:

Italic is used for:

- New terms where they are defined
- Pathnames, filenames, URLs, and program names

Constant Width Bold is used for:

- Typed user input
- Emphasis within code samples and tables

Constant Width is used for:

- C++, CIL, and C# source code
- Assembler and CIL code
- Symbol and macro names

 This icon designates a note, which is an important aside to the nearby text.

 This icon designates a warning relating to the nearby text.

How to Contact Us

Please address comments and questions concerning this book to the publisher:

O'Reilly & Associates, Inc.
1005 Gravenstein Highway North
Sebastopol, CA 95472
(800) 998-9938 (in the United States or Canada)
(707) 829-0515 (international/local)
(707) 829-0104 (fax)

There is a web page for this book, which lists errata, examples, or any additional information. You can access this page at:

http://www.oreilly.com/catalog/sscli

To comment or ask technical questions about this book, send email to:

bookquestions@oreilly.com

For more information about books, conferences, Resource Centers, and the O'Reilly Network, see the O'Reilly web site at:

http://www.oreilly.com

Acknowledgments

David Stutz

This is my first attempt at a book. Thanks to my wife Beth, who bemusedly watched from her experienced vantage without making too many sarcastic comments, and to those who showed me the details, especially our editors Brian Jepson and John Osborn. I also thank Brian, Geoff, John, and Ted for their patience during occasional personal lacunae induced by two of the truly important things in life: winemaking and music-making.

Special thanks go to those who spent so much effort commenting on drafts, including Jan Kotas, John Norwood, Vladimir Fedorov, Eric Albert, and the rest of the Rotor team: Geoff, Barry, Mario, Stephe, and Pankaj. Jan, Vlad, and Barry kept me from telling outright technical lies (although I'm sure that I've slipped a few by them), and John's detailed review comments were invaluable.

Many of the implementers of Microsoft's .NET Framework also helped with the task of reviewing the text, including Jim Miller, Chris Brumme, Patrick Dussud, Ian Carmichael, Alan Shi, and George Bosworth. For both reviewing this book, and for transforming our original COM runtime proposal into today's CLI, thanks!

Microsoft Research provided much help in getting the word out about Rotor. In particular, the Cambridge research lab, run by Roger Needham with the help of his crack University Relations group of Pierre-Yves Saintoyant, Van Eden, and Bruno Quarta, along with Greg O'Shea, were indispensable. Just as important were reviewers and agitators external to Microsoft, including Peter Drayton, Jason Whittington, Jim Bennett, Chris Sells, Gary Nutt, Chris Tavares, and all of our O'Reilly technical reviewers. I'm sure that I've missed people here; to any of these, and to the web denizens who sent comments on posted chapters: thanks! We have been looking at Rotor's code for years, and your externally focused viewpoint helped give us a fresh perspective.

Finally, I'd like to thank Antonio Cisternino, Werner Vogels, Damien Watkins, and Yahya Mirza for helping to move the early Rotor community forward, and Miguel de Icaza for supporting and promoting the CLI standard within the open source community.

Ted Neward

This marks the fourth time I've written acknowledgments for a book, and I'm amazed each time at just what a good deal an author gets: people spend hours of sacrifice, dedication, hard work, and effort supporting an author's endeavors, and in return get their names mentioned in a brief paragraph or two.

I'm tremendously grateful to John Osborn, the .NET editor at O'Reilly & Associates, for introducing me to this project. At dinner one night while teaching in Boston, on the heels of *C# in a Nutshell*, John asked me if I was interested in speaking with somebody at Microsoft who was looking for an author to write about Rotor. I couldn't say yes fast enough and spent an anxious week waiting for John to get ahold of David Stutz and introduce the two of us. I flew up to Redmond a week later, met Dave and the rest of the Rotor team, and the results of that meeting rest in your hands. My deepest thanks to John for the opportunity.

To my coauthors, Dave and Geoff, I cannot express in words how much fun I've had on this project. I've enjoyed working with both of you and the rest of the Rotor team, in ways I never would have predicted.

It seems that every DevelopMentor instructor/author spends at least a sentence or two praising Don Box and Mike Abercrombie for the incredible and wonderful environment they created there; I'm no exception. I have never met a more supportive, technically sharp yet incredibly eloquent group of individuals in my life. Guys, you all humble me. In particular, I want to thank Jason Whittington and Peter Drayton, two guys who've labored through the Rotor code with me. If you ever get the chance to hear either one of them speak, do so.

Finally, I owe staggering debts of gratitude to my students, past, present, and future, for listening to (and encouraging!) my rants on technology, challenging me when I needed to be challenged, and exploiting all the weak points in my arguments; my wife Charlotte and my two sons, Michael and Matthew, who surrendered their husband and father to yet another book; and to my father, Lance Neward, who bought that Apple][+ back in 1978 instead of a new Volvo—no other single decision he has made, aside from marrying my mother, has so dramatically altered my life.

Geoff Shilling

This is my first time writing a book, and what a ride it has been. I wish to express my appreciation to my coauthors, David and Ted, for all their hard work, and to the folks at O'Reilly who were willing to go ahead with this project. To our editors Brian Jepson and John Osborn—I'm still not sure how you put up with us.

We had great help in reviewing and improving the drafts, and I'm very grateful for everyone who gave their time and insight to help us get it right. Barry, Eric, and Jan —thank you for answering the endless series of questions and correcting those misconceptions I had.

Special thanks go to everyone at Microsoft who made Rotor possible in the first place: to Paul Maritz for driving the idea forward, and to Yuval Neeman and David Treadwell for their ongoing support. Thanks to Jeff Ranck, who helped us through the twisty world of licenses and to the entire CLR team who supported us from the start, even if they weren't quite sure what we were doing with their code. To the team at the Microsoft Research Cambridge University Relations team—Pierre-Yves Saintoyant, Greg O'Shea, Van Eden, and Bruno Quarta, and the head of the lab, Rodger Needham—thank you very much for your support in bringing Rotor to the broader community. And thanks to Jim Miller for his ongoing support for everything Rotor.

To the best team I have ever had the privilege to lead: thank you. Barry Bond, John Norwood, David Stutz, Stephen Walli, Jan Kotas, Eric Albert, Vladimir Fedorov, Mario Chenier, and Pankaj Kakkar—you guys really made Rotor and this book a great experience.

Finally, I wish to thank my wife Ann for supporting me (and tolerating me) throughout this project.

CHAPTER 1

Introducing the CLI Component Model

The programmer of the 21st century has a lot to worry about.

For one thing, useful software is far more complex than ever before. No longer is it acceptable to simply, present a simple terminal-based command prompt or a character-based user interface; users now demand rich, graphical user interfaces with all sorts of visual goodies. Data can seldom be structured to fit in flat files in a local filesystem; instead, the use of a relational database is often required to support the query and reporting requirements that computer users have come to depend on, as well as the ongoing transformations that shape and reshape long-lived data. A single computer once sufficed for application deployment, on which data sharing was accomplished using files or the clipboard; now most computers on the planet are wired for networking, and the software deployed on them must not only be network-aware, but must also be ready to adapt to changing network conditions. In short, building software has moved beyond being a craft that can be practiced by skilled individuals in isolation; it has become a group activity, based on ever more sophisticated underlying infrastructure.

Programmers no longer have the luxury of being able to complete an entire project from scratch, using tools that are close to the processor, such as assemblers or C compilers. Few have the time or the patience to write intermediate infrastructure, even for things as simple as an HTTP implementation or an XML parser, much less the skills to tune this infrastructure to acceptable levels of performance and quality. As a result, great emphasis is now placed on reusable code and on reusable components. The operating system plus a few libraries no longer suffices as a toolkit. Today's programmer, like it or not, relies on code from many different sources that works together correctly and reliably, in support of his applications.

Component software, a development methodology in which independent pieces of code are combined to create application programs, has arisen in response to this trend. By combining components from many sources, programs can be built more quickly and efficiently. However, this technique places new demands on programming tools and the software development process. Reliance on components that were created by untrusted or unknown developers, for example, makes it essential to have stringent control over the execution and verification of code at runtime. In our era of ubiquitous network connectivity, complex component-based software is often updated on-the-fly without local intervention and sometimes maliciously. Ask any virus victim about the necessity of preserving the sanctity of her computers and data, or talk to an unsophisticated computer user about the baffling loss of stability that comes from installing and uninstalling applications on his system, and you will discover that component-based software often contributes as much to the problem as to the solution.

For many years, the business promises of component software and its expected efficiencies were offset by the complexity of combining components from many sources in a safe way. Within the last 10 years, however, we have seen the successful commercialization of virtual execution environments that host *managed components*. Managed components are simply software parts that can be developed and deployed independently, yet safely coexist within applications. They are "managed" because of their need for a virtual execution environment that provides runtime and execution services. These environments, to match component requirements, focus on presenting an organizational model that is geared towards safe cooperation and collaboration, rather than on exposing the physical resources of the processors and operating systems on which they are implemented.

Virtual execution environments and managed components, such as the ones abstractly portrayed in Figure 1-1, provide advantages to three different software communities: programmers, those who build programming tools and libraries, and those who administer software built to run within them. To programmers using managed components to build complex applications, the presence of tools and libraries translates to less time spent on integration and communications tasks and more productivity. To tool builders such as compiler writers, the presence of supporting infrastructure and a high-definition, carefully specified virtual machine translates to more time available for building tools and less time worrying about infrastructure and interoperability. Finally, administrators and computer users reap the benefits and control that come from using a single runtime infrastructure and packaging model, both of which are independent of processor and operating system specifics.

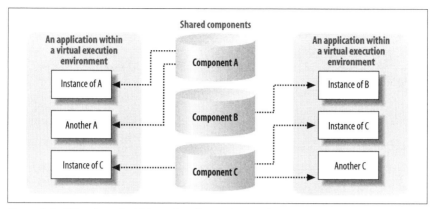

Figure 1-1. When hosted within a virtual execution environment, components can collaborate safely

The CLI Virtual Execution Environment

The ECMA Common Language Infrastructure (CLI) is a standardized specification for a virtual execution environment. It describes a *data-driven architecture*, in which language-agnostic blobs of data are brought to life as self-assembling, typesafe software systems. The data that drives this process, called *metadata*, is used by developer tools to describe both the behavior of the software as well as its in-memory characteristics. The CLI *execution engine* uses this metadata to enable managed components from many sources to be loaded together safely. CLI components coexist under strict control and surveillance, yet they can interact and have direct access to resources that need sharing. It is a model that balances control and flexibility.

 ECMA, the European Computer Manufacturers Association, is a standards body that has existed for many years. Besides issuing standards on its own, ECMA also has a strong relationship with ISO, the International Standards Organization, and based on this relationship, the CLI specification has been approved as ISO/IEC 23271:2003, with an accompanying technical report designated as ISO:IEC 23272:2003. The C# standard has also been approved, and has become ISO/IEC 23270:2003.

The CLI specification is available on the web sites mentioned in the Preface, and is also included on the CD that accompanies this book. It consists of five large "partitions" plus documentation for its programming libraries. At the time that the CLI was standardized, a programming language named C# was also standardized as a companion effort. C# exploits most of the features of the CLI, and it is the easy-to-learn, object-oriented language in which we have chosen to implement most of the small examples in this book. Formally, the C# and CLI specifications are independent (although the C# specification does refer to the CLI specification), but practically, both are intertwined, and many people consider C# to be the canonical language for programming CLI components.

Virtual execution in the CLI occurs under the control of its execution engine, which hosts components (as well as code that is not component-based) by interpreting the metadata that describes them at runtime. Code that runs in this way is often referred to as *managed code*, and it is built using tools and programming languages that produce CLI-compatible executables. There is a carefully-specified chain of events that is used to load metadata from packaging units called assemblies and convert this metadata into executable code that is appropriate for a machine's processor and operating system. A simplified version of this chain of events is shown schematically in Figure 1-2 and will form the basis of the rest of this book. It is also described in Partition I of the CLI specification in great detail. (Section 8, describing the Common Type System, and section 11, describing the Virtual Execution System, are particularly good background sources.)

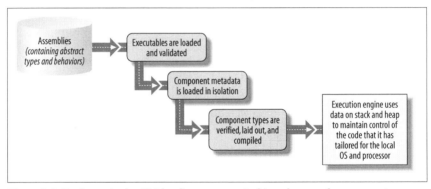

Figure 1-2. Each step in the CLI-loading sequence is driven by metadata annotations computed during the previous step

In some ways, the CLI execution engine is similar to an operating system, since it is a privileged piece of code that provides services (such as loading, isolation, and scheduling) as well as managed resources (such as memory and IO) for code that is executing under its control. Furthermore, in both the CLI and in operating systems, services can either be explicitly requested by programs or else made available as an ambient part of the execution model. (*Ambient services* are services that are always running within an execution environment. They are important because they define a large part of the runtime computational model for a system.)

In other ways, the CLI resembles the traditional toolchain of compiler, linker, and loader, as it performs in-memory layout, compilation, and symbol resolution. The CLI specification takes pains to describe in detail not only how managed software should work, but also how *unmanaged* software can coexist safely with managed software, enabling seamless sharing of computing resources and responsibilities. Its combination of system and tool infrastructure is what makes it a unique and powerful new technology for building component-based software.

Fundamental Concepts in the CLI Specification

Behind the CLI specification and execution model are a core set of concepts. These key ideas were folded into the design of the CLI both as abstractions and as concrete techniques that enable developers to organize and partition their code. One way to think of them is as a set of design rules:

- Expose all programmatic entities using a unified type system.
- Package types into completely self-describing, portable units.
- Load types in a way that they can be isolated from each other at runtime, yet share resources.
- Resolve intertype dependencies at runtime using a flexible binding mechanism that can take version, culture-specific differences (such as calendars or character encodings), and administrative policy into account.
- Represent type behavior in a way that can be verified as typesafe, but do not require all programs to be typesafe.
- Perform processor-specific tasks, such as layout and compilation, in a way that can be deferred until the last moment, but do not penalize tools that do these tasks earlier.
- Execute code under the control of a privileged execution engine that can provide accountability and enforcement of runtime policy.
- Design runtime services to be driven by extensible metadata formats so that they will gracefully accommodate new inventions and future changes.

We'll touch on a few of the most important ideas here, and revisit them in detail as we progress through the book.

Types

The CLI categorizes the world into types, which programmers use to organize the structure and behavior of the code that they write. The component model used to describe types is powerfully simple: a type describes fields and properties that hold data, as well as methods and events that describe its behavior (all of which will be discussed in detail in Chapter 3). State and behavior can exist at either the *instance* level, in which components share structure but not identity, or at the *type* level, in which all instances (within an isolation boundary) share a single copy of the data or method dispatch information. Finally, the component model supports standard object-oriented constructs, such as inheritance, interface-based polymorphism, and constructors.

The structure of a type is captured as metadata that is always available to the execution engine, to programmers, and to other types. Metadata is very important because it enables types from many people, places, and platforms to coexist peacefully, while remaining independent. By default, the CLI loads types only as they are needed; linkages are evaluated, resolved, and compiled on demand. All references within a type to other types are symbolic, which means that they take the form of names that can be resolved at runtime rather than being precomputed addresses or offsets. By relying on symbolic references, sophisticated versioning mechanisms can be constructed, and independent forward-versioning of types can be achieved within the binding logic of the execution engine.

A type can inherit structure and behavior from another type, using classic object-oriented, single-inheritance semantics. All methods and fields of the base type are included in the derived type's definition, and instances of the derived type can stand in for instances of the base type. Although types may have only one base type, they may additionally implement any number of interfaces. All types extend the base type, System.Object, either directly or through their parents' lineage.

The CLI component model augments the concepts of field and method by exposing two higher-level constructs for programmers: properties and events. Properties allow types to expose data whose value can be retrieved and set via arbitrary code rather than via direct memory access. From a plumbing perspective, properties are strictly syntactic sugar, since they are represented as methods internally, but from a semantics perspective, properties are a first-class element of a type's metadata, which translates to more consistent APIs and to better development tools.

Events are used by types to notify external observers of interesting occurrences within their implementations (for example, notification of data becoming available or of internal state changes). To enable external observers to register interest in an event, CLI *delegates* encapsulate the information necessary to perform a callback. When registering an event callback, a programmer creates one of two kinds of delegate: either a *static delegate* that

COM and the CLI

Standardized component packaging and runtime interoperability have long been essential to software designers looking for reuse, as demonstrated by the early use of punch-card decks as reusable libraries of computing routines. The twin goals of unified packaging and fine-grained interoperability were the reason that the Component Object Model (COM) was developed at Microsoft.

The resulting "interface-based" approach to binary component packaging has been used successfully by countless software producers to deploy their APIs and modular pieces of code. Unlike the CLI, COM is a component model that is almost completely based on shared conventions, rather than on a shared execution engine. COM components share the barest runtime infrastructure and cooperate on a per-component basis. This approach can be very useful, and it is particularly well-suited to environments in which the programmer must squeeze every last bit of performance out of very limited computing resources or in which large existing code bases wish to expose a component façade.

Using nothing more than COM's shared conventions, fine-grained binary interoperability between components has become commonplace in software running on the Windows operating system. It is used widely and successfully as a way for applications to expose their internals for the purpose of programmability and also as a standard way to publish APIs. Some of the systems facilities of Windows are also exposed via COM interfaces, and many third-party "controls" exist that are sold as reusable parts.

There is a definite downside to the COM approach, however. In its model, the implementer is responsible for every last detail of runtime operation, and must very carefully conform to complex cooperative protocols to operate correctly. This code is both redundant and prone to bugs, since the protocols are difficult to implement correctly.

Much of the complexity associated with COM can be eliminated by providing shared underlying services for use by component builders, just as operating systems provide shared underlying services for the benefit of all programs using machine resources. (Garbage-collected memory, for example, is the kind of service that can radically reduce the amount of cooperation required between components.). In 1997, a companion runtime for COM was proposed that would provide a *class model* along with *common runtime services* for COM programmers, both to increase productivity (no longer would programmers have to write the same support mechanisms over and over again) and to enable greater safety, efficiency, and stability. The original name for this runtime was Component Object Runtime (COR), which can still be found embedded in a few function names in the Shared Source CLI.

Microsoft took COR further than the original, limited proposal for a companion runtime to COM and decided to pursue a general-purpose virtual execution environment. This process culminated in the standardization of the CLI.

encapsulates a pointer to a static method of a type, or an *instance delegate* that associates an object reference with a method on which that object will be called back. Delegates are typically passed as arguments to event registration methods; when the type wants to raise an event, it simply performs a callback on its registered delegates.

Types, from a minimalist perspective, are a hierarchal way to organize programming modules using fields to hold data and methods to express behavior. Above this simple, yet complete, model, properties, events, and other constructs provide additional structure with which to build the shared programming libraries and runtime services that distinguish the CLI.

A shared type system and intermediate language

Types in the CLI are built from fields and methods at the lowest level, but how are fields and methods themselves defined? The CLI specification defines a processor-agnostic intermediate language for describing programs, as well as a common type system that provides the basic datatypes for this intermediate language. Together, these two entities form an abstract computing model. The specification embellishes this abstract model with rules that describe how it can be transformed into native instruction streams and memory references; these transformations are designed to be efficient and to capture and accurately represent the semantics of many different programming languages. The intermediate language, its types, and the rules for transformation form a broad, language-independent way to represent programs.

The intermediate language defined in the CLI specification is called the Common Intermediate Language (CIL). It has a rich set of opcodes, not tied to any existing hardware architecture, which drive a simple-to-understand abstract stack machine. Likewise, the Common Type System (CTS), defines the base set of types that embody standardized cross-language interoperability. To fully realize the benefits of this language-agnostic world, high-level compilers need to agree on both the CIL instruction set and its matching set of datatypes. Without this agreement, different languages might choose different mappings; for example, how big is a C# int, and how does it relate to a Visual Basic Integer? Is that the same as a C++ long? By matching the instruction set to the types, these choices are made considerably simpler; choices about exactly which instructions and types to use are, of course, in the hands of compiler implementers, but the presence of a well-thought-out specification means that making these choices is considerably more straightforward. By using this approach, the resulting code can interoperate with code and frameworks written in other languages, which results in more effective reuse. Chapter 3 discusses the CLI type system in great detail, while Chapter 5 covers CIL and how it is converted into native instructions.

Portable packaging for types: assemblies

With its type system and its abstract computational model, the CLI enables the idea that software components, written at different times by different parties, can be verified, loaded, and used together to build applications. Within the CLI, individual components are packaged into units called *assemblies*, which can be dynamically loaded into the execution engine on demand either from local disk, across a network, or even created on-the-fly under program control.

Assemblies define the component model semantics for the CLI. Types cannot exist outside of assemblies; conversely, the assembly is the only mechanism through which types can be loaded into the CLI. Assemblies are in turn made up of one or more *modules*—a packaging subunit in which information resides—plus a chunk of metadata describing the assembly called the *assembly manifest*. While assemblies can be made up of multiple modules, most often an assembly will consist of one module.

To ensure that assemblies aren't tampered with between the time they were compiled and the time they are loaded, each assembly can be signed using a cryptographic key pair and a hash of the entire assembly, and this signature can be placed into the manifest. The signature is respected by the execution engine, and ensures that assemblies won't be tampered with and that damaged assemblies won't be loaded. If a hash generated at runtime from the assembly doesn't match the hash contained in the assembly's manifest, the runtime will refuse to load the assembly and raise an exception before the potentially bad code has a chance to do anything.

In many ways, assemblies are to the CLI what shared libraries or DLLs are to an operating system: a means of bounding and identifying code that belongs together. Thanks to the full-fidelity metadata and symbolic binding approach found in the CLI, each component can be loaded, versioned, and executed independently of its neighbors, even if they depend on each other. This is crucial, since platforms, applications, libraries, and hardware change over time. Solutions built from components should continue to work as these components change. Assemblies are discussed in Chapter 3 and Chapter 4.

Component isolation: application domains and remoting

As important as the ability to group code together into components is the ability to load these components in a way that they can work together and yet be protected from malicious or buggy code that might exist in other components. Operating systems often achieve *isolation* by erecting protected address spaces and providing communication mechanisms that can bridge them; the address spaces provide protected boundaries, while the communications mechanisms provide channels for cooperation. The CLI has similar constructs for isolating executing code, which consist of application domains and support for remoting.

Assemblies are always loaded within the context of an application domain, and the types that result are scoped by their application domain. For example, static variables defined in an assembly are allocated and stored within the application domain. If the same assembly is loaded into three different domains, three different copies of the type's data for that assembly are allocated. In essence, application domains are "lightweight address spaces," and the CLI enforces similar restrictions on passing data between domains as operating systems do between address spaces. Types that wish to communicate across domain boundaries must use special communications channels and behave according to specific rules.

This technique, referred to as *remoting*, can be used to communicate between application domains running on different physical computers (and running different operating systems on different processors). Just as often, the remoting mechanisms are used to isolate components within domains that exist in a single process on a single machine. Components that wish to participate in remoting can be Serializable, in which case they can be passed from domain to domain, or alternatively can extend the System. MarshalByRefObject type, in which case they can communicate using proxy objects that act as relays. Application domains, remoting, and the details of loading will be covered in Chapter 4.

Naming conventions for version-flexible loading

Because all types and their code live within assemblies, there needs to be a well-defined set of rules describing how the execution engine will discover and use assemblies when their types are needed. Assembly names are formed from a standard set of elements, which consist of an assembly base name, a version number, a culture (for internationalization), and a hash of the public key that represents the distributor of the assembly. Compound names ensure that software built from assemblies will accommodate version changes gracefully. When compiled, each assembly also carries references to the compound names of other assemblies that it was compiled against and remembers the versioning information for each of those assemblies. As a result, when loaded, assemblies request very specific (or semantically-compatible) versions of the assemblies on which they depend. The *binding policy* used to satisfy these requests can be influenced by configuration settings but is never ignored.

Assemblies are normally found in one of two places: in a machine-wide cache known as the Global Assembly Cache (GAC) or on a URL-based search path. The GAC is effectively a per-machine database of assemblies, each uniquely identified by its four-part name. The GAC can be, but doesn't have to be, a filesystem directory; a CLI implementation must be able to put multiple versions of the same assembly into the GAC and track them. The search path is essentially a collection of URLs (usually filesystem directories) that are searched when an assembly is requested for loading. The loading process and how it can be implemented is detailed in Chapter 4.

JIT compilation and typesafety

The execution model described by the CLI implies that the act of compiling high-level type descriptions should be separated from the act of turning these type descriptions into processor-specific code and memory structures. This separation introduces a number of important advantages to the computing model, such as the ability to easily adapt code to new operating systems and processors after the fact, as well as the ability to independently version components from many different sources. It also introduces new challenges. For example, because all types are represented using CIL and the CTS, all types must be transformed into native code and memory structures before they can be used; in essence, the entire application must always be recompiled before it can be run, which can be a very expensive proposition.

To amortize the cost of transforming CIL into native code, both in terms of time taken to load and in terms of memory required, types in a CLI-based application are typically not loaded until they are needed, and once a type is loaded, its methods are not translated until they are needed for execution. This process of deferring layout and code generation is referred to as just-in-time (JIT) compilation. The CLI does not absolutely require last-minute JIT compilation to occur, but deferred loading and compilation are implied at some point in an application's lifecycle, to convert the CIL into native code. One can imagine an installation utility that might perform compilation, for example. The way that JIT compilation can be implemented to conform to the CLI is discussed in Chapter 5.

The most important reason that JIT compilation is built into the CLI execution model is not obvious. The transformation from abstract component to running native code, under the control of the execution engine's own loader and compiler is what enables the execution engine to maintain control at runtime and run code efficiently, even when calling back and forth between code written in C++ and code written in a managed language. The traditional pipeline of compilation, linking and loading, continues to exist in the CLI, but as we have seen, each toolchain element must make heavy use of clever techniques (such as caching) because deferred use leads to higher runtime costs. These higher costs are well worth bearing because deferral also results in comprehensive control over the behavior of executing components.

Since execution in the CLI is based on the incremental loading of types, and since all types are defined using a platform-neutral intermediate language, the CLI execution engine is constantly compiling and adding new behavior as it runs. CIL is designed to be verifiably typesafe, and since compilation into native code is performed under the control of the privileged execution engine, typesafety can be verified before a new type is given a chance to run. Security policy can also be checked and applied at the time that CIL is transformed into native code, which means that security checks can be injected directly into the code, to be executed on behalf of the system while methods are executing. In short, by deferring the loading, verification, and compilation of components until runtime, the CLI can enforce true *managed execution*.

Managed execution

Type loading is the trigger that causes the CLI's toolchain to be engaged at runtime. As part of this loading process, the CLI compiles, assembles, links, validates executable format and program metadata, verifies typesafety, and finally even manages runtime resources, such as memory and processor cycles, on behalf of the components running under its control. The tying together of all of these stages has led the CLI to include infrastructure for name binding, memory layout, compilation and patching, isolation, synchronization, and symbol resolution. Since the invocation of these elements is often deferred until the last possible moment, the execution engine enjoys high-fidelity control over loading and execution policies, the organization of memory, the code that is generated, and the way in which the code interacts with the underlying platform and operating system.

Deferred compilation, linking, and loading facilitate better portability both across target platforms and across version changes. By deferring ordering and alignment decisions, address and offset computation, choice of processor instructions, calling conventions, and of course, linkage to the platform's own services, assemblies can be much more forward-compatible. A deferred process, driven by well-defined metadata and policy, is very robust.

The execution engine that interprets this metadata is trusted system code, and because of this, security and stability are also enhanced by late loading. Every assembly can have a set of permissions associated with it that define what the assembly is permitted to do. When code in the assembly attempts to execute a sensitive operation (such as attempting to read from or write to a file, or attempting to use the network), the CLI can look at the call stack and walk it to determine if all of the code currently in scope has appropriate rights—if code on the stack doesn't have correct permissions, the operation can be rejected, and an exception can be thrown. (Exceptions are another mechanism that enables simpler interactions between components; the CLI was designed to not only support a wide range of exception semantics within the execution engine, but also to integrate tightly with exception signaling from the underlying platform.) Managed execution is discussed at length in Chapter 6 and Chapter 7.

Enabling data-driven extensibility with metadata

CLI components are self-descriptive. A CLI component contains definitions for every member contained within it, and the guaranteed runtime availability of this information is one factor that helps make virtualized execution highly adaptable. Every type, every method, every field, every single parameter on every single method call must be fully described, and the description must be stored within the assembly. Since the CLI defers all sorts of linkages until the moment they are needed, tools and programs that wish to manipulate components or create new ones by working with metadata have a tremendous amount of flexibility. The same kinds of tricks played by the CLI can be used by code built on top of the CLI, which is a windfall for tools and runtime services.

To get information about types, programmers of the CLI can use the reflection services of the execution engine. Reflection provides the ability to examine compile-time information at runtime. For example, given a managed component, developers can discover the structure of the type, including its constructors, fields, methods, properties, events, interfaces, and inheritance relationships. Perhaps more importantly, developers can also add their own metadata to the description, using what are called *custom attributes*.

Not only is compile-time information available, but it can be used to manipulate live instances. Developers can use reflection to reach into types, discover their structure, and manipulate the contents of the types based on that structural information. For methods, the same is true; developers can invoke methods dynamically at runtime. The capabilities of this metadata-driven style of programming, and how it can be implemented, are touched on in Chapter 3, and examined in more detail in Chapter 8.

A CLI Implementation in Shared Source: Rotor

In the summer of 2001, a small team of developers in Redmond announced plans for a Microsoft rarity: a freely-available software distribution containing modifiable, redistributable, source code. This distribution, named the Shared Source CLI (SSCLI, also known affectionately by its code name, "Rotor"), was to contain a fully-functional CLI execution engine, a C# compiler, essential programming libraries, and a number of relevant developer tools. It had been quietly under development alongside the commercial .NET framework and represented an important facet of Microsoft's developer tool strategy. In particular, the SSCLI had three goals to meet: to validate the portability of the CLI standard, to help people learn about and understand Microsoft's commercial CLR offering, and to stimulate long-term academic interest in the CLI. Above all else, the SSCLI was to match the ECMA standard so that anyone who wished to understand or implement this standard would have a guide.

Although the SSCLI is nominally the subject of this book, the CLI standard is its heart. The SSCLI helps us illustrate how and why the CLI is such an interesting piece of work. The distribution itself is a large body of code, and as such, it can provide a significant leg up for researchers and experimenters working in the area of developer tools or systems design, as well as those teaching computer science. This book attempts to act as a top-level guide to the code for such people, giving information beyond the theory of the CLI to facilitate hacking and to explain the conventions of the code base. The CLI standard will be important for years to come, and there is no better way for you to understand it fully than by browsing, building, observing, and tweaking a running implementation.

While Rotor demonstrates one way to build a portable, programming language–independent version of the CLI standard, it is certainly not the only way. Alternate implementations exist at the time of writing, including two from Microsoft (the commercial .NET Framework and a version for the small devices that is called the "Compact Framework"), and two third-party, open source implementations, one from Ximian (called Mono) and one from the DotGNU project (called Portable.NET). Rotor itself, to provide additional developer tools and facilities, implements more than just the standard. To clarify what is contained in the distribution, Figure 1-3 contains a pictorial representation of the differences between Microsoft's commercial offering (.NET CLR), the CLI and C# specifications, and Rotor.

The SSCLI, as shown in Figure 1-3, is a superset of the CLI standard, and the Microsoft commercial offering is, in turn, a superset of the SSCLI.

Rotor is a large collection of code built by many people over a number of years, and because of this, it is complex and stylistically variable. In terms of scale, it is comparable to the largest familiar source code distributions such as XFree86, Mozilla, and OpenOffice. As with these distributions, getting started in the code can be an intimidating prospect. This book will help make this task easier, beginning with this brief tour of the distribution itself.

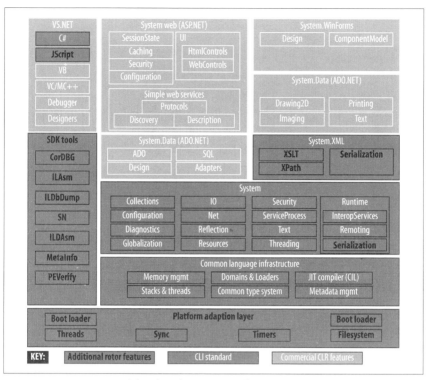

Figure 1-3. Components of the Shared Source CLI distribution

The SSCLI is built using a combination of C++ and C#, with a smattering of assembler for processor-specific details. The distribution is built as a three step process. First, a platform-specific C++ compiler is used to build a Platform Adaptation Layer (PAL), which is a library that hides the differences between operating system APIs behind a single set of programming abstractions. After this, a set of build tools (including the C# compiler) that are needed to build the SSCLI are built and linked against the PAL library. Finally, the rest of the distribution is built using these tools and the PAL.

Table 1-1 lists some of the interesting subdirectories to visit in the SSCLI source code, which is on the CD that accompanies this book (it can also be downloaded from *http://msdn.microsoft.com/net/sscli*).

Table 1-1. Important subdirectories of the distribution and their contents

Subdirectory	Contents
/build	Contains built executables and libraries
/clr/src	Home to many core subdirectories
/bcl	The base class libraries, written in C#

Table 1-1. Important subdirectories of the distribution and their contents (continued)

Subdirectory	Contents
/csharp	A C# compiler, written in C++
/classlibnative	Programming libraries implemented in C++
/debug	Support for managed debugging
/dlls/mscorsn	Strongname crypto code
/fjit	The SSCLI JIT compiler
/fusion	Code for locating versioned files
/ilasm	A CIL assembler
/ildasm	A CIL disassembler
/inc	Shared include files
/md	Metadata facilities
/toolbox/caspol	Source to the *caspol* security utility
/tools	Home to many-utility programs
/clix	The SSCLI managed executable launcher
/gac	Source to the *gacutil* cache utility
/peverify	The *peverify* CIL verification utility
/sos	The SOS debugging extension library
/strongname	The *sn* code-signing utility
/vm	The CLI execution engine
/docs	Documentation
/fx/src	Home to additional managed libraries
/net/system/net	The networking library
/regex/system/text	The regular expressions library
/jscript	A complete JScript compiler that compiles to CIL code, written in C# (a managed managed code compiler!)
/managedlibraries/remoting	Additional remoting support to what is found in the *bcl* directory
/pal	Multiple operating system–specific implementations of the PAL
/palrt	Low-level APIs that support the SSCLI implementation but are not operating system–specific
/samples	Sample programs that use the CLI
/tests	Extensive tests and test infrastructure
/tools	Tools used to build the SSCLI distribution

The subdirectories can be divided into four distinct conceptual areas, as follows:

- The CLI execution engine
- Component frameworks that both wrap and extend the execution engine

- A portability layer (the PAL) used to move from one operating system to another
- Tools, tests, compilers, documentation, and utilities for working with managed code

Let's examine each of these areas in turn, focusing on where to find their implementation.

The CLI execution engine

The execution engine is the heart of the CLI. It contains the component model, as well as runtime services, such as exception handling, and automatic heap and stack management. In many respects, this is the big kahuna; it is the code that we refer to when we speak of "the runtime" or "the virtual execution environment." JIT compilation, memory management, assembly and class loading, type resolution, metadata parsing, stack walking, and other fundamental mechanisms are implemented here. This code can be found in *sscli/clr/src* and in the four directories *vm*, *fjit*, *md*, and *fusion*, in which the bulk of the execution engine resides.

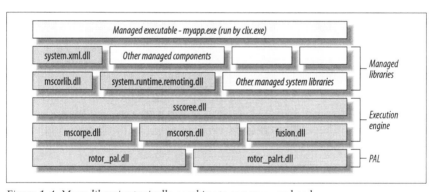

Figure 1-4. Many libraries typically combine to run managed code

The execution engine, as shown in Figure 1-4, is built as a set of dynamically loadable libraries rather than as a standalone executable. The *clix* program launcher (or any program that wishes to use the services of the execution engine) loads the main shared library, *sscoree*, to create an instance of the CLI in process and then feeds this instance a start-up assembly to be executed. As a result, there is no main in the execution engine; it is packaged to be hosted by other programs. The execution engine depends on a number of other shared libraries, which include libraries that are broken because they are replaceable, such as the crypto code necessary to load and build signed assemblies that is located in *mscorsn*, as well as libraries that are potentially useful in many different places, such as the PAL, which can be found in *rotor_pal* and *rotor_palrt*. Finally, code that may not always be needed is also packaged into separately loaded libraries, such as *mscordbc*, which implements debugger support.

Programming libraries in the CLI

The shared infrastructure of the CLI includes not only standardized, low-level capabilities such as metadata, the common intermediate language, and the common type system, but also high-level, productivity-oriented class libraries. The contents of these libraries are briefly summarized by functional area in Table 1-2.

Table 1-2. High-level elements included in CLI standard libraries

Category	Facilities
Productivity libraries	Text formatting, regular expressions, collections, time, dates, file and network IO, configuration, diagnostics, globalization, isolated storage, XML
Execution engine libraries	Isolation domains, asynchronous callbacks, stackwalks, stack traces, garbage collector, handles, environment, threads, exceptions, monitor-based synchronization, security, verification, reflection, serialization, interop with native code
Type-related libraries	Primitive types, value types, delegates, strings, arrays
Extended numerics library	Decimal numbers, double and single precision floating point numbers, math
Programming language support	Compiler services, custom metadata attributes, resource reclamation

These libraries provide an interface to the facilities of the underlying operating system but in a way that has been tailored to exploit the services and conventions of the CLI, increasing programmer productivity through their consistency and quality.

These APIs also serve another, less obvious role: they facilitate component integration by exposing programming services and conventions that will promote good component hygiene through their use. Services that minimize the amount of bookkeeping that is necessary for component builders to implement, or that minimize the need for complex intercomponent management protocols, make for smoother and safer integration (and less code to write). The less a component needs to rely on other components and the fewer things that a component must do on behalf of other components, the more likely an application will be bug-free, simple to read, and robust. To realize the true promise of component-based software, components need to be built to rely on managed execution within an environment designed with these principles in mind.

One might think of the CLI libraries as a modern equivalent to the C runtime library. They do not attempt to provide all things to all programmers;

instead, they are a core set of components for which nearly every programmer will find a use. Since the base libraries, found in *sscli/clr/src/bcl*, are specified to be part of any CLI implementation, they form a basis for portable application implementations. Additional libraries, found in the *sscli/fx*, *sscli/clr/src/classlibnative*, and *sscli/managedlibraries* directories, are either optional standard libraries or specific to the SSCLI. At this point in time, all of the libraries in the SSCLI are also found in the commercial Microsoft .NET Frameworks.

 Explorers of the programming libraries will find that, besides the documentation found in *sscli/docs* that is specific to the Rotor distribution and to its utilities, there is a separately downloadable file archive (which is also contained on the CD for this book) containing documentation for the class libraries. This documentation is derived from the documentation used in the Microsoft .NET Framework SDK, although it has been edited and converted to simple HTML files.

The Platform Adaptation Layer

The PAL is an interesting piece of software with more uses than might meet the eye at first glance. Of course, as is typical of any adaptation or driver layer in a large piece of code that is meant to run on many operating system platforms, the first goal of the PAL was to isolate implementers from the details of various operating systems. The choice in the case of the SSCLI was obvious: since it had started as Win32–specific code, the PAL was designed to present a subset of the Win32 API (which can be seen in *sscli/pal/rotor_pal.h*). This implementation is by no means complete, as it needs to provide only the calls that are actually made by the CLI. Do not attempt to use the PAL as a general Win32 emulation layer, because it is incomplete!

The PAL is, of course, the place where the work to bring Rotor to new platforms would begin, since the tools that are used to build Rotor depend on the PAL for their operating systems, resources. To see what is involved, examine the *sscli/pal/unix* directory. There is a significant amount of work having to do with providing a common exception-handling mechanism, common threading, a shared handle manager, IO, synchronization, debugging, and more. Specialized host processes, such as web servers or databases, might very well have their own similar runtime needs, which might need to take the semantics of the PAL into consideration. Because of this and because the PAL defines how operating system resources are used, understanding the various PAL implementations will be important for many people.

In addition to the PAL, there is a directory named *sscli/palrt/src*, which contains a library implementation of Win32 APIs that are needed by the SSCLI but are not dependent on the operating system for implementation. This library also includes a small number of PAL-specific APIs. It is a true hodge-podge of facilities, but to give it flavor, it contains decimal arithmetic, a stub implementation of some of the Microsoft COM component model, array-handling, memory management, and numerous other utility functions.

The most interesting aspect of the PAL has to do with execution engine control. The SSCLI is designed to run cooperatively with native code within native processes, which means that many operating system calls need to be caught to give the execution engine a chance to maintain bookkeeping information for the use of runtime systems, such as the garbage collector or the security system. This is a critical use of the PAL layer; the SSCLI implementation is built in terms of the abstractions that are presented by the PAL and without them, it could not maintain isolation, security, and control. For example, both threading and exception handling are implemented in the PAL and both of these are critical to the execution engine at runtime, since it uses exception frames to track managed code and the stacks associated with threads to store diffuse structures that hold the state of many of its services. Details of this aspect of the PAL will be covered at length in Chapter 6, while the PAL's design itself is the topic of Chapter 9.

Tools, compilers, tests, documentation, and utilities

A significant percentage of the code in Rotor consists of support infrastructure that is used to build, test, and use its CLI implementation. The PAL, which we have just discussed, is such code. There are numerous additional developer tools, utilities, and test programs that can be found in various spots within the distribution. These fall into the broad categories of utilities for managed development and utilities for building the distribution.

As far as managed development goes, many of the tools in the Rotor distribution will be familiar to any programmer who has spent time with the SDK for the Microsoft .NET Framework because the two implementations share their basic set of utilities, such as linker, assembler, and disassembler. The *sscli/clr/src*, *sscli/clr/src/tools*, and *sscli/clr/src/toolbox* directories contain directories for these utilities, as well as for utilities that are unique to developing and running managed code with the SSCLI, such as *clix.exe*. Programmers should consult the documentation in *sscli/docs* to see whether features are shared between the Rotor version of a utility and its .NET Framework counterpart; not all features were ported.

The build system used to bootstrap Rotor can be found in *sscli/tools*. These tools are built against the PAL and are used to track dependencies, drive the build process, and assemble the libraries and executables, once built, into the *sscli/build* directory. Dependencies in Rotor are convoluted, as they are with most large projects, and so these tools are quite important. To understand how they are used and how developers should interact with them when modifying code, see *sscli/docs/buildtools* directory.

Once the SSCLI is built, it can be tested by using the tests in the *sscli/tests* directory. Of particular note are the PAL tests, found in *sscli/tests/palsuite*, which can be used to verify new PAL implementations or changes to an existing PAL, and the developer Build Verification Tests (BVT) found in *sscli/tests/bvt*, which can be used to check work being done in the execution engine. There are also tests for other areas such as the base class libraries; most of these, along with the BVTs, use the test harness found in *sscli/tests/harness* and documented in *sscli/docs/testing_overview.html*.

Documentation and technical notes for Rotor can be found in *sscli/docs*. This directory contains material that is useful for browsing the sources, for modifying code, and for understanding both the architecture of the CLI and the specific implementation choices that were made when building the SSCLI. There is also a detailed specification included for the PAL that would be very useful to anyone porting Rotor to new platforms. It is well worth taking some time to browse this directory.

Scoping This Book

This book focuses on how the CLI component model and its underlying execution engine are implemented in the SSCLI. The requirements that the resulting mechanisms place on the operating system, and general porting issues, are briefly discussed. Discussions of compilers, languages, and frameworks, however, are lacking, as well as non–component-oriented uses of the CLI, which fortunately can be found in the numerous other books on the .NET Framework and the CLI. Size and scope, along with the fact that the authors wanted to actually see this book in print, dictated the more focused approach.

A disclaimer is also called for: the numerous C++ samples in this book taken from the SSCLI source code have been considerably cleaned up, becoming pseudo-code in the process. This was done to remove ugly macros, error-handling, and asserts that pepper the Real Code, and to make the code more readable. If you are planning to add to or modify the SSCLI code, you should be aware of the invariants that must be maintained and adopt the same programming conventions and error handling methods used by the developers of the SSCLI. See Appendix D for a short description of these requirements.

Summary

The CLI is the first virtual execution environment designed from the ground up to be shared by many different programming languages. Platform providers, framework builders, and programmers are not forced into all-or-nothing language decisions just to take advantage of the facilities that make component-based computing work, such as exceptions, garbage collection, reflection, code access security, and data-driven extensibility. Using the CLI, it is easy to incorporate preexisting code into component-based programming efforts, which results in increased interoperability and shared infrastructure.

The CLI's standardized format for packaging, describing, and deploying components is tied to neither operating system nor implementation language. This is important because this format forms the foundation for the CLI's data-driven architecture. Data-driven mechanisms increase programmer productivity because they enable diverse programs, libraries, and tools to interact seamlessly and to evolve over time. A data-driven component model is as future-proof as today's technology allows.

The abstract instruction set and the type system that outline the CLI's virtual execution model offer a tempting glimpse of the Holy Grail: software that runs everywhere. The designers of the CLI certainly anticipated a world in which multiple implementations and multiple versions of their standard would run both side-by-side and on many platforms. Yet in this world, each implementation is likely to expose unique frameworks, services, utilities, tools, or language features that augment the basic capabilities, using the CLI's excellent support for interoperability. What will result is akin to C language development, in which one rarely finds significant applications built on top of the standard runtime alone. Instead, applications judiciously combine standard facilities with either platform-specific libraries or libraries designed specifically for cross-platform use. Most significant CLI programs will combine standard components with either platform-specific components or third-party components designed specifically for cross-platform use.

The CLI's language-agnostic approach, its data-driven architecture, and its virtual execution model were developed to create an arena in which components could cooperate effectively without sacrificing their security and autonomy. Its unfolding chain of metadata creates an environment in which it is possible to reason about the behavior of components and inject safeguards into their code before running them. Each stage in the CLI's execution model involves receiving data from the prior stage and transforming or augmenting it before passing it on to another stage. This book describes this entire chain of stages and the execution engine in which they are implemented, from its initial bootstrap sequence to the death of its last managed resource.

CHAPTER 2

Getting Started with Rotor

The expertise needed to build a virtual machine spans disciplines as diverse as systems design, compiler theory, and hardware architecture. Understanding how and why this is true is important, both for those using virtual machines to solve day-to-day problems and for those extending or implementing them. The purpose of this book is to explain the CLI specification in these terms, drawing on Rotor's source code for examples and clarification.

Before getting to these details, we'll take a detailed look at building, running, debugging, and modifying managed code with Rotor. A simple example will demonstrate these concepts: a managed component that echoes its input back to the console. This example will form a recurring basis for continuing discussions of Rotor's implementation in the chapters that follow.

A Simple Component Assembly

Consider the simple CLI component in Example 2-1, which consists of a single type named Echo. The Echo type has a single property named EchoString, and a single method, DoEcho.

Example 2-1. A simple CLI component expressed in C# code

```
public class Echo
{
  private string toEcho = null;

  public string EchoString {
    get { return toEcho; }
    set { toEcho = value; }
  }

  public string DoEcho()
  {
```

Example 2-1. A simple CLI component expressed in C# code (continued)

```
    if (toEcho == null)
      throw new Exception("Alas, there is nothing to echo!");
    return toEcho;
  }
}
```

This component is written using the C# programming language and can be compiled into a CLI component using any C# compiler. C# was chosen for examples in this book, because it was developed as a companion language for the CLI standard and has direct syntax for many of the features found in the CLI.

 The SSCLI source code distribution includes several compilers in addition to the C# compiler that will be used in this book. Most notably, there is a full JScript compiler that is itself written in C#. Although there are no JScript samples in this book, the source code for this compiler (found in the *jscript* directory) is worth browsing, since the typeless dynamic semantics of the language differ greatly than from those of C#. The implementation techniques used to support features such as runtime expression evaluation demonstrate alternative design approaches.

If you are unfamiliar with C#, don't worry. Readers familiar with any high-level, component oriented programming languages such as Java should have no problem reading and understanding these very simple examples. Many good online tutorials and books are available for those who would like to learn C#; the O'Reilly web site *http://www.ondotnet.com* is one good place to start.

Before we can compile and run the code for the Echo component, we need to prepare Rotor for first use.

Configuring the Environment

Rotor is packaged as a compressed file archive, which can be expanded using your archiving utility of choice. On FreeBSD, *tar* comes with the system, while on Windows or Mac OS X, there are a number of options: *gnutar* or *StuffIt* are good alternatives on the Mac, or *WinZip* on Windows. (See the *readme* that comes with the tarball for details on expansion.) For example, this command would do the trick:

```
$ gnutar xvfz sscli_20021101.tgz
```

After profuse disk activity, unarchiving will leave a directory named *sscli* in its wake, containing more than 12,000 files and directories, that contain over 3.5 million lines of code. (And this is before unarchiving the optional reference tarball!)

This tutorial switches freely between the Windows shell (*cmd.exe*) and the two major flavors of Unix shell: *sh* and *csh*. A Windows prompt will be represented as >, while a *bash* shell (or other *sh* compatible shell) will be represented as $, and *tcsh* (or equivalent) will be %. You may notice that the directory paths shown change in a similar fashion.

To tame this huge volume of code, the first thing that you will need to do after expanding the archive is to set up a working environment within a command-line shell. Rotor is designed for tinkering: it is assumed that you will be working with multiple versions of the CLI on a single machine as you experiment, make modifications, and use instrumented versions of the runtime for debugging, profiling, or tracing. To make side-by-side operation easy, configuration is done using environment variables that are easy to set and to change.

Within the root of the *sscli* directory, three script files stand ready to configure the runtime environment: *env.bat*, *env.sh*, and *env.csh*. The first of these is for use from the Windows command shell, while the second two are for use from within Unix shells, differing only in their syntax. (Those who worship according to *sh*, *ksh*, or *bash* will opt for *env.sh*, while those who prefer the *csh* or *tcsh* way of life will use *env.csh*.) Running the file on Windows is as simple as firing up *cmd.exe* and typing:

```
> env
```

From Unix, you would *source* the appropriate script, as follows:

```
$ source env.sh
```

One of three different build variants can be established using command-line arguments to these scripts. In the *checked* build, symbols are generated for debugging and no compiler optimizations are used when building code. Some extra instrumentation is also built into the CLI execution engine. This mode is slow but very useful when debugging. *Free* mode, in contrast, is built without debugging instrumentation. It is also built using compiler optimizations so that it can be as fast as possible and will have the best performance of the three variants. *Fastchecked* is a compromise between the free and checked: it preserves debug symbols and instrumentation but also uses some compiler optimizations.

Whenever you run code using the SSCLI or use tools from within the distribution, you'll need to set up your environment first. There are several runtime configuration parameters that depend on values found in environment variables or are directory-specific. This bit of legerdemain may seem a bit awkward and unnecessary at first, but it is done to support side-by-side execution. Using Rotor, it is possible to run assemblies built from differing versions of the CLI (including your own custom versions!) without issues. By using version-specific command shells that have had their environments tailored to specific instances of the Rotor build, you can easily switch between versions by switching between terminal windows.

Passing the mode as a parameter to one of the *env* scripts will set up corresponding environment values. If no mode is specified, fastchecked is the default. Since most users of Rotor will want debug symbols, fastchecked is a good option for most purposes, as it was designed as a compromise between execution speed and source-level debugging. Users who are primarily debugging and spelunking through the Rotor code, however, may prefer the debug checked build, since the optimizations of fastchecked may cause some source lines to appear out of sync with compiled code.

You will see the mode printed in response to your command. From an instance of *csh*, for example:

```
% source env.csh checked
CheckedEnvironment
```

On Windows, you'll get more information:

```
> env free
CLR environment (C:\sscli\clr\bin\rotorenv.bat)
Building for Operating System - NT32
            Processor Family - x86
                   Processor - i386
          Build Environment = C:\sscli\rotorenv
                  Build Type - free
```

With your environment in place, you'll want to build the distribution. Rotor is distributed without any binaries, and so you must build it to do anything more than browse through source code. Fortunately, this is straightforward, and there are only a few prerequisites: you'll need quite a bit of disk space (over a gigabyte is best), and you'll need to have suitable development tools (including *perl*) in your execution path. Appendix A describes these prerequisites in detail, as well as how to build Rotor on all supported operating systems.

Of course, if you'd like to skip the Appendix, the simplest option is to do a complete build. There is a shell script for this purpose in the *sscli* directory named *buildall*, along with a matching *.cmd* file for Windows. Using the shell in which you've prepared the environment, from the *sscli* directory, type:

```
% buildall -c
```

Feel free to take a break at this point, because the build process is lengthy! After lots of stimulating disk exercise, during which over half a gigabyte of disk space is consumed, you'll have the Shared Source CLI, along with its rich set of accompanying tools and examples. To verify that the build was successful (after typing *rehash* if you are using a *csh*), try typing:

```
> csc -?
```

If all has gone well, you'll see the usage message for the C# compiler scroll by. At this point, you're ready to compile the Echo component.

Creating an Echo Component

To compile the C# Echo component into an executable on-disk library, use the following invocation of the C# compiler (assuming that you've saved it into a file named *echo.cs*):

```
> csc -t:library -debug echo.cs
```

This command will produce a file named *echo.dll* that serves as a container for a CLI assembly that contains the Echo type. The -debug switch causes a second file to be created, *echo.ildb*, which contains line number and symbol information for the *cordbg* debugger.

 If you try to compile *echo.cs* without command-line switches, compilation will fail, because Echo doesn't define a method named Main, which is needed by convention to create standalone executables in C#.

Using the *ildasm* disassembler that comes with the SSCLI, you can verify that *echo.dll* contains both metadata tables and CIL code for the Echo type:

```
> ildasm -all echo.dll

// Microsoft (R) Shared Source CLI IL Disassembler.  Version 1.0.0003.0
// Copyright (C) Microsoft Corporation 1998-2002. All rights reserved.

// PE Header:
// Subsystem:                    00000003
// Native entry point address:   0000240e
// Image base:                   00400000
// Section alignment:            00002000
```

```
// File alignment:          00000200
// Stack reserve size:      00100000
// Stack commit size:       00001000
```

(MUCH more follows, spewing across pages of output)

Note that *echo.dll* is a well-formed PE/COFF executable. Many only slightly interesting details that relate to the file's structure scroll by, until you reach output about the Echo type itself. Stripped to its essence (and liberally edited for readability), it looks like this:

```
.class public auto ansi beforefieldinit Echo
       extends System.Object
{
  .field private string toEcho
  .method public hidebysig specialname
          instance string get_EchoString() cil managed
  {
    // CIL stripped for clarity
  }
  .method public hidebysig specialname
          instance void set_EchoString(string 'value') cil managed
  {
    // CIL stripped for clarity
  }

  .method public hidebysig
          instance string DoEcho() cil managed
  {
    // CIL stripped for clarity
  }

  .method public hidebysig specialname rtspecialname
          instance void  .ctor() cil managed
  {
    // CIL stripped for clarity
  }

  .property instance string EchoString()
  {
    .get instance string Echo::get_EchoString()
    .set instance void Echo::set_EchoString(string)
  } // end of property Echo::EchoString
} // end of class Echo
```

The Echo type has a single field, a string named toEcho, a property named EchoString, and a method named DoEcho. It also has a constructor, which was automatically produced by the C# compiler. Everything that a compiler would need to do type checking and other compile-time validation is part of the definition. No external resources are needed, such as header files or linker maps. Types in the CLI are self-contained and self-describing. Unlike traditional compilation toolsets, in which names, structural informa-

---

tion, source code, and object code often reside in separate places, CLI executables contain all of their information in a single file.

If ypu expand the DoEcho implementation, you can see that the simple, three-line C# method has been converted into 12 CIL opcodes by the C# compiler (the comments have been removed for clarity):

```
.method public hidebysig instance string DoEcho( ) cil managed
{
  .maxstack  2
  .locals init ([0] string CS$00000003$00000000)
  IL_0000:  ldarg.0
  IL_0001:  ldfld      string Echo::toEcho
  IL_0006:  brtrue.s   IL_0013

  IL_0008:  ldstr      "Alas, there is nothing to echo!"
  IL_000d:  newobj     instance void /
  [mscorlib]System.Exception::.ctor(string)
  IL_0012:  throw

  IL_0013:  ldarg.0
  IL_0014:  ldfld      string Echo::toEcho
  IL_0019:  stloc.0
  IL_001a:  br.s       IL_001c

  IL_001c:  ldloc.0
  IL_001d:  ret
} // end of method Echo::DoEcho
```

CIL is an intermediate representation of the behavior originally expressed in the C# program, and is the target representation for compilers and other utilities that wish to express behavior natively in terms of the CLI runtime's services. CIL itself is a simple language to read and understand, particularly for those with some experience working with assembly language. It is fully described in the third partition of the ECMA specification, for those who would like to dig deeper. (There are also a number of books that cover the subject, including *.NET IL Assembler* by Serge Lidin, published by Microsoft Press.)

One key to understanding CIL is to realize that the instruction set is stack-based. So, for example, when the first instruction ldarg.0 (load argument zero) executes, it pulls the first argument passed to the method (which in this case is a this pointer to the Echo instance being called) and pushes it onto the execution stack. This value is then used by the next instruction ldfld (load instance field contents), which takes a single operand, the name of the field to load, dereferences it, and stores the result on the stack. In the example, ldfld takes the this pointer from the top of the stack and uses it to dereference the named field: Echo::toEcho.

Those familiar with assembly language might start to grow a bit skeptical: just how wide is this stack? Is it 32-bit? 64-bit? The beauty of the CLI execution model and the CIL instruction set is that implementation details, such as the stack's size, are irrelevant. CIL was not designed for direct execution, but rather for compilation into code native to whatever processor is at hand. Alignment issues are also something that the CLI programmer can rely on the JIT compiler to take care of automatically.

Other CIL Tools

CIL is a *lingua franca* for CLI structure and behavior, and every CLI component can be shown as CIL. In fact, files containing CIL component descriptions can be built by hand and assembled directly into an executable by using the *ilasm* utility, without using any higher-level compiler. The *ilasm* assembler is a counterpart to *ildasm*, and its file format is often used as a target by compilers that wish to target the CLI. In fact, the output from *ildasm* can be recompiled by *ilasm*, a capability called "round-tripping." It is easy to capture the dump to a file and "round-trip" the Echo component from its compiled form to CIL and back again:

```
> ildasm -out=roundtrip.il echo.dll
> ilasm -dll roundtrip.il
```

CIL is also easy to manipulate and examine statically. As an example of this, you might examine the *peverify* tool that comes with the Rotor distribution. This utility verifies that the combination of metadata and CIL within an executable's assemblies is typesafe. Its code can be found in *sscli/clr/src/tools/peverify*.

The rest of the method is fairly easy to understand. The brtrue.s (branch short if true) instruction is used to test the results of the ldfld to see whether the topmost element on the execution stack is non-null. If it is, there is a jump to the label IL_0013, which can be found in the column of labels on the lefthand side of the CIL instructions. Otherwise, the ldstr (load string) instruction loads a reference to the constant string Alas, ... onto the execution stack, where it is used as the sole parameter to the constructor for a System.Exception, created by the newobj instruction that follows it. With an Exception object on the stack, the throw instruction terminates execution of this method and unwinds the stack, looking for exception handlers. The instruction sequence for the nonexception path results in a reference to the string value from the Echo::toEcho field being pushed onto the stack with ldloc.0. It is returned to the original caller of the method with ret.

The ECMA specification for the CLI contains an excellent summary of the complete set of CIL opcodes. See Partition III for details.

Exercising the Echo Component

Given the lengthy dissassembled output, *echo.dll* appears to contain a valid CLI component. Without a program that takes advantage of its capabilities, however, this component and the assembly in which it is contained are of little use. Here is code that will put Echo through its paces:

```
public class MainApp {
  public static void Main( ) {
    Echo e = new Echo( );
    e.EchoString = "Echo THIS!";
    System.Console.WriteLine("First echo is: {0}", e.DoEcho( ));
    e.EchoString = null;
    System.Console.WriteLine("Second echo is: {0}", e.DoEcho( ));
  }
}
```

This simple program instantiates an Echo component, sets its EchoString property, and calls DoEcho, printing the results to *stdout*. It then sets EchoString to null, and calls DoEcho again.

 To find out more about any of the tools or utility programs being discussed in this chapter, browse the documentation that comes as part of the SSCLI. The file *sscli/docs/index.html* has links to individual web pages for every program in the distribution. These pages document syntax and command-line arguments, as well as general usage.

To compile and run the code, save it into a file named *main.cs* and feed it to the compiler, passing *echo.dll* on the command line as a referenced component. The program can be executed by using the managed code launch utility, *clix*:

```
% csc -t:exe -r:echo.dll -debug main.cs
Microsoft (R) Visual C# Shared Source CLI Compiler version 1.0.0003
for Microsoft (R) Shared Source CLI version 1.0.0
Copyright (C) Microsoft Corporation 2002. All rights reserved.

% clix main.exe
First echo is: Echo THIS!

Unhandled Exception: System.Exception: Alas, there is nothing to echo!
   at Echo.DoEcho( ) in /Users/dstutz/first_echo/echo.cs:line 12
   at MainApp.Main( )in /Users/dstutz/first_echo/echo.cs:line 7
```

As you can see, the program does precisely what it should, echoing the first string and then blowing up with an unhandled exception! Because you compiled both files using the -debug switch, the resulting stack trace contains line number information about the problem, but to find out more about the exception and what is causing it, you can drop into the managed code debugger, *cordbg*:

```
% cordbg main.exe
Microsoft (R) Shared Source CLI Test Debugger Shell Version 1.0.0003.0
Copyright (C) Microsoft Corporation 1998-2002. All rights reserved.

(cordbg) run main.exe
Process 638/0x27e created.
[thread 0xa0000dec] Thread created.
[thread 0xb6150] Thread created.
[thread 0xa0000dec]
003:   Echo e = new Echo( );
(cordbg)
```

The debugger loaded *main.exe* and automatically ran until the first line of code in Main. Note that to get to this point, the CLI has fired up three managed threads (of which much more will be said in later chapters). The debugger prints out the current line, and then waits patiently for instructions. To see command options, you can type:

```
(cordbg) ?
```

This will give you a list of all possible debugger commands. Typing *show* (**sh**) will display the source code for the current method:

```
(cordbg) sh
001: public class MainApp {
002:   public static void Main( ) {
003:*  Echo e = new Echo( );
004:   e.EchoString = "Echo THIS!";
005:   System.Console.WriteLine("First echo is: {0}", e.DoEcho( ));
006:   e.EchoString = null;
007:   System.Console.WriteLine("Second echo is: {0}", e.DoEcho( ));
008:   }
```

The asterisk indicates current position. By typing *continue* (**cont**), you can watch the exception happen:

```
(cordbg) cont
First echo is: Echo THIS!
First chance exception generated: (0x00d74378) <System.Exception>
Unhandled exception generated: (0x00d74378) <System.Exception>
  _className=<null>
  _exceptionMethod=<null>
  _exceptionMethodString=<null>
  _message=(0x00d72e54) "Alas, there is nothing to echo!"
  _innerException=<null>
```

```
_helpURL=<null>
_stackTrace=(0x00d743b8) array with dims=[24]
_stackTraceString=<null>
_remoteStackTraceString=<null>
_remoteStackIndex=0x00000000
_HResult=0x80131500
_source=<null>
_xptrs=0x00000000
_xcode=0xe0524f54

012:        throw new Exception("Alas, there is nothing to echo!");
```

Using *where* (**wh**) to view a trace of the execution stack and *print* (**p**) to exam-ine the state of the instance of Echo, you can see that the null string field is causing the problem:

```
(cordbg) wh
Thread 0xa0000dec Current State:Normal
0)* echo!Echo::DoEcho +0140 in /Users/dstutz/echo.cs:12
1)  main!MainApp::Main +01cc in /Users/dstutz/main.cs:7

(cordbg) p this
this=(0x00d72e48) <Echo>
  toEcho=<null>
```

Although the commands might be foreign, this debugger interaction should be familiar to any programmer. Based on the information discovered, you could correct Main by adding a try block around calls to the Echo component, which would give the program a chance to recover from runtime exceptions.

Bootstrapping the Loading Process

To bootstrap the loading process, the *clix* application launcher receives the name of a managed executable and runs that executable by loading the CLI execution engine, loading the executable file, and putting them to work. We will take *clix* apart in much more detail in Chapter 4, but the executive sum-mary goes something like this:

1. *clix* loads the execution engine into its process space by dynamically loading the *sscoree* module. Under Windows, this file is named *sscoree. dll*; on the Mac, it is *libsscoree.dylib*; and on FreeBSD, it is *libsscoree.so*.

2. *clix* then finds the file named in its command-line argument and loads it into memory.

3. Finally, *clix* feeds the loaded file to a function exposed by the *sscoree* module named _CorExeMain2. When the function returns, the managed executable has exited, and it's time to shut off the lights and go home.

Once the file is passed to the execution engine, the CLI begins the business of loading and JIT-compiling assemblies as they are needed.

Debugging the Rotor Execution Engine

If you run *clix* itself under a debugger, rather than running the managed executable under a managed debugger, you can see the workings of the execution engine in great detail. On a Unix system, using *gdb*, for example, this would look as follows:

```
$ gdb clix
GNU gdb 5.1-20020408 (Apple version gdb-231) (Tue Aug 13 21:37:39 GMT 2002)
Copyright 2002 Free Software Foundation, Inc.
GDB is free software, covered by the GNU General Public License, and you are
welcome to change it and/or distribute copies of it under certain
conditions.
Type "show copying" to see the conditions.
There is absolutely no warranty for GDB.  Type "show warranty" for details.
This GDB was configured as "powerpc-apple-macos10".
Reading symbols for shared libraries . done
(gdb) l
30      #ifdef __cplusplus
31      extern "C"
32      #endif
33      int __cdecl PAL_startup_main(int argc, char **argv);
34
35      #ifdef __cplusplus
36      extern "C"
37      #endif
38      int __cdecl main(int argc, char **argv) {
39          if (PAL_Initialize(argc, argv)) {
```

This looks promising. Rather than C# code, there is now a call to an entirely different main function that begins with a call to PAL_Initialize. This code, of course, is the Rotor implementation for *clix*, which will launch and run *main.exe*. Using *gdb*'s run command, you can cause this to happen:

```
(gdb) r main.exe
Starting program: /Users/dstutz/sscli/build/v1.ppcfstchk.rotor/clix main.exe
[Switching to process 652 thread 0xb03]
Reading symbols for shared libraries ...... done
Reading symbols for shared libraries .... done
Reading symbols for shared libraries . done
Reading symbols for shared libraries . done
First echo is: Echo THIS!

Unhandled Exception: System.Exception: Alas, there is nothing to echo!
   at Echo.DoEcho() in /Users/dstutz/echo.cs:line 12
   at MainApp.Main() in /Users/dstutz/main.cs:line 7

Program exited with code 0124.
(gdb)
```

Hmm, the debugger didn't catch the exception in this case but just bailed out. Why?

The unfortunate truth is that managed code and unmanaged code cannot easily be debugged from within the same debugger. (We will see ways to examine JIT-compiled code and execution engine structures in Chapter 5, but using these facilities with native debugging facilities is not easy.) Of course, this lack of symbolic information for managed code doesn't stop us from listing and running the unmanaged code for the execution engine under the debugger!

```
(gdb) l Launch
143     DWORD Launch(WCHAR* pRunTime, WCHAR* pFileName, WCHAR* pCmdLine)
144     {
145         HANDLE hFile = NULL;
146         HANDLE hMapFile = NULL;
147         PVOID pModule = NULL;
148         HINSTANCE hRuntime = NULL;
```

The *clix* application contains a function named Launch, from which the CLI execution engine is dynamically loaded and called. To run the C# code for Main, *clix* maps the *main.exe* into memory and then hands the image to a function named _CorExeMain2, which will load and run the code. By placing a breakpoint at this point, you can actually trace through this transition into managed code, but from the perspective of the CLI implementer rather than the perspective of the C# programmer:

```
(gdb) l 253,275
253         // load the runtime and go
254         hRuntime = ::LoadLibrary(pRunTime);
255         if (hRuntime == NULL)
256         {
257             nExitCode = ::GetLastError();
258             DisplayMessage(MSG_CantLoadEE, nExitCode, pRunTime);
259             goto Error;
260         }
261
262         __int32 (STDMETHODCALLTYPE * pCorExeMain2)(
263                 PBYTE   pUnmappedPE,         // -> memory mapped code
264                 DWORD   cUnmappedPE,         // Size of memory mapped
code
265                 LPWSTR  pImageNameIn,        // -> Executable Name
266                 LPWSTR  pLoadersFileName,    // -> Loaders Name
267                 LPWSTR  pCmdLine);           // -> Command Line
268
269         *((VOID**)&pCorExeMain2) =
                            (LPVOID)::GetProcAddress(hRuntime, /
                            "_CorExeMain2");
270         if( pCorExeMain2 == NULL)
271         {
272             nExitCode = ::GetLastError();
273             DisplayMessage(MSG_CantFindExeMain, nExitCode, pRunTime);
274             goto Error;
275         }
```

```
(gdb) b 262
Breakpoint 1 at 0x1f5c: file /Users/dstutz/sscli/clr/src/tools/clix/clix.
cpp, line 262.

(gdb) r main.exe
Starting program: /Users/dstutz/sscli/build/v1.ppcfstchk.rotor/clix main.exe
[Switching to process 709 thread 0xb03]
Reading symbols for shared libraries ...... done
Reading symbols for shared libraries .... done

Breakpoint 1, Launch(unsigned short*, unsigned short*, unsigned short*)
(pRunTime=0x93bc0, pFileName=0x93c40, pCmdLine=0
x92e48) at /Users/dstutz/sscli/clr/src/tools/clix/clix.cpp:269
269          *((VOID**)&pCorExeMain2) =
                              (LPVOID)::GetProcAddress(hRuntime, "_
CorExeMain2");
```

At this point, put a breakpoint in RaiseException, which you know will be
called when the Echo component uses the throw statement from within
DoEcho. Continuing, hit this breakpoint:

```
(gdb) b RaiseException
Breakpoint 2 at 0x1a21ec: file ../exception.c, line 101.

(gdb) c
Continuing.
Reading symbols for shared libraries . done
Reading symbols for shared libraries . done
First echo is: Echo THIS!

Breakpoint 2, RaiseException (dwExceptionCode=1, dwExceptionFlags=0,
                             nNumberOfArguments=3763490644,
lpArguments=0xd66960)
                             at ../exception.c:101

101          ENTRY("RaiseException (dwCode=%#x, dwFlags=%#x, nArgs=%u,
pArgs=%p)\n"
```

The first "Echo THIS!" output is among *gdb*'s output; now you know that
you are at the same exact spot that you were in *cordbg*: the Echo component
is raising an exception, because its field has a null value. Examining a
slightly cleaned up version of the stack trace, let's look for the nested calls to
Main and DoEcho:

```
(gdb) bt
#0  RaiseException (dwExceptionCode=1, dwExceptionFlags=0,
nNumberOfArguments=3763490644, lpArguments=0xd66960) at ../ex
ception.c:101
#1  0x07244a2c in RaiseTheException(OBJECTREF, int)
                    at /Users/dstutz/sscli/clr/src/vm/excep.cpp:2089
#2  0x07277b80 in JIT_Throw(Object*) (obj=0xd66960)
                    at /Users/dstutz/sscli/clr/src/vm/jitinterface.cpp:4944
#3  0x02e6d46c in ?? ()
```

```
#4   0x02e6c438 in ?? ()

// many frames omitted

#13 0x00001fa8 in Launch(unsigned short*, unsigned short*, unsigned short*)
                      (pRunTime=0x93bc0, pFileName=0x93c40,
pCmdLine=0x92e48)
                   at /Users/dstutz/sscli/clr/src/tools/clix/clix.cpp:277
#14 0x0000219c in PAL_startup_main (argc=-531476652, argv=0x1)
                   at /Users/dstutz/sscli/clr/src/tools/clix/clix.cpp:411
#15 0x00001a90 in main (argc=2, argv=0xbffff7b4)
                   at ../../../src/inc/palstartup.h:45
#16 0x00001998 in _start (argc=2, argv=0xbffff7b4, envp=0xbffff7c0)
                   at /SourceCache/Csu/Csu-45/crt.c:267
#17 0x00001818 in start ()
```

Looking at this stack trace in some detail, notice that at the point that the exception is being raised, you are 17 function calls deep in the CLI execution engine. Frames 3 and 4, although they do not have symbols for *gdb* to display, are actually the calls to the JIT compiled versions of DoEcho and Main. (In Chapter 5, we will examine debugging techniques that can be used to verify this. For now, experts among you may examine the raw code produced by the JIT-compiler by using *gdb*'s disassemble command on the addresses shown in the stack trace.) The JIT-compiled code for DoEcho (frame 3) calls the JIT_Throw helper function to actually raise its managed exception. Far, far up the stack, in frame 13, is the original call to Launch and, even higher, *clix*'s call to main.

Choosing a Debugger

The same debugging sequence demonstrated in *gdb* can be performed in the *ntsd*, *cdb*, *windbg*, or Visual Studio debuggers on Windows. In *ntsd*, *cdb*, and *windbg*, for example, the following sequence of commands will yield similar results:

```
0:000> bp rotor_pal!PAL_RaiseException
0:000> g
0:000> k
```

The first sets a breakpoint in the PAL at RaiseException, the second continues execution, and the third looks at a stack trace once the breakpoint has been hit. In Chapter 5, we will talk about special debugger extensions and how to use them, but for the most part, you should simply use the debugger that you are most comfortable with to work with Rotor!

Don't worry if this doesn't make a lot of sense yet. It will, shortly. The Rotor implementation of the CLI runtime is composed of large quantities of C, C#, and C++ code, mixed together in complex ways. Wringing order from this apparently chaotic mass of code is the mission that this book sets out to complete.

Observing Managed Execution

Because so much of what's happening in the execution engine is low-level, self-modifying code, trying to keep track of what's going on can be awkward. Rather than constantly walk through code in a debugger, readers can take advantage of a number of tracing and diagnostic facilities that exist in Rotor.

To demonstrate the use of tracing, we will use it to observe the JIT compiler in action. First, modify *main.exe* to contain a try block, as follows:

```
public class MainApp {
  public static void Main( ) {
    try {
      Echo e = new Echo( );
      e.EchoString = "Echo THIS!";
      System.Console.WriteLine("First echo is: {0}", e.DoEcho( ));
      e.EchoString = null;
      System.Console.WriteLine("Second echo is: {0}", e.DoEcho( ));
    } catch {
      System.Console.WriteLine("Caught and recovered from bad Echo.");
    }
  }
}
```

When you run this program, you will see:

```
% csc -t:exe -r:echo.dll -debug main2.cs
Microsoft (R) Visual C# Shared Source CLI Compiler version 1.0.0003
for Microsoft (R) Shared Source CLI version 1.0.0
Copyright (C) Microsoft Corporation 2002. All rights reserved.

% clix main2.exe
First echo is: Echo THIS!
Caught and recovered from bad Echo.
```

Scattered throughout the code that implements the CLI execution engine are thousands of calls to chunks of code such as the following that are conditionally compiled for logging and debugging:

```
#if defined(_DEBUG) || defined(LOGGING)
  const char *szDebugMethodName;
  const char *szDebugClassName;
  szDebugMethodName = compHnd->getMethodName(info->ftn, &szDebugClassName );
#endif
```

```
#ifdef _DEBUG
  static ConfigMethodSet fJitBreak;
  fJitBreak.ensureInit(L"JitBreak");
  if (fJitBreak.contains(szDebugMethodName, szDebugClassName,
                         PCCOR_SIGNATURE(info->args.sig)))
    _ASSERTE(!"JITBreak");

  // Check if need to print the trace
  static ConfigDWORD fJitTrace;
  if ( fJitTrace.val(L"JitTrace") )
    printf( "Method %s Class %s \n",szDebugMethodName, szDebugClassName );
#endif
```

In fact, this code snippet was taken directly from *sscli/clr/src/fjit/fjitcompiler.cpp*, which is where the implementation of Rotor's JIT compiler can be found. Whenever a new method is compiled in a build in which _DEBUG and LOGGING are defined (such as checked and fastchecked), the JIT compiler executes this #ifdef code. To see it in action, create an environment variable named COMPlus_JitTrace, and set its value to 1. You should then see the following when you run *main2.exe*:

```
$ export COMPlus_JitTrace=1
$ clix main2.exe
Method SetupDomain Class System.AppDomain
Method .cctor Class System.Runtime.Remoting.Proxies.RealProxy
Method .ctor Class System.AppDomainSetup
Method .ctor Class System.Object
Method SetupFusionStore Class System.AppDomain
Method get_Value Class System.AppDomainSetup
Method .cctor Class System.String

(Many more messages follow)

Method Main Class MainApp
Method .ctor Class Echo
Method set_EchoString Class Echo
Method DoEcho Class Echo
Method .cctor Class System.Console

(Many more messages follow)

Method CorrectnessEnabled Class System.BCLDebug
Method get_CurrentDomain Class System.AppDomain
Method .cctor Class System.Threading.Thread
First echo is: Echo THIS!
Caught and recovered from dysfunctional Echo.

(Many more messages follow)

Method Finalize Class System.Object
Method Dispose Class System.IO.TextWriter
Method Finalize Class System.Threading.Thread
```

The very first method to be JIT-compiled when *main2.exe* is run is AppDomain::SetupDomain. Is this surprising? Not really. Remember that much of the Rotor CLI implementation is written in C#. To run any program, some of this C# code will be loaded and executed. As part of that execution sequence, it will be JIT-compiled from the CIL in its assembly, just like any other managed code. This is what happens in this trace.

The entire trace is actually quite enlightening, but we won't print all 1300-plus lines here. Instead, we included only a few of the important parts in the previous listing, including the lines in which the MainApp and Echo types are compiled, as well as the point at which their output is emitted to the console. Note how many methods are compiled between the time that DoEcho is run and the time the characters emerge on the console!

There is actually a vast diagnostic logging subsystem in Rotor with a number of different facilities defined, each of which can be enabled for logging. The diagnostic variable named LogFacility is a bitmasked field mapping to 32 different logging categories, defined in *sscli/clr/src/inc/loglf.h*. These flags can be combined to trace very specific parts of the execution engine. The LogLevel diagnostic variable is used in conjunction with LogFacility to indicate the level of detail which the execution engine should provide. Both LogLevel and LogFacility have default behavior that results in maximum logging.

One approach to setting these variables is to use environment variables, as you did with the JIT trace. First, turn off the JIT trace:

```
$ export COMPlus_JitTrace=0
```

Then, to turn on allocation tracing in the garbage collector, which by looking at the header file you know has a flag value of 0x100, type the following:

```
$ export COMPlus_LogEnable=1
$ export COMPlus_LogToConsole=1
$ export COMPlus_LogFacility=0x100
$ clix main2.exe
TID 72c: Executing program with command line 'main2.exe'
TID 72c: Allocated    64 bytes for REF_TYPE 00b6f8a4 System.
OutOfMemoryException[mscorlib.dll]
TID 72c: Allocated    64 bytes for REF_TYPE 00b6f8e4 System.
StackOverflowException[mscorlib.dll]
TID 72c: Allocated    64 bytes for REF_TYPE 00b6f924 System.
ExecutionEngineException[mscorlib.dll]
TID 72c: Allocated  2064 bytes for REF_TYPE 01aa0018 System.Object[]
TID 72c: Allocated  4096 bytes for REF_TYPE 01aa0840 System.Object[]
TID 72c: Allocated    20 bytes for REF_TYPE 00b6f964 System.
SharedStatics[mscorlib.dll]
TID 72c: Allocated    80 bytes for REF_TYPE 00b6f978 System.
AppDomain[mscorlib.dll]
```

```
TID 72c: Allocated    12 bytes for VAL_TYPE 00b6f9c8 System.Int32[mscorlib.
dll]
TID 72c: Allocated    136 bytes for REF_TYPE 00b6f9d4 System.String[mscorlib.
dll]

(and on and on...)
```

An interesting thing to notice in this example is that allocation order is quite different from JIT compilation order. In fact, the first thing to be allocated is the Exception object for out-of-memory errors! Many delightful factoids can be gleaned by examining execution traces.

Log settings can also be made by using a configuration file that is tied to the build of the CLI being used, such as *sscli/build/v1.<arch>.<buildmode>.rotor/rotor/rotor.ini*. For example, to watch every log message available, with output going to both the console and a file named *my.log*, the *rotor.ini* file in the *rotor* subdirectory of the appropriate *build* subdirectory (*v1.x86fstchk.rotor* for the fastchecked build on x86) would look like this:

```
[Rotor]
LogEnable=1
LogLevel=10

LogToConsole=1
LogToFile=1
LogFile=C:\Rotor\rotor.log
```

Be warned that running with extremely high log levels generates copious amounts of output during execution. Running at LogLevel=10, *main2.exe* generates many megabytes of text. As a result, not only will a log file fill extremely quickly (or scroll by in the console window far too quickly to read), but execution will slow down due to the amount of console I/O taking place. There are more instructions and a number of logging examples in the file *docs/techinfo/logging.html* that will help you navigate and use this facility efficiently.

Looking Ahead

Within the rest of the book, we will focus in detail on each of the elements we have already touched on: types, assemblies and metadata, JIT compilation, managed execution, automatic memory management, and the platform adaptation layer. In the next chapter, we begin by examining the notion of type within the CLI and the execution engine, and how the CLI guarantees typesafety within the managed environment.

CHAPTER 3

Using Types to Describe Components

Types are the universal abstraction that enables CLI-based programs to interact with the operating system, with foreign code, and with the world of the microprocessor. Below the CLI lurks a world of address spaces, threads, instructions, interrupts, and registers, defined by the operating system and microprocessor being used. Above the CLI, high-level programming languages project component-based abstractions that help to ease programmer interactions with those painfully concrete low-level constructs. Types are the organizational principle that bridges these two worlds safely, efficiently, and consistently. To understand how the CLI creates native code and maintains control over its execution, it is first important to understand its *type system*.

Types and Type Systems

The notion of a type system can be difficult to define. For most programmers, the old adage, "I can't tell you what it is, but I know it when I see it" describes their definition of a type system. Intuitively, we know that primitive types, classes, structs, and such are part of a type system, and that languages will enforce certain rules regarding the use of these types. But to actually say, in formal terms, what a type system is and entails is difficult. Nonetheless, most programmers, regardless of their background, will be able to infer some interesting details about the CLI type system from Example 3-1, even if they're not familiar or comfortable with C#.

Example 3-1. The Echo component revisited

```
using System;
namespace SampleEcho {
  public enum EchoVariation { Louder, Softer, Indistinct }
  public struct EchoValue {
    public string theEcho;
    public EchoVariation itsFlavor;
```

Example 3-1. The Echo component revisited (continued)

```
    }
  public interface IEchoer {
    void DoEcho(out EchoValue[] resultingEcho);
  }

  public class Echo : IEchoer {
    private string toEcho = null;
    private static int echoCount = 0;
    private const System.Int16 echoRepetitions = 3;

    public delegate void EchoEventHandler(string echoInfo);
    public event EchoEventHandler OnEcho;

    public Echo(string initialEcho) {
      toEcho = initialEcho;
    }
    public string EchoString {
      get { return toEcho; }
      set { toEcho = value; }
    }
    public void DoEcho(out EchoValue[] resultingEcho) {
      if (toEcho == null) {
        throw(new Exception("Alas, there is nothing to echo!"));
      }
      resultingEcho = new EchoValue[echoRepetitions];
      for (sbyte i = 0; i < echoRepetitions; i++) {
        resultingEcho[i].theEcho = toEcho;
        switch (i) {
          case 0:
            resultingEcho[i].itsFlavor = EchoVariation.Louder;
            break;
          case 1:
            resultingEcho[i].itsFlavor = EchoVariation.Softer;
            break;
          default:
            resultingEcho[i].itsFlavor = EchoVariation.Indistinct;
            break;
        }
      }
      if (OnEcho != null) {
        OnEcho(System.String.Format("Echo number {0}", echoCount));
      }
      echoCount++;
      return;
    }
  }
}
```

Casual users of C, C++, or Java will find much here that feels familiar and intuitive. For example, the Echo component contains a number of type definitions: the enumerated type `EchoVariation`, the struct `EchoValue`, the interface `IEchoer`, and the class `Echo`. We can see some fields, some methods, some code, and so forth—much of this is intuitive and familiar, even if we've never put formal definitions to it.

Type, Object, and Component

We need to draw a distinction between the terms type, object, and component. These terms are frequently used throughout the industry, often with vague or differing meanings. They are also used in very specific ways in the ECMA CLI specification. Taking the time up front for definitions will help ensure a common understanding of what is meant by these terms in this book.

Type

A *type* is a specification that describes how a piece of unadorned data will be interpreted within the CLI execution engine. Types provide a way to classify both the shape of data and the ways that operations on that data should be expected to behave. The use of types has proven to be indispensable for the construction of reliable software on a large scale; their use results in a classification system that can be used to automate and enrich most aspects of the programming process, from compilation and linking to ensuring correct runtime behavior.

In the CLI, types are always used to access and manipulate data, which results in a typesafe environment. Typesafety is achieved jointly by cooperation between compilers and the execution environment. Within the CLI, every object, every variable, and every piece of data used as part of the frameworks has a type associated with it from the time that it is allocated by the execution engine to the time that it is no longer used. A typesafe compiler for the CLI, such as the Rotor JIT compiler, will restrict the kind of code that it emits to code that always obeys the rules of the typesystem and execution environment. From a practical perspective, this gives the CLI a way to maintain control over managed code.

To put it simply, the CLI seeks to ensure through analysis that a program will behave "according to the rules." If there are no semantic violations of the set of verification rules defined in the ECMA specification, then that program is defined to be typesafe. For example, if a variable is declared to be an unsigned 32-bit integer, then in a typesafe program, there will be no code that attempts to assign a string to it:

```
int x;
x = "12"; // this would not be typesafe
```

In addition to things like simple assignment compatibility checks, a strongly-typed environment ensures that methods called on a type are actually declared as part of that type. For example, while System.String has a method called IndexOf on it, an integer (an instance of System.Int32) does not:

```
int x = 12;
x.IndexOf("1"); // also illegal
```

The C# compiler will reject both of these code fragments, and even if the programmer somehow fools the compiler or build illegal CIL manually without a compiler, the execution engine will still recognize that System.Int32 doesn't have this method and reject the compiled code. (The verification step that performs this check is something we will cover later.) Both the compiler and the execution engine enforce typesafety. The C# compiler does checking to provide the programmer with warnings and error messages at compile time. The execution engine does checking so that it can protect the system against buggy compilers, poor component design, and malicious code. By this careful attention to the rules, a level playing field for components is maintained.

Object

A very careful discussion of the terms "type" and "object" can be found in Section 7 of the first partition of the ECMA specification:

> Types describe values and specify a contract that all values of that type shall support. Because the CTS supports Object-Oriented Programming (OOP) as well as functional and procedural programming languages, it deals with two kinds of entities: objects and values. Values are simple bit patterns for things like integers and floats; each value has a type that describes both the storage that it occupies and the meanings of the bits in its representation, and also the operations that may be performed on that representation. Values are intended for representing the corresponding simple types in programming languages like C and also for representing non-objects in languages like C++ and Java.

Objects have more to them than values. By this definition, each object is self-describing, which is to say that a reference to its type is explicitly available from its in-memory representation. It has an identity that distinguishes it from all other objects, and it has memory associated with it that can store other entities (which may be either object references or values). While the contents of this memory may be changed, the identity of an object never changes.

This book will continue to use the word "object" in a very specific way rather than the general sense that object-oriented programming languages and programmers often do. For the purposes of this book, objects are values that match the criteria in the previous paragraph, which are classified as type System.Object in the CLI typesystem, and are used according to this type's specification within the CLI execution engine.

Many Objects Make an Object

As you browse the source code, you will discover three files that each seem to implement object base classes: *clr/src/bcl/system/object.cs*, *clr/src/vm/comobject.cpp*, and *clr/src/vm/object.cpp*. The first of these, *object.cs*, fits together with the code in *comobject.cpp* to form a hybrid implementation of the CLI type System.Object, in which the methods marked with an InternalCall attribute are implemented in C++. The file named *object.cpp* contains the execution engine's private view of objects in a C++ class named Object. When a CLI object of type System.Object is created using the CIL instruction newobj, the code emitted by the JIT compiler causes a C++ Object to be created. Confusing, but true.

To make things even clearer, a fourth class, CObjectHeader, can be found in *clr/src/vm/gcsmp.cpp*. This class represents the way that objects appear when they are laid out in the garbage collector's heap.

There are many different ways to look at an "object" in Rotor!

Not surprisingly, the CLI component model is about objects. Objects in the Shared Source CLI implementation are represented at runtime by the C++ class Object, found in the filename *object.h* in the *clr/src/vm* directory. A quick examination of this header file reveals that Object is closely tied to the CLI's implementation details—think of objects as "the thing represented by the System.Object class in the CLI" and you'll never be confused. Within the CLI environment, all object types descend from this special base type, whose type definition is shown here in C#:

```
public class System.Object
{
    // Constructors
    public Object();

    // Methods
    public virtual bool Equals(object obj);
    public static bool Equals(object objA, object objB);
    public virtual int GetHashCode();
    public Type GetType();
    public static bool ReferenceEquals(object objA, object objB);
    public virtual string ToString();
}
```

When using the CLI component model, all object types (and value types!) are descendants of System.Object, which means that a reference to any value can be placed into an Object reference:

```
int x = 12;
string s = "Hello";
```

```
Object o = x;
System.Console.WriteLine(o.ToString( )); // prints "12"
o = s;
System.Console.WriteLine(o.ToString( )); // prints "Hello"
```

Note that, as the preceding code fragments imply, each and every type within the CLI has the methods Equals, GetHashCode, ToString, and others defined for it—how this is possible for "primitive types" like int is discussed later, when we talk about value types. Also note that the assignment of x to o causes a copy of the value 12 to be placed into o; changing the value of o doesn't change the original value of x.

Component

Components are the abstract units of interoperability and reuse for programmers working with languages that target the CLI. They are defined using types and manipulated using high-level computer languages or CIL. The most important aspects of components, as discussed in Chapter 1, are their packaging as autonomous, replaceable units and their capability of adapting over time while maintaining type-correct behavior. Because of these characteristics, components are replaceable; they can be modified and redeployed without requiring changes to other components with which they collaborate or to the execution engine.

Since we've tied up the word "object" for a restricted concept (an instance of the CLI System.Object type), the word "component" will need to serve in a more general conceptual role. To make up for the very specific definition of "object" in the previous section, we use the word "component" where other people might frequently say "object." We'll try to be as clear and consistent as possible.

To programmers, components can be intuitively understood as "separable units." Take, for example, the Echo example earlier in this chapter. The component revolves around four types: an enumerated type, a value type, an interface, and an implementation class. Example 3-2 shows how these types can be used in code.

Example 3-2. Using the Echo component

```
using System;
using SampleEcho;

namespace MainSampleProgram
{
  class EchoProgram
  {
    static void Main(string[] args)
    {
```

Example 3-2. Using the Echo component (continued)

```
    Echo myEcho;
    EchoValue[] result;

    if (args.Length > 0) {
      myEcho = new Echo(args[0].ToString( ));
    } else {
      throw new Exception("Hi mom!");
    }

    // Set up an event handler and hook to component
    Echo.EchoEventHandler handler =
      new Echo.EchoEventHandler(CallMe);
    myEcho.OnEcho += handler;

    try {
      System.Console.WriteLine( );
      myEcho.DoEcho(out result);
      System.Console.WriteLine("Main program received echo!");
      for (int i = 0; i < result.Length; i++) {
        Console.WriteLine("{0}: {1}, {2}", i,
          result[i].theEcho, result[i].itsFlavor);
      }
    }
    catch (System.Exception e) {
      System.Console.WriteLine("Caught exception: {0}", e.Message);
    }
  }

  static void CallMe(string msg) {
    System.Console.WriteLine(msg);
  }
  }
}
```

In this example, the program creates instances of the types defined in the Echo component and works with them. The four types defined as part of the Echo component—IEchoer, Echo, EchoValue, and EchoVariation—are each declared as part of the SampleEcho namespace. The program also uses the Echo component as a source of notifications. The program registers the static CallMe method as the recipient of notifications from the Echo component, and when those notifications are received, prints the string that is passed as a parameter to System.Console.WriteLine, another component.

If some of the surrounding terminology or code (events, delegates, namespaces, and so on) are unfamiliar, fear not—all of these terms and code will be discussed in greater detail throughout the remainder of this and other chapters. The key here is the difference between the overall component (Echo), and the many types that are used, including, but not limited to, object types.

Type Systems, More Formally Defined

The role of the type system in the CLI is twofold: it provides a logically consistent and unchanging conceptual foundation for programmers, and it ensures that programs can be checked for correctness at runtime. This latter role, enforcer of typesafety, helps to prevent tampering, and is an effective way to help ensure a robust, stable, and secure runtime environment. It is absolutely required when building services and applications that combine components from many sources.

In general, modern software engineering aims to ensure that a system behaves correctly as specified—that is, as its creator intended. We accomplish this through a variety of means, some formal, some less so. At the far end of the spectrum are powerful tools and/or methodologies, such as algebraic specification languages and denotational semantics. These techniques use mathematics to prove that a given program will behave precisely as specified. While powerful, these approaches tend to be cumbersome and awkward to work with and frequently require a tremendous degree of skill on the programmer's part.

On the other end of the spectrum, we can put automatic checking into software tools that any programmer (or even nonprogrammer) can utilize—compilers, linkers, source-code analyzers, and so on. Some of these tools include model checkers, tools that scan finite-state systems (firmware, for example) for errors, and runtime monitoring, in which a system can dynamically detect when a component is misbehaving by comparing its behavior against the component's specification. By and large, however, the most popular mechanism is type verification.

A system that checks (either statically or at runtime) to make sure that all types are being used correctly, as defined in their type descriptions, is said to be *strongly typed*. Strongly typed systems avoid erroneous or malicious computation by prohibiting operations that cannot be verified as typesafe; the ECMA specification contains a number of rules that define exactly what this means in the context of the CLI. When a component is JIT-compiled in the CLI's execution engine, the compiler not only produces executable code, but also performs verification of that code using the rules specified in the ECMA specification. By ensuring that all loaded components are typesafe, the execution engine provides an important guarantee of integrity to component programmers.

There are many benefits to using type systems:

Detecting errors
> This is the most obvious advantage, by which types are used to detect areas of code in which the programmer has inadvertently asked for

incorrect behavior—making a method call on a type that doesn't exist, for example. It is better to detect this kind of error during development than at runtime, since you can rely on tools to do very complete checks.

Maintenance

This is an extension of error detection, in which programmers use typechecking as a powerful tool to support the refactoring of code. Instead of relying on programmer-centric disciplines when changing code to support new features or results, a programmer can simply change a type's definition and run the compiler. The compiler will find the places where the code is no longer consistent, giving the programmer a well-defined and precise list of what needs to be changed to support the modification. While this technique might arguably fall into the category of slothful engineering practice, it is nonetheless very common.

Abstraction

Strongly typed systems can enforce programmer discipline in ways that other tools simply cannot. This is particularly true within object-oriented systems that support inheritance (either interface-based or implementation-based)—when a method expects a parameter of type Person, for example, the typechecker enforces that only Persons, and derived types, will be accepted. This in turn gives the programmer a powerful means to differentiate between Persons and other types, such as Lists, Forms, and XmlReaders, making code clearer and more intentional.

Documentation

Types are also handy when reading programs, since the structure of type declarations helps offer hints regarding their usage and behavior. This sort of documentation is especially useful because, unlike comments, there is no way for it to become outdated or inaccurate.

Efficiency

If the type of an argument can be extracted at runtime, then optimizations can be made on that type to increase program speed, reduce memory footprints, or both.

Security

A typechecker can enforce a policy that says that types are not to be used in ways which would allow for malicious code to subvert the program or act in other undesirable ways. Some languages may choose to allow programmers to override a strict policy for the purposes of interfacing with code that is not typesafe; in this case, it is important to permit these programmers to make explicit assertions about their intentions, prove that they are authorized to make such assertions, and then include these assertions in the type-checking process.

A strongly typed system can offer all of these benefits, without inconveniencing the programmer in the least.

Consider again the Echo component listed in Example 3-1. Drilling down a bit farther, notice that the Echo object type contains several type members: the string field named toEcho, and the two number fields named echoCount and echoRepetitions. The echoCount type member is also static, which means that its value is shared across all instances of the component, rather than being stored on a per-instance basis.

Of course, the Echo object type consists of type members besides its fields. There is a property named EchoString, a method named DoEcho, and an event named OnEcho. There is also a constructor for the class; constructors for both instances and classes are another important kind of type member.

Method parameters and return values are also typed. The DoEcho method, for example, has a void return type and actually returns its computed results by passing them an out parameter that is an array of EchoValue structures. Under the covers, this out parameter is represented as a managed pointer, which is one of several ways that the CLI encapsulates pointers for safe use.

When the DoEcho method is called, the implementation raises an event after it has successfully manufactured the array to be passed back to its caller. Events are an interesting kind of type member that take advantage of another reference type called a delegate. Like managed pointers, a delegate encapsulates a pointer in a special-purpose way; it contains a function pointer that refers to a method for one or more specific component instances. When an event is *raised*, each instance contained in the delegate has its method invoked. Besides the delegate, there is another kind of reference type in this sample: the interface named IEchoer. Interfaces describe a set of operations that can be implemented by a component and are implemented by providing methods that define these operations. How reference types are used is what distinguishes them—delegates and interfaces, for example, can both refer to method signatures, but the purposes for which they were designed are very different, as we will see.

Values, and references to them, can be woven together and accessed in many different ways. The managed pointer used in DoEcho, for example, encapsulates a pointer to an array, which is a reference type that contains values and is accessed by index rather than by name. The array itself is composed of structures, which are compound value types. So, in this example, the parameter is a reference type that refers to another reference type that contains compound value types that are themselves composed of simple values. This intermixing of diverse types is a powerful, yet easily understood, way for programmers to access the capabilities of the underlying operating system, of frameworks from many sources, and the services of the CLI itself.

Types as Contracts

Types act as *contracts* between the programmer and the execution engine, through which the programmer can describe storage requirements, dependencies, and behaviors. Type contracts are far deeper than mere structure, since the CLI includes not only structural descriptions in component type information, but also the intermediate code needed to generate native method implementations. In addition, types specify details about how components will interact with the execution engine at runtime. The ECMA specification contains a detailed definition of the word "contract" as it relates to types. The short gloss would be: contracts consist of concrete, well-described details of implementation that types assert they abide by.

The execution engine can vouch for the integrity of components that it loads at runtime because of the presence of type contracts. Likewise, components that have no knowledge of other components' structure or behavior can depend on type contracts and related runtime mechanisms to guide their interactions. Tools, for example, can load and manipulate components by examining and annotating component type contracts; this style of programming is sometimes called *meta-programming*, and the actual type contracts themselves are represented by what is called *component metadata*.

Metadata is, simply put, the data used to describe types at runtime, their behavior, and layout information that will be needed at runtime to load the component that they represent. Compilers and tools typically emit metadata by using a standard set of APIs to write to, and read from, in-memory data structures. When the tool wishes to save metadata, the in-memory structures are compressed and written out as binary data, although tools can also choose to follow the more tedious route of writing the ECMA executable file format directly to disk.

Metadata is structured within the execution engine itself as named tables that are mapped either from secondary storage into memory or populated on the fly. These tables are fundamental to the execution engine, since without them, there would be no way to comprehend the type structures used in any given executable. The representation of metadata in the Shared Source CLI is optimized for read-only access because the component contract is usually used while running programs that utilize a given component rather than modify its structure. Load time is often the most critical optimization scenario.

 The code for the metadata system can be found in *clr/src/md*. There are a number of interesting tables, and their relationships are explained in the documentation for the unmanaged metadata APIs that can be found in the .NET Framework SDK.

Anyone who has used a relational database will feel at home while looking at the metadata implementation; the data itself takes the form of either heaps (for variable-length data such as strings) or tables (for fixed-length data such as field definitions). These heaps and tables are accessed by using persistable tokens, which contain a reference to a specific location within a specific table or heap. As you can see from Example 3-3, there are a number of different kinds of token—each has a specific role in describing the structure of types, and each has its own table or heap and a unique record format.

Example 3-3. Types of metadata tokens (defined in clr/src/inc/corhdr.h)

```
typedef enum CorTokenType
{
    mdtModule           = 0x00000000,     //
    mdtTypeRef          = 0x01000000,     //
    mdtTypeDef          = 0x02000000,     //
    mdtFieldDef         = 0x04000000,     //
    mdtMethodDef        = 0x06000000,     //
    mdtParamDef         = 0x08000000,     //
    mdtInterfaceImpl    = 0x09000000,     //
    mdtMemberRef        = 0x0a000000,     //
    mdtCustomAttribute  = 0x0c000000,     //
    mdtPermission       = 0x0e000000,     //
    mdtSignature        = 0x11000000,     //
    mdtEvent            = 0x14000000,     //
    mdtProperty         = 0x17000000,     //
    mdtModuleRef        = 0x1a000000,     //
    mdtTypeSpec         = 0x1b000000,     //
    mdtAssembly         = 0x20000000,     //
    mdtAssemblyRef      = 0x23000000,     //
    mdtFile             = 0x26000000,     //
    mdtExportedType     = 0x27000000,     //
    mdtManifestResource = 0x28000000,     //

    mdtString           = 0x70000000,     //
    mdtName             = 0x71000000,     //
    mdtBaseType         = 0x72000000,     // no table
} CorTokenType;
```

When metadata is referred to within CIL or during runtime in the execution engine, it is done by using 32-bit integers that combine a RID or a heap pointer with the CorTokenType that designates its type. Example 3-4 (which is defined in *clr/src/inc/corhrd.h*) contains the macro definitions used to access the two individual parts of a token, its RID, and its type.

Example 3-4. The structure of a metadata token

```
typedef ULONG32 mdToken;          // Generic token

// Build / decompose tokens.
//
```

Example 3-4. The structure of a metadata token (continued)

```
#define RidToToken(rid,tktype) ((rid) |= (tktype))
#define TokenFromRid(rid,tktype) ((rid) | (tktype))
#define RidFromToken(tk) ((RID) ((tk) & 0x00ffffff))
#define TypeFromToken(tk) ((ULONG32)((tk) & 0xff000000))
#define IsNilToken(tk) ((RidFromToken(tk)) == 0)
```

Metadata tokens are inserted directly into component CIL, and because of this, the metadata for a component must itself be verified as part of certifying the code as "safe." For example, method signatures are part of the metadata representation of a component, and these method signatures themselves are used to drive the code that passes parameters on the stack—if it were possible to modify the metadata, it would be possible to circumvent the security mechanisms put in place by the execution engine, and the component model would not provide the guarantees needed for safe integration and interoperability.

CLI metadata is also extensible. This is very important for developer tools, which need to annotate types, for a variety of purposes; for example, an implementation of a language that supports checked exceptions (as Java does) would want to annotate method metadata with the exception types thrown so that callers could be checked to ensure they handle those exception types. Also, tools or languages can add abstractions that are not natively supported by the CLI by adding custom metadata; again, a given language might support the concept of runtime-mutable types by marking compiled types with attributes indicating their mutability and providing necessary runtime constructs around those types to provide the façade of mutability. Custom attributes, as well as custom modifiers on signatures, are offered.

Since type contracts are the primary way that independently developed assemblies probe and utilize each other's resources, it is desirable that the logical structure that they are capable of describing is rich enough to support interesting component-to-component interactions, such as event handling, inheritance, and data member access.

Types and Their Behavior

The CLI specifies a neutral instruction set, CIL, whichdescribes component structure and behavior. CIL is never executed directly in the SSCLI—it must be translated into native microprocessor instructions before it can be used. (The instruction set was designed to be compiled before being executed, but it would be possible for a CLI implementation to interpret it, albeit slowly.) Example 3-5 contains a portion of the CIL for the DoEcho method of the Echo component.

Example 3-5. Beginning of the Echo component's DoEcho method in CIL

```
.method /*0600000A*/ public hidebysig newslot final virtual instance
    void DoEcho([out] valuetype SampleEcho.EchoValue/* 02000004 */[]&
            resultingEcho) cil managed
{
    // Code size       184 (0xb8)
    .locals /*11000003*/ init (int8 V_0, int8 V_1)
    IL_0000:  ldarg.0
    IL_0001:  ldfld      string
        SampleEcho.Echo/* 02000006 */::toEcho /* 04000008 */
    IL_0006:  brtrue.s   IL_0013

    IL_0008:  ldstr      "Alas, there is nothing to echo!" /* 70000091 */
    IL_000d:  newobj     instance void
        [mscorlib/* 23000001 */]System.Exception/* 01000009 */
        ::.ctor(string) /* 0A000003 */
    IL_0012:  throw

    IL_0013:  ldarg.1
    IL_0014:  ldc.i4.3
    IL_0015:  newarr     SampleEcho.EchoValue/* 02000004 */
    IL_001a:  stind.ref
    IL_001b:  ldc.i4.0
    IL_001c:  stloc.0
    IL_001d:  br.s       IL_007d
    // etc.
```

The CIL in Example 3-5 is printed using the assembler format introduced in the ECMA specification and generated using *ildasm* with the -tokens switch to display the value of metadata tokens. In this snippet, the tokens are printed as comments of the form /* 0n0000nn */ (in which the character *n* is meant to represent nonzero numeric digits). It shows just how many metadata tokens are typically embedded into CIL by language compilers. The loading of type-dependent information is completely data-driven, based on these tokens.

Rather than compile nonportable constructs like offsets or addresses into the code, the metadata for the type is examined by the JIT compiler when it is needed by using the tokens to navigate the in-memory table structure. The JIT compiler decides how to map these neutral representations of the types into runtime data structures and compiled code when the types are needed.

By deferring compilation decisions, types can safely be propagated from architecture to architecture in dormant form. The presence of complete descriptive metadata also means that the compiled code can take advantage of a great deal of structural information to avoid extra indirection, expense, and, most importantly, fragility. Cross-component binding, including such arcana as alignment and ordering, can be taken care of by the JIT compiler rather than being a packaging issue. Of course, the downside of this approach is that the code needs to be compiled every time dormant components are brought to life—this can be mitigated by caching, but the SSCLI does not implement such a cache.

Type Evolution Through Versioning

Type evolution is a key issue for all programmers. Although they might often want to deny it, at some point in its lifetime, a given software component invariably breaks or ceases to be useful in a changing environment. In time, all components must be supplemented, rewritten, or replaced.

In the face of versioning, pre-CLI environments begin to break down. Because environments like C++ or Java have no explicit support for versioning in their formal model, developers are left to invent their own mechanism. It begins simply, usually some form of version number embedded as a string inside of the code in question or else as a "version number" field inside of a common structure; when the class or library is loaded, it is the developer's responsibility to verify that the version that was loaded was an acceptable version. Unfortunately, no standardized behavior is specified, and developers are left to their own devices as to what should happen if the numbers don't match as expected.

The story gets worse—the version number exists as part of the class, but this is static, opaque data to the loader. For most operating systems or execution environments, the first class or executable file to match the base criteria (the filename, usually) is what's loaded, even if multiple copies of the same file can be found along the loader's list of directories from which to load code. This leaves the developer in an even nastier quandary—the right file is there, but because an earlier (wrong) version is there earlier on the PATH, the correct version is never loaded. A developer might then diagnose the problem, put the right version into the right place, but then this breaks an older application that depends on the older version.

This problem, colloquially and accurately referred to in the Windows world as "DLL Hell," essentially stems from a single problem: the criteria by which the operating system or execution environment loader selects the correct component to load are too narrow and underspecified. Only limited information is captured about one component's dependency on another, and because of this, when multiple implementations are present, loaders have no ability to differentiate correctly between alternative implementations.

Within the CLI, this problem is addressed by taking the problem of versioning (and its associated partner, that of *binding*, or the process by which the criteria for loading a component is evaluated) to a more formal and complex definition. As opposed to C++, in which versioning is nonexistent and binding is left up to the C++ environment to handle in an "implementation-dependent manner," the CLI specifies the rules by which a component can declare an identifying four-part tuple: a version number, locale (internationalization) information, a "strong name" that corresponds to a cryptographic public key, and the component's name. In addition, as we will see in Chapter 4, the CLI provides specific rules describing the process by which a component is evaluated as a possible candidate for loading and use by client code.

The issue of versioning is not one that the runtime alone can solve, however—developers must still make certain conscious decisions regarding type design and implementation. Programmer decisions are undoubtedly the largest factor in how well a type can survive versioning.

Component Self-Description

The fact that CLI defines components via the use of metadata, thereby making these components entirely self-describing, is the most important design point for the entire CLI. Much of the functionality and capability provided by the CLI is keyed off of this ability for components to stand alone, yet provide complete information about themselves. The ability to defer binding decisions, as discussed in the previous section, leads to better versioning behavior and smoother evolution. The ability to defer layout and compilation decisions is also important.

Consider, if you will, two tiny programs that do the same thing, one written in C++ and one written in C#. Both define a Point component, presenting a traditional Cartesian (x/y) coordinate location. Code for both is in Example 3-6 and Example 3-7.

Example 3-6. C++ and C# Point components

```
class Point
{
public:
  double x;
  double y;

  Point();
};

Point::Point()
  : x(0), y(0)
{ }

int main(int argc, char* argv[])
```

Example 3-6. C++ and C# Point components (continued)

```
{
  Point* p = new Point;
  p->x = 12;
  p->y = 24;
  return 0;
}
```

Example 3-7. A C# Point component

```
public class Point
{
  public double x;
  public double y;
}

class App
{
  static void Main( )
  {
    Point p = new Point( );
    p.x = 12;
    p.y = 24;
  }
}
```

Despite their source-level similarities, the compiled formats between the two are strikingly different; a C++ compiler might emit the x86 assembly code found in Example 3-8.

Example 3-8. Assembly code for C++ Point class

```
        // Point* p = new Point;
        // allocate the memory from ::new( )
        // and call Point::Point( )
push      10h
call      operator new
add       esp,4
mov       dword ptr [ebp-0ECh],eax
mov       dword ptr [ebp-4],0
cmp       dword ptr [ebp-0ECh],0
je        main+66h
mov       ecx,dword ptr [ebp-0ECh]
call      Point::Point
mov       dword ptr [ebp-0F4h],eax
jmp       main+70h
mov       dword ptr [ebp-0F4h],0
mov       eax,dword ptr [ebp-0F4h]
mov       dword ptr [ebp-0E0h],eax
mov       dword ptr [ebp-4],0FFFFFFFFh
mov       ecx,dword ptr [ebp-0E0h]
mov       dword ptr [p],ecx
```

Example 3-8. Assembly code for C++ Point class (continued)

```
    // p->x = 12;
    // x is at offset 0 (8 bytes long) from the start of p
mov         eax,dword ptr [p]
mov         dword ptr [eax],0
mov         dword ptr [eax+4],40280000h
    // p->y = 24;
    // y is at offset 8 (8 bytes long) from the start of p
mov         eax,dword ptr [p]
mov         dword ptr [eax+8],0
mov         dword ptr [eax+0Ch],40380000h
```

A C# compiler produces the CIL in Example 3-9, which looks very different.

Example 3-9. Synopsized CIL for the C# component in Example 3-7

```
.class public auto ansi beforefieldinit Point
       extends [mscorlib]System.Object
{
  .field public float64 x
  .field public float64 y
} // end of class Point

.class private auto ansi beforefieldinit App
       extends [mscorlib]System.Object
{
  .method private hidebysig static void  Main( ) cil managed
  {
    .entrypoint
    // Code size       37 (0x25)
    .maxstack  2
    .locals init (class Point V_0)
    IL_0000:  newobj     instance void Point::.ctor( )
    IL_0005:  stloc.0
    IL_0006:  ldloc.0
    IL_0007:  ldc.r8     12.
    IL_0010:  stfld      float64 Point::x
    IL_0015:  ldloc.0
    IL_0016:  ldc.r8     24.
    IL_001f:  stfld      float64 Point::y
    IL_0024:  ret
  } // end of method App::Main

} // end of class App
```

In particular, note that the C++ version has layout information built into the code that it produces; it calculated the offset of x and y from the beginning of the Point object in memory, then looked up the contents of memory at [p] plus the offset. If a later revision of the Point class were to change its declaration so that another field were added to Point and that field happened to be placed at the top of the class declaration rather than at the bottom, all of the offsets would change—and the client code would suddenly break, either plugging in bad values or crashing entirely. Likewise, if this code were deployed on a different microprocessor, it would not work. Abstract information about the Point class is compiled away, leaving no metadata for other tools or a runtime to utilize later.

The CIL version of this code, however, doesn't rely on layout information being compiled into the code. Rather than calculating the offset in memory for the stfld instruction, a metadata token is emitted instead, in this case the metadata token for Point::x and Point::y. At load time, when the type Point is loaded, these tokens will serve as the necessary lookup points to determine precisely where in the layout of a Point instance the values of x and y are located. Even if Point changes its definition so that x and y are completely reversed, because the CLI doesn't depend on physical offsets, but names from the metadata, the client code can continue to function as before. In short, the brittleness introduced by C++ due to its insistence on removing all unnecessary overhead falls away and leaves you with more robust code in the face of changes. Because the CLI uses metadata to describe its components, types, and type members, no hard data that could break in a subsequent revision or use needs to be introduced—the CLI represents a significant step forward in the area of component adaptability.

More on Value Types

As has been pointed out, not everything can be a reference. Within an individual component, for example, there must be real data—the numbers, strings, and so on that our programs manipulate to achieve some useful result. *Value types* are the abstraction that the CLI component model uses to represent the real data of a program to programmers and tools. Without value types, components would be nothing but empty shells—without values, not much can be done. All useful computational work eventually boils down to working with values.

Bytes, characters, integers (of all sizes), floating-point numbers, decimal numbers, enumerated values, and booleans are all value types. A value type, by ECMA Specification definition (Partition I, 7.2.1), is "represented as a sequence of bits"—in other words, values are actual data rather than an address to a location that contains data.

An instance of a value type can be used as a field of a type, as a parameter, as a method return value, or as a variable. When allocated as part of an object or within an array, the value lives within the object on the heap. When declared as a variable or used as a parameter, value types live on the stack.

When passed as a parameter to a method, by default, a copy, rather than the address, of the value type is created and sent to the recipient of the method; in short, value types are passed by value. Example 3-10 shows a C# declaration from the Echo component that uses two different kinds of value types.

Example 3-10. A compound value type from the Echo component

```
public struct EchoValue {
    public string theEcho;
    public EchoVariation itsFlavor;
}
```

As this sample shows, value types can be grouped together into compound values—in C#, this is done using the struct keyword. Since we are dealing with "real data," value types have features that can be used for interop with data structures that already exist—it is possible to designate with great precision how to lay out a value type in memory, both in terms of ordering and alignment. In general, developers will not want or need to do this—layout is something best left to the JIT compiler unless interop with unmanaged code is needed, but it is definitely possible to take fine-grained control over this. (To be complete, it should be mentioned that it is possible to do explicit layout for nonvalue types, but value types are by far and away the most common use for this feature.)

You can define values to act as representatives from a bounded set of choices; in many programming languages, these are called *enumerated types*. In practical terms, enumerated types are used to offer a strongly typed set of values, possibly in the form of a bitmask; in the case of the Echo component in Example 3-1, the component wishes only to provide three levels of volume: Louder, Softer, and Indistinct (which we presume to be more quiet than Softer—we're assuming that it's not indistinct because we've gone deaf listening). While it certainly would be possible to describe the volume of the echo using integer values (perhaps using decibels as the units of measurement?), this isn't always a practical or preferred design approach. Within the CLI, enumerations are always a value type, backed by a built-in integer value type for storage; this integer type is included in an enum's metadata.

Working with Values

There are two principal issues with which developers working with the CLI must be acquainted: the concept of *type coercion* and *conversion*, and the process by which a value can be given reference semantics where necessary or desired, called boxing (and its reverse operation, unboxing).

Coercion and conversion

Frequently, when working with values, the need to "convert" a value of one size or format into a value of a different size or format arises—for example, you may want to convert a character value into a 4-byte integer representing the Unicode character code for that character, or you may want to take a 4-byte integer value and store it in a floating-point value, most likely in preparation for performing floating-point arithmetic on that value.

Therefore, it's both desirable and necessary to provide rules by which a value of one value type can be converted to another type: this is known as *coercion*. Formally, "coercion takes a value of a particular type and a desired type and attempts to create a value of the desired type that has equivalent meaning to the original value."[*] In more practical language, compilers insert coercion operations when a value of one type is assigned to a storage location that has a different type, as in Example 3-11.

Example 3-11. Safe implicit type coercion

```
int x = 24;
long y;
y = x; // coercing x from 32 bits to 64 bits
```

In this example, the 32-bit value stored in the location named x is being extracted, a 64-bit value is created, assigned 24, and stored back into the location named y. The two values are of different types, even though they have equivalent meanings. (Also note that the two values are equivalent, even though they are not identical.)

Within the CLI, two types of coercion are discussed. *Widening coercion* occurs when a value is assigned to a value type that is larger than the original type, such as storing a 32-bit signed integer into a 64-bit signed integer location. *Narrowing coercion* is when the reverse takes place: storing a 32-bit signed integer into a 16-bit signed integer location. The former, as in Example 3-11, is usually a benign operation—no information is lost, since the value can be represented completely using the smaller of the two types. The latter, in Example 3-12, is dangerous, since it might result in loss of information.

Example 3-12. Dangerous narrowing coercion

```
System.Int32 x = 32000;
System.Byte y;
y = (System.Byte)x; // coercing x from 32 bits to 8 bits, with info loss
```

---

[*] Partition I, 7.3.2.

Narrowing coercion will sometimes result in a loss of information—if the 32-bit integer stores a value that cannot be represented in 8 bits of information, for example, then the assignment will result in a different value than the original. For this reason, narrowing coercion operations are usually required to be explicitly coded by the programmer (usually through a cast or similar operation), whereas widening coercions can be implicitly (and safely) done by the language itself. The CLI provides the ability to check for narrowing coercions that lose information and throw a System. OverflowException at runtime when they occur.

Boxing/unboxing

By default, when an instance of a value type is passed from one location to another as a method parameter, it is copied in its entirety. At times, however, developers will want or need to take the value type and use it in a manner consistent with reference types. In these situations, the value type can be *boxed*: a reference type instance will be created whose data is the value type, and a reference to that instance is passed instead. Naturally, the reverse is also possible: taking the boxed value type and dereferencing it back into a value type—this is called *unboxing*.

CIL's box instruction is a typesafe operation that converts a value type instance to an instance of a reference type that inherits from System.Object. It does so by making a copy of the instance and embedding it in a newly allocated object. For every value type defined, the type system defines a corresponding reference type called the *boxed type*. The representation of a boxed value is a location where a value of the value type may be stored—in essence, a single-field reference type whose field is that of the value type. Note that this boxed type is never visible to anyone outside the CLI's implementation—the boxed type is silently generated by the CLI itself, and is not accessible for programmer use. (It is purely an implementation detail that would have no real utility were it exposed.)

In the Echo example component, there is a single place where a box instruction is generated by the C# compiler, which is highlighted in the excerpt in Example 3-13.

Example 3-13. An excerpt from the Echo component

```
if (OnEcho != null) {
  OnEcho(System.String.Format("Echo number {0}", echoCount));
}
```

If you're hard-pressed to spot the boxing operation in this line of code, it's because it occurs implicitly in C#. In fact, the operation is implicit in most languages, much as widening coercions can be. This code snippet, deep in the DoEcho method, contains a call to String.Format, which is a method whose implementation takes a variable number of arguments, each of unknown type. To make this work, parameters are specified to be as generic as possible; they are typed as System.Object. When the method is called, the parameters take on more specific types, which results in them being cast (or boxed) to the ultimate base class, System.Object. Because echoCount is declared as an int, which is a value type, echoCount will be boxed before being passed to the Format method. The Format method invokes ToString on what appears to be an object, but the runtime looks up and invokes System. Int32's ToString virtual method dynamically. (If you want to see the box operation for yourself, run *ildasm* against the *echo.dll* executable and examine the CIL for this method.)

Example 3-14 shows how boxing is performed within the execution engine. A call to the JIT_Box function is emitted by the JIT compiler when the box instruction is discovered in the stream of opcodes being compiled.

Example 3-14. Implementation of the box instruction (simplified from clr/src/vm/ jitinterface.cpp)

```
Object* JIT_Box(CORINFO_CLASS_HANDLE type, void* unboxedData)
{
  TypeHandle clsHnd(type);
  MethodTable *pMT = clsHnd.AsMethodTable( );
  OBJECTREF newobj;
  pMT->CheckRestore( );

  // You can only box things that inherit from valuetype or Enum.
  if (!CanBoxToObject(pMT))
    COMPlusThrow(kInvalidCastException, L"Arg_ObjObj");

  newobj = FastAllocateObject(pMT);

  CopyValueClass(newobj->GetData( ), unboxedData, pMT,
                 newobj->GetAppDomain( ));

  return(OBJECTREFToObject(newobj));
}
```

In this code, an object is allocated using FastAllocateObject, and the value class or Enum being boxed is copied into this object using CopyValueClass. CopyValueClass is a simple wrapper for CopyValueClassUnchecked, which is shown in Example 3-15. It is notable, because it uses layout information to copy actual values into the object instance; this layout information was computed from the type's metadata when the type was loaded by the execution engine.

Example 3-15. Implementation of CopyValueClassUnchecked (simplified from clr/src/vm/object.cpp)

```cpp
void CopyValueClassUnchecked(void* dest, void* src, MethodTable *pMT)
{
  // "Blit" any data that can be copied it directly as bytes
  switch (pMT->GetClass()->GetNumInstanceFieldBytes())
  {
  case 1:
    *(UINT8*)dest = *(UINT8*)src;
    break;
  case 2:
    *(UINT16*)dest = *(UINT16*)src;
    break;
  case 4:
    *(UINT32*)dest = *(UINT32*)src;
    break;
  case 8:
    *(UINT64*)dest = *(UINT64*)src;
    break;
  default:
    // The number of bytes in the data are not a "natural" size
    memcpyNoGCRefs(dest, src, pMT->GetClass()->GetNumInstanceFieldBytes());
      break;
  }

  // Now, if the value being copied contains object references,
  // tell the GC about copied references.
  if (pMT->ContainsPointers()) {
    CGCDesc* map = CGCDesc::GetCGCDescFromMT(pMT);
    CGCDescSeries* cur = map->GetHighestSeries();
    CGCDescSeries* last = map->GetLowestSeries();
    DWORD size = pMT->GetBaseSize();
    do {
      // Offset to embedded references in this series must be
      // adjusted by the VTable pointer, when in the unboxed state.
      size_t offset = cur->GetSeriesOffset() - sizeof(void*);
      OBJECTREF* srcPtr = (OBJECTREF*)(((BYTE*) src) + offset);
      OBJECTREF* destPtr = (OBJECTREF*)(((BYTE*) dest) + offset);
      OBJECTREF* srcPtrStop = (OBJECTREF*)((BYTE*) srcPtr +
                                  cur->GetSeriesSize() + size);
      while (srcPtr < srcPtrStop) {
        SetObjectReferenceUnchecked(destPtr,
                ObjectToOBJECTREF(*(Object**)srcPtr));
        srcPtr++;
        destPtr++;
      }
      cur--;
    } while (cur >= last);
  }
}
```

The code automating the copy is fairly straightforward, thanks to the presence of metadata. Contiguous instance data is copied from the value type into the object instance based on the number of "instance field bytes." Note that the grungy details of garbage collection must be dealt with; this will be discussed much more deeply in Chapter 7.

unbox is a CIL instruction that corresponds to box. It converts an object whose runtime type has been boxed (which is possible only via the box instruction—again, it's impossible to directly create a boxed type) back to an instance of a value type. Example 3-16 shows the code for the JIT_Unbox function.

Example 3-16. Implementation of the unbox instruction (Simplified from clr/src/vm/jitinterface.cpp)

```
LPVOID JIT_Unbox(CORINFO_CLASS_HANDLE type, Object* obj)
{
  TypeHandle typeHnd(type);

  RuntimeExceptionKind except;
  if (obj != 0) {
    if (obj->GetMethodTable() == typeHnd.AsMethodTable())
      return(obj->GetData());
    else {
      LPVOID ret = JIT_Unbox_Helper(type, obj);
      if (ret != 0)
        return(ret);
    }
    except = kInvalidCastException;
  } else
    except = kNullReferenceException;

  FCThrow(except);
}
```

When an unbox instruction is encountered, a call to the JIT_Unbox function is emitted by the JIT compiler. Not surprisingly, the JIT_Unbox function takes the object passed to it and unwraps the data contained in the instance using the GetData method. JIT_Unbox_Helper is a simple function that encapsulates conversion between primitive types and enums.

More on Reference Types

Reference types tie computational behavior directly to their heap-allocated state. There are three important classifications of reference types within the CLI: objects, interfaces, and encapsulated pointers, each of which can be found within the Echo component of Example 3-1. Enumerating these elements, the Echo class itself is an object type that implements an interface, contains a delegate, and uses a managed pointer to pass an out parameter.

General Principles

Recall that the definition of a value type is tied to its data, which are types that are "represented as a sequence of bits." The location of the value's data is directly embedded into a value type instance. Conversely, a reference type "describes values that are represented in the location of a sequence of bits," according to the ECMA specification. A reference type's value data is never manipulated directly by clients but is always accessed indirectly.

A reference is essentially a small piece of memory that points to the actual location of the reference type—in many ways, it's fair to think of the reference as a pointer. However, references have several advantages over pointers in the classic C/C++ sense:

References are strongly-typed

An object instance cannot be assigned to a reference unless it is assignment-compatible; this means a programmer cannot assign a Person object to a Department reference unless the type Person inherits from Department (an unlikely scenario).

References cannot be incorrectly assigned

A reference cannot point to a memory location that is not occupied by an object of that specific (or compatible) type; similarly, a reference cannot be "manufactured" to point to an arbitrary location in memory.

References cannot dangle

As long as a reference points to an object, that object cannot be deallocated. Therefore, a reference will always either be good or null, which is a reference literal value that points nowhere.

These tie into another aspect that separates reference types from value types. With a value type, because the instance of the value type is the data in question (remember, a value type is "represented as a sequence of bits"), allocation of a value type occurs as soon as the value type is declared within the code:

```
struct Size
{
  public int x;
  public int y;
}

class App
{
  static void Main()
  {
    Size s1, s2;
    int diff;

    diff = s1.x - s2.x;
  }
```

As soon as s1 and s2 are needed for the computation of diff, the compiler allocates enough memory to represent them, in this case on the method's stack. On the other hand, in many programming languages, objects (instances of reference types), must be allocated in a distinct operation using object-specific syntax. For example, the code below creates only a reference for s, without creating an object instance for it:

```
class Size
{
  public int x;
  public int y;
}

class App
{
  static void Main( )
  {
    Size s;
  }
}
```

Creating the actual object would require the explicit use of the new operator:

```
class App
{
  static void Main( )
  {
    Size s = new Size( );
  }
}
```

Similarly, in this code, only one object exists, even if it is referenced by two references:

```
class App
{
  static void Main( )
  {
    Size s = new Size( );
    Size t = s;
  }
}
```

Observant readers will notice that in none of these code samples is there any mention of deallocation of the object pointed to by s. This is because, as we have seen, the CLI is a garbage-collected system—the CLI itself takes responsibility for the deallocation and destruction of objects allocated during the CLI's lifetime. This is also how the CLI guarantees that a reference will never dangle—it ensures that as long as one reference to an object exists from reachable code, the object will continue to exist, as well. How this works will be explored in Chapter 7.

Interfaces

An interface, unlike other reference types, is simply a contract of behavior that will be present on any type that implements it. It provides a strongly typed definition that must be completely implemented on any concrete object instance whose type claims to implement it. For example, the Echo component defines an interface, IEchoer, which promises, in this case, that the component will implement a single method called DoEcho which returns void and sets the output parameter resultingEcho to some value:

```
public interface IEchoer {
    void DoEcho(out EchoValue[] resultingEcho);
}
```

Any implementation of IEchoer must therefore have a DoEcho method that matches this signature. What an interface provides is the ability to partition types into categories of related functionality—of all types in the system, those that can echo messages should in turn implement the IEchoer interface, all types that can compare instances of themselves against other instances of other types should implement the IComparable interface, and so on.

Interfaces can define any member type, including properties, methods, and events:

```
interface IPerson {
  string FirstName {
    get; set;
  }
  string LastName {
    get; set;
  }

  void Eat();
}
```

This interface specifies that any type that wishes to provide "person-like" behavior must provide two string properties—one called FirstName, one called LastName—and a method matching the Eat signature.

The fact that the CLI provides the ability to specify interfaces as more than just methods is a very useful semantic detail and is worth examining in more detail. Historically, interfaces in other languages (specifically, C++ and Java) have provided contracts for all three elements as method declarations on an interface—that is, state is represented as accessor and mutator, also known as *getter* and *setter* methods; behavior is represented as nonstate-related methods; and notification involves a *callback interface* that interested client components must implement somehow. In code, this can be boiled down as such:

```
/*
 * Fictitious C++ RS-232 Serial Port component class; to make
 * this an "interface" in C++, these would be pure virtual
```

```
    */
class SerialPort
{
public:
  SerialPort();
  ~SerialPort();

  // State methods
  //
public:
  // Getter/setter for the baud rate on the serial port
  //
  int getBaud();
  void setBaud(int newBaudValue);

  // Flow control state
  //
  bool getFlowControl();
  void setFlowControl(int newFlowControlValue);

  // Behavior methods
  //
public:
  void send(int data);
  int read();

  // Notification methods
  //
public:
  class Callback
  {
  public:
    // Called when data is ready to be read
    //
    virtual void onDataReady() = 0;
  };

  void registerListener(const Callback& listener);
  void removeListener(const Callback& listener);
};
```

Java code can be similarly imagined. The key here is that the interface's contract can be expressed using only method declarations and definitions, even
though the method calls aren't particularly expressive of the intent. The
state methods, for example, are reflected as nothing more than methods in
the metadata, as are the behavioral methods and the notification methods.
In short, only by examining the naming patterns of the method names can
you ascertain what the intent of the interface is.

Within the CLI (again, using C# as the language), the interface can be
coded more clearly and intentionally:

```
public interface SerialPort
{
  public int Baud
  {
    get;
    set;
  }

  public bool FlowControl
  {
    get;
    set;
  }

  public void send(int data);
  public int read( );

  public delegate void DataReadyDelegate( );
  public event DataReadyDelegate OnDataReady;
}
```

Here, the intent of each is much clearer, but more importantly, the intent is fully captured in metadata, again making SerialPort entirely self-descriptive: any tool, from compiler to code-generation tool, will have full awareness of the fact that Baud and DataReadyDelegate are state of the serial port component, while things like send and OnDataReady are behavioral—no convention involving method names is required.

Delegates and Managed Pointers

Delegates and managed pointers are both *encapsulated pointers*, which are reference types that augment an internal reference with additional information to enable unique CLI features. Take, for example, the references to code that are called *function pointers*.

Function pointers are supported as a first-class construct by the CLI. However, function pointers, used to refer to a method of an object, are not enough to capture the locations of both the method code and the object's instance data. Because the need to capture both locations together is very common in object-oriented code, to represent events and for the purpose of passing callback functions as method parameters, the designers of the CLI invented delegates for this purpose. Delegates are essentially the object-oriented equivalent of function pointers (more specifically, they are a special kind of closure), and as you can see from Example 3-17, they bundle a method pointer and a reference to a specific object instance, into a single type.

Example 3-17. The elements of a delegate (defined in clr/src/bcl/system/delegate.cs)

```
public abstract class Delegate : ICloneable, ISerializable
{
    // _method is the MethodInfo representing the target
    private IntPtr _methodPtr;

    // _target is the object we will invoke on
    private Object _target;

    // additional implementation omitted
```

Because the delegate contains an object reference, it can rely on the metadata for this object to maintain typesafety at runtime. Note that the class is abstract—the Delegate class is used to derive other delegate types, most notably the MulticastDelegate that is used to implement events in the CLI.

Managed pointers might be a little harder to understand than delegates, although they work under a similar principle. (And unless you are one of the lucky readers who are building compilers, you'll probably never need to understand the details.) There are a number of places where compilers and development tools need to work with pointers directly—for example, when they are allocating new chunks of memory. However, the execution engine needs to preserve typesafety at all times and, because of this, cannot pass pointers directly to the compiler. To solve this problem, a mechanism similar to delegates is used—a "raw" pointer is stored alongside type information that enables the JIT to verify that the pointer will be used properly and to create code accordingly.

There are a number of CIL instructions that result in pointer manipulation that are informed by metadata in this way, including the box and unbox instructions, allocation-related instructions such as newarr and newobj, and more esoteric instructions such as mkrefany.

An implementation that shows this technique is the value type TypedReference, seen in Example 3-18. Note that both the pointer (which is somewhat confusingly called Value in this code) and the type information are stored generically in integers. At this level of implementation, the execution engine has no abstractions to fall back on—the ugly details of mapping are exposed directly.

Example 3-18. The elements of a typed reference (from clr/src/bcl/typedreference.cs)

```
public struct TypedReference
{
    private int Value;
    private int Type;

    // additional implementation omitted
```

A managed pointer is used in the Echo component in Example 3-1 to represent the "out" parameter to the DoEcho method. If you examine the CIL and the metadata for the component, you will find that a stack location is allocated, into which the newarr opcode places a newly allocated instance of an array of value types. This array is then filled with return values and is available on the heap until all references to it are dropped, at which point it becomes available for garbage collection.

The key to managed pointers, delegates, and all other encapsulated pointers is that they are opaque. Since their inner data contents are not accessible, and since their implementations are completely contained within the code implementing the CLI, the execution engine can guarantee that their use is safe despite the fact that their use equates to manipulating addresses directly.

Identity and Equality for Reference and Value Types

As part of a discussion of type, we should examine the difference between object *identity* and object *equality*. Tests for both identity and equality are used throughout the Rotor CLI implementation. Of the two, identity is particularly important, being found in many of the runtime services such as code access security and garbage collection.

Identity is a property of an object's location—the memory address at which the object's data is located describes the value's identity, rather than the data contained at that address. Equality, on the other hand, is a measure of the value's contents—the data for two objects, rather than their locations, determines whether they are equal. This implies that two values that are identical must also be equal, but the reverse does not necessarily hold. For example, consider this snippet of C#:

```
System.Object A, B, C, D;
A = "A string";
B = A;
C = "A String";
D = "A different string";
```

Figure 3-1 shows the results schematically.

A and B, since their data share the same location, are identical, as well as equal. A and C, although their data are in different locations, both contain bitwise matching data, and therefore they are equal, even though they aren't identical. Finally, A and D, having unmatched data in different locations, are neither identical nor equal.

Within the CLI, the properties of identity and equality are provided via two methods on the base System.Object type: ReferenceEquals, which provides identity comparison capabilities, and Equals, which provides equality comparison. Since the Equals operation is heavily dependent on the semantics of

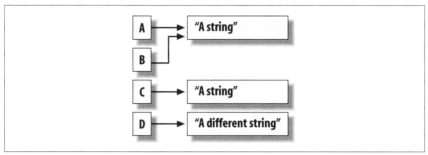

Figure 3-1. Identity versus equality

a given component, it is not unusual for its behavior to be replaced or augmented in derived types. Identity, on the other hand, is a simple test that
rarely needs to be overridden. Both Equals and ReferenceEquals may sometimes be mapped to operators in programming languages, although this is
purely in the hands of the language's designers.

The code used to implement Equals and ReferenceEquals for System.Object
should help drive home the difference between equality and identity. First,
Example 3-19 is the simple, one-line C# method that compares two references to determine whether they represent the identical object.

Example 3-19. ReferenceEquals tests for identity (defined in clr/src/bcl/system/object.cs)

```
public static bool ReferenceEquals (Object objA, Object objB) {
  return objA == objB;
}
```

Identity is easy to test for! (Assuming that no sneaky programmer has overridden the equality operator...)

Equality, on the other hand, is trickier. Example 3-20 shows the generic test
that is the default behavior for managed objects in the CLI. (Note that the
implementation of this object method is C++ code rather than C#.)

*Example 3-20. Object's equality test (simplified from clr/src/vm/comobject.cpp "internal
call" implementation)*

```
BOOL ObjectNative::Equals(Object *pThisRef, Object *pCompareRef)
{
  if (pThisRef == pCompareRef)
    return TRUE;

  // NULL cannot be a valid "this" pointer
  if (pThisRef == NULL || pCompareRef == NULL)
    return FALSE;

  MethodTable *pThisMT = pThisRef->GetMethodTable();
```

Example 3-20. Object's equality test (simplified from clr/src/vm/comobject.cpp "internal call" implementation) (continued)

```
// If it's not a value class, don't compare by value
if (!pThisMT->IsValueClass())
  return FALSE;

// Make sure they are the same type.
if (pThisMT != pCompareRef->GetMethodTable())
  return FALSE;

// Compare the contents (size - vtable - sink block index).
BOOL ret = !memcmp((void *) (pThisRef+1), (void *) (pCompareRef+1),
                   pThisRef->GetMethodTable()->GetBaseSize() -
                   sizeof(Object) - sizeof(int));
  return ret;
}
```

The code first checks for identity—if the two object references passed as arguments are identical, they will always be equal. If they are not identical, additional tests are performed to make sure that the objects being compared are values of the same type, since values of differing types cannot equal each other. As stated previously, reference types can certainly test for equality, but to do this, a type must replace the default implementation found in Object, which implements equality only for value types. Eventually, if all tests are passed, the contents of the two objects are compared directly, and if they match, the two values are determined to be equal.

Type Interoperability

Because the CLI type system regards interoperability with native code as an important goal, CLI consumers can expose their own component frameworks or unique features of an underlying operating system without compromise. Unlike execution environments that claim to provide "write once, run anywhere" facilities, the CLI was designed to augment existing system abstractions with its type system rather than fully duplicate such facilities in a new layer. To implement this approach, it follows that CLI types must not only be consistent among themselves, but must also be capable of representing the complete set of native constructs provided by the underlying system and microprocessor, and of using these constructs within its component model.

Built-in Types

Built-in types are perhaps the simplest form of type interoperability to understand: they are directly understood by the CLI execution engine, and have obvious value type equivalents. For example, the built-in type System. Int32 represents a 4-byte signed integer. These types are commonly mapped directly to types that the microprocessor implements in hardware by a given CLI implementation. In the ECMA specification, these mappings and the semantics associated with them are termed the "virtual execution system."

The actual constants used to represent built-in types within the JIT compiler are shown in Example 3-21.

Example 3-21. The map used to convert abstract CLI types into processor-specific types (defined in clr/src/vm/jitinterface.cpp)

```
static const BYTE map[] = {
  CORINFO_TYPE_UNDEF,
  CORINFO_TYPE_VOID,
  CORINFO_TYPE_BOOL,
  CORINFO_TYPE_CHAR,
  CORINFO_TYPE_BYTE,
  CORINFO_TYPE_UBYTE,
  CORINFO_TYPE_SHORT,
  CORINFO_TYPE_USHORT,
  CORINFO_TYPE_INT,
  CORINFO_TYPE_UINT,
  CORINFO_TYPE_LONG,
  CORINFO_TYPE_ULONG,
  CORINFO_TYPE_FLOAT,
  CORINFO_TYPE_DOUBLE,
  CORINFO_TYPE_STRING,
  CORINFO_TYPE_PTR,              // PTR
  CORINFO_TYPE_BYREF,
  CORINFO_TYPE_VALUECLASS,
  CORINFO_TYPE_CLASS,
  CORINFO_TYPE_CLASS,            // VAR (type variable)
  CORINFO_TYPE_CLASS,           // MDARRAY
  CORINFO_TYPE_BYREF,          // COPYCTOR
  CORINFO_TYPE_REFANY,
  CORINFO_TYPE_VALUECLASS,     // VALUEARRAY
  CORINFO_TYPE_INT,            // I
  CORINFO_TYPE_UINT,           // U
  CORINFO_TYPE_DOUBLE,         // R

  // put the correct type when we know our implementation
  CORINFO_TYPE_PTR,            // FNPTR
  CORINFO_TYPE_CLASS,          // OBJECT
  CORINFO_TYPE_CLASS,          // SZARRAY
  CORINFO_TYPE_CLASS,          // GENERICARRAY
  CORINFO_TYPE_UNDEF,          // CMOD_REQD
  CORINFO_TYPE_UNDEF,          // CMOD_OPT
  CORINFO_TYPE_UNDEF,          // INTERNAL
};
```

In addition to the basic types one would expect to see in this list, void, bool, char, and various sizes of floating-point and integral numbers, the CLI also defines several other built-in types that carry additional structure or semantics. OBJECT, arrays, strings, and VALUECLASS aren't too surprising, along with the several flavors of CLASS, since these are important fundamentals for the component model. The natively sized flavors of integers, and floating-point numbers that take on whatever word size the underlying hardware's CPU uses, are also to be expected.

More interestingly, there are several varieties of pointer that show up in this map: function pointers, BYREF, PTR, and REFANY. Pointer types are fully supported by the CLI, despite the fact that they can cripple the advantages of typesafety. The CLI both provides a broad set of types to work with and the rules of engagement that define best practices—in this case, "don't use pointers unless you understand that your code will not be verifiably typesafe, and because of this, you will be completely responsible for maintaining typesafety in place of the CLI execution engine." To use trusted code within the CLI implementation that manipulates addresses and interoperates with unmanaged code, pointers must be called out as a special case or else represented like any other primitive type. The designers of the CLI opted for the single mapping, which had the side effect of greatly enhancing interoperability—in many cases, well-defined pointers can be used within typesafe code. For example, function pointers to methods are used extensively and exposed as delegates. Typed references and managed pointers are additional typesafe constructs that are available to compiler writers.

All of the types in Example 3-21 form the backbone of the CLI type system, since to be useful, the CLI must ultimately translate abstract types and their behavior into native instructions, datatypes, and data layouts represented by addresses and offsets. This list is used by the internals of the CLI and is never exposed directly to consumers, who see CLI runtime services, CIL and metadata, or interoperability facilities in their place.

Wrapper Classes, Marshaling, and Interop

An interoperability requirement that makes a good sample case is the use of opaque handles in APIs. Opaque handles are forms of names. They are pointers or indexes to data whose structure is not meant to be visible to the clients of a programming API, but is important internally to that API. Handles are dispensed to clients to track resources that belong to the API's implementation; they are stored and returned to other runtime routines as parameters by clients when they need to programmatically refer to the original resource. Because handles are often used to represent operating-system entities, the CLI needs to be able to interact with and use them without intrinsic knowledge of the structure of the resources that they represent. In this case, how should typed abstractions like handles (or semaphores, or...) be represented in the CLI?

The usual approach has been to enable call-level interop so that API calls can be embedded directly into "wrapper classes," which themselves can be managed code. This kind of use places additional requirements on the runtime services used by components—explicit layout of memory regions must be possible, finalization becomes important during garbage collection for cleanup, exception mechanisms need to coexist peacefully, threading and thread sensitivity must be recognized...the list goes on and on. A discussion of this kind of interop will be found in the chapters on extending the SSCLI. From the perspective of types, low-level resources can be represented as managed pointers, callbacks, or components themselves. Much more will be said about these techniques later.

 Wrapped APIs and value types are clearly essential for programming languages that do not support components. A major design point for the CLI is enabling a language agnostic approach—just because this book concentrates on the component model, this point should not be lost. Classes that are not instantiable and have only static methods, for example, make great wrappers; the component model can accommodate these cases. The ECMA specification has an extensive and more formal discussion of its typesystem in its sections on the Common Language Specification and the Common Type System.

Using Types in Data-Driven Code

Earlier, in the section entitled "Type, Object, and Component," we saw how the loading and compilation process of the CLI is data-driven, with many decisions made by examining embedded metadata tokens at the last possible moment. This technique is not limited to the JIT compiler—it can be used by custom programs as well. The use of type information to drive program decisions is called *introspection* or *reflection*—the component's code is reflecting on its own structure and making decisions based on this information.

Programs with sufficient permissions can create, manipulate, and examine type metadata, either from managed code (using the System.Reflection family of types) or from unmanaged code (using the unmanaged APIs described in *clr/src/inc/metadata.h* that are outside the CLI specification). Type descriptions can be used to defer decisions until runtime, enabling looser linkages between components and more robust load-time adaptations.

This last point deserves a bit more in the way of explanation—specifically, the idea of using component metadata to promote looser coupling between components may be a new concept for many. Consider, for a moment, a desire to take an existing in-memory object instance and save its current state to some secondary storage stream (e.g., the filesystem, or sent as part of an HTTP request, or even to a binary field in a database.) Under formal, object-oriented approaches, this is common behavior across types and therefore should be represented as a base type from which derived types inherit this functionality.

On closer examination, however, serious problems begin to creep in. To begin with, this base type knows absolutely nothing of the derived type's data, yet it's the derived type's data that needs to be stored (along with any further derived types that in turn derive from the derived type). In addition, because we also look to use inheritance as a mechanism for unifying commonality among domain types (Employee is a Person, whereas Department is not), this in turn begs the argument for multiple inheritance within the system, a road the C++ community already went down and discovered significant issues with.

Within a single-inheritance environment, like Java, one possible solution is to create an interface that serves as a well-understood "flag" to components that indicate that this type wants to participate in this "object-to-disk" behavior. A type inherits this "marker interface," which has no methods, and when instances of this type are passed to the "object-to-disk" APIs, this flag is checked to ensure that this type does, in fact, want to be stored.

In turn, this approach has some significant flaws. For starters, the level of granularity on an interface is again centered on methods. If the component wants or needs to indicate some additional information about its desire to be stored to disk, it needs to specify a method in the interface, called by the storing APIs, to obtain that information. This in turn means the components wishing to be stored must implement those methods, making this an intrusive operation—in essence, it "pollutes" the API of the component with code that isn't domain-related.

What we really want for this system, at this point, is the ability to place information at the type level into the code, available to interested parties, but otherwise a non-intrusive (and non-polluting) specification.

Custom attributes were designed exactly for this purpose. Attributes are metadata that is attached to various facets of types, using either special language syntax or tools that enable after-the-fact type annotation. The Serializable attribute, for example, could be attached to the Echo component with the very simple one-line declaration shown in Example 3-22, creating a capability for this component simply by the act of annotating it.

Example 3-22. C# syntax of the serializable attribute

```csharp
[ Serializable( ) ]
public class Echo : IEchoer {
    // Rest of component declaration would follow
}
```

At runtime, when the now-serializable component is asked to serialize its state, a serialization engine can use the component's metadata to determine exactly how to read and write the values of the type to or from an external representation. The state of the component can be freeze-dried using such a technique and then reloaded later. Note that like component assemblies, serialized component state can persist across runtime incarnations of the component itself; serialized state information saved by Version 1 of a component may very well be reloaded into Version 3 of the same type. By making the process data-driven, a well-designed component can adapt to this eventuality.

Example 3-23 contains the code from the SSCLI that implements serialization.

Example 3-23. Code from the serialization engine (defined in clr/src/bcl/system/runtime/ formatter.cs)

```csharp
protected virtual void WriteMember(String memberName, Object data)
{
    if (data==null) {
        WriteObjectRef(data, memberName, typeof(Object));
        return;
    }

    Type varType = data.GetType( );

    if (varType==typeof(Boolean)) {
        WriteBoolean(Convert.ToBoolean(data), memberName);
    } else if (varType==typeof(Char)) {
        WriteChar(Convert.ToChar(data), memberName);
    } else if (varType==typeof(SByte)) {
        WriteSByte(Convert.ToSByte(data), memberName);
    } else if (varType==typeof(Byte)) {
        WriteByte(Convert.ToByte(data), memberName);
    } else if (varType==typeof(Int16)) {
        WriteInt16(Convert.ToInt16(data), memberName);
    } else if (varType==typeof(Int32)) {
        WriteInt32(Convert.ToInt32(data), memberName);
    } else if (varType==typeof(Int64)) {
        WriteInt64(Convert.ToInt64(data), memberName);
    } else if (varType==typeof(Single)) {
        WriteSingle(Convert.ToSingle(data), memberName);
    } else if (varType==typeof(Double)) {
        WriteDouble(Convert.ToDouble(data), memberName);
```

Example 3-23. Code from the serialization engine (defined in clr/src/bcl/system/runtime/ formatter.cs) (continued)

```
  } else if (varType==typeof(DateTime)) {
    WriteDateTime(Convert.ToDateTime(data), memberName);
  } else if (varType==typeof(Decimal)) {
    WriteDecimal(Convert.ToDecimal(data), memberName);
  } else if (varType==typeof(UInt16)) {
    WriteUInt16(Convert.ToUInt16(data), memberName);
  } else if (varType==typeof(UInt32)) {
    WriteUInt32(Convert.ToUInt32(data), memberName);
  } else if (varType==typeof(UInt64)) {
    WriteUInt64(Convert.ToUInt64(data), memberName);
  } else {
    if (varType.IsArray) {
      WriteArray(data, memberName, varType);
    } else if (varType.IsValueType) {
      WriteValueType(data, memberName, varType);
    } else {
      WriteObjectRef(data, memberName, varType);
    }
  }
}
```

Because the metadata for any object instance is available through the reflection APIs, the code to implement the writing out of values is nearly trivial. If the serialization engine wants to provide additional services later, like the ability to optionally encrypt the serialized data, then the attribute could be enhanced to include a boolean Encrypt flag, defaulted to false. But because this is not an intrusive part of the client wishing to be serialized, the client component suffers no substantive changes to its own implementation—a change to the metadata attribute would be the worst required.

Summary

We will have much more to say about the data-driven approach to execution used in the CLI in later chapters. For now, it is important to note that metadata-rich types are the abstraction that makes this approach possible.

The type system of the CLI is designed to promote maximal flexibility in a language-agnostic approach to component integration. By creating completely self-descriptive components and preserving their metadata as the executable representation, no intrinsic binding to the underlying platform is created until the JIT compiler is run. Using this approach, a single executable can adapt to a variety of platforms, environments, and system versions over time. Armed with more intimate knowledge about how this is possible in the type system of the CLI, we can now turn our attention to how types are packaged and distributed as stored component assemblies.

CHAPTER 4

Extracting Types from Assemblies

Types attain their full power as an integration mechanism when they are packaged in a form that can be easily transported from machine to machine and reconstituted safely. The CLI devotes a great deal of its design to enabling exactly this scenario, using a packaging approach based on *assemblies*. Assemblies are central to understanding components, since as we saw in the discussion of metadata, the component architecture of the CLI is data-driven: the data found in assemblies is a blueprint for all of the types that will populate the execution engine at runtime. Although such metadata can be synthesized directly at runtime, it is far more common to find it in the form of a file on disk, in which form it can propagate from machine to machine and from microprocessor to microprocessor, via traditional disk-to-disk copy or via network download.

Type Packaging

Assemblies are the basic unit of packaging and code security for the CLI runtime. The requirement that most influenced their design was the need for packaging that would allow self-contained components to be moved easily from location to location and yet still interoperate with high fidelity. To accommodate this, assemblies took on the following characteristics, which will serve to guide us further in our examination of the CLI:

Assemblies are self-describing
> Assemblies, to enable data-driven execution, are completely self-descriptive and preserve full-fidelity metadata.

Assemblies are platform-independent
> The CLI achieves a good measure of platform independence by ensuring a well-known, standard format for assemblies.

Assemblies are bound by name
> Clients locate assemblies by querying for a four-part tuple that consists of a human-friendly name, an international culture, a multipart version number, and a public key token.

Assembly loading is sensitive to version and policy
> Assemblies are loaded using tunable binding rules, which allow programmers and administrators to contribute policy to assembly-loading behavior.

Assemblies are validated
> Each time an assembly is loaded, it is subjected to a series of checks to ensure the assembly's integrity.

We'll examine each of these concepts in turn.

Assemblies Are Self-Describing

Assemblies contain blueprints for types in the form of metadata and CIL, which are referred to as *modules*. A module is a single file containing the structure and behavior for some or all of the types and/or resources found in the assembly. An assembly always contains at least one module but has the capacity to include multiple modules if desired, usually to gain packaging and performance flexibility.

The types exposed by an assembly are actually represented in the metadata as redirections to the modules that contain the types; it is not possible to expose types without modules. Allowing multiple modules in a single assembly makes it easier to isolate changes as requirements evolve. In particular, resources or types that are either infrequently accessed or are frequently changed can be contained in separate files.

As you can see from Figure 4-1, the modules in an assembly can also contain *resources*, which is a squishy term for passive data (meaning anything that isn't intended as executable code or metadata). Resources are typically packaged as part of the assembly to take advantage of its namespace, as well as the locality and trust that come from being within, rather than outside, its logical boundaries. Both types and resources are optional; assemblies that contain types with no resources are common, while assemblies that contain resources can be useful only for tasks such as localization.

Like the type-describing modules that they contain, assemblies themselves have metadata that describe their structure. This metadata takes the form of a *manifest* that itemizes the contents of the assembly, contains the compound name for the assembly, describes public types that the assembly exports, and describes types that the assembly will import from other

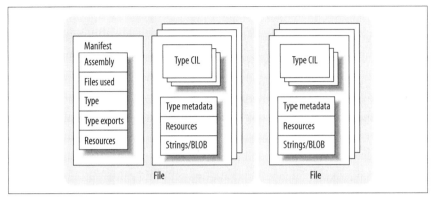

Figure 4-1. Assemblies can use one or more modules, but only one contains a manifest

assemblies. Manifests are built using the same metadata table mechanisms that are used to describe types—to see this in action, look in *assembly.cpp* and *assemblymd.cpp* in the *sscli/clr/src/vm* directory.

 As we've already seen, there are several tools that are part of the SSCLI distribution whose implementation can help illuminate the structure of modules and assemblies. The first of these is *ildasm.exe*, the CIL disassembler, whose code can be found in *sscli/clr/src/ildasm*. The job of *ildasm* is fairly simple: take a file and disassemble it into its component parts. All source is displayed as CIL, and complete metadata tables can be dumped. As a development and diagnostic tool, *ildasm* is peerless. More importantly, however, to the Rotor experimenter, *ildasm* provides the ability to examine CLI metadata from both a black-box and white-box perspective; developers can use it to examine the metadata of compiled assemblies, as well as use the code that comprises *ildasm* as a template from which to build their own unmanaged applications and tools that examine CLI executables. Another useful tool to examine is *al.exe*, the assembly linker, which is used to piece together different modules into a single assembly and whose code can be found in *sscli/clr/src/csharp/alink*.

Usually, the assembly manifest is built when the source is compiled; to see this in action, take the Echo component from Chapter 3 and compile it into a library using the C# compiler. After it has successfully compiled, run the *metainfo* tool against the single-module assembly contained in *echo.dll* by typing:

```
> metainfo -assem echo.dll
```

The -assem switch restricts the output of *metainfo* to show only assembly metadata, which means that you'll see something similar to the following:

```
Microsoft (R) Shared Source CLI Runtime Meta Data Dump Utility
Version 1.0.0002.0
Copyright (C) Microsoft Corporation 1998-2002. All rights reserved.
//////////////////////////////////////////////////////////////////

File echo.dll:
Assembly
-------------------------------------------------------
        Token: 0x20000001
        Name : echo
        Public Key    : 00 24 00 00 04 80 00 00  ...
        Hash Algorithm : 0x00008004
        Major Version: 0x00000001
        Minor Version: 0x00000000
        Build Number: 0x00000000
        Revision Number: 0x00000000
        Locale: <null>
        Flags : [SideBySideCompatible] [PublicKey]  (00000001)
        CustomAttribute #1 (0c000001)
        -------------------------------------------------------
                CustomAttribute Type: 0a000001
                CustomAttributeName:
                  System.Reflection.AssemblyKeyFileAttribute ::
                                    instance void .ctor(class /
                                        System.String)
                Length: 13
                Value : 01 00 08 65 63 68 6f 2e   73 6e 6b 00 00 > echo.snk <
                ctor args: ("echo.snk")

        CustomAttribute #2 (0c000002)
        -------------------------------------------------------
                CustomAttribute Type: 0a000003
                CustomAttributeName:
                  System.Diagnostics.DebuggableAttribute ::
                                    instance void .ctor(bool,bool)
                Length: 6
                Value : 01 00 01 01 00 00                    >         <
                ctor args: ( <can not decode> )
```

This dump shows the values of the assembly's attributes. If you instead run the following against the component, you'll see a great deal more of the metadata:

```
> ildasm –metainfo echo.dll
```

The results are too lengthy to include here, but in the *ildasm* output, you'll be able to see assembly versioning and dependency information, in addition to imported and exported types. If this were a multimodule assembly spread out over several files, you would get information for every module.

The *ildasm* program provides a superset of the functionality found in *metainfo*. As is the case with many small utility programs, each has its role, and this role is governed by programmer taste. Some think that the -assem switch, for example, is the easiest way to get to assembly attributes. Playing with each comparatively is a fine way to fritter away a few moments of free time.

Assemblies are, at their core, the metadata that comprises their manifests (which, of course, transitively include type metadata and behavior, as well as resources). The distinction between an assembly and a module is important; in particular, it must be stressed that "assembly" and "file" are not equivalent terms. The CLI is built on top of abstractions that can be used in many different situations on many different platforms, and because of this, there are cornerstone concepts that do not correspond directly to common operating system abstractions. Since assemblies can be made up of multiple files, one cannot always point to a file that corresponds to the assembly. In our example, *Echo.dll* happens to be a file that comprises the entire assembly and contains both the singleton module and the assembly manifest, but this will not always be the case. You might decide to split the implementation into two modules, one for backward compatibility and one containing new code, for example. Or you might decide to localize using a separate module to contain resources. The important thing to remember is that assemblies and their manifests always refer to modules.

Assemblies Are Location-Agnostic

On-disk assemblies can be successfully loaded on many different machine architectures. This isn't magic, but it is fundamental to portability. An easy-to-try experiment is to compile an assembly using the SSCLI on Windows, and then load and run it on FreeBSD, and vice versa. You should also be able to take an assembly produced using the SSCLI and examine it using the .NET Framework SDK tools. Using a shared format is a venerable and well-understood way to begin a quest for interoperability.

The persistent structure for an assembly and its types is very different than what it will eventually become in memory. In the Chapter 2 tutorial, we briefly saw that the file format is based on the PE/COFF executable format, but most of the interesting structure is entirely contained within a single opaque .text section. Because of this, the ECMA format does not rely heavily on the PE/COFF headers and file structure.

The Microsoft Portable Executable (PE) file format is the format used by Microsoft Win32-based operating systems for storing executable resources (DLLs and EXEs). PE depends, in turn, on the Common Object File Format (COFF), which is an even older executable format. A complete description of the PE/COFF format, besides being excruciatingly dull, is beyond the scope of this book; however, the segmented format is well-documented in a specification that can be found on Microsoft's MSDN web site.

Within the Rotor code base, the task of loading, parsing, and verifying the PE file structure falls to a single class called (cleverly enough) PEFile, located in *sscli/clr/src/vm/pefile.h* and *pefile.cpp*. A PEFile instance is a C++ class wrapper around a Portable Executable image. This image doesn't have to exist on disk; it can in fact be created around an image that the program hosting the execution engine has mapped into memory already or created directly. The PEFile itself is fairly simple: once created, the PEFile provides an easy way to obtain various headers—the Win32 headers (an instance of an IMAGE_NT_HEADERS struct), the COR headers (an instance of an IMAGE_COR20_HEADERS struct), and instances to metadata objects (an instance of an IMDInternalImport interface).

Examining the PEFile class doesn't take long; there's not much to PEFile beyond verifying the structural integrity of the file and then using it to obtain the sections of a file to be picked apart further by hand. Within Rotor, the principal aim is to get at the part of the PE file where the IMAGE_COR20_HEADER lives, as shown in Example 4-1 (which is defined in *clr/src/inc/corhdr.h*).

Example 4-1. The IMAGE_COR20_HEADER

```
typedef struct IMAGE_COR20_HEADER
{
    // Header versioning
    ULONG                   cb;
    USHORT                  MajorRuntimeVersion;
    USHORT                  MinorRuntimeVersion;

    // Symbol table and startup information
    IMAGE_DATA_DIRECTORY    MetaData;
    ULONG                   Flags;
    ULONG                   EntryPointToken;

    // Binding information
    IMAGE_DATA_DIRECTORY    Resources;
    IMAGE_DATA_DIRECTORY    StrongNameSignature;

    // Regular fixup and binding information
    IMAGE_DATA_DIRECTORY    CodeManagerTable;
```

Example 4-1. The IMAGE_COR20_HEADER (continued)

```
    IMAGE_DATA_DIRECTORY    VTableFixups;
    IMAGE_DATA_DIRECTORY    ExportAddressTableJumps;

    // Precompiled image info (internal use only - set to zero)
    IMAGE_DATA_DIRECTORY    ManagedNativeHeader;
} IMAGE_COR20_HEADER;
```

PEFile has a method called GetCORHdr that can be used to obtain this simple header, which further segments the mapped file using the following typedef:

```
    typedef struct _IMAGE_DATA_DIRECTORY {
        ULONG   VirtualAddress;
        ULONG   Size;
    } IMAGE_DATA_DIRECTORY, *PIMAGE_DATA_DIRECTORY;
```

Important fields include the version numbers and the entry point, as well as the segment addresses for the metadata, the resources, and the digital signature, if present. Note that there is no segment address for the code itself; the entrypoint token will be resolved like every other metadata token, via the metadata segment, by the ExecuteMainMethod method of ClassLoader. The token is resolved to a MethodDef, its calling convention and signature are verified, and, eventually, the method is given control by the execution engine.

Loading Assemblies by Name

Assemblies are as self-contained as possible to impart independence and maximize their chances at being versionable. The types in an assembly are exposed as public or are purely internal to the assembly; there are no friend constructs to complicate binding relationships. To ensure adaptability, they attach to their surrounding environment at runtime by binding to names, rather than addresses or offsets.

Types are the universal abstraction that drives execution in the CLI, and types use other types by referring to them by name. Fully qualified type names combine the assembly name and the base type name, plus an optional namespace prefix, if present. The name of the type is scoped by the assembly, and types are joined together (or bound) by name.

Although the namespaces that components populate appear to be hierarchically structured, they are not. (This differs, in particular, from Java, in which package structure is mapped directly to the filesystem.) The namespace prefix in a fully qualified name is just an optional string that can precede a type's name and typically follows a hierarchal naming convention used by developer tools to group types together. They are purely conventional, and they are not isolated; multiple assemblies can contribute to the same namespace.

The loose coupling that comes from name-based binding is consistent with adaptability over time. To remain viable over time, the assembly must be capable of propagating itself through future generations, no matter how harsh conditions become. The best way to do this robustly in the face of changing conditions is to meticulously describe all parts of the system and develop ways to make small changes, while still remaining compatible with the overall system. It is precisely this ability to make small changes transparently and swap component implementations in and out behind names that enables clever programmers to ensure good release-to-release binary compatibility.

Example 4-2 shows how assembly names are represented in the System. Reflection namespace.

Example 4-2. The elements of assembly names (simplified from clr/src/bcl/system/ reflection/assemblyname.cs)

```
public sealed class AssemblyName : ICloneable,
                                   ISerializable, IDeserializationCallback
{
    private String             _Name;
    private byte[]             _PublicKey;
    private byte[]             _PublicKeyToken;
    private CultureInfo        _CultureInfo;
    private String             _CodeBase;         // Location for file
    private Version            _Version;

    private StrongNameKeyPair             _StrongNameKeyPair;
    internal Assembly                     _Assembly;
    private AssemblyHashAlgorithm         _HashAlgorithm;
    private AssemblyVersionCompatibility _VersionCompatibility;
    private AssemblyNameFlags             _Flags;
}
```

The full name of an assembly includes four parts; all but the base name itself are optional. A full assembly name typically consists of the filename minus its extension plus version information in a format that concatenates major version, minor version, build number, and revision number into a dot-separated string. After this, the localized culture of the assembly can be referenced by including a two-character abbreviation (dictated by IETF RFC-1766). Culture information is particularly important when resources or localizable strings are included as part of the assembly. Finally, a public key or a public key token (an abbreviated form of the public key formed using a cryptographic hash) that identifies the developer of the assembly can be included. This is used when exploiting the CLI's support for cryptographic *strongnames*. When the parts of the full name are combined in a canonical way, the result is called the *displayname* of the assembly. Displaynames can be either complete or partial. Strongnames are optional, and if they are used, they have a radical effect on the binding regimen used; the rules for finding strongnamed libraries supplement the rules for finding libraries without strongnames, and enable sharing scenarios that wouldn't otherwise exist.

An assembly's display name can be seen within managed code by interrogating the FullName property of the System.Reflection.Assembly instance for the assembly. Printed, it appears as "*assembly-name*, Version=*x.x.x.x*, Culture=*culture*, PublicKeyToken=*token*"; the assembly for the Echo component, for example appears as:

```
echo, Version=0.0.0.0, Culture=neutral, PublicKeyToken=null
```

when displayed. As you can see, the assembly is unsigned, and no version number has been assigned to it.

To set the other three parts of the assembly name, the SSCLI uses assembly-level custom attributes to directly emit the values into the assembly manifest.

 The implementation of assembly-level attributes is strictly a compiler convention, ad can be found in *assemblyattributes.cs* in the *bcl/system/reflection* directory. Assembly-level attributes are not implemented in the same way as custom attributes, which is a shortcoming of the current CLI specification. It is possible to use the more general custom attribute mechanism for module-level attributes, but not for assembly level attributes.

So to set the version and strongname signature of the Echo component, you could use the following attributes at the top of the *Echo.cs* file:

```
[assembly: AssemblyVersion("1.0.0.0")]
[assembly: AssemblyKeyFile("echo.snk")]
```

in which echo.snk is a file containing a cryptographic public key/private key pair generated by the *sn.exe* utility. This would then change the display name of Echo to:

```
echo, Version=1.0.0.0, Culture=neutral, PublicKeyToken=fcd14a8abe06f0d2
```

Of course, the value of PublicKeyToken will vary given unless readers use the exact same public key/private key token file used to generate the example. Throughout this chapter, whenever we show a public key token, you should assume that your own will differ.

Assembly names were constructed with as many parts as they have to support versioning and side-by-side loading. Embedding the version number into the name permits the CLI to highlight dependencies as part of its component-to-component contract.

Alternatively, public key tokens allow two assemblies of the same name from different parties to coexist. There are repercussions to this technique, however; in the presence of many versions of a single assembly, name resolution and binding rules become quite complex.

Binding to Versioned Assemblies

Of course, it is possible to manually load assemblies from code using the Load or LoadFrom methods of the Assembly type, but the more normal case is that assemblies are loaded as they are needed. The assembly loading code, like so many of the other portions of the CLI, follows the principle of deferred actions: by deferring a costly action until it is actually needed, you can avoid performing it unnecessarily. If an application rarely calls a method or rarely accesses a named resource, the assembly will rarely be loaded. In fact, an application can be built to run successfully with assemblies that are referenced, but not deployed. Debugging code, or optional features, might benefit from this treatment.

Once a call is made to a method in an assembly, the first step in binding is to decide what version of the assembly, containing the type, should be used. To determine this, the execution engine consults the manifest of the assembly that made the call, where it can find an exact version specifier in the table of external references. Once this version number is procured, the CLI hunts down a file that corresponds to it using the loosely defined runtime service that is referred to in the SSCLI code base as *fusion*.

 "Fusion" was the codename for the assembly loader at the development of the Microsoft .NET Framework, and because of this, you will see many comments and variable names that contain the word. There is also a directory in the SSCLI distribution, named *sscli/clr/src/fusion*, in which you'll find some of the code used during assembly loadtime. (This code is deployed as the *fusion.dll* shared library that is dynamically loaded by the SSCLI at runtime.) However, the configuration and loading code that can be found in this library is augmented by a fair amount of code that resides in the execution engine directory (*sscli/clr/src/vm*). Like many projects, the SSCLI has accreted partial layers of imperfectly factored subsystems over time. When searching for implementation details, one way to approach the division of code between fusion and the execution engine is to remember that the CLI is concerned with loading types from assemblies, while fusion is concerned with locating and loading files.

The execution engine checks to see whether the appropriate assembly is already loaded, since once an assembly is loaded, it can never be reloaded within a given application domain. (Application domains will be discussed later in this chapter.) If the assembly is not loaded, but is strongly named and fully qualified, a machine-wide cache, called the Global Assembly Cache (GAC), is checked. Details about the GAC are, for the moment, irrelevant—just recognize it as a common place for assemblies to live. If the assembly is found in the GAC, it is loaded; otherwise, the execution engine then searches for codebase elements in configuration files, which specify locations from which assemblies can be loaded. If no codebase locations are provided, the execution engine will look in the appbase as a last resort, which is a variety of likely locations in the filesystem. By default, the appbase is the relative root directory from which the application was executed.

Key-Based Binding to Assemblies

The CLI supports the use of cryptographic signatures as a way to uniquely identify assemblies. The presence of the AssemblyKeyFileAttribute in an assembly's metadata denotes that it is strongly named, and that this attribute will be used as a part of the loading process to verify that the assembly being loaded is identical to the referenced assembly. It is possible to turn off this verification, and during development, this is an important configuration option, since code under development is usually both trusted and broken at the same time, and the time spent signing and verifying strongnames could almost certainly be better be spent fixing bugs!

The verification mechanism for strongnames requires the build process to have access to both the public and private elements of a cryptographic key pair at the time that it builds an assembly. The public key becomes part of the assembly name, and a cryptographic hash of the metadata of the assembly is calculated using the private key and is inserted into the assembly. At load time, the execution engine uses the public key to extract a hash value for the assembly being verified that is then compared against a direct cryptographic hash of the metadata, proving that the producer of the assembly had access to the private key. The implementation of the strongname crypto code can be found in *strongname.cpp* in the *clr/src/dlls/mscorsn* directory. It is used by the execution engine from files such as *assembly.cpp*.

The Shared Source CLI is not intended for use as a secure environment, although the source code does provide a good example of how a secure execution environment might be built. For example, strongname verification is turned off by default in the SSCLI for several important public keys, which means that no assembly built as part of the SSCLI can be trusted with respect to origin. Since you have control of access to the Rotor source code on your machine, you are the only person who understands the level of trust to impart to your own build output. If you want to make Rotor secure, you will need to audit source code modifications, restrict access to keypairs used to build the execution engine, do the work necessary to establish trust relationships between the execution engine and its assemblies, and, in general, pay a lot of attention to the process used to build and deploy the executables that comprise the built output of the distribution.

The GAC, as mentioned previously, is part of the extended search path for assemblies. To be found in the GAC, an assembly must have a public key. Public keys are normally attached by dropping an `AssemblyKeyFile` attribute into a C# source file and compiling; the C# compiler will extract the key pair from the key file and sign the assembly. (An assembly with a public key does not have to be signed to be in the GAC, although such a delay signed assembly must still have a public key attached. Since it cannot be safely loaded, it can be used only with verification turned off.) In the SSCLI implementation, which supports running many different versions of the CLI on a single machine, the GAC is implemented as a subdirectory of the build directory; in the SSCLI, the GAC is tied to the directory structure of the particular version of *sscoree.dll* that is being used.

Sharing Assemblies on a Computer

The GAC essentially represents a machine-wide library of assemblies for use by any CLI process. It is, in essence, the communal pool of shared assemblies. Like any communal resource, there are strict rules for use, to protect the peace and to ensure correct behavior. If a programmer doesn't wish to play by these rules or has no need to share an assembly, then she may simply place her assembly in the same directory as the managed executable that needs it, and it will be found and loaded from there.

Within the Rotor source base, as mentioned previously, the GAC is implemented as a subdirectory of the build tree. In particular, the Rotor binaries will be in a directory named something like *v1.x86chk* (with the directory name changing according to version, platform, and the kind of build being used). The *GAC* subdirectory will be in the *assembly* subdirectory underneath that location. Exploring this subdirectory reveals that each assembly is placed into further subdirectories, first separated by the assembly name as a subdirectory, then the assembly's version number and public key token. For example, the *GAC* directory looks something like the following on Windows:

```
Directory of C:\sscli\build\v1.x86fstchk.rotor\assembly\GAC

11/02/2002  02:53 AM    <DIR>          .
11/02/2002  02:53 AM    <DIR>          ..
11/02/2002  02:53 AM    <DIR>          ISymWrapper
11/02/2002  02:53 AM    <DIR>          Microsoft.JScript
11/02/2002  02:53 AM    <DIR>          Microsoft.Vsa
11/02/2002  02:53 AM    <DIR>          System
11/02/2002  02:53 AM    <DIR>          System.Runtime.Remoting
11/02/2002  02:53 AM    <DIR>          System.Runtime.Serialization.
Formatters.Soap
11/02/2002  02:53 AM    <DIR>          System.Xml
```

These are the assemblies that ship with Rotor out of the box. Drilling down into the System directory, you'll find something like this:

```
Directory of C:\sscli\build\v1.x86chk.rotor\assembly\gac\system

11/02/2002  02:53 AM    <DIR>          .
11/02/2002  02:53 AM    <DIR>          ..
11/02/2002  02:53 AM    <DIR>          1.0.3300.0__b77a5c561934e089
```

Drilling down one level further:

```
11/02/2002  02:53 AM    <DIR>          .
11/02/2002  02:53 AM    <DIR>          ..
11/02/2002  02:53 AM           675,840 System.dll
11/02/2002  02:53 AM               203 __AssemblyInfo__.ini
```

And, sure enough, running *ildasm* on the *System.dll* contained in this directory reveals that the version number of *System.dll* is 1.0.3300.0, and its public key token matches that of the other half of the subdirectory name. (The *.ini* file is just text information about the assembly, and doesn't contain anything magical or, in fact, particularly interesting. It is simply information about the assembly that can, for the most part, already be obtained by the assembly metadata itself or easily computed. It is used as a cache.)

Having demonstrated this implementation detail, however, it is important to once again note that the GAC is communal property, and dropping compiled assemblies into this GAC subdirectory without using the proper utility

---

program is strongly discouraged; the mechanism chosen by a CLI implementer is entirely in his hands and is almost guaranteed to vary from one platform to the next.

To manage moving assemblies in and out of the GAC, the Rotor code base ships with a utility that eases management details, known creatively as *gacutil*. (The source for *gacutil* can be found in the directory *sscli/clr/src/tools/gac*; examining the source reveals that it is actually a thin wrapper around the IAssemblyCache and IAssemblyEnum interfaces.) This utility provides the ability to install, remove, and enumerate the various assemblies stored in the GAC, as well as the ability to manage traced reference counts, which keep assemblies from being accidentally uninstalled. Example 4-3 is an example of how to enumerate the assemblies currently in the GAC by using its -l option.

Example 4-3. Using gacutil to examine the default shared assemblies in the SSCLI

```
> gacutil -l

Microsoft (R) Shared Source CLI Global Assembly Cache Utility.
  Version 1.0.0003.0
Copyright (C) Microsoft Corporation 1998-2002. All rights reserved.

The Global Assembly Cache contains the following assemblies:
        ISymWrapper, Version=1.0.3300.0,
          Culture=neutral, PublicKeyToken=b03f5f7f11d50a3a, Custom=null
        Microsoft.JScript, Version=7.0.3300.0,
          Culture=neutral, PublicKeyToken=b03f5f7f11d50a3a, Custom=null
        Microsoft.Vsa, Version=7.0.3300.0,
          Culture=neutral, PublicKeyToken=b03f5f7f11d50a3a, Custom=null
        System, Version=1.0.3300.0,
          Culture=neutral, PublicKeyToken=b77a5c561934e089, Custom=null
        System.Runtime.Remoting, Version=1.0.3300.0,
          Culture=neutral, PublicKeyToken=b77a5c561934e089, Custom=null
        System.Runtime.Serialization.Formatters.Soap, Version=1.0.3300.0,
          Culture=neutral, PublicKeyToken=b03f5f7f11d50a3a, Custom=null
        System.Xml, Version=1.0.3300.0,
          Culture=neutral, PublicKeyToken=b77a5c561934e089, Custom=null
```

Binding Scenarios

For many programmers, strict versioning, strongnames, the GAC, and domain-based isolation are unfamiliar ground. Many developers are still living the "good ol' days" of C++, in which the results of running any given program are configuration-dependent and, as a result, trying to make sense of the CLI approach to management, deployment, and loading policies is

Factoring Assemblies by Culture

Another way to factor assemblies is to centralize the parts that are not locale-dependent and break locale-specific parts into files that can be loaded on demand. Assemblies that use this technique are referred to as *culture neutral*.

For those who wish to build "culture neutral" assemblies, the Shared Source CLI provides command-line utilities, including the *resgen.exe* program for building managed resources and *resourcecompiler.exe* for building unmanaged string resources. See the tools documentation in the SSCLI distribution for details of how to use these tools to build resource-only assemblies.

Managed code that is designed to be global can be built in a way that leverages the infrastructure for finding and binding to assemblies that already exist in the CLI. Because of this, most of the advantages that come from the use of this infrastructure (such as loosely coupled, strongly versioned, configurable binding) also accrue to the code being globalized.

The globalization support that is part of the SSCLI is a hidden gem and comprises a very complete set of components that can be found in *sscli/clr/src/bcl/system/globalization*. It is not only interesting to consider the implementation of these components on their own, but also to notice how they are tied into the low-level implementation of the execution engine and the frameworks. Because of their role, they relate directly to resource loading, to the implementation of datatypes such as strings, and to marshaling mechanisms. Unfortunately, covering the details of the globalization code is outside of the scope of this book, but it is definitely worth browsing.

---

bewildering. Using the Echo component that we've been developing so far as an example will help demonstrate how versioning the GAC and the loading policies of the CLI can serve useful and beneficial purposes.

Step one: Baseline

The first step is, of course, to establish the baseline functionality with which most programmers are familiar. In this case, this is the standard "everything-in-one-directory" scenario used up until this point for all code examples. *Echo.cs* is compiled into *Echo.dll* and rests in the current directory:

```
using System;

namespace SampleEcho {
  public enum EchoVariation { Louder, Softer, Indistinct }
  public struct EchoValue {
    public string theEcho;
    public EchoVariation itsFlavor;
  }
```

```
      public interface Echoer {
        void DoEcho(out EchoValue[] resultingEcho);
      }

      public class Echo : Echoer {
        private string toEcho = null;
        private static int echoCount = 0;
        private const System.Int16 echoRepetitions = 3;

        public delegate void EchoEventHandler(string echoInfo);
        public event EchoEventHandler OnEcho;

        public Echo(string initialEcho) {
          toEcho = initialEcho;
        }
        public string EchoString {
          get { return toEcho; }
          set { toEcho = value; }
        }
        public void DoEcho(out EchoValue[] resultingEcho) {
          if (toEcho == null) {
            throw(new Exception("Alas, there is nothing to echo!"));
          }
          resultingEcho = new EchoValue[echoRepetitions];
          for (sbyte i = 0; i < echoRepetitions; i++) {
            resultingEcho[i].theEcho = toEcho;
            switch (i) {
              case 0: resultingEcho[i].itsFlavor = EchoVariation.Louder; break;
              case 1: resultingEcho[i].itsFlavor = EchoVariation.Softer; break;
              default: resultingEcho[i].itsFlavor = EchoVariation.Indistinct;
break;
            }
          }
          if (OnEcho != null) {
            OnEcho(System.String.Format("Echo number {0}", echoCount));
          }
          echoCount++;
          return;
        }
      }
    }
```

MainProgram.cs is compiled, referencing *Echo.dll* as part of the compilation step, and also resides in the current directory:

```
using System;
using SampleEcho;

namespace MainSampleProgram {
  class EchoProgram {
    static void Main(string[] args) {
      SampleEcho.Echo myEcho;
      SampleEcho.EchoValue[] result;
```

```
      if (args.Length > 0)
        myEcho = new SampleEcho.Echo(args[0].ToString( ));
      else
        myEcho = new SampleEcho.Echo("Hi mom!");

      // Set up an event handler and hook to component
      SampleEcho.Echo.EchoEventHandler handler =
        new SampleEcho.Echo.EchoEventHandler(CallMe);
      myEcho.OnEcho += handler;

      try {
        myEcho.DoEcho(out result);
        System.Console.WriteLine("Main program received echo!");
        for (int i = 0; i < result.Length; i++)
          Console.WriteLine("{0}: {1}, {2}", i,
                            result[i].theEcho, result[i].itsFlavor);
      }
      catch (System.Exception e) {
        System.Console.WriteLine("Caught exception: {0}", e.Message);
      }
    }

    static void CallMe(string msg) {
      System.Console.WriteLine(msg);
    }
  }
}
```

Executing *MainProgram.exe* produces what we'd expect:

```
> clix mainprogram
Echo number 0
Main program received echo!
0: Hi mom!, Louder
1: Hi mom!, Softer
2: Hi mom!, Indistinct
```

The *Echo.dll* assembly could also be placed into a subdirectory whose name is the same as the assembly (minus extension), from which it would also be successfully loaded.

Step two: The GAC

The Echo component has turned out to be an extremely useful component, so much so that Echo needs to be shared with other assemblies that also desire echoing behavior. Echo could be copied into private code bases for each application, but this loses a large part of the benefit of shared libraries; instead, we want to share it from a single place, the GAC. To do this, Echo needs to be installed into the GAC:

```
> gacutil -i echo.dll

Microsoft (R) .NET Global Assembly Cache Utility.  Version 1.0.1.0
Copyright (C) Microsoft Corporation 1998-2002. All rights reserved.

Failure adding assembly to the cache: Attempt to install an assembly
without a strong name
```

Recall that in order for an assembly to be stored into the GAC, it needs to be either strongly named or partially signed with verification turned off. Both of these options are most easily accomplished by creating a keypair using the *sn* utility and referencing the keyfile from *Echo.cs*. (There are also command-line options on the C# compiler and the *al* assembly linker to do this.) Add this line to *Echo.cs* and generate a key with sn -k echo.snk:

```
// Echo.cs

[assembly: System.Reflection.AssemblyKeyFile("echo.snk")]

// rest as before
```

Recompiling *Echo.cs*, gacutil will now accept the assembly as installable. Unfortunately, running *MainProgram* yields an exception, since the assembly it was compiled against was "echo, Version=0.0.0.0, Culture=neutral, PublicKeyToken=null," and there is no assembly that matches that criteria. *MainProgram* needs to be recompiled against the new, strongly named Echo.

Once that's done, to prove that *MainProgram* will in fact pull the component out of the GAC, try deleting *Echo.dll* from the current directory; *MainProgram* should still run. In fact, once the assembly has been put into the GAC, it will be preferentially loaded from the GAC rather than from the local directory.

Step three: Versioning

Having deployed the Echo component into the public arena, however, another concern arises—what happens if and when Echo needs to support new functionality? This is precisely what versioning and versioning-aware load policies are for. Add a version number to *Echo.cs*, Version 1.0, and recompile it:

```
// Echo.cs

[assembly: System.Reflection.AssemblyVersion("1.0.0.0")]
// rest as before
```

To test versioning-bound load policies, it's helpful to make sure the version (which will be changing in just a moment to illustrate the side-by-side capabilities of the CLI) is what's expected; to do this, *MainProgram* will display the complete display name of the Echo assembly when it first references Echo:

```
// MainProgram.cs, in class EchoProgram

    static void Main(string[] args) {
      Console.WriteLine("Echo assembly: " +
                        typeof(SampleEcho.Echo).Assembly.FullName);
      // . . . as before . . .
    }
```

Recompile *MainProgram*, install echo v1.0.0.0 into the GAC, delete the local *Echo.dll*, and run *MainProgram*. It works as expected.

Step four: Side-by-side versioning

Echo has reached a state where it needs to be versioned; it now looks to echo messages back five times, instead of the previous version's three (the echoRepetitions field, a constant, has been changed from 3 to 5). To do this, the AssemblyVersion attribute changes its value:

```
// Echo.cs

[assembly: System.Reflection.AssemblyVersion("2.0.0.0")]
// ...

public class Echo : Echoer {
  // ...
  private const System.Int16 echoRepetitions = 5;
  // ...
}

// rest as before
```

Again, recompile *Echo.cs* and install the new echo component into the GAC.

As a point of experimentation, before moving on, consider what's just taken place: there are now two entirely different (as far as the CLI is concerned) versions of the same component now living in the GAC; running *gacutil -l* proves this. And, if the CLI supports version-aware binding, then *MainProgram*, which was originally compiled against v1.0.0.0 of the Echo component, should still load and run against the still-installed *echo.dll* v1.0. 0.0 version, which it will.

If you're using Windows, don't forget to run *MainProgram.exe* and *MainProgramv1.exe* under *clix*. In many cases, you can run SSCLI assemblies at the Windows command prompt without *clix* (this runs them using the .NET CLR). However, the examples in this chapter need to bind against assemblies that can only be found in the SSCLI's GAC, and if you run them with the .NET CLR, it will not find them. This also raises the question of which version of *gacutil* you're running. If you see "Shared Source CLI Global Assembly Cache Utility" in the banner when you run it, you've got the right one. If not, run *env.bat* to make sure your environment is properly set up for the SSCLI.

Save the current *MainProgram* to *MainProgramv1.exe* or something similar, and recompile *MainProgram* against v2 of *echo.dll*. Delete *echo.dll* out of the current directory, and each version of *MainProgram* in turn binds to the current version of echo stored in the GAC. It should be noted before moving on that versioning the main program and its libraries, as shown here, does not need to be done at the same time; it is also certainly possible to version them one at a time, in an uncoordinated fashion.

Configuring How Assemblies Load

In addition to the very complete versioning scheme detailed previously, administrators and developers can add their own configuration guidance into the mix. The policy used when binding to an assembly can be specified on a per-application, per-assembly, or per-machine basis.

The need for this is obvious. Frequently, developers won't make the final determination about which component version an application needs to work correctly. Service packs, bug fix releases, and product upgrades all occur long after the developer has shipped the product to manufacturing for release. One of the key weaknesses, in fact, that most shared library systems have is the evolutionary nature of the machines on which they exist. On Windows platforms, this phenomenon is known by the unpleasant name "DLL Hell," but it exists quietly in every software environment that relies on shared, dynamically loaded libraries.

Developers, administrators, and users must all occasionally influence how their assemblies load. They need the ability to not only upgrade an assembly to a later version, but also to revert from an upgraded assembly back to the original version (due to unworkable bugs found in the new release, or even just incomplete backwards incompatibility).

When components are loaded from their dormant state, the loading process takes local environmental information into account, as well as information provided by the programmer and by the administrator of the system. Because the CLI doesn't mandate any specific mechanism, different CLI implementations are left up to their own devices. By default, the SSCLI examines the runtime version number that has been placed in the metadata header by the compiler, and uses this hint to first load the correct version of the CLI, and then load the assembly into it.

 Rotor expects to find v1.0.0 in the assembly's metadata header, which is a special number that should also be supported by other CLI implementations. If this number isn't supported, executables that run on the SSCLI won't load into other CLI implementations. This is because other CLI implementations will first attempt to match the assembly to their execution engine. Only after this fails will they fall back to using v1.0.0.

The simplest form of configuration in Rotor takes the form of XML configuration files. There are also many settings of interest to developers that can be configured by using either XML files or environment variables; these are listed in Rotor's online documentation. The XML files are the most important of the two mechanisms because they allow an administrator or developer to influence binding policy in a structured way.

Configuration files are named, by convention, using the same name as the entry point assembly that they configure, with the extension ".config". For example, a configuration file for the *MainProgram.exe* assembly from the previous example would be *MainProgram.exe.config*. In addition, the SSCLI offers the ability to provide *publisher policy* configuration information on a per-assembly basis and *machine policy* configuration information that applies to the entire machine.

 Because there can be multiple versions of the SSCLI running side-by-side, machine-wide policy is per-installation, and the configuration file for machine policy is stored in the *machine.config* file in the *config* subdirectory of the version-specific SSCLI build directory.

The basic format of the part of a configuration file used to configure binding parameters looks something like the following:

```
<configuration>
  <runtime>
    <assemblyBinding xmlns="urn:schemas-microsoft-com:asm.v1">
```

```
        <!-- assembly-related configuration goes here -->
      </assemblyBinding>
    </runtime>
  </configuration>
```

Other sections (such as `system.runtime.remoting` configuration elements) appear as children of the `configuration` root element. Note that the namespace declaration on the `assemblyBinding` element is crucial, since Microsoft CLI implementations look specifically for assembly-related configuration elements that use this namespace.

Services and applications are also free to store their own private information within configuration files, much as *.properties* files are used in Java or *.ini* files are used in Windows.

Influencing binding policy

Users and administrators can drive the assembly-binding policy in a configuration file by creating `dependentAssembly` elements as children of the `assemblyBinding` element that in turn contain `assemblyIdentity` elements to identify which assembly they wish to influence and `bindingRedirect` elements to indicate the versioning redirection. Multiple `dependentAssembly` elements can be declared as children of the `assemblyBinding` element, but each `dependentAssembly` element can describe only one assembly.

To see this in action, recall that the *MainProgram.exe* application from the previous example currently uses Version 2.0.0.0 of the `Echo` component. Unfortunately, Version 2.0.0.0 has a horrible bug within it, and the developer of *MainProgram* cannot (or will not) release a version of *MainProgram* that depends on Version 1.0.0.0 of `Echo`. The administrator or user needs to essentially redirect *MainProgram*'s load-request for 2.0.0.0 of `Echo` back to Version 1.0.0.0. To do so, the administrator writes *MainProgram.exe.config*, similar to the following:

```
<configuration>
  <runtime>
    <assemblyBinding xmlns="urn:schemas-microsoft-com:asm.v1">
      <dependentAssembly>
        <assemblyIdentity name="echo"
                          publicKeyToken="fcd14a8abe06f0d2"
                          culture="neutral" />
        <bindingRedirect oldVersion="2.0.0.0"
                         newVersion="1.0.0.0" />
      </dependentAssembly>
    </assemblyBinding>
  </runtime>
</configuration>
```

Once again, remember that public key tokens will differ from what is printed.

When run, *MainProgram*, even though its assembly reference indicates that it requires the use of "echo, Version=2.0.0.0, ..." will in fact load and run "echo, Version=1.0.0.0," and only echo three times instead of five (which was version 2's behavior):

```
> ildasm MainProgram.exe

// Microsoft (R) .NET Framework IL Disassembler.  Version 1.0.1.0
// Copyright (C) Microsoft Corporation 1998-2002. All rights reserved.

.assembly extern mscorlib
{
  .publickeytoken = (B7 7A 5C 56 19 34 E0 89 )
  .ver 1:0:3300:0
}
.assembly extern echo
{
  .publickeytoken = (FC D1 4A 8A BE 06 F0 D2 )
  .ver 2:0:0:0
}
.assembly MainProgram
{
  .hash algorithm 0x00008004
  .ver 0:0:0:0
}

(dump elided for clarity)

> clix MainProgram.exe

Echo assembly: echo, Version=1.0.0.0, Culture=neutral,
PublicKeyToken=fcd14a8abe
06f0d2
Echo number 0
Main program received echo!
0: Hi mom!, Louder
1: Hi mom!, Softer
2: Hi mom!, Indistinct
```

This is powerful and is important to the successful evolution of a system over time. Versioning is a constant balancing act between the robust, conservative policy of always binding to the original versus the "politically correct" policy of binding to a version that contains fixes (such as security patches) or new features. Unfortunately, no one has discovered how to make this choice automatic; the best that can be done is to offer control over the configuration of the binding process.

Validating Assemblies for Consistency

Since the CLI uses a data-driven architecture for its services, there are many codepaths in the SSCLI that perform consistency checks on data. When we examine JIT compilation, for example, we will see how the metadata for individual types is validated and how the CIL is verified. Each layer of data that drives the execution engine must be loaded and checked before it is used so that the next layer can be guaranteed a good-clean life.

Keeping with this principle, assemblies are loaded from disk in a way that guards against changes, malicious or unintentional, made while the assembly has lain dormant. When they are loaded, they are first checked for consistency by the PEVerifier class, the code for which is shown in Example 4-4.

Example 4-4. PEVerifier validation (simplified from clr/src/vm/peverifier.cpp)

```
BOOL PEVerifier::Check( )
{
#define CHECK(x) if ((ret = Check##x( )) == FALSE) goto Exit;

#define CHECK_OVERFLOW(offs) {                                    \
    if (offs & CLR_MAX_RVA)                                       \
    {                                                            \
        Log("overflow\n");                                       \
        ret = FALSE;                                             \
        goto Exit;                                               \
    }                                                            \
}

  BOOL ret = TRUE;
  m_pDOSh = (PIMAGE_DOS_HEADER)m_pBase;
  CHECK(DosHeader);

  CHECK_OVERFLOW(m_pDOSh->e_lfanew);
  m_pNTh = (PIMAGE_NT_HEADERS) (m_pBase + m_pDOSh->e_lfanew);
  CHECK(NTHeader);

  m_pFh = (PIMAGE_FILE_HEADER) &(m_pNTh->FileHeader);
  CHECK(FileHeader);

  m_nSections = m_pFh->NumberOfSections;

  m_pOPTh = (PIMAGE_OPTIONAL_HEADER) &(m_pNTh->OptionalHeader);
  CHECK(OptionalHeader);

  m_dwPrefferedBase = m_pOPTh->ImageBase;

  CHECK_OVERFLOW(m_pFh->SizeOfOptionalHeader);
  m_pSh = (PIMAGE_SECTION_HEADER)((PBYTE)m_pOPTh + m_pFh->SizeOfOptionalHeader);
```

```
  CHECK(SectionHeader);
  CHECK(Directories);
  CHECK(ImportDlls);
  CHECK(Relocations);
  CHECK(EntryPoint);

Exit:
  return ret;

#undef CHECK
#undef CHECK_OVERFLOW
}
```

The CHECK macro in this code simply results in calls to segment-specific verification functions, all of which are also found in *peverifier.cpp*. They each encode very specific rules, depending on the segment; this is a useful file to read if you are looking for specifics of the CLI format.

PE validation, which is what check does, is distinct from metadata validation, which is also very important. Metadata tokens are essentially a form of indirect addressing, and because they are directly embedded into both CIL and attribute values for assemblies, they must be consistent with the tokens found in their assemblies to be valid. CIL and the metadata tables themselves are checked for consistency in several stages. We will take a careful look at how this is done in Chapter 5.

Application Domains

Application domains (also frequently called "app domains") are critical to understanding assembly loading within the execution engine. They tend to be a bit mysterious and are often described in terms of their similarity to process address spaces, since they scope the visibility of components and resource handles, as well as provide a security and fault isolation barrier. But from our component model implementation point of view, they are not mysterious at all; application domains are the architectural elements that are responsible for loading and unloading assemblies into the execution engine. In addition, while assemblies are resident in memory, application domains provide for isolation on their behalf.

Although the isolation provided by application domains may bear some passing similarities to an operating system address space, they actually coexist within a single address space for a process. Because of this, all domains in a process share execution engine services such as the garbage collector. Application domains provide the means for externalizing references to their components, which means that their components can set up channels of communication between one another under a programmer's control. Because component instances can pass such externalized references among themselves, threads of execution can traverse app domain boundaries; the execution engine carefully monitors these transitions to maintain isolation.

Assemblies are always loaded within the context of an app domain. All communication to and from external processes or components in other domains is mediated by the presence of a component's domain; the execution engine has *remoting* and *marshaling* machinery that enforces isolation under the control of the app domain. When the cost of using this machinery is too high or when it is unnecessary, managed processes have the alternative of caching their assemblies in a domain that is reserved for the purpose of sharing assemblies. This is a special case, and it should be used only when necessary, since it compromises the protection afforded by domain isolation.

There are three well-known domains in every SSCLI process. The first is called the *system domain*, which is essentially a bootloader for types that are integral to the loading process, such as System.AppDomain and System. Exception. The system domain loads and maintains a single assembly, named mscorlib, which contains only trusted types and is not available for use for any other purpose. The system domain provides programmers with a way to root their searches for assemblies—there is a closure across all loaded types, which emanates from the system domain.

For nonsystem types that need to be shared, there is another special domain called the *shared domain*. Assemblies loaded in the shared domain are said to be domain-neutral, and their types are made directly available within every domain in the process. To be eligible for loading within this domain, an assembly must be strongly named and highly trusted. Advantages to being domain-neutral include resource savings in load time and memory consumption, and possibly lower marshaling costs. Note that not everything in the shared domain is shared; even when assemblies use it to cache their execution engine data structures and JIT-compiled code, individual domains still maintain private instances of the statics needed by the assembly's types.

Normal types, such as your own unshared executables and shared libraries, load into a *default domain*. However, programmers may also choose to partition and isolate application-defined boundaries by creating their own application domains programmatically, either directly from managed code or else from unmanaged code hosting the execution engine. When multiple domains are used in this way, if a single type is loaded into more than one domain, each domain will contain an independent set of execution engine data structures to represent the type. This is necessary because the loading parameters may vary from domain to domain. Both class loaders and the security engine, which we will learn about in later chapters, are in cahoots with the implementation of app domains.

 See *appdomain.cpp* in *sscli/clr/src/vm* for the implementation of AppDomain and the two special domains, SystemDomain and SharedDomain. All three C++ classes share a common superclass named BaseDomain, which implements many of their basic mechanisms.

One of the most important features of application domains is that they provide the only way to unload types (and the dependent resources of these types) from the execution engine. When a domain is unloaded, it carefully reclaims all of the resources associated with it before removing itself from service. A domain tracks both managed and unmanaged object instances and resources, and to clean these up and implement unloading, load activity for these entities must be carefully tracked and contained in the first place.

Agile Components

Despite all of these precautions, in some very special cases, it is both permissible and desirable to leak object state across app domain boundaries. Components that behave in this way are called *agile*, since they can effectively move from domain to domain. Some important agile components include:

Strings
These are both common and have immutable state once loaded. This means that performance gains can be had by copying and caching their state across domains.

Security objects
These are part of the execution engine infrastructure even though they are implemented as managed code. Security objects are backed by the global state of the execution engine itself, and because they can get to their state from within any domain, they qualify as agile.

Localization tables
These are very large, and duplicating them on a per-domain basis would be expensive, so they are implemented as agile.

Components that are part of the remoting infrastructure
These components must, by the nature of the service that they provide, be able to cross domain boundaries. They too are part of the execution engine infrastructure and are implemented as managed components.

The set of agile components is important but limited. They are often loaded into the system domain, since this domain can act as a home for trusted components that need to be available in every context. The complexities of implementing agile components, which include limits such as a strict ban on holding any references to non-agile components, restrict their representational possibilities.

Bootstrapping the Assembly Load Process

Executing the code stored within an assembly is a chicken-and-egg scenario. The assembly cannot execute until it has been resolved, loaded into the CLI, verified, and JIT-compiled. The CLI itself is simply a body of code, contained in assemblies that must be loaded into the process space and run. Fortunately, this is a classic bootstrapping problem, and implementation solutions abound. For the SSCLI implementation, a special entry point into the primary assembly is all that is needed, along with some initial security conditions, which are attached to the assembly as data.

The bootstrap API makes hosting the CLI a simple thing to do, as evinced by Rotor's program launcher, *clix.exe*, whose code can be found in *sscli/clr/src/ tools/clix*, and whose main function, Launch, appears without error handling in Example 4-5.

Example 4-5. The Launch function of clix.exe

```
DWORD Launch(WCHAR* pRunTime, WCHAR* pFileName, WCHAR* pCmdLine)
{
  HANDLE hFile = NULL;
  HANDLE hMapFile = NULL;
  PVOID pModule = NULL;
  HINSTANCE hRuntime = NULL;
  DWORD nExitCode = 1;
  DWORD dwSize;
  DWORD dwSizeHigh;
  IMAGE_DOS_HEADER* pdosHeader;
  IMAGE_NT_HEADERS32* pNtHeaders;
  IMAGE_SECTION_HEADER*   pSectionHeader;
  WCHAR exeFileName[MAX_PATH + 1];

  // open the file & map it
  hFile = ::CreateFile(pFileName, GENERIC_READ, FILE_SHARE_READ,
                      0, OPEN_EXISTING, 0, 0);
  hMapFile = ::CreateFileMapping(hFile, NULL, PAGE_WRITECOPY, 0, 0, NULL);
  pModule = ::MapViewOfFile(hMapFile, FILE_MAP_COPY, 0, 0, 0);
  dwSize = GetFileSize(hFile, &dwSizeHigh);
```

Example 4-5. The Launch function of clix.exe (continued)

```
// check the DOS headers
pdosHeader = (IMAGE_DOS_HEADER*) pModule;
if (pdosHeader->e_magic != IMAGE_DOS_SIGNATURE ||
    pdosHeader->e_lfanew <= 0 ||
    dwSize <= pdosHeader->e_lfanew + sizeof(IMAGE_NT_HEADERS32)) {
  // Error logic here
}

// check the NT headers
pNtHeaders = (IMAGE_NT_HEADERS32*) ((BYTE*)pModule + pdosHeader->e_lfanew);
if ((pNtHeaders->Signature != IMAGE_NT_SIGNATURE) ||
    (pNtHeaders->FileHeader.SizeOfOptionalHeader !=
        IMAGE_SIZEOF_NT_OPTIONAL32_HEADER) ||
    (pNtHeaders->OptionalHeader.Magic != IMAGE_NT_OPTIONAL_HDR32_MAGIC)) {
  // Error logic here
}

// check the COR headers
pSectionHeader = (PIMAGE_SECTION_HEADER)
    Cor_RtlImageRvaToVa(pNtHeaders, (PBYTE)pModule,
                        pNtHeaders->OptionalHeader
                            .DataDirectory[IMAGE_DIRECTORY_ENTRY_COMHEADER]
                            .VirtualAddress,
                        dwSize);
if (pSectionHeader == NULL) {
  // Error logic here
}

// load the runtime and go
hRuntime = ::LoadLibrary(pRunTime);

__int32 (STDMETHODCALLTYPE * pCorExeMain2)(
        PBYTE   pUnmappedPE,            // -> memory mapped code
        DWORD   cUnmappedPE,            // Size of memory mapped code
        LPWSTR  pImageNameIn,           // -> Executable Name
        LPWSTR  pLoadersFileName,       // -> Loaders Name
        LPWSTR  pCmdLine);              // -> Command Line

*((VOID**)&pCorExeMain2) = ::GetProcAddress(hRuntime, "_CorExeMain2");
nExitCode = (int)pCorExeMain2((PBYTE)pModule, dwSize,
                        pFileName,              // -> Executable Name
                        NULL,                   // -> Loaders Name
                        pCmdLine);              // -> Command Line
```

With this code, an assembly is loaded, fed to the CLI, executed, and the return code is fed back to the operating system. To be fair, much of the code in *clix* is error-handling and message-display, which has been edited out, as well as some memory-management and string-parsing, but these sections of code make for uninteresting reading.

Why is *clix* necessary? On Windows, the commercial .NET Framework uses a tiny executable entrypoint to launch managed executables directly, without the need for a helper program. This executable stub consists of a `jmp` instruction that transfers control to _CorExeMain and is defined as part of the image's file format.

There are two reasons that Rotor doesn't do this. First, such a mechanism cannot be done portably (although platform-specific code could certainly be written for the purpose). Second, and more importantly, to enable many versions of the CLI to easily run side-by-side, the Rotor team opted use a simple and configurable helper program that is tied to the version being run, rather than more complex launch mechanisms.

clix performs the following steps when hosting the runtime:

1. Registers the *rotor_palrt* library using `PAL_RegisterLibrary`. The *rotor_pal* and *rotor_palrt* libraries combine to provide the PAL implementation that is needed to run the SSCLI.

2. Obtains the assembly name to feed to the CLI as the executing assembly. Within *clix*, this is obtained from the command line.

3. Obtains the name of the execution engine to be loaded. In the case of *clix*, this is obtained by working from the full path to *clix.exe* and stripping out the program name.

4. Loads the *sscoree* library and obtains the function pointer for _CorExeMain2. A host could of course choose to bind directly against the CLI library but would then be unable to take advantage of running against newer versions of the CLI.

5. Call_CorExeMain2 with the mapped file for the assembly to be loaded, and let the CLI execution engine take over.

Having loaded the CLI into the process space, the call from *clix* to _CorExeMain2 will cause the CLI to initialize itself, through a call to `CorEEInitialize`, to create the system and default domains and other necessary internal bookkeeping constructs, and ultimately to call `ExecuteMainMethod` on the `ClassLoader` instance for the assembly.

Example 4-6. Bootstrap assembly loading

```
HRESULT ClassLoader::ExecuteMainMethod(Module *pModule, PTRARRAYREF *stringArgs)
{
    MethodDesc          *pFD = NULL;
    Thread *            pThread = NULL;
    BOOL                fWasGCDisabled;
```

Example 4-6. Bootstrap assembly loading (continued)

```
IMAGE_COR20_HEADER *    Header;
mdToken                 ptkParent;

// error handling and HRESULT return calculation omitted

Header = pModule->GetCORHeader( );

// Disable GC if not already disabled
pThread = GetThread( );
fWasGCDisabled = pThread->PreemptiveGCDisabled( );
if (fWasGCDisabled == FALSE)
  pThread->DisablePreemptiveGC( );

// This thread keeps the process alive, so it can't be a background thread
pThread->SetBackground(FALSE);

// Must have a method def token for the entry point.
if (TypeFromToken(Header->EntryPointToken) != mdtMethodDef) {
  // bail out if not
}

// Get properties and the class token for MethodDef
pModule->GetMDImport( )->GetParentToken(Header->EntryPointToken,&ptkParent);

if (ptkParent != COR_GLOBAL_PARENT_TOKEN) {
  EEClass* InitialClass;
  OBJECTREF pThrowable = NULL;

  NameHandle name;
  name.SetTypeToken(pModule, ptkParent);
  InitialClass = LoadTypeHandle(&name,&pThrowable).GetClass( );

  pFD = InitialClass->FindMethod((mdMethodDef)Header->EntryPointToken);
} else {
  pFD = pModule->FindFunction((mdToken)Header->EntryPointToken);
}

RunMain(pFD, 1, stringArgs);

// more code follows
```

Notice how the code in Example 4-6 demonstrates (which summarized from clr/src/vm/clsload.cpp) the use of metadata tokens. The entrypoint for an executable assembly is stored as a method metadata token. Because method tokens can be one of several types, however, this means effectively that the entrypoint can be either a method of a type or a global method, and so this is tested by the if (ptkParent != COR_GLOBAL_PARENT_TOKEN) statement. If this token has a parent token, in this case an enclosing type token, that equals the constant token value COR_GLOBAL_PARENT_TOKEN (which represents the containing module instead of a specific type, in essence making this a global function), the enclosing type doesn't need to be loaded. Either way, the ClassLoader pulls out the MethodDesc for the method and calls it by passing it to RunMain, which checks to make sure that the entrypoint signature conforms to CLI conventions, and then calls into the MethodDesc directly:

```
RetVal = (__int32)(pFD->Call(&stackVar));
```

Note the use of the IMAGE_COR20_HEADER in Example 4-6 to retrieve the entrypoint token. As we saw in Example 4-1, this struct is a map that yields the location of important data about disk layout. Also note the operational details: a garbage collection pass should not be happening when the main entrypoint is called, and the thread that the code will be running on must not be marked as "background," since background threads do not keep the execution engine alive.

Securing Against Harmful Assemblies

The SSCLI supports Code Access Security (CAS), which is a component-aware approach to security that extends traditional OS security concepts. The goal for the SSCLI is to provide a level playing field for the components themselves, to enable code from many sources to be combined into applications. Since programs run under the control of the execution engine, and since component code is verified when it is JIT compiled, it is possible for the CLI execution engine to intervene when components misbehave. Because this is possible, the runtime enforcement mechanisms of code access security have real teeth. They would not be possible without managed execution as their foundation.

Code access security combines *permissions* with *evidence* and *policy*. There are two parts to CAS: the assembly load phase and the runtime enforcement phase. We will talk briefly about the load phase at this point and defer the discussion of how runtime enforcement is achieved until Chapter 6.

Permissions represent specific capabilities, such as the ability to read a file. Permissions are used in *permission grants* and *permission demands*, which are runtime actions that are tracked and enforced by the CAS service within the execution engine. A permission grant (henceforth referred to as just a "grant") is an authorization based on some combination of policy and evidence; a demand is a check for the corresponding grant.

Within an assembly, permissions may be associated with resources, code identity, or user identity, and are granted to code on a per-assembly basis rather than on a per-user or per-process basis. Permissions are applied to code either declaratively, in which case custom attributes specify behavior in conjunction with policy, or imperatively, in which case code is written to manipulate the CAS service directly to specify behavior. There are numerous resource permissions built into the SSCLI, such as the `FileIOPermission`, the `EnvironmentPermission`, and the `UIPermission`. There is also support for code identity permissions based on strongname. Finally, there is very basic skeletal support for generic user identities and authorization, as well as role-based identities. To see how these are implemented and to learn about others, look in the *sscli/clr/src/bcl/system/security/permissions* directory.

The programmer responsible for an assembly provides the nucleus around which the CAS service operates. In the assembly's code, either as attributes or as direct API calls, security requirements are specified through grants and demands. On top of this nucleus, the user or administrator who is responsible for the runtime well-being of its applications must also have a say in specifying security requirements and behaviors. In the CAS service, this is referred to as *policy* and is implemented as a set of XML configuration files (much like the versioning configurations that we examined earlier in this chapter).

Evidence is information about the assembly to be loaded and is used by the CLI in conjunction with policy to make binding decisions about which permissions to grant and which to deny. Evidence is implicitly trusted information, and the execution engine has built-in support for certain types of evidence, such as digital signatures or the directory from which an assembly is loaded. Assemblies can also provide additional evidence in the form of *permission set requests*, which are useful because they allow programmers who create components to provide evidence on their own behalf. The evidence to support permission set requests can be put into an assembly in serialized form, to be deserialized when the CAS engine prepares to audit the evidence at runtime.

An assembly's set of grants is determined by combining evidence, assembly demands, and policy at runtime. In order for this to be secure, a careful loading sequence must be followed, during which evidence and policy are created in preparation for their interpretation. One of the great advantages of the CLI's data-driven model is that the persistent representation of assemblies can accommodate this carefully specified mechanism in a way that allows new or custom data to be added after the fact. Evidence is an example of the sort of annotation for which this capability is important, since the runtime conditions under which a component is used may change drastically over the years.

Evidence attached to code is itself represented as components, and is extensible. Of course, custom evidence will be taken into consideration only if the policy being applied looks for it during the loading process, but the execution engine has been designed to allow for this kind of extension. Assemblies can contain custom evidence directly as serialized data or can provide it programmatically.

Summary

In many ways, assemblies are what programmers think of as components. In their on-disk form, they are durable atoms that can move, as needed, from CLI to CLI and from application version to application version. As a key element of the CLI component model, they are the packages within which types are named and implemented, and from which types are extracted. Assemblies also define the unit of isolation for the code access security model, which facilitates safe interactions between independently developed components by enforcing isolation (in conjunction with the execution engine).

Binding to disk-based assemblies is usually name-based, and the namespace used to bind to assemblies provides scoping flexibility as systems evolve over time. While the common path is to load from disk, it is also important for compilers and tools to have the ability to create assemblies on the fly, and dynamic assemblies are supported for this purpose. Dynamic assemblies can be used to create new on-disk assemblies programmatically or create new in-memory assemblies that can be run immediately.

Once an assembly has been loaded into the CLI either dynamically or by using an application domain, its types and security data are ready to be converted from their passive PE format into the runtime structures that drive the CLI. Each type will be loaded and compiled in turn from the assembly on demand, which is the subject of the next two chapters.

CHAPTER 5

Synthesizing Components

In CLI component-based applications, references between types are represented symbolically using names, as we saw in Chapter 4. This chapter investigates how a set of running components can be synthesized just-in-time by following these symbolic names. Just-in-time synthesis customizes component structure and behavior to a local environment. Using this technique, the execution engine can create optimizations and adaptation wrappers for the benefit of the component.

A gap exists between the CLI's logical representation of a component, expressed as assembly metadata and CIL, and the physical structure and machine instructions needed to execute on an actual microprocessor. To create components and run the behaviors associated with them, the execution engine must bridge this gap and convert the logical representation into data types and instructions that the underlying CPU can understand. CIL must be transformed into opcodes and operands; component metadata must be realized as in-memory data structures that fit both the microprocessor's conventions and any constraints imposed by the host operating system. In short, the execution engine must play by the rules imposed by the hardware and operating system at runtime.

In a traditional approach to compilation, a *compiler frontend* parses high-level type descriptions and converts them into an intermediate representation, performing data layout at the same time. The *back-end* then converts the CIL to a flow graph, optimizes it, and produces relocatable native code along with two sets of symbols: *imports*, which will be used to locate foreign addresses during linkage, and *exports*, whose addresses will likewise be provided for the use of other modules. At *link time*, multiple modules are combined into a single executable image, addresses and offsets contained within their code are recalculated as necessary, and symbolic names are resolved by patching these recalculated addresses into the compiled code.

Once the linker has produced a complete executable image, a *loader* is responsible for placing it into virtual memory with execution permissions, as well as performing any remaining relocations (such as taking care of dynamically loadable libraries).

While this approach has proven to be effective for many years, it has weaknesses when it comes to deployment. In particular, at the moment that code is generated, data structures are laid out, names are bound to addresses, or the implementation is tied to processor-specific details. This approach is more brittle than it needs to be, especially when components must adapt within systems that change over time. The designers of the CLI wanted to alleviate this brittleness by allowing compilation, layout, and linkage to be deferred until the last possible moment, totally sidestepping many of the issues that come from changes in the execution environment. To do this, the jobs performed by compiler, linker, and loader had to be redistributed. Although compilers still produce intermediate language in the form of CIL, the execution engine has become responsible for all other tasks. In addition, CLI metadata is not thrown away as it used by these compilers, but is instead kept for later use by runtime services. (We will see some of the ways that they use it in Chapter 7 and Chapter 8.) Many gains result from this approach, including improved security and reduced on-disk code size. We will discuss these as we discuss how compilation and linkage happen within the SSCLI.

The Anatomy of a Component

Given an instance of a managed component, how is it concretely represented within the CLI's execution engine? We know that we can get a detailed look at the logical structure of a component by running *ildasm* and viewing the metadata for its type members; however, this tool shows logical structure only. This is not enough; the decision process used by the execution engine to turn these elements into actual memory locations that contain processor instructions or data cannot be predicted by examining metadata alone (except for rare cases in which explicit layout information has been provided by the programmer).

The physical way in which Rotor maintains an object instance and its related type information is quite complex, and the elements that compose its parts are split across many different regions of memory. Figure 5-1 shows the anatomical detail, in gruesome detail. We will spend most of this and the next two chapters dissecting the parts contained in this diagram.

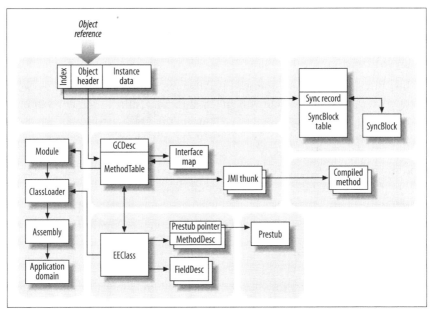

Figure 5-1. The structure of an object and its type is complex

To understand how the execution engine augments CLI metadata through the application of environment-specific layout rules, we will examine the elements of an object instance, and work our way backwards through the data structures that represent its type and their creation. Although this might seem like putting the cart before the horse, it gives us a chance to appreciate the large differences between the abstract world of the CLI and its concrete realization within a specific operating system/processor pair.

Component Instance Structure

Object instances, although they appear to be tightly consolidated units in high-level programming languages, are actually not represented as monolithic chunks of contiguous memory within the SSCLI. Of course, an object can be represented with a single, pointer-sized reference in memory, as anyone who has looked at the parameters associated with CIL's opcodes can attest. Given that component references of this form are the only tangible manifestation for managed objects, it stands to reason that it is possible to find and navigate the important data structures associated with such instances by starting from references to them.

As we saw in the first chapter, component instances are created within the CLI's garbage-collected heap by CIL instructions such as newobj or newarr. (Chapter 7, which covers memory management, will cover this heap in detail; however, to talk about runtime representation, we will present a basic understanding of internal layout without delving into how the memory is allocated or managed.) Every component instance created in this way contains a reference to a table of function pointers called a `MethodTable`, whose entries point to code for method implementations. (In many ways, `MethodTable` is an imprecise name for this structure, because it will end up holding far more than just methods when all is said and done.) The `MethodTable`, since it contains per-type data, can be shared by all instances of a given type; all component instances contain a reference to a `MethodTable` in their first available memory location.

When you are holding a reference to a component, you are actually holding a pointer to its `MethodTable`. While instance-specific data resides in the garbage collector's heap, or on a thread's stack, all of the type description information, compiled code, and execution engine context that goes along with that instance data resides in memory belonging to the execution engine. All of it is accessed by using the object's `MethodTable` pointer, behind which lives the bewildering maze of type information shown in Figure 5-1.

Before diving into this type information, however, we should examine the structure of the instance data. Recall that reference types have a small amount of overhead associated with each object instance (for synchronization support, for example). Intuitively, one would expect to find that overhead clearly delineated in a core C++ class somewhere, perhaps in the CLI implementation of `System.Object`. Unfortunately, it's not quite that easy.

Looking in *clr/src/vm/object.h*, which represents the structure and implementation of the most generic type, `System.Object`, only one field, the `MethodTable` pointer mentioned earlier, is defined in the C++ `Object` class, as shown in Example 5-1.

Example 5-1. The C++ class that represents objects within the execution engine

```
class Object
{
  protected:
    MethodTable    *m_pMethTab;
    // many method declarations follow
};
```

The impression given by this C++ class—that there is a single, pointer-sized field shared by every object—is wrong because not all of the data for a given instance of every component lies in the heap. There is an additional "invisible" field in every component instance that is used for memory bookkeeping, and the minimum size of an object is actually larger than 8 bytes, as we will find out in our discussion of heap traversal in the "Reclaiming Memory" section of Chapter 7. These implementation factoids aside, the simple case holds true in many situations: an instance can often be found completely on the heap. If the instance does not use execution engine services that tack on additional state, the instance data will be a simple single block of memory. However, any instance, once it has been created, may use execution engine services (such as automatic thread synchronization) that dynamically allocate control structures and then associate them with an instance. These structures are allocated in memory that is private to the execution engine rather than in the garbage collector's heap, making matters more complex. To solve this problem, instance data and instance control structures are split, and the control structures are accessed using what is called the instance's *sync block index*. The name is something of a misnomer, since the sync block can contain many things besides synchronization data, but like the MethodTable pointer, it is a field that is contained in every component instance.

To "see" the sync block index, look at the implementation of the GetHeader method of Object, shown below (again, from *clr/src/vm/object.h*):

```
ObjHeader   *GetHeader()
{
    return ((ObjHeader *) this) - 1;
}
```

If this construct is unfamiliar, don't panic. It is an approach that is sometimes used in C/C++, in which there is an anonymous slot before the MethodTable reference that can be cast to an ObjHeader. This allows every object reference to carry information that's not formally part of the Object class. C++ compilers often put vtable references in front of the object's address for similar reasons: given a pointer to user-visible data, the internal implementation of the language knows where to find associated administrative data very quickly (in this sample case, the vtable for virtual method dispatch). Pictorially, the technique looks something like Figure 5-2.

Looking at *clr/src/vm/syncblk.h*, the class definition of ObjHeader reads as follows:

```
class ObjHeader
{
  private:
    DWORD   m_SyncBlockValue;       // the Index and the Bits
  public:
    DWORD GetHeaderSyncBlockIndex()
    {
        // Pull the value out before checking it to avoid race condition
        DWORD value = m_SyncBlockValue;
        if (value & BIT_SBLK_IS_APPDOMAIN_IDX)
          return 0;
        return value & MASK_SYNCBLOCKINDEX;
```

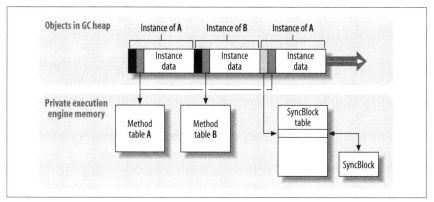

Figure 5-2. The ObjHeader and Object for instances lie back-to-back in the heap

```
  }
  // Ditto for setting the index, which is careful not to disturb
  // the underlying
  // bit field -- even in the presence of threaded
  // access.
  void SetIndex(DWORD indx)
  {
    LONG newValue;
    LONG oldValue;
    while (TRUE) {
      oldValue = *(volatile LONG*)&m_SyncBlockValue;
      newValue = (indx |
              (oldValue & ~(BIT_SBLK_IS_APPDOMAIN_IDX | /
                    MASK_SYNCBLOCKINDEX)));

      if (FastInterlockCompareExchange((LONG*)&m_SyncBlockValue,
                         newValue,
                         oldValue) == oldValue) {
        return;
      }
    }
  }
}
```

ObjHeader and Object, although they are distinct C++ classes, are actually allocated as a pair and located back-to-back at the beginning of every component instance. In the code for ObjHeader note that the field m_syncBlockValue is a compound value that can contain a number of different things: a LONG value used as an index, some bitflags and a bit used as a spinlock (which is a lock that can be taken by actively looping until the bit becomes available using an atomic test-and-set opcode). Because of this, it is important to be careful when changing the value contained in the field—the call to FastInterlockCompareExchange guards against race conditions.

Additional instance state is accessed by using the index portion of m_syncBlockValue; if it is 0, there is no additional state. If it has a nonzero value, then there will be an entry at the corresponding offset in the table contained in the global variable named g_pSyncTable. For more details as to how this lazy initialization works and the things that it can contain, such as locks and hash values, see the comments in *clr/src/vm/syncblk.h.*

ArrayBase and other derived types such as StringObject or StringBufferObject will contain additional fields tacked onto the instance, such as lowerbound or length, and, in general, component instances will include storage for the instance data that they encapsulate. Do note, however, that JIT-compiled components make no guarantees about ordering of the layout within an object instance; the compiler is free to make optimal choices. We will see how type members such as fields are created by the JIT compiler later in this chapter.

The Hierarchy of Runtime Metadata

Besides the instance data itself, it is important to have an instance's type information available at runtime; this information can be explicitly queried by the programmer using methods of System.Object, and it is also needed for the normal workings of the execution engine during compilation, garbage collection, virtual dispatch, and other runtime services.

Assembly loading in the SSCLI, as we've seen, is the first step in the process of converting type descriptions from their original format (which is designed to be used for persistent storage) into in-memory structures and opcode sequences. Once an assembly has been loaded in this way, its type metadata becomes available in a different, pointer-based format, which can easily be combined with information about the ambient execution environment to plan the layout of types in memory. This layout format is described below; it is divided into two different structures, one of which contains "hot" data that needs to be quickly available during program execution (such as method pointers or information used by the garbage collector), and the other which contains "cold" data such as structural information about sizes and members that is typically needed only by compilers or by the CLI reflection APIs. MethodTable, which we've already seen, contains the hot data, while EEClass contains the cold. These structures are split to achieve better locality of reference and take advantage of processor caches, when possible.

More about MethodTables

MethodTable is a complex data structure that consists of a header followed by the variable-length table of method and interface pointers that is the origin of its name. It also has a companion class, named GCDesc, which optionally lives before the header at a negative offset and, if it is needed, is allocated with the `MethodTable` as a pair. (`GCDesc` will be discussed in Chapter 7, since it is an important piece in the garbage-collection puzzle.) The header portion of `MethodTable` is shown in Example 5-2, and Figure 5-1 shows the back-to-back relationship of the `MethodTable` and the `GCDesc`.

Example 5-2. The header portion of MethodTable (defined in clr/src/vm/class.h)

```
class MethodTable
{

  union
  {
     WORD         m_ComponentSize;      // Array or value class size, or zero
     DWORD        m_wFlags;
  };

  DWORD           m_BaseSize;           // Base size of instance of this class
  EEClass*        m_pEEClass;           // class object

  union
  {
     LPVOID*      m_pInterfaceVTableMap; // subtable for interface/vtable mapping
     GuidInfo*    m_pGuidInfo;           // cached guid inforation for interfaces
  };

  WORD            m_wNumInterface;      // number of interfaces in interface map
  BYTE            m_NormType;           // The CorElementType for this class
  Module*         m_pModule;
  WORD            m_wCCtorSlot;         // slot of class constructor
  WORD            m_wDefaultCtorSlot;   // slot of default constructor
  InterfaceInfo_t* m_pIMap;             // pointer interface map for classes.

  union
  {
     // valid only if EEClass::IsBlittable() or EEClass::HasLayout() is true
     UINT32       m_cbNativeSize;       // size of fixed portion in bytes
  };

  DWORD           m_cbSlots;            // total slots in this vtable
  SLOT            m_Vtable[1];          // vtable slots follow - variable length

  // rest of MethodTable elided for brevity
};
```

The `MethodTable` is all about navigating object layout at runtime, whether to dispatch to methods or fetch instance data. As a result, `MethodTable` is a data structure that has been optimized for high performance. Contains unions because of flag bits overlaid onto integers, or GUIDs, which are overlaid onto interface maps. Note that the `m_pEEClass` pointer links the hot data of the `MethodTable` to the cold data stored in an `EEClass` instance associated with the type. Also note the kind of information that is in this header: sizes, slot counts, "maps," and indexes for distinguished methods, such as constructors (m_wDefaultCtorSlot and m_wCCtorSlot). Indexes, maps, and pointers are effectively computed shortcuts that enable fast traversal of important type data structures.

Notice the last data item declared in MethodTable, the SLOT array m_Vtable. Again, on the surface, it would appear that this is a single-element array of SLOT structures; this is deceptive. In fact, this is another performance-friendly trick used especially frequently within C code. When the MethodTable is allocated, the actual array of SLOTs will be placed at the end of the MethodTable instance, allowing the m_Vtable to essentially hang off the end of the MethodTable object. Pictorially, this looks like the diagram in Figure 5-3.

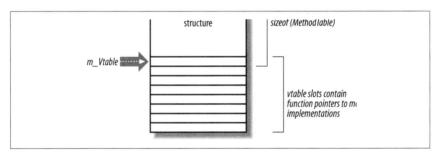

Figure 5-3. A MethodTable in memory has its length customized to the type that it represents

The reason for using this technique is performance, just as it was for ObjHeader in the object instance. In both cases, lookup needs to be as fast as possible, since the MethodTable stores frequently accessed data. While the obvious thing to do would be to allocate the SLOT array using a separate dynamic allocation and then store the pointer in m_Vtable, this would require an extra pointer indirection; this implementation requires no such indirection, since the beginning of the table lies at a fixed offset from the beginning of the object.

The order of the vtable slots in m_Vtable is carefully computed, as we will see below. Each slot contains a pointer to an executable piece of code in the form of a function that follows the standard CIL calling convention (more on that to follow). There are three sections in the array of slots: the static methods for the type being described, followed by any inherited methods that it has, followed by any *introduced methods*, which are methods defined by the type directly. Embedded within any or all of these three subsections are ranges of the table that constitute interface implementations. How this table is built will be covered in detail in the later section "Laying Out Method and Interface Tables"; it is a somewhat complex process.

EEClasses

Compared to `MethodTable`, `EEClass` is quite large, but it is also more straight-forward. Near the top of the class definition, we find a number of struct def-initions that begin with the prefix `bmt`, which stands for `BuildMethodTable`; these are used, along with a few of the `EEClass` fields, when constructing the type's `MethodTable` in the function of that name. Further down in the defini-tion is the heart of the data structure, which contains the following fields, as shown in Example 5-3.

Example 5-3. Some of the fields in the EEClass used by the execution engine. (defined in clr/src/vm/class.h)

```
WORD m_wNumInterfaces;
WORD m_wNumInstanceFields;
WORD m_wNumStaticFields;
WORD m_wNumGCPointerSeries;
WORD m_wNumHandleStatics;

DWORD m_dwNumInstanceFieldBytes;

ClassLoader *m_pLoader;
MethodTable *m_pMethodTable;
FieldDesc *m_pFieldDescList;

DWORD m_dwAttrClass;
DWORD m_VMFlags;

BYTE m_MethodHash[METHOD_HASH_BYTES];

SecurityProperties m_SecProps ;

mdTypeDef m_cl; // CL is valid only in the context of the module (and its scope)

MethodDescChunk *m_pChunks;

WORD m_wThreadStaticOffset;  // Offset which points to the TLS storage
WORD m_wContextStaticOffset; // Offset which points to the CLS storage
WORD m_wThreadStaticsSize;   // Size of TLS fields
WORD m_wContextStaticsSize;  // Size of CLS fields

static MetaSig *s_cctorSig;
```

Again, we find a number of fields that contain structural information for the type: not only things like counts of interfaces (`m_wNumInterfaces`) and static fields (`m_wNumStaticFields`), but also less obvious, but highly impor-tant, things like `m_wNumGCPointerSeries`, which will contain the number of places where the object references cna be found in an instance of this type. (This instance is used by the JIT compiler when it computes the contents of the GCDesc structure.) Likewise, the size and offset for storage to be allocated for fields that are static relative to the thread of execution (*thread local storage* or TLS) or the type itself (*class local storage* or CLS), are kept in the fields m_wThreadStaticOffset, m_wThreadStaticsSize, m_wContextStaticOffset, and m_wContextStaticsSize.

The list of FieldDesc entries (m_pFieldDescList) contains complete information about fields that are declared by the type represented by this EEClass. To find inherited fields, you must visit the parent EEClass instances by walking the chain of superclasses, starting with m_parentClass. The FieldDesc structure itself (defined in *clr/src/vm/field.h*) is quite compact; Example 5-4 shows its two data fields.

Example 5-4. The FieldDesc structure (defined in clr/src/vm/field.h)

```
union {
    struct {
        unsigned char m_mb_begin;
    } offset1;
    struct {
        unsigned m_mb                  : 24;

        // 8 bits...
        unsigned m_isStatic            : 1;
        unsigned m_isThreadLocal       : 1;
        unsigned m_isContextLocal      : 1;
        unsigned m_isRVA               : 1;
        unsigned m_prot                : 3;
        unsigned m_isDangerousAppDomainAgileField : 1;
        // application domain agility was discussed in Chapter 4
    } u;
};

union {
    struct {
        unsigned char m_dwOffset_begin;
    } offset2;
    struct {
        // Note: this has been as low as 22 bits in the past & seemed to be OK.
        // we can steal some more bits here if we need them.
        unsigned m_dwOffset       : 27;
        unsigned m_type           : 5;
    } v;
};
```

Again, because of efficiency concerns (remember, there will be one of these for every field of every type throughout the entire CLI), FieldDesc is as compact as it can possibly be. As a result, key administrative information (such as whether it is a static field, whether it is thread-local or class-local, and so on) is kept in bitfields, sharing with fields that can spare the room.

It should go without saying that if readers playing with Rotor seek to add elements to the `FieldDesc` structures or to the `MethodDesc`, described below, careful and extensive testing must be done to ensure that everything still works as planned. For example, the `m_mb` field is used to hold the metadata token of the field, and that token requires 24 bits. Taking another bit from the high bits of the union `u` will have disastrous consequences, since it would be accidentally stomping over the high bits of the metadata token.

Method information is also stored in the `EEClass`, in batched form, using `MethodDescChunk` structures that are chained together; a single `MethodDescChunk` is, as its name implies, a "chunk" of `MethodDesc` entries strung together for rapid access. As with fields, finding `MethodDesc` information introduced by superclasses requires walking the inheritance chain. As with `FieldDesc`, `MethodDesc` is a compact structure marked with few data fields and many accessor methods to manipulate those fields. Consider the (very brief and heavily edited) definition of `MethodDesc` in Example 5-5, edited from *clr\src\vm\method.hpp*.

Example 5-5. The MethodDesc structure is conceptually part of the EEClass (defined in clr/src/vm/method.hpp)

```
// Stores either a native code address or an IL RVA (relative virtual address).
// The high bit is set to indicate IL. If an IL RVA is held, the native address
// is assumed to be the prestub address. (See Figure 5-1)
DWORD_PTR       m_CodeOrIL;

// Returns the slot number of this MethodDesc in the vtable array.
WORD            m_wSlotNumber;

// Flags.
WORD            m_wFlags;

// The args that fit in an ARG_SLOT are inline. The ones that don't fit in an
// ARG_SLOT are allocated somewhere else (usually on the stack) and a pointer to
// that area is put in the corresponding ARG_SLOT. ARG_SLOT is guaranteed to be
// big enough to fit all basic types and pointer types. Basically, one has
// to check only for aggregate value-types and 80-bit floating point values or
// greater.
//
ARG_SLOT Call(const ARG_SLOT *pArguments);
ARG_SLOT Call(const ARG_SLOT *pArguments, BinderMethodID mscorlibID);
ARG_SLOT Call(const ARG_SLOT *pArguments, MetaSig* sig);
INT64 Call(const BYTE *pArguments, MetaSig* sig);

ARG_SLOT CallOnInterface(const ARG_SLOT *pArguments);
ARG_SLOT CallOnInterface(const ARG_SLOT *pArguments, MetaSig* sig);
```

Example 5-5. The MethodDesc structure is conceptually part of the EEClass (defined in clr/src/vm/method.hpp) (continued)

```
INT64 CallOnInterface(const BYTE *pArguments, MetaSig* sig);

INT64 CallDebugHelper    (const BYTE *pArguments, MetaSig* sig);

ARG_SLOT CallTransparentProxy(const ARG_SLOT *pArguments);
```

That is, quite literally, the sum of fields within the MethodDesc structure, with the caveat that there is an additional hidden field that precedes the MethodDesc at a negative offset. This field, which contains a *thunk*, is a critical and interesting piece of the SSCLI's runtime plumbing. It is discussed in the later section entitled "Verifying and Compiling CIL."

Within MethodDesc, the Call methods are of paramount interest, since they represent the path that the execution engine will use to execute a method on a type—for example, during reflection-based invocation, or at the point that an assembly's .entrypoint method is called during startup. Note that this does not imply that all method calls will come through Call. In fact, most JIT-compiled code will call an actual method body and bypass the MethodDesc entirely. Only when a method is invoked by name must the call be made explicitly using the MethodDesc.

The SecurityProperties that will be used when loading the class can be also be seen in this structure, as well as a pointer to a ClassLoader, which plays a critical role in the loading process; it synthesizes the runtime structures for the type, including this EEClass, from the assembly.

 Readers familiar with Java may wonder about the relationship between this ClassLoader and Java's ClassLoader architecture; even worse, they may draw dangerous inferences based on the similarity of the names. In point of fact, there is no relationship beyond their shared name. Both entities load classes in their respective execution environments—from there, however, all details wildly diverge.

The final thing to note at this point is the MetaSig for the class constructor, found in s_cctorSig. This will be used to start up the managed type once it is loaded and an instance of the type has been requested.

To summarize, component instances always contain a MethodTable pointer, which references a MethodTable that itself always contains a pointer to an EEClass. Although these two structures are separated for runtime efficiency, both are logically part of the same runtime data. The EEClass and the MethodTable (along with the optional SyncTable entry in some cases) define the structural properties of a class at runtime, and are initialized from the metadata found in a component's assembly. Referring once again to Figure 5-1, the `MethodTable` pointer, the one-to-one relationship between `EEClass` and `MethodTable`, and the optional `SyncTable` entry can all be seen.

Viewing the Type, Method, and Interface Tables

Having taken a quick tour of the elements that comprise the runtime structures used to describe types, it's time to examine how they are created and populated during the load of an assembly.

The `Echo` component, viewed from the debugger, will act as our concrete example of the class structure at runtime. Besides the physical layout of its structs, statics, and fields, the component has an interface, inherited methods, and introduced methods to deal with. Interfaces and virtual methods are both represented by contiguous chunks of method SLOTs, called *vtables*, a term that is borrowed from C++ that refers to the table of function pointers used to implement dispatch tables for virtual method calls. The `Echoer` interface, as an example, contains a single virtual method, and so its vtable will have a single corresponding SLOT. The `Echo` class, on the other hand, has a constructor, a class constructor, a property (which will have two method SLOTs, one for the get implementation and another for the set implementation), an event handler (which will also have two method SLOTs), and finally, an introduced method named `DoEcho`. `Echo` also inherits all of the fields and methods of its superclass, which is `System.Object`. Taking these into account, `Echo` will have an inherited vtable for `System.Object`, and six new SLOTs added to the end of the `MethodTable` to hold its introduced methods and constructors. Thus, the final vtable for the `Echo` class will look, schematically, like Figure 5-4.

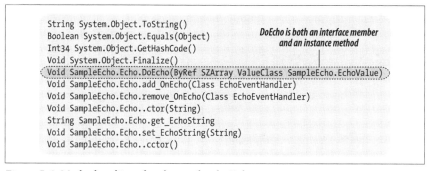

```
String System.Object.ToString()
Boolean System.Object.Equals(Object)                 DoEcho is both an interface member
Int34 System.Object.GetHashCode()                        and an instance method
Void System.Object.Finalize()
Void SampleEcho.Echo.DoEcho(ByRef SZArray ValueClass SampleEcho.EchoValue)
Void SampleEcho.Echo.add_OnEcho(Class EchoEventHandler)
Void SampleEcho.Echo.remove_OnEcho(Class EchoEventHandler)
Void SampleEcho.Echo..ctor(String)
String SampleEcho.Echo.get_EchoString
Void SampleEcho.Echo.set_EchoString(String)
Void SampleEcho.Echo..cctor()
```

Figure 5-4. Method and interface layout for the Echo componen

Consider the code that exercises the `Echo` component, shown in Example 5-6.

Example 5-6. Exercising the Echo component

```
using System;
using SampleEcho;

namespace MainSampleProgram
{
  class EchoProgram
  {
    static void Main(string[] args)
    {
      Echo myEcho;
      EchoValue[] result;

      if (args.Length > 0) {
        myEcho = new Echo(args[0].ToString());
      } else {
        throw new Exception("Hi mom!");
      }

      // Set up an event handler and hook to component
      Echo.EchoEventHandler handler =
        new Echo.EchoEventHandler(CallMe);
      myEcho.OnEcho += handler;

      try {
        System.Console.WriteLine();
        myEcho.DoEcho(out result);
        System.Console.WriteLine("Main program received echo!");
        for (int i = 0; i < result.Length; i++) {
          Console.WriteLine("{0}: {1}, {2}", i,
            result[i].theEcho, result[i].itsFlavor);
        }
      }
      catch (System.Exception e) {
        System.Console.WriteLine("Caught exception: {0}", e.Message);
      }
    }

    static void CallMe(string msg) {
        System.Console.WriteLine(msg);
    }
  }
}
```

Using the Windows *windbg* debugger, for which the SSCLI distribution contains a managed code extension, you can easily view the EEClass, MethodTable,
and MethodDesc structures allocated by Rotor as part of executing EchoProgram.
This debugger extension is written in such a way that can be used from other
debuggers as well (such as GDB and NTSD—this is covered in *docs/debugging/
sos.html*); the sources for it can be found in *sscli\clr\src\tools\sos*. While it

would certainly be possible to do the kind of spelunking that we are about to undertake in a debugger that didn't use these extensions, it would involve manually walking data structures and would be considerably less easy.

 Since we are dealing with translations to native microprocessor instructions, a few samples will be shown in assembler; the target processor that we've selected is Intel x86 because of its widespread use. Readers unfamiliar with x86 assembly language may be feeling a bit uncomfortable at this point, since this seems to imply that an in-depth understanding of x86 is a core requirement to understanding the chapter. As it turns out, however, only a passing familiarity with x86 is needed, and it's entirely possible that readers familiar with just the concepts of an assembly language will still be able to carry through with flying colors. In fact, one of the authors proudly claims never to have written any sort of x86 assembly language program except as a final assignment in college, while another author is really fluent only in assembly languages that were popular before many readers of this book were born. Fear not!

Besides debugger extensions, there are two configuration file settings that may be useful for watching the construction of runtime type descriptions: BreakOnClassBuild and BreakOnClassLoad. By specifying a type name as the parameter for these configuration variables, you can cause the execution engine to drop into the debugger when a particular class is built or loaded. (These settings work only in debug-enabled builds; see the documentation on logging that accompanies the Rotor distribution for details.)

Using WinDbg and the SOS debugger extension

At this point, a minitutorial on debugging seems as though it would be useful. We will illustrate techniques using the latest *windbg* debugger (Version 4.0.0018.0) from Microsoft, which can be downloaded from Microsoft's Platform SDK download area on *http://msdn.microsoft.com*. Recent Windows operating systems ship with a copy of the *ntsd* debugger as part of the standard distribution, which is the original command-line program on which *windbg* is based (and with which it is command-compatible). Which one you choose to use is purely a matter of GUI versus command line. The Rotor-specific extensions that are demonstrated can also be used from GDB on platforms that support it, although the syntax is slightly different.

The obvious first step is to fire up the debugger. The easiest way to do this is to make sure that *windbg.exe* is on your path, and fire it up from the command line:

```
> windbg clix.exe MainProgram.exe
```

A few things need to be done before you can get to spelunking—most notably, you need to tell *windbg* about Rotor-specific extensions and where to find debug symbols. (You did remember to build the SSCLI checked build, to enable all of those debugging hooks, right? The fast checked build is the default, but to really experience debugging paradise, checked is the way to go.)

To set the extension into motion in a command window that has been prepared using the *env* script for the SSCLI, you should be able to type:

```
0:000> !sos.help
```

If the extension is loaded, this will return help on all the commands available in the extension:

```
0:000> !sos.help
Loaded sos extension DLL
Strike : Help
IP2MD <addr>        | Find MethodDesc from IP
DumpMD <addr>       | Dump MethodDesc info
// list of commands continues
```

The output from this command has been truncated. It is summarized in Table 5-1.

Table 5-1. Commands in the SOS debugger extension

Command	Description
IP2MD <addr>	Converts an instruction pointer address into the corresponding MethodDesc (used to move from JIT-compiled code into the execution engine's data structures)
DumpMD <addr>	Dumps the contents of a MethodDesc
DumpMT [-MD] <addr>	Dumps a MethodTable (use-MD to see MethodDescs for each method)
DumpClass <addr>	Dumps the contents of a type
DumpModule <addr>	Dumps the contents of a module
DumpObj <addr>	Dumps the contents of an object
u [<MD>] [IP]	Disassembles code, showing managed symbols where possible (this is especially useful for examining JIT-compiled code)
Threads	Lists managed threads
ThreadPool	Lists stats about the threadpool
DumpStack [-EE] [top stack [bottom stack]]	Dumps the stack, showing information about JIT-compiled code
DumpStackObjects [top stack [bottom stack]]	Finds object references on the stack and lists them
EEStack [-short] [-EE]	Lists stacks
SyncBlk [-all|#]	Dumps the syncblock table

Table 5-1. Commands in the SOS debugger extension (continued)

Command	Description
DumpDomain [<addr>]	Lists stats for an application domain, along with the assemblies and modules that it contains
Token2EE	Finds EE info for token
Name2EE	Finds EE info about name (expressed in C# form)

If the extension is not loaded, or if you are not using an SSCLI command window, the same thing can be done by using the .load command to load the extension DLL into WinDbg's process space, as follows:

```
0:000> .load C:\sscli\build\v1.x86chk.rotor\int_tools\sos.dll
0:000> !sos.help
```

The fully qualified pathname is necessary unless sos.dll is on what's called the *debugger extension path,* which is read from an environment variable called _NT_DEBUGGER_EXTENSION_PATH at the time the debugger starts up; this is one of the things that the standard Rotor environment prompt sets up for you automatically.

As you can see, there are a large number of commands available; we won't go over all of them, but a little experimentation will reveal their usage and purpose in short order.

Loading the executable for debugging

At this point, the executable is not yet loaded. Furthermore, since *clix.exe* dynamically loads the PAL and the SSCLI execution engine as shared libraries (you will remember that this is how versioning of the execution engine can be accomplished), there is not yet a way to actually view any PAL or execution engine routines. Instead, a couple of options are open to us. One is to set a deferred breakpoint on a common routine, execute the program, and wait:

```
0:000> bp rotor_pal!pal_writefile
0:000> g
```

When new modules are loaded (in this case, the *rotor_pal* module), the debugger will look to see whether there are breakpoints that should be set. Once it has set them, the breakpoints will function as expected. Alternatively, you can single-step through the *clix* code, and once you see a message that *sscoree.dll* is loaded, you can set a breakpoint or step into the _CorExeMain2 routine. A third technique is to use an environment variable from the set shown in Table 5-2 to trigger a break from within the execution engine code itself; this is probably the simplest method and is very convenient to use against debug-enabled builds. Whichever technique you choose, you should at this point be able to view and manipulate SSCLI routines directly.

Table 5-2. Environment variables can be used to trigger breakpoints

Configuration setting	Values	Comment
COMPlus_BreakOnEELoad	0 or 1	Break on startup
COMPlus_BreakOnEEShutdown	0 or 1	Break on shutdown
COMPlus_BreakOnClassBuild	Classname	Break when loading classname
COMPlus_JitBreak	class::method	Break before compiling method
COMPlus_JitHalt	class::method	Break when method executes

If *windbg* complains of an inability to see source files, either set the _NT_ SOURCE_PATH environment variable before starting it, or add a directory using the File → Source File Path menu item. At a minimum, you should add the SSCLI source directory. In a similar vein, symbols must be on the _NT_SYMBOL_ PATH (or else defined using the File → Symbol File Path menu item). Again, this is something the Rotor *env.bat* script will establish for you automatically when it is run.

Halting execution

At this point, you could set a breakpoint on ClassLoader::FindTypeHandle and watch each and every type get loaded into Rotor, but you are likely to find that this becomes slightly tedious after the tenth or twentieth type to be loaded, particularly in view of the fact that there are still hundreds of types left to go before you get to Echo, the type we're interested in seeing. Again, there are a couple of ways to go about this.

A quick-and-dirty way would be to set a breakpoint on SystemDomain:: ExecuteMainMethod (in *appdomain.cpp*). Since this method is the entrypoint for *MainProgram.cs*, you know that when Echo and its related types are loaded, this function will be called. A better approach is to use the environment variable configuration tactic to inform the execution engine specifically which type you would like to examine. Referring to Table 5-2, note that by setting COMPlus_JitHalt to EchoProgram::Main (remembering that CLR environment variable names are case-sensitive) and then running the program under the debugger, the debugger will return control to exactly where you want to poke around.

Viewing internal structures

Once the Echo type has been loaded, you can view the internal implementation details for the loaded type using the SOS DumpClass command. DumpClass, however, requires the address of an EEClass instance to dump, and we don't happen to have one of those handy. Fortunately, it is possible to get class pointers from a number of other SOS commands; for example, Name2EE can be used, after which it is simple to pass it to DumpClass:

```
0:000> !sos.Name2EE Echo3.dll SampleEcho.Echo
---------------------------------------
MethodTable: 07431f7c
EEClass: 06ea85d8
Name: SampleEcho.Echo

0:000> !sos.DumpClass 0x06ea85d8
Class Name : SampleEcho.Echo[echo3.dll]
mdToken : 02000005 (c:\prg\RotorBook\code\ch03\echo3.dll)
Parent Class : 02bd7edc
ClassLoader : 000ca008
Method Table : 07431f7c
Vtable Slots : 5
Total Method Slots : b
Class Attributes : 100001 :
Flags : 3100021
NumInstanceFields: 2
NumStaticFields: 1
ThreadStaticOffset: 0
ThreadStaticsSize: 0
ContextStaticOffset: 0
ContextStaticsSize: 0
FieldDesc*: 07431e14
      MT    Field  Offset             Type      Attr    Value Name
07431f7c 4000008       4             CLASS  instance          toEcho
07431f7c 400000a       8             CLASS  instance          OnEcho
07431f7c 4000009      30      System.Int32    static 00000000
echoCount
```

As you can see, quite a lot of information is available here; of the most interest is verification of what you wrote earlier, that static fields occupy their own slot in the MethodTable (see the last line in the DumpClass output). Note also that this isn't the complete MethodTable; to see that, use the DumpMT command with the -MD switch to see a summary of each of the MethodDesc structures in the table:

```
0:000> !sos.DumpMT -MD 0x07431f7c
EEClass : 06ea85d8
Module : 000ca148
Name: SampleEcho.Echo
mdToken: 02000005  (c:\prg\RotorBook\code\ch03\echo3.dll)
MethodTable Flags : 40000
Number of IFaces in IFaceMap : 1
Interface Map : 07431fe0
Slots in VTable : 11
---------------------------------------
MethodDesc Table
   Entry  MethodDesc   JIT   Name
```

```
00762073 00762078   None   [DEFAULT] [hasThis] String System.Object.
ToString()
79608030 79608035   None   [DEFAULT] [hasThis] String System.Object.
ToString()
79607ef0 79607ef5   None   [DEFAULT] [hasThis] String System.Object.
ToString()
073f0ae4 00762118   EJIT   [DEFAULT] [hasThis] Void System.Object.Finalize(
)
07431f23 07431f28   None   [DEFAULT] [hasThis]
    Void SampleEcho.Echo.DoEcho(ByRef SZArray ValueClass SampleEcho.
EchoValue)
07431e5b 07431e60   None   [DEFAULT] [hasThis]
    Void SampleEcho.Echo.add_OnEcho(Class EchoEventHandler)
07431e83 07431e88   None   [DEFAULT] [hasThis]
    Void SampleEcho.Echo.remove_OnEcho(Class EchoEventHandler)
07431eab 07431eb0   None   [DEFAULT] [hasThis] Void SampleEcho.Echo..
ctor(String)
07431ed3 07431ed8   None   [DEFAULT] [hasThis]
    String SampleEcho.Echo.get_EchoString()
07431efb 07431f00   None   [DEFAULT] [hasThis]
    Void SampleEcho.Echo.set_EchoString(String)
07431f4b 07431f50   None   [DEFAULT] Void SampleEcho.Echo..cctor()
```

And there, in glowing detail, is the Echo class MethodTable—constructors, property methods, event methods, the "whole nine yards," as they say. From here, we could follow each of the MethodDesc structures and poke around further, but we'll leave that as an exercise you can do on your own. Enjoy!

Laying Out Method and Interface Tables

Building up the runtime layout (including vtables) described by the MethodTable and the EEClass for a component is a complex process, with much attention paid to optimization. Most of the work is done by the ClassLoader class, which starts by determining the number and types of fields and methods on the component; this information will be used to allocate memory and dictate offsets when creating instances. The ClassLoader then traces the relationship of the component description being loaded to its parent (because parents contribute their own member types) and resolves ambiguities or plumbing details such as method overrides. Layout is done in *clsload.cpp*, *class.cpp*, and *method.cpp* (all in the *clr/src/vm* subdirectory) and is controlled by a central ClassLoader method named LoadTypeHandleFromToken. This method begins with a module and a metadata token for the type being loaded, and returns an EEClass (and, by extension, it returns a fully formed MethodTable, because an EEClass points to its associated MethodTable):

```
HRESULT ClassLoader::LoadTypeHandleFromToken(
    Module *pModule, mdTypeDef cl, EEClass** ppClass, OBJECTREF *pThrowable)
```

```
{
  EEClass *pClass;
  EEClass *pParentClass;
  mdTypeDef  tdEnclosing = mdTypeDefNil;
  DWORD       cInterfaces;
  BuildingInterfaceInfo_t *pInterfaceBuildInfo = NULL;
  IMDInternalImport* pInternalImport;
  LayoutRawFieldInfo *pLayoutRawFieldInfos = NULL;
  HENUMInternal   hEnumInterfaceImpl;
  mdInterfaceImpl ii;
```

Note pClass and pParentClass, which are the first order of business. After
getting the metadata for the module and checking to see that the type is
actually defined in the module, you need to load both the EEClass for the
type's parent superclass, if it has one and for the type itself. (System.Object
is the only type in the entire CLI that won't have a superclass.) The call to
GetEnclosingClass yields the EEClass for the type rather than the parent; the
name is a bit confusing:

```
pInternalImport = pModule->GetMDImport( );
hr = LoadParent(pInternalImport, pModule, cl, &pParentClass, pThrowable);
hr = GetEnclosingClass(pInternalImport, pModule, cl,
                              &tdEnclosing, pThrowable);
```

Verification code ensuring that the right metadata is present has been omitted from this walk-through. We skip directly to the next important step,
which is to populate the EEClasses with data:

```
hr = EEClass::CreateClass(pModule, cl, fHasLayout, fIsAnyDelegateClass,
                              fIsEnum, &pClass);
pClass->SetParentClass (pParentClass);
```

After ensuring that a bogus EEClass was not created (not shown), the interfaces of the type are loaded and resolved:

```
// Now load all the interfaces
hr = pInternalImport->EnumInit(mdtInterfaceImpl, cl, &hEnumInterfaceImpl);
cInterfaces = pInternalImport->EnumGetCount(&hEnumInterfaceImpl);
if (cInterfaces != 0) {
  DWORD i;

  // Allocate the BuildingInterfaceList table
  pInterfaceBuildInfo = (BuildingInterfaceInfo_t *)
    _alloca(cInterfaces * sizeof(BuildingInterfaceInfo_t));

  for (i = 0; pInternalImport->EnumNext(&hEnumInterfaceImpl, &ii); i++) {
    mdTypeRef crInterface;
    mdToken    crIntType;

    // Get properties on this interface
    crInterface = pInternalImport->GetTypeOfInterfaceImpl(ii);

    // Validate the token
```

```
        crIntType =
             RidFromToken(crInterface)&&pInternalImport->
IsValidToken(crInterface)
                ? TypeFromToken(crInterface) : 0;

        switch(crIntType) {
          case mdtTypeDef:
          case mdtTypeRef:
          case mdtTypeSpec:
            break;
          default:
            // Blow up
        }

        // Load and resolve interface
        NameHandle myInterface(pModule, crInterface);
        pInterfaceBuildInfo[i].m_pClass =
                            LoadTypeHandle(&myInterface, pThrowable).
GetClass();
    }
  }
  pClass->SetNumInterfaces ((WORD) cInterfaces);
```

The activity is straightforward: if there are interfaces, enumerate them, check them, and then load their types. After they've been loaded, remember how many there were.

After this, the fields of the class requiring explicit layout will be built by enumerating those fields and accumulating metadata while the enumeration is being performed:

```
if (fHasLayout) {
  ULONG          cFields;
  HENUMInternal  hEnumField;
  hr = pInternalImport->EnumInit(mdtFieldDef, cl, &hEnumField);
  if (FAILED(hr)) return hr;

  cFields = pInternalImport->EnumGetCount(&hEnumField);

  pLayoutRawFieldInfos =
          (LayoutRawFieldInfo*)_alloca((1+cFields) *
sizeof(LayoutRawFieldInfo));

  hr = CollectLayoutFieldMetadata(cl,
                                  nstructPackingSize,
                                  nstructNLT,
                                  fExplicitOffsets,
                                  pClass->GetParentClass(),
                                  cFields,
                                  &hEnumField,
                                  pModule,
                                  &(((LayoutEEClass *) pClass)->m_
LayoutInfo),
```

```
                              pLayoutRawFieldInfos,
                              pThrowable);
        pInternalImport->EnumClose(&hEnumField);
    }
```

After this, dependencies are loaded (which is omitted here), and the *piece de resistance* is performed: the construction of the method table itself:

```
hr = pClass->BuildMethodTable(pModule, cl, pInterfaceBuildInfo,
                              pLayoutRawFieldInfos, pThrowable);
```

BuildMethodTable, like LoadTypeHandleFromToken, is given a module and a token, along with both the interface and layout information gathered up to this point. The implementation of the method is massive, taking up much of *class.cpp*, and because of this, we will only touch on highlights. It is a method of EEClass and has the effect of creating the MethodTable that corresponds to the EEClass. It uses the bmt* struct definitions found in EEClass to pass bundles of related state from subfunction to subfunction, rather than force each subfunction to have parameter lists that run for half a page. The structs and the subfunctions are just ways of structuring the data and the code to make it slightly more modular; in pattern terminology, the bmt structures are *parameter objects*.

The method begins by resolving and gathering together all structural data about interfaces, method implementations, and class members for the type. This is used to call PlaceMembers, which computes where in physical memory the members will go, and gather important facts about the members, such as how they will use the security service or what calling convention they will use.

With this member layout data in hand, work begins on the interface map, which is an array that is shared between all of the types in an application domain. Every interface type loaded in the application domain has a corresponding entry in this array. Remember that an interface is represented by a reference to a vtable that contains SLOTs for each of its methods, in order. An interface has no instance data—it is always dependent on a companion instance to provide it with its method implementations. To make this work, the MethodTable for the instance keeps a pointer in m_pIMap and a count in m_wNumInterface that it uses to track the interfaces that it implements—this is the interface map, and it is built from the following struct:

```
typedef struct
{
    enum {
        interface_declared_on_class = 0x1
    };

    MethodTable* m_pMethodTable;        // Method table of the interface
```

```
        WORD         m_wFlags;
        WORD         m_wStartSlot;              // starting slot of interface vtable
    } InterfaceInfo_t;
```

There is a backpointer to the MethodTable, some flags, and the offset within the vtable at which the contiguous entries for the interface will be found. While the elements of this struct are not complicated, the layout of the vtable to accommodate it is—the vtable must follow a set of semantic rules, which can be found in the ECMA Specification document. For example, virtual methods must be laid out in a very specific relationship to the virtual methods of a type's supertype; the supertype specifies the layout for the first part of the vtable, and then the type can introduce its virtuals. (See the discussion of the Common Type System in Partition I of the ECMA CLI Specification for both layout and vtable details.)

Method layout and interface maps

Recall that a method call can be made through one of two possible method-bearing types—either via an object or an interface. In code, this translates into the difference shown here:

```
Echo echo = new Echo( ); // echo is a class reference type
Echoer echoer = echo;    // echoer is an interface reference type
```

Even though both variables refer to the same object instance, one is a reference of type Echo and the other is a reference of the interface type Echoer. This is important because the CLI draws a distinction between them; in particular, it is possible to create explicit interface method definitions, which would look something like the following in C#:

```
interface IFoo
{
  void Method( );
}

class FooImpl : IFoo
{
  public void Method( ) { ... }
  void IFoo.Method( ) { ... }
}
```

When calling Method on a FooImpl reference, the public Method will be invoked; however, when invoking through an IFoo reference type, the explicit interface method definition (noted as IFoo.Method in the class definition) is invoked instead. C# allows for overloading method calls based on the calling type. Internally to the CLI, such methods are simply distinct method bodies in the component's MethodTable, but in order for interfaces to stand alone, the subsection of the table dedicated to a given interface must be located contiguously in memory. And this requirement, along with performance, is to blame for the complexity of method layout.

The simplest approach might be to have a table of interfaces stored within the MethodTable, containing a list of structures, each structure describing the interface methods and their SLOT indexes in the class's vtable. At runtime, the execution engine would look up the interface reference type in the object's interface table, look up the method desired, and jump to that location in the vtable. Clear and straightforward, perhaps, but also slow and wasteful—not only would each type need its own table of interfaces, which would introduce additional allocation overhead, but the cost of traversing the structure would also be high.

Suppose we improve on this approach a bit: since the compiler has *a priori* knowledge of the interface's metadata (specifically, the complete set of methods supported on that interface), let the compiler assign a fixed offset for those methods. If IFoo has three methods (Bar, Quux, and Baaz), then Bar would always be the first method in the interface's little table, Quux the second, and so forth. Now, instead of doing an expensive lookup to ascertain the offset of the method, it can be generated at compile-time, and potentially baked into efficient instruction sequences when the code is JIT-compiled.

The problem that arises here is matching implementations to interfaces; if IFoo defines a method called Bar, IRestaurant also defines a method called Bar, and a class then implements both IFoo and IRestaurant. There might be one, two, or three methods all named Bar sporting the same signature. What happens to the table-driven approach then? How can we keep the fixed order of methods in the interfaces?

Fortunately, nobody ever said that there must be only a single SLOT pointing to a given method definition. In the SSCLI, interfaces are aggressively laid on top of one another where possible, as well as on top of the underlying class's method sets. If no overlap can be exploited, a given method body will then occupy multiple slots in the vtable. In the case where one public Bar method is defined in a class implementing IFoo and IRestaurant, for example, there may be three actual copies of the pointer to the method's stub (which itself contains a pointer to the compiled code). One of these might be in the class's own method set, one in the interface table for IFoo, and one in the interface table for IRestaurant. The application domain responsible for a type keeps track of the multiple method implementations in an interface map, as shown in Figure 5-5.

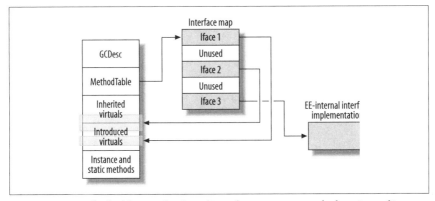

Figure 5-5. A method table uses the shared interface map to store the locations of its interface vtables

More examples will help make this clearer. Suppose that there are two interfaces and three object types, as follows:

```
interface Iface1 {
  void Method1( );
  void Method2( );
}

interface Iface2 {
  void Method2( );
  void Method3( );
}

class Type1 : Iface1 {
  void Method1( ) { // do something };
  void Method2( ) { // do something else };
}

class Type2 : Type1, Type2 {
  void Method3( ) { // do yet another thing };
}

class Type3 : Type2 {
  void Iface2.Method2( ) { // override Method2 for Iface2 };
}
```

Let's walk through this:

- Interface Iface1 is a simple interface consisting of two methods, Method1 and Method2. Its corresponding interface map is equally simple: two slots, one for each of the two aforementioned methods.

- The class Type1, which implements Iface1, has two methods in its method set, both of which correspond precisely to the interface map laid out by Iface1. Thus, its method table will be a precise overlay—the interface map for Iface1 can be laid directly on top of the methods implemented by Type1, with no duplication required.

- Interface Iface2 is also a simple map consisting of the two methods Method2 and Method3. Note, however, that for our own purposes (the execution engine won't notice this until later), we will have to deal with the fact that Method2 here and Method2 in Iface1 are the same signature. This will produce some interesting results.

- The class Type2 inherits from Type1, and also implements the interface IFace2. This means that there are four interface maps laid out on Type2: one for Type1, one for Iface1, one for Iface2, and one for Type2. Fortunately, we can share some implementations among these four interface maps. For starters, the Type1 map can lay directly on top of the same methods inherited from Type2 (which will always be the case in inheritance relationships). Iface1 also neatly conforms to the layout of those first two methods, so it can lay directly on top of the same area covered by the Type1 map. Iface2 needs Method2 and Method3 (in that order), but if Type2's Method3 came right after its Method2, and if Type2's implementation is appropriate for the Iface2.Method2 implementation (which it is—there is no explicit interface method definition here), then we can lay Iface2 on top of Method2 and Method3. Finally, Type2's interface map stretches across all three methods.

- Naturally, we've saved the most complex for last: Type3. Type3 inherits from Type2 but explicitly overrides the interface method definition for the Method2 call on Iface2. This presents a problem—it means that the Iface2 map can't lie directly on top of the Type2 implementation of Method2. No matter how convoluted the rearranging, there is no way to keep the interface maps in order without duplicating method entries. So, Type3 will need to have a duplicate slot for Method3, since the Iface2.Method2 method has been overridden, but the Type2 version of Method3 has not. (Note that this means this layout looks no different even if Method3 is explicitly overridden in Type3—either one is sufficient to force duplication. Similar effects would happen if Type2 overrode an Iface1 method.)

Schematically, all of the above appears in Figure 5-6.

An interface pointer for Iface2 in Type3 will have a different offset than the this pointer for the same instance. To dispatch virtual calls through this interface, the following takes place:

- The object's this pointer is loaded.
- The pointer to the MethodTable is dereferenced.
- The interface map is pulled out of the MethodTable.

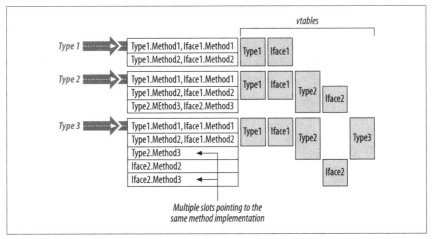

Figure 5-6. Vtable SLOT layout shares method bodies between classes and interfaces

- The vtable for Iface2 is found in the interface map.
- The actual call is made through one of the vtable SLOTs.

After members have been placed and interface maps built, final tasks are performed, such as placing instance fields and bookkeeping functions like noting data for the garbage collector, security needs, or marking this type as "resolved." The computation and layout of type information is involved, but since the type structures contain the information that drives the execution engine, this is understandable. Laying out the method tables and interface maps is by far the most complex part of the whole procedure, so pat yourself on the back, take another deep swig of your favorite caffeinated beverage, and let's press on.

Verifying and Compiling CIL

After the EEClass and its related MethodTable have been laid out, all of the type information necessary for compilation and most of the runtime structures necessary for execution are finished. At this point, the execution engine is ready to compile and execute the code for the type. But what is it that triggers JIT compilation?

In traditional toolchains (such as that of C++), compilation often occurs as far forward as the language can make it—the C++ compiler wants to eliminate as much information as possible from being needed at runtime, so as to minimize the amount of processing required. Frequently, this approach results in situations in which the assumptions used while compiling no longer apply—methods are compiled that are never called in a normal run of the program, for example, or precomputed layouts cannot be used against newer libraries.

The CLI adheres to a principle of maximal deferral: compilation (along with many other activities) does not occur until the last possible moment. In the case of method compilation, the "last possible moment" is the moment that a method is required to run. We need some kind of tripwire to inform us of this event, something that will fire just before method execution, giving the CLI a chance to invoke the JIT compiler on the CIL for that method. It would be possible to track all method invocations and force JIT compilation when necessary, but this would be a naïve implementation and would perform poorly, since only a small number of method invocations actually need to trigger compilation in a typical application.

The CLI chooses an approach that uses an indirect call to a helper function called the *prestub helper*. Although a type's MethodTable will eventually contain pointers to the native functions that implement its method bodies, every SLOT is initially loaded with a thunk that will trigger both JIT compilation and backpatching of the MethodTable when it is called. This tiny, method-specific piece of code is called a *stubcall*. With each SLOT holding a pointer to a stubcall, any call via the MethodTable will set method compilation into motion.

 Thunk is a term that is used for different, but similar, concepts in systems programming. Some refer to the use of automatic marshaling as thunking; others call nullary helper functions thunks. We use it here according to prevailing parlance at Microsoft, in which a thunk is a small helper function that is typically inserted automatically by a compiler, loader, or some other piece of runtime machinery.

The prestub helper, which will do the actual work of compilation, is called by the stubcall in an unusual way. When an as-yet-uncompiled method is called, the stubcall does nothing more than place the address of the method's MethodDesc on the stack or into a register and then jump to the prestub helper. The MethodDesc is needed during compilation, because it contains all of the method-specific information needed for code generation. But rather than look up its address from within the code of the prestub helper, Rotor actually uses the stubcall to record the location of the MethodDesc by attaching the code for each stubcall directly to the body of its MethodDesc as a small piece of assembly code. This assembly code is created during the initialization of the MethodDesc, using a processor-specific function. The code for the x86 version can be found in *clr/src/vm/i386/cGenCpu.h*, and looks like this:

```
inline void emitStubCall(MethodDesc *pMD, BYTE *stubAddr) {
    StubCallInstrs *pInstrs = ((StubCallInstrs*)pMD) - 1;
    pInstrs->m_op = 0xe8; // CALL NEAR32
    pInstrs->m_target = (UINT32)(stubAddr - (BYTE*)pMD);
}
```

As you can see, the code for the stubcall is emitted at a negative offset to the main body of the MethodDesc, and consists of nothing but a call instruction and the address of the prestub helper, which is passed as a parameter at runtime. The call instruction will cause the address of the following MethodDesc to be pushed onto the stack as though it were a return address. This is a hack, of course, since the address pushed is not a return address at all and does not contain executable code. Like many low-level mechanisms, the call instruction just happens to do the right thing, and using it enabled a compact and efficient solution for triggering compilation, especially on the x86 processor architecture.

The prestub helper function itself, which can be found in the MethodDesc::DoPrestub method in *clr/src/vm/prestub.cpp*, is quite long and involved; it is worth stepping through the entire function to understand it, although we will provide only a brief synopsis here. (One way to do this is to set the global configuration flag PreStubHalt to true to force a debugger break, using either an environment variable or a config file.)

All of the pre- and post-processing of method calls needed by the execution engine is set up in the prestub:

- The security engine and the remoting service are each given the opportunity to intercept calls.
- The profiler is given an opportunity to gather data and even modify the CIL of the method.
- If it is the first time that a type has been used, ensure that its constructor is called.
- The SLOT for which the method body is being created is backpatched.

There are other specialized checks performed, such as checking to see whether the method call is an unboxing operation, in which case the appropriate unwrapping code is generated or other similar details. All in all, the prestub mechanism is vital to JIT compilation. Understanding its interaction with the execution engine will be very important to readers who are interested in understanding the Zen of Rotor's JIT compiler.

Once the prestub helper has compiled a method, the address of the method body is not inserted directly into the MethodTable, since the memory that contains it may later be reclaimed and recycled, as discussed in the "Code Pitching" sidebar in Chapter 7. Instead, yet another thunk is created that is contained in a JittedMethodInfo structure. This snippet of code is called the *JMI thunk*, and it points to the method body compiled by the prestub helper. The JMI thunk is an indirection; it does nothing but call the method body or act as a *tombstone*, in the case that the compiled code has been disposed of, safely causing recompilation.

Finally, having triggered compilation and generated code, the original SLOT for the method is rewritten to point to the JMI thunk. *Backpatching* is the name used for this update to the SLOT value that reflects the address of the JMI thunk. Every SLOT is backpatched on demand, using the mechanism just described, when a method call is dispatched through it. Even when there are multiple SLOTs in a MethodTable pointing to a single method, they are each backpatched when used (although in this case, they will all share the same JMI thunk thanks to a check in the prestub helper).

The PowerPC stubcall mechanism is similar to the x86 version, although it contains more instructions. To understand it, you need to know that the PowerPC, by convention, passes the address of an indirect call in register 12. Since method calls use the MethodTable function pointer, they qualify as indirect calls, and because of this, a first-time method call will have register 12 set to contain the address of its stubcall. The PPC stubcall code can be found in *clr/src/vm/ppc/cGenCpu.h*, and looks like this:

```
inline void emitCall(LPBYTE pBuffer, LPVOID target)
{
    UINT32* p = (UINT32*)pBuffer;
    p[0] = 0x7D8B6378; // mr r11, r12
    p[1] = 0x818C0010; // lwz r12, 16(r12)
    p[2] = 0x7D8903A6; // mtctr r12
    p[3] = 0x4E800420; // bctr
    p[4] = (UINT32)(size_t)target; // <actual code address>
    FlushInstructionCache(GetCurrentProcess(), p, 16);
}
```

The most important thing to note is the bctr instruction, which jumps to the *prestub helper* after copying the address of the MethodDesc into a scratch register. The final call to FlushInstructionCache is needed because this code is emitted dynamically, and on the PowerPC, the act of code generation requires a flush of the instruction cache.

Referring to Figure 5-1 to recap what we just went over will probably be very helpful at this point. The MethodTable for a type initially holds pointers to *stubcalls*, which are each at a negative offset from their corresponding MethodDesc. These stubcalls are created at the same time that a MethodDesc is loaded and contain code that jumps to the prestub helper where compilation will be performed. When a method body is compiled by the prestub helper, the dispatching MethodTable SLOT is backpatched to contain a pointer to a JMI thunk, which, in turn, points to the compiled code. Each method call dispatched via the backpatched SLOT, from this point on, will consist of an indirect call plus a jump.

Verification and JIT Compilation

To verify that code is typesafe, the JIT compiler must walk through the CIL to ensure that every instruction behaves according to the rules specified in the ECMA spec. This may sound strangely similar to what needs to happen when CIL is transformed into native code—the JIT-compiler must step through, producing native instructions that implement the abstract description. Because these two activities *are* basically the same, JIT compilation and verification proceed apace, and are intermixed. And because code that is JIT compiled is not compiled until the last possible moment, both compilation and verification are just-in-time activities, which means that both can result in runtime exceptions. Programmers should be prepared for this eventuality.

We've already seen both PE verification and metadata verification in Chapter 4, the first checking the file format for consistency and the second checking the integrity of the metadata tables. The third and final kind of verification is CIL verification, which will ensure that there is a valid CIL instruction stream for each method, and that all potential code paths through it are typesafe. The ECMA specification very carefully describes the process of CIL verification, along with an accompanying set of *verification types*. Only verification types need to be considered during the verification process, since their use covers the semantics of all types—verification types are more basic than the set of CIL types.

Verification and compilation in the SSCLI are performed as a single-pass algorithm. As the JIT compiler works through a section of CIL, it verifies that the operands are valid for the operations being performed and that the stack won't either underflow or overflow when the code is executed. At every potential branch, the JIT makes sure that the types on the stack will be treated consistently by each fork of the branch—no path should interpret the type of a stack entry in a different way. To assure that this is true, the JIT uses an internal data structure to remember the stack states associated with each branch.

 The JIT compiler uses a number of different stack-structured variables internally to track the state of a compilation while it is in progress. These stacks are of course different from the CIL stack and the native microprocessor stack. Don't be confused by the presence of so many stack-structured entities; we will be clear as to which we are referring to.

To do its verification and compilation in a single pass, the JIT compiler processes the CIL stream for a method in an order that ensures that the state of the stack is always known rather than stepping from beginning to end. This reordering is accomplished by deferring compilation of the parts of the CIL stream that carry unknown state and noting those locations as "places to come back to." The data structure used to keep these deferrals is called the *split stack* in the code, and it varies in size depending on the number and type of branchpoints encountered. When both the split stack is finally empty and the working opcode stream is exhausted, the complete method has been both verified and compiled into native instructions successfully. (This algorithm also has the happy side effect of eliminating dead code, which is never compiled.) To see the code that implements this verification algorithm, examine *sscli/clr/src/fjit/fjitverifier.cpp*.

The main method that performs compilation is FJit::jitCompile in *clr/src/fjit/fjit.cpp*. To start compilation, the JIT sanity checks exception handling for the method by checking that no try block, filter, or handler extends beyond the end of the method or has a size of 0. Locals are initialized to 0, or to null in the case of references. The compiler also checks to see that no handler or filter is colocated within the corresponding try block, and that the type tokens used in any typed catch blocks are valid. After these checks, whenever a try block for exception handling is encountered, the compiler pushes the try address, along with the starting offsets of matching catch, filter, finally, and/or fault blocks onto its split stack for verification, while also remembering the stack state that will be expected at these points (which will always consist of a lone object on the stack, thanks to the way that the exception handling opcodes work).

The compiler then begins stepping through the CIL instructions, starting at the method's entrypoint. As it compiles code for a given opcode, the compiler takes care of tracking both stack contents and branching state for the use of the verifier. When the verifier encounters a branching instruction, its next action is dependent on the type of branch. The simplest example is an unconditional branch; the verifier will check to see whether the target offset has already been jitted, and if it has, will make sure that the stack state matches what is already expected. If the branch target has not been JIT-compiled, the verifier will remember the stack state and continue at the target offset. If the split stack is empty, the compilation of the method is finished; otherwise, a new offset is fetched and compilation resumes. Variations on this simple formula also exist for conditional branches and for leave, throw, ret, and switch instructions—these rules describe the overall execution of the verification algorithm.

Along with these bookkeeping and verification operations, the SSCLI compiles the CIL instructions one at a time. Compilation is simple in the SSCLI and designed for maximum ease of portability, as well as approachability. The compiler has a buffer into which it places its output, which consists of a stream of native microprocessor instructions. CIL opcodes drive a switch statement whose case statements represent the entire set of CIL opcodes; for each case, the JIT compiler emits a corresponding sequence of instructions into its buffer. Beyond the opportunistic enregistering of top-of-stack that was already mentioned, there are essentially no compiler optimizations. (To *enregister* a value means to place it in a machine register.)

As an example of code emission, let's look at a representative CIL opcode, the add.ovf instruction, which adds two numbers from the stack, checking for overflow and leaving its result as a single entry on the stack. For the SSCLI, all instructions are defined in a table named *opcode.def* that can be found in the *sscli/clr/src/inc* directory. In this file, there is an entry that looks like the following:

```
OPDEF(CEE_ADD_OVF, "add.ovf", Pop1+Pop1, Push1, InlineNone, IPrimitive,
    1, 0xFF, 0xD6, NEXT)
```

The first entry in this macro is the name that will be used in code for this instruction, followed immediately by a human-readable string for the use of tools. This is followed by the stack behavior that the opcode will exhibit (which in this case is two pops followed by a push), along with parameter characteristics and implementation details, such as whether it is a *primitive*, and how the instruction is encoded in the CIL. The final field categorizes the control flow implications of the instruction and is used during verification.

The information encoded by this macro is used to drive the JIT compiler, which can be found in *sscli/clr/src/fjit/fjit.cpp*. In this file, there is a large switch statement that discriminates between opcodes and calls out to the appropriate compilation function. For our example instruction, the switch arm is quite simple:

```
switch (opcode) {
    // omitted many cases
    case CEE_ADD_OVF:
        JitResult = compileCEE_ADD_OVF();
        break;
```

Most of the arms have similar functions that emit opcode-specific code, along the lines of the compileCEE_ADD_OVF function in our example. This function appears in the same file as the switch, and looks like the following:

```
FJitResult FJit::compileCEE_ADD_OVF()
{
    OpType result_add;
    BINARY_OVERFLOW_RESULT(topOp(),topOp(1), CEE_ADD_OVF, result_add);
    TYPE_SWITCH_INT(topOp(), emit_ADD_OVF, ());
    POP_STACK(2);
    pushOp(result_add);
    return FJIT_OK;
}
```

The BINARY_OVERFLOW_RESULT is a verification check that is contingent on the types of operands on the stack. It checks that the two operands match and sets the value of the result_add variable to the expected type of the result. TYPE_SWITCH_INT then calls lower-level macros based on the types of operands:

```
#define TYPE_SWITCH_INT(type, emit, args)                 \
    switch (type.enum_()) {                               \
        case typeI4:                                      \
            emit##_I4 args;                               \
            break;                                        \
        case typeI8:                                      \
            emit##_I8 args;                               \
            break;                                        \
        default:                                          \
            FJIT_FAIL(FJIT_INTERNALERROR);                \
    }
```

For example, if the stack has 4 byte integers on it, the emit_ADD_OVF_I4 macro is called:

```
#define emit_ADD_OVF_I4()                           \
{                                                   \
    LABELSTACK((outPtr-outBuff),2);         \
    callInfo.reset();                               \
    emit_tos_arg( 1, INTERNAL_CALL );               \
    emit_tos_arg( 2, INTERNAL_CALL );               \
    emit_callhelper_I4I4_I4(ADD_OVF_I4_helper); \
    emit_pushresult_I4();                           \
}
```

The LABEL_STACK macro in this sequence captures the state of the stack during compilation, using a StackEncoder (defined in *clr/src/fjit/fjit.h*), to support garbage collection. It is used whenever calls to helper functions are used, and the operation will record the locations of object references on the stack. (While on the subject of garbage collection, any time a backward-branching instruction is compiled, the JIT compiler emits a call to the garbage collector's polling helper function. We will see how both the stack encoding information and the polling helper are used by the garbage collector in Chapter 7.)

After recording references, callInfo, which is an accumulator used by some of the emit macros used to support different calling conventions, is reset, and the native code to do the addition and push the result is emitted. (The emit_tos_arg macro is sometimes used to enregister the top-of-stack value, but since in this case the add.ovf operation is implemented using an internal function, the arguments should be passed on the stack using the __cdecl calling convention rather than being put into registers. INTERNAL_CALL is defined as false to cause correct behavior.) The address of the ADD_OVF_I4_helper is placed into the instruction stream in the buffer along with an x86 call instruction, and finally, the return value is pushed back onto the stack.

Compilation and verification for this particular opcode are complete at this point.

The JIT compiler actually has several layers of macros that are used during code emission. At the core is a set of primitive helper functions that are designed to be easily ported, which are augmented by processor specific macros. The simple and highly portable macros can be used while doing quick and dirty ports to new processors, and can then be improved over time. All of the macros discussed to this point are part of this layer that is portable across JIT implementations. See Appendix C for a summary of the details.

The layered approach to compilation uses file- and directory-naming conventions to define processor-specific elements. At the top level, the *sscli/clr/src/fjit* directory contains a file named *fjitcore.h*, which is the main file for the JIT compiler, and which defines the calling convention and also acts as the root of a processor-specific tree of include files. This file, in turn, includes *fjit.h*, which is a key header file that imports the opcodes defined by *sscli/clr/src/inc/openum.h* and listed in *opcode.def*. This file also describes the linkages between the JIT compiler, the execution engine, and the code manager; declares entry points for helper code; and defines the reduced set of data types and the stack encoding mechanism used by the type verification process. Understanding the contents of this header is critical to understanding the JIT compiler.

In addition to *fjit.h*, the *fjitdef.h* header file contains machine-independent code emitter macros, which are themselves tied to the actual processor being used by a naming convention: the appropriate *<processor>def.h* and *<processor>fjit.h* files are switched at compile-time. For example, when building the JIT compiler for an x86 processor, the *x86def.h* and *x86fjit.h* files would be switched into the build. For the Power PC processor, the files to use would be *ppcdef.h* and *ppcfjit.h*.

The *<processor>def.h* file is itself wrapped by another header, *c<processor>def.h*, which wraps the macros to make them available to C++ code. (Again, for x86, the file is *cx86def.h*, while for Power PC it is *cppcdef.h*.) This file is a low-level and machine-specific collection of macros that encapsulate details about the processor, such as opcodes, in addition to things like special formats. Porting this file represents the minimal amount of work that can be done to target a new processor.

One additional file rounds out the scheme: the *<processor>fjit.h* file. In this file, macros can be redefined to get processor-specific performance gains. Returning to our example, although the add.ovf instruction doesn't use the processor-specific macro layer, the closely related add instruction (which performs addition without checking for overflow) does. In *x86fjit.h*, the emit_ADD_I4 macro is redefined to take advantage of x86 specific instructions:

```
#define emit_ADD_I4()        \
    enregisterTOS;       \
    x86_pop(X86_ECX);        \
    x86_barith(x86OpAdd, x86Big, x86_mod_reg(X86_EAX, X86_ECX));    \
    inRegTOS = true
```

As you can see, this macro has intimate knowledge of the processor's instruction set and conventions. The x86_pop and x86_barith macros can be found in *x86def.h*, and are defined in terms of the generic cmdByte macro.

> The Rotor JIT compiler for the PowerPC does not implement as many low-level macros as the x86 JIT compiler does, and its more generic nature causes it to generate code of lower quality. Improving the quality of code generation by implementing more of these macros would be an interesting and informative project.

The use of processor-specific helper functions also deserves discussion. Remember that the arguments in emit_ADD_OVF_I4 were readied for an INTERNAL_CALL; in the case of add.ovf, the call takes the form of a C function that can be found in *fjitdef.h*. The emit_callhelper macro eventually bottoms out into the x86_call_reg macro, which emits x86 microprocessor instructions to call the helper function:

```
int HELPER_CALL ADD_OVF_I4_helper(int i, int j) {
    int i4 = j + i;
    // if the signs of i and j are different, then we can never overflow
    // if the signs of i and j are the same, then the result
    // must have the same sign
    if ((j ^ i) >= 0) {
        // i and j have the same sign (the sign bit of j^i is not set)
        // ensure that the result has the same sign
        if ((i4 ^ j) < 0) {
            THROW_FROM_HELPER_RET(CORINFO_OverflowException);
        }
    }
    return i4;
}
```

Because the arguments for this function were pushed earlier in the CIL stream using opcodes whose compiled behavior "matches" that of the helper call, the arguments are already in the right spot on the stack for the function invocation. As you can see, the function simply checks for the conditions that would cause an overflow, and either throws an exception or adds the two arguments together.

For those who really enjoy gory details, the call to the helper function that is compiled using the THROW_FROM_HELPER_RET macro must actually invoke an interpreter that revisits the processor instruction stream, since it needs to reconstruct the structure of the stack to find exception handlers. To see this, look in the processor-specific directories in *sscli/clr/src/vm*; the files beginning with the *gms* prefix contain the implementation.

The way that verification errors are returned from the verifier is interesting. It is a clean and consistent way to back out of an uncomfortable situation and is worth a quick peek, which is shown in Example 5-7, and defined in *clr/src/fjit/fjit.cpp*.

Example 5-7. How JIT verification exceptions are handled

```
FJitResult FJit::jitCompileVerificationThrow( )
{
  outBuff = codeBuffer;
  outPtr  = outBuff;
  *(entryAddress) = outPtr;

  // Emit prolog
  unsigned int localWords = (localsFrameSize+sizeof(void*)-1)/ sizeof(void*);
  emit_prolog(localWords, zeroWordCnt);
  mapInfo.prologSize = outPtr-outBuff;

  // Beginning of function code
  mapping->add(0,(unsigned)(outPtr - outBuff));

  // Jit a verification throw
  emit_verification_throw(ver_failure_offset);

  // End of the function code
  mapping->add(1, (unsigned)(outPtr-outBuff));

  // Generate the epilog
  if (!CALLER_CLEANS_STACK) {
    // Callee pops args for varargs functions
    emit_return(methodInfo->args.isVarArg( ) ? 0 : argsFrameSize );
  } else
    // If __cdecl calling convention is used the caller is responsible
    // for clearing the arguments from the stack
    emit_return(0);

  // Fill in the intermediate IL offsets (in the body of the opcode)
  mapping->fillIn( );

  mapInfo.methodSize = outPtr-outBuff;
  mapInfo.epilogSize = (outPtr - outBuff) - mapping->pcFromIL(1);
```

Example 5-7. How JIT verification exceptions are handled (continued)

```
//Set total size of the function
*(codeSize) = outPtr - outBuff;

return FJIT_VERIFICATIONFAILED;
}
```

This function creates a method body that will throw a verification exception when it is called. It is a clever use of the JIT tools that we've seen already; when a verification error is detected, the compilation process continues, but the body of the method that is returned and executed does nothing more than throw an exception.

Calling Conventions in Managed Code

Once the CIL has been verified and compiled, the native code for the method can be safely executed. Since the CLI, like every modern execution environment, supports programming languages that use recursion, the stack is used to track execution state. Every method call has an activation record on this stack containing its arguments, return value, local variables, and other bookkeeping information such as a security object (which is used by the code access security engine). The structure of Rotor's activation records is shown for both Intel x86 processors and Motorola PowerPC processors in Figure 5-7.

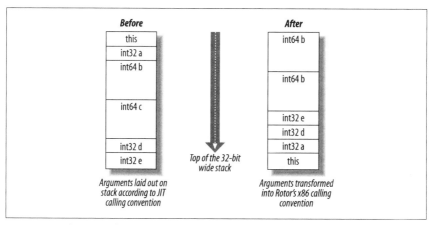

Figure 5-7. Elements of an SSCLI stack frame, for the X86 and PPC architectures

As methods call other methods, the stack is maintained cooperatively using a variety of calling conventions. All calls begin with the setup of the *callsite* (the stack context associated with a method call by the caller). Parameters are always a part of the callsite, since they can clearly be pushed only by the caller because the method being called knows nothing of them. Past this, however, different calling conventions use different mechanisms; why they differ is often a matter of history, of small performance gains, or of codified personal tastes, and their differences can seem quite arbitrary. Nonetheless, they exist, and how they interoperate in the SSCLI is described in the following sections.

The JIT Calling Convention

The standard calling convention used in code produced by the JIT compiler is referred to as the *JIT calling convention*. From the perspective of CIL, there are four possible ways to call code: the jump instruction (which is not verifiable, and so we won't cover it here) and three flavors of the call opcode: call, calli, and callvirt. Each of these has slightly different semantics, and each can additionally be modified to be a *tailcall* (which reuses the same activation record during recursive calls rather than profligately generating new records). The call instruction is nonvirtual, executing precisely the method targeted by the instruction, versus callvirt, which calls indirectly through a vtable. Both instructions take a token as an argument, the lookup of the method is the only difference—in the case of callvirt, the table of method pointers is selected at runtime instead of always being part of the component that is called in the case of call. For indirect calls, calli, a function pointer is loaded on the stack and control is dispatched to it. Note that once any of these have been compiled, all use the JIT calling convention.

In the JIT calling convention, all arguments, as well as the return value, are passed on the stack, and nothing that is passed in is registered. (The CLI is an abstract stack machine, after all—there are no registers in it.) Arguments are initially pushed in a CLI-specified order, and if the call has a variable number of arguments, a varargs token is pushed before the arguments. After the arguments, the return address is pushed automatically. Finally, if the call is an instance method call, the object's this pointer will be the last argument pushed, and the first argument found, on the stack. If there is no this pointer, the return buffer (which is also optional) will be the first element. Remember, neither the this pointer nor the return buffer will always be present.

x86 as a Native Calling Convention Example

The JIT calling convention is a simple, abstract calling convention. Unfortunately, its simplicity is not the last word. Each processor-specific build of the SSCLI converts the JIT calling convention into a different native calling convention. We will talk about how this is done for the x86 JIT in this section; the PowerPC JIT compiler that ships as part of Rotor uses a very similar, but not identical, approach.

The JIT compiler produces code that specifically targets the local micropro-cessor and its native stack. There is no separate CIL stack implementation; the CIL stack is simply an abstraction. Because of this, the execution con-text for managed code coexists on the stack along with the execution con-text for unmanaged code that may have run as part of the CLI implementation or as calls to external services. In order for this to work smoothly, all code, whether JIT-compiled or natively compiled, needs to obey the same rules with respect to local calling conventions, nonlocal returns (such as exceptions) and use of "dangerous" data types such as pointers.

 The choice of native calling convention in the SSCLI was driven by the desire for minimal rewriting of code that was inherited from Microsoft's commercial CLI implementation. As an example of how this decision has impacted the JIT compiler's calling convention, the stub implementations depend on stable locations for both the this pointer and for the return value of a method when either is present. To change this invariant, the stubs would have to be rewritten. Likewise, the order in which arguments are pushed onto the stack is slightly unusual; this too is driven by the desire for minimal code churn. As we said, the choices that drive implementation decisions can seem capricious...

In the x86 JIT compiler, when a call, calli, or callvirt instruction is encountered, the arguments will have been pushed onto the stack by pre-ceding CIL instructions, as discussed earlier. At this point, the compiler will locate two of the arguments that will fit into four bytes, to hoist them into the ECX and EDX registers. The stack is compacted, and the holes out of which arguments were hoisted are removed, after which EDX is pushed back onto the stack, followed by ECX. Cleanup in the SSCLI is __cdecl-style: the caller will clean up the stack on return, and the hoisting of arguments will be a remnant of the x86-oriented convention called __fastcall in previous implementations.

The following example may help make this clear, since it is a bit convo-luted. The instance method:

```
void MyFunc(int32 a, int64 b, int64 c, int32 d, int32 e)
```

will be transformed as shown in Figure 5-8. The first two four byte quanti-ties, a and d, are moved to the top of the stack beneath the this pointer.

For x86 functions with a variable number of parameters, a VarArg token is passed along with the arguments to the function, as described in the previ-ous discussion of the JIT calling convention. The signature of each call to a vararg function is described in the method metadata, and the token can be

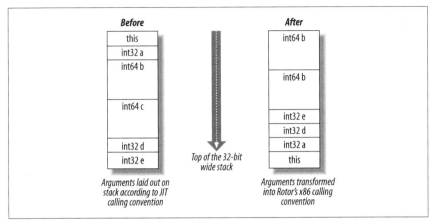

Figure 5-8. Transforming the JIT-calling convention to Rotor's x86 calling convention

used to find this signature and examine it. The signature doesn't include the this pointer or the return buffer pointer, and as before, the stubs and the garbage collector expect to find them at fixed offsets, so they are pushed onto the stack after the token. All other arguments are pushed onto the stack before the VarArg token from left to right and there is no reordering to pull out 4-byte arguments, as there is in the "normal" convention.

The location of activation records on the stack cannot be predicted in advance, but many of the important and oft-accessed elements of the record can be determined at compile-time. To take best advantage of this, a frame pointer is kept, and offsets into the frame are used—the security object for a frame lives at a standard offset, for example, and the location of object references, which is tracked for use by the garbage collector, is noted by the compiler and placed into a table. Exception tables, which are an optional part of the frame, are also treated this way.

Besides parameter values, return values, and instance pointers, things like the security object and exception tables populate the activation frame for a method. The prolog of a call is where these entities are managed, and where the code to move the two hoisted register values onto the stack can be found. It also does other things, as can be seen in the x86-specific version of the prolog shown in Example 5-8.

Example 5-8. The x86 method prolog (Defined in clr/src/fjit/i386/x86fjit.h)

```
#define x86_emit_prolog(locals, zeroCnt)                            \
    x86_push(X86_EBP);                                              \
    x86_mov_reg(x86DirTo, x86Big, x86_mod_reg(X86_EBP, X86_ESP));   \
    x86_push(X86_ESI);  /* callee saved, used by newobj and calli*/ \
    x86_barith(x86OpXor, x86Big, x86_mod_reg(X86_ESI, X86_ESI));    \
    x86_push(X86_ESI);  /* security obj == NULL */                  \
```

Example 5-8. The x86 method prolog (Defined in clr/src/fjit/i386/x86fjit.h) (continued)

```
    if (locals) {                                              \
        x86_mov_reg_imm(x86Big, X86_ECX, locals);              \
        int emitter_scratch_i4 = (unsigned int) outPtr;        \
        x86_push_imm(0);                                       \
        x86_loop();                                            \
        cmdByte(emitter_scratch_i4-((unsigned int) outPtr)-1); \
    }
```

This code saves the frame pointer on the stack, sets the new frame pointer, saves the ESI register (which is used to pass back new objects from the newobj or newarr opcodes and pass the function pointer for indirect calls in string copy operations), and then allocates a spot on the stack for the method's security object, which will be populated lazily, if needed. If there are locals, it grows the stack to accommodate them, and then initializes their values to 0.

The x86_emit_prolog macro is of course one of the processor-specific redefinitions of generic JIT macros that were previously discussed in the compilation section. In the generic version of the prolog, which can be found in *fjitdef.h* and is shown in Example 5-9, the simplest presentation of the bare bones of the calling convention can be seen.

Example 5-9. The generic version of the method prolog (defined in clr/src/fjit/fjitdef.h)

```
#define emit_prolog(locals)              \
{                                        \
   setup_frame();                        \
   storeEnregisteredArguments();         \
   ON_X86_ONLY(if (locals))              \
      grow(locals ON_PPC_ONLY(+1), true);\
   if ( ALIGN_ARGS )                     \
      alignArguments();                  \
}
```

The prolog sets up the frame, takes care of any callee-saved register, and grows the stack for locals as needed, initializing them to 0. Each of these actions is handled by other functions or macros, such as the PowerPC-specific setup_frame shown in Example 5-10.

Example 5-10. The PowerPC version of setup_frame is called by the generic version of emit_prolog (defined in clr/src/fjit/ppc/ppcdef.h)

```
#define ppc_setup_frame()                \
{                                        \
  ppc_mfspr(R0, PPC_MOVE_LR);            \
  ppc_stw(R0, R1, 0x8);                  \
  if (mapInfo.savedIP )                  \
  {                                      \
```

Example 5-10. The PowerPC version of setup_frame is called by the generic version of emit_prolog (defined in clr/src/fjit/ppc/ppcdef.h) (continued)

```
    ppc_stw(R28, R1, 0x4);                              \
    ppc_b( 1, 0, SAVE_RET_ADDR);                        \
    storedStartIP = outPtr;                             \
    ppc_mfspr(R28, PPC_MOVE_LR);                        \
  }                                                     \
  ppc_stw(R30, R1, ((unsigned)(-4)&0xFFFF));           \
  ppc_or( R30, R1, R1, 0 );                            \
  ppc_stwu(R29, R1,((unsigned)(-8)&0xFFFF));           \
}
```

The code that uses offsets in the activation record is isolated into what is called the *code manager*. In the SSCLI distribution, the code manager can be found in *fjit_eetwain.cpp* (which roughly stands for "FJIT Execution Engine Technology Without An Important Name"). The code manager knows intimate details about stack layout, and because of this, is used whenever the stack needs to be traversed or pried open. We will see it used in Chapter 6 and Chapter 7 in conjunction with stack walks, exception handling, and garbage collection.

One of the functions of the code manager can be used as an example of offset-based access to the activation record, as shown in Example 5-11.

Example 5-11. Relative access to stack activation records (defined in clr/src/vm/fjit_eetwain.cpp)

```
OBJECTREF* Fjit_EETwain::GetAddrOfSecurityObject(
                PREGDISPLAY    ctx,
                LPVOID         methodInfoPtr,
                size_t         relOffset,
                CodeManState   *pState)
{
    unsigned char* compressed = (unsigned char*) methodInfoPtr;
    Fjit_hdrInfo hdrInfo;
    crackMethodInfoHdr(compressed,  (SLOT)relOffset, &hdrInfo);
    PVOID* pFrameBase = getInternalFP(GetRegdisplayFP(ctx));
    return GetAddrOfSecurityObjectInternal(pFrameBase);
}
```

Of course, the important line in this function is the last, which calls GetAddrOfSecurityObjectInternal, which is defined as:

```
    OBJECTREF* GetAddrOfSecurityObjectInternal(PVOID* internalFP)
    {
      return (OBJECTREF*)(internalFP + offsetof(prolog_data, security_obj) /
        sizeof(void*) + 1);
    }
```

This short function uses the current register value of the frame pointer to find the base of the activation record. The prolog_data struct, defined in *ifjitcompiler.h*, is used to pull out the address of the security object itself. This struct varies from processor to processor, based on the calling convention. For example, the x86 version looks like this:

```
struct prolog_data {
    unsigned security_obj;
    unsigned callee_saved_esi;
};
```

Clearly the two elements that it contains rely heavily on specifics of the x86 compiler. Porting Rotor to other processors requires that equal attention be paid to the specific characterizations of each of them.

Other Calling Conventions

Another thing that will be seen during compilation is the use of *stubs*, which are pre-built helper functions that can be joined together using the StubLinker class to create pre- and post-processing for method calls. Stubs are often used for performance-critical purposes and have detailed knowledge of the conventions used by a specific JIT compiler. Like the code manager, stubs are linked tightly to the compiler. To see the collection of stubs used in the SSCLI implementation, look in the *sscli/clr/src/vm/i386* directory. You will find templates for exception-handling stubs, security stubs, array accessors, and marshaling stubs (used by P/Invoke), as well as even more esoteric ones used for very implementation-specific purposes such as multicasting delegates.

In non-jitted code such as helper functions and stubs, other calling conventions are often utilized, and because of this, you will not see a completely homogenous stack at runtime. All calls in jitted code still obey the JIT calling convention, but calls between non-jitted components can and do obey other conventions. The file *method.hpp* contains an enum that holds additional calling conventions supported by the SSCLI execution engine for managed code:

```
enum MethodClassification
{
    mcIL        = 0, // IL
    mcECall     = 1, // ECall
    mcNDirect   = 2, // N/Direct
    mcEEImpl    = 3, // special method; implementation provided by EE
    mcArray     = 4, // Array ECall
};
```

We've already seen how JIT calls use the stack, but what about the others here? The enum essentially describes where the code for the call is coming from—each type of call differs, either because interop dictates another calling convention or because the execution engine has a high degree of control over the callsite and can make execution more efficient. It is interesting that all of these use the same JIT calling convention described above, from the perspective of the JIT-compiled code; the stubs do their conversion internally.

One of the important calling conventions in the SSCLI implementation (which appears in the enum above as mcECall for historical purposes) is referred to within the distribution as the *FCall*. It is a very efficient call to code that is internal to the execution engine and can be recognized in C# code as methods that are marked with the MethodImplOptions.InternalCall method attribute. FCalls are mapped onto C++ functions in the execution engine using a table that can be found in *clr\src\vm\ecall.cpp*. Each entry in this table is an ECFunc struct, as follows:

```
struct ECFunc {
    LPCUTF8             m_wszMethodName;
    LPHARDCODEDMETASIG m_wszMethodSig;
    LPVOID             m_pImplementation;
    MethodDesc*        m_pMD;              // for reverse mapping
    unsigned           m_intrinsicID : 8;
    ECFunc*            m_pNext;            // linked list for hash table
};
```

The mapping is from m_wszMethodName to m_pImplementation. All functions being called are implemented within the execution engine itself; thus, the calls do not need to perform parameter marshaling or checks of other kinds. You will see references to "ECalls" in the code base in places, such as the ECFunc table (and in the MethodClassification enum already shown). This name is obsolete, and all ECalls are now FCalls. The order of parameters to an FCall needs to match the JIT calling convention, and to ensure this, FCalls are implemented using the FCDECL and FCIMPL series of macros that can be found in *fcall.h*. The native code for an FCall needs to be written in a very rigorous way—it should protect against causing GC and throw exceptions only from its top-level function using special macros. FCalls, while fast, are also expert-only territory and are very prone to bugs because of the many rules that must be followed while masquerading as managed code; the unmanaged code in an FCall implementation must use the same calling convention and stack management regimen as managed code.

It may be tempting to extend Rotor using the FCall convention for performance-critical code or as an integration mechanism for already existing C++. This is almost certainly a bad idea. The trend in Microsoft's commercial CLI implementation is to move away from using this mechanism, both because implementing correct calls is difficult and because it increases the size of the core system library.

If a call with type mcNDirect is going through the CLI P/Invoke mechanism, it can be recognized in C# by the DllImport method attribute. (N/Direct is an obsolete code name for what became the P/Invoke feature; readers who recognize the name from previous Microsoft products should pretend not to notice.) The code for the method is generated by NDirect:: GetNDirectMethodStub; it is code that handles argument marshaling, as described in the discussion of P/Invoke in the ECMA Specification. *Corinfo. h* contains an enum for the "external" calling conventions recognized by the P/Invoke stub. These flags affect the marshaling behavior of the stub, depending on the calling convention being matched. P/Invoke also does parameter marshalling. The stub that marshals the arguments first adjusts the state of the execution engine (because the execution engine needs to record whether execution is outside the scope of execution engine control on a given thread); it then calls the method that can reside in any native DLL on the system.

The code for both mcEEImpl and mcArray type calls is generated directly: by the execution engine for delegate multicasters in the mcEEImpl case and by GenerateArrayOpStub for multidimensional array getters and setters in the mcArray case. There are other fascinating uses of stubs in the SSCLI, including things such as profiling. The last one that we will examine is used by the remoting service, which provides application domain isolation. Using the EEClass for a given type, the remoting service produces what is called a *transparent proxy*, which is an object that looks exactly like another type but has a special implementation that forwards operations to a companion object of the "real" type. Several interesting functions in *remoting.cpp* use the runtime type information structures we have already seen to synthesize the look alike proxy: see for example, CTPMethodTable::CreateTPOfClassForRP. The method calls on the transparent proxy are JIT-compiled like any other method and use the TPStub, seen in Example 5-12, to implement their behavior (and defined in *clr/src/vm/i386/remotingx86.cpp*).

Example 5-12. A stub for cross application domain access to components

```
Stub *CTPMethodTable::CreateTPStub( )
{
  if (s_pTPStub == NULL) {
```

```
    pStubLinker = CTPMethodTable::NewStubLinker( );

    CodeLabel *ConvMD = pStubLinker->NewCodeLabel( );
    CodeLabel *UseCode = pStubLinker->NewCodeLabel( );
    CodeLabel *OOContext = pStubLinker->NewCodeLabel( );

    EmitCallToStub(pStubLinker, OOContext);
    EmitJumpToAddressCode(pStubLinker, ConvMD, UseCode);
    pStubLinker->EmitLabel(OOContext);
    EmitSetupFrameCode(pStubLinker);

    s_pTPStub = pStubLinker->Link( );

    g_dwOOContextAddr = (DWORD)(size_t)(s_pTPStub->GetEntryPoint( ) +
                                   pStubLinker->GetLabelOffset(OOContext));
  }

  if(NULL != s_pTPStub) {
    CVirtualThunkMgr::InitVirtualThunkManager(
                               (const BYTE *) s_pTPStub->GetEntryPoint( ));
  }
  if (pStubLinker)
    delete pStubLinker;

  return(s_pTPStub);
}
```

What is interesting in this stub is that its creation is entirely automatic; the stub and its EEClass are created by interpreting metadata. A StubLinker is created, and again, knowledge of the calling convention is used in the various emit functions to create a customized, data-driven method body.

Emitting Components Dynamically

In an interesting twist, not only does the CLI provide the facilities to examine all this structure and metadata at runtime via the System.Reflection namespace, it also provides the ability to emit entirely runtime-synthesized types via the System.Reflection.Emit namespace. This means, quite literally, that it becomes possible to build these types "on the fly," as it were. While we won't do a complete tutorial on System.Reflection.Emit (other sources cover this API in some detail), it does prove interesting to follow the System.Reflection.Emit calls and see how they end up in this same structure we've just been diving through.

The API

What follows here is a simple `Reflection.Emit` program, which dynamically produces, the "Hello World" sample that every programming textbook defines. (Note that we don't reuse the `Echo` sample because to emit even something as simple as `Echo` would occupy several pages of pure code.)

```
using System;
using System.Reflection;
using System.Reflection.Emit;


class App
{
  static void Main( )
  {
    AssemblyName an = new AssemblyName( );
    an.Name = "HelloReflectionEmit";

    AppDomain ad = AppDomain.CurrentDomain;
    AssemblyBuilder ab = ad.DefineDynamicAssembly(an, /
                      AssemblyBuilderAccess.Run);

    ModuleBuilder mb = ab.DefineDynamicModule(an.Name, "Hello.exe");

    TypeBuilder tb = mb.DefineType("Hello.Emitted", TypeAttributes.Public |
                                      TypeAttributes.Class);

    MethodBuilder mthb = tb.DefineMethod("Main",
                          MethodAttributes.Public |
                          MethodAttributes.Static,
                          typeof(int),
                          new Type[] { typeof(string[]) });

    ILGenerator ilg = mthb.GetILGenerator( );

    ilg.Emit(OpCodes.Ldstr, "Hello, World!");
    ilg.Emit(OpCodes.Call,
      typeof(Console).GetMethod("WriteLine", new Type[]{typeof(string[])}));
    ilg.Emit(OpCodes.Ldc_I4_0);
    ilg.Emit(OpCodes.Ret);

    Type t = tb.CreateType( );

    ab.SetEntryPoint(mthb, PEFileKinds.ConsoleApplication);

    Console.WriteLine("Finished--executing Hello");

    ad.ExecuteAssembly("Hello.exe");
  }
}
```

Emitting a dynamic assembly requires only seven steps:

1. Often (although we don't do so here), a new application domain will be created, to allow the host to unload the domain and its dynamically-defined assembly when desired.

2. From that application domain, create an `AssemblyBuilder` by calling `DefineDynamicAssembly`, passing in the `AssemblyName` for the dynamic assembly and the access restrictions—can this assembly be saved, run, or both?

3. Define each module (usually 1:1) for the assembly.

4. Generate the desired types (in this case, the type "Emitted" in the namespace "Hello"). Note that the type's attributes are described using `TypeAttributes` in the second parameter to the `DefineType` call.

5. Define methods using `MethodBuilder` (and fields using `FieldBuilder`, and events using `EventBuilder`, and so on), again making sure to pass in the desired attributes and, as necessary, the signature of the element being defined—in this case, the signature of the `Main` method needs to take an array of strings (`typeof(string[])`), and returns an `int`.

6. For methods, emit the CIL opcodes directly to the method body.

7. Call `CreateType` to finish, and the type is ready—in our case, we set the entrypoint for the assembly, then ask our application domain to execute it.

The results are pretty much as would be expected—the assembly is defined and executed, printing "Hello, World" to the console. Note that *Hello.exe* exists only in memory—to save it would require creating the `AssemblyBuilder` with the `AssemblyBuilderAccess.Save` attribute and saving the type using `Save` on the `AssemblyBuilder`.

It is important to note here that the `Reflection.Emit` structures closely mirror those of the underlying structures they generate—assemblies contain one or move modules, which in turn contain types, which in turn contain fields, methods, properties, events, and so on. In fact, the metadata token itself is available from these APIs—you can get the `MethodToken` from a `MethodBuilder` by calling `GetToken`–adding the line

```
Console.WriteLine("{0:X}", mthb.GetToken().Token);
```

right after the `CreateType` call prints out `0x06000001`. (As verification, save the emitted assembly to disk and run *ildasm* against it—Main is, in fact, `0x06000001`.)

The implementation

To provide this functionality, the `Reflection` types, and especially the `Invoke` methods found on them, have to have extensive knowledge of `EEClass`,

MethodTable, and other internal structures. Finding that link is something of an interesting dive through the Rotor-Base-Class-Library-to-VM chain. While we won't trace the entire set of methods, we'll touch on a few of the interesting ones.

Working in top-down fashion, we start with the call to AppDomain. DefineDynamicAssembly. From the source, stored in the file *clr\src\bcl\system\appdomain.cs*, we see that this is a wrapper around another call:

```
public AssemblyBuilder DefineDynamicAssembly(
    AssemblyName        name,
    AssemblyBuilderAccess   access)
{
    StackCrawlMark stackMark = StackCrawlMark.LookForMyCaller;
    return InternalDefineDynamicAssembly(name, access, null,
                                         null, null, null, null, /
                                         ref stackMark);
}
```

This internal method, in turn, sets the key pair on the assembly (if provided), demands a security permission (if security evidence was provided), and then makes a call to another internal method, nCreateDynamicAssembly, whose declaration is also found in *appdomain.cs*:

```
[MethodImplAttribute(MethodImplOptions.InternalCall)]
private extern AssemblyBuilder nCreateDynamicAssembly(AssemblyName name,
                Evidence identity,
                ref StackCrawlMark stackMark,
                PermissionSet requiredPermissions,
                PermissionSet optionalPermissions,
                PermissionSet refusedPermissions,
                AssemblyBuilderAccess access);
```

But, as can plainly be seen, no implementation is found—instead, the MethodImplAttribute indicates that this is an *internal call*, meaning this is the point of entry into the execution engine code itself. However, the SSCLI doesn't have a method named nCreateDynamicAssembly anywhere within it—so where, precisely, will you jump off to?

Defined in *clr/src/vm/ecall.cpp* is a set of tables that map methods marked as internal calls to their actual function entry points; sure enough, in one of these tables, an entry named nCreateDynamicAssembly is found:

```
static
ECFunc gAppDomainFuncs[] =
{
    // . . .
    {FCFuncElement("nCreateDynamicAssembly",    NULL,
        (LPVOID)AppDomainNative::CreateDynamicAssembly)},
    // . . .
};
```

This is the trampoline, then, that takes calls bound to the name nCreateDynamicAssembly and substitutes the entry point for the CreateDynamicAssembly method of the C++ class AppDomainNative. Tracking this further, then, takes you to *clr/src/vm/appdomainnative.cpp*, in which CreateDynamicAssembly rips through the arguments handed to it, finds the VM-level pointer for the given application domain, creates a new Assembly structure, and adds it to the application domain.

A number of interesting functions are defined in *vm/ecall.cpp*; one is the trampolined call that occurs when TypeBuilder is asked to create a new type. This in turn routes to:

```
static
ECFunc gCOMClassWriter[] =
{
    {FCFuncElement("InternalDefineClass",    NULL,
        (LPVOID) COMDynamicWrite::CWCreateClass)},
    // . . .
};
```

which is in turn defined in *clr/src/vm/comdynamic.cpp*. (Again, don't let the "COM" prefixes here throw you—remember, Rotor was derived from the original CLR sources, which were developed under the presumption that . NET would be the next generation of COM.) This method calls against a RefClassWriter class (defined in *clr/src/vm/reflectclasswriter.h*), which in turn is a wrapper around our old friends IMetaDataEmit and IMetaDataImport, the interfaces to the metadata subsystem in Rotor. These take the generated CIL for the type, store it into the CLI metadata formats, which are suitable for consumption by the very mechanisms we've just discussed, the class loader and JIT compiler.

Summary

Assemblies are loaded on demand, using the techniques outlined in Chapter 4. As new components are called for by application domains in the execution engine, runtime specifications are built from their metadata for in-memory layout. This information includes specifications for static and per-instance data, as well as method-dispatching tables. The dispatch tables are constructed to initially contain thunks that will trigger code compilation, rather than the method code for class behaviors that will eventually populate them. By using thunks in this way, compilation is deferred until the last possible moment, reducing startup costs.

The combination of on-demand loading and deferred compilation is called JIT compilation. Class loaders and the SSCLI JIT compiler work in conjunction with high-level language compilers to create component types. Source languages are parsed and converted into a combination of metadata and language-agnostic CIL opcodes rather than being converted directly into native microprocessor instructions, and this combination of metadata and CIL is transformed at runtime into in-memory layouts, native microprocessor instructions, and tables for the CLI's garbage collector and exception-handling facility. The facilities of the runtime that do layout and compilation are also available to programmers in the CLI's reflection facility.

From the perspective of the CLI component model, the stage of a component's lifecycle during which it is loaded and compiled is a moment when layout and behavior are transformed from an abstract representation into concrete, directly executable forms. To ensure that these forms continue to be safe, the SSCLI JIT compiler intermixes type verification with compilation, using a unique one-pass algorithm. In the SSCLI, the actual implementation of the verifier and compiler is also layered for maximum portability and simplicity.

Having converted a component into native code, addresses, and offsets, it remains to be seen how this code can be run under the watchful eye of the execution engine without "losing control," which is the topic of Chapter 6.

Regulating the Execution Engine

We've now seen how the CLI transforms high-level type descriptions into processor-specific code. This chapter examines what happens once this code has begun to run and what the execution engine needs to do to remain in control. Without a foolproof way to retain control, all of the unpacking, rejiggering, checking, compiling, and linking of types that has been described to this point would be for nought. The runtime boundaries that are erected by the execution engine are one of its most desirable features, since they enable components to cooperate while remaining safely isolated.

Rotor piggybacks on two operating system abstractions, *threads* and *exceptions*, to control the execution state for a given process. Threads and exceptions are both related to the execution stack: a thread is home to the memory that makes up an execution stack, while exceptions create structure for that memory using a convention that helps protect its integrity at runtime.

Threads

Most programmers think of threads as a way to separate well-defined tasks into independent chunks of code, usually in conjunction with matching synchronization constructs. This usage is supported by the CLI, of course; chunks of code can run "on" threads whose schedules are dictated by the operating system's threading implementation and by intertask dependencies. But threads in the CLI have another equally important role: they are the primary data structure for maintaining execution engine information about executing code. Besides representing concurrent execution and synchronization, the thread structures within the CLI provide a way to associate the microprocessor's execution stack with related runtime data. This runtime data is a trove of bookkeeping information, which includes security annotations, garbage-collection markers, program variables, and many other things.

Inside the execution engine, threads are implemented on top of *PAL threads*, which abstract away system-specific threading details. (Threads are one of the least standardized system services. Because of this, the PAL's implementation is both difficult and important.) In the discussion that follows, we will draw a distinction between PAL threads and *managed threads*. A managed thread is an instance of the Thread type, while a PAL thread is a preemptively scheduled execution unit that exists within an address space and can have private state associated with it. Managed threads wrap PAL threads; they are high-level types within the CLI that encapsulate lower-level semantics. Managed threads always have a corresponding PAL thread, but PAL threads do not need to have a corresponding managed thread.

The ability of PAL threads to maintain private per-thread state is important, because the execution engine tracks "interesting" threads (defined, rather myopically, as threads that have executed managed code) by associating an instance of Thread with the underlying PAL thread using this per-thread state. From the perspective of the managed code, the Thread type has a field named m_ThreadHandle, which contains a HANDLE to its PAL thread that it uses to control and schedule execution on this thread. Since there is no PAL call to enable navigating from a thread handle to a managed thread, the execution engine maintains a ThreadStore that can be used to enumerate managed threads from both managed and unmanaged code.

To facilitate interoperability between unmanaged and managed code, managed threads mix the execution state of managed and unmanaged code on a single stack. PAL threads that become associated with managed code are used by the execution engine to maintain exception handlers, scheduling priorities, and a set of structures that the underlying platform uses to save context whenever it preempts the thread's execution. (The thread context holds important details, such as the values held in machine registers and the state of the current execution stack.)

There are many places in which unmanaged code calls managed code, and vice versa, as illustrated by Figure 6-1. Three scenarios, in particular, are common:

- Much of the execution engine is written in unmanaged code, and JIT helper functions and large parts of the base class libraries frequently call or are called by JIT-compiled code.
- Managed components can be instantiated and called by native applications that wish to host the CLI.
- Previously unknown threads can enter the runtime from the "outside."

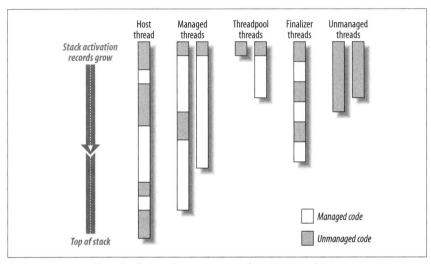

Figure 6-1. Many threads of control can coexist within a managed process

Managed threads must be prepared to behave gracefully in the face of manipulation in any of these scenarios. Since components are free to call external routines using ECMA's *platform invocation* (P/Invoke) mechanism and pass component references to these external routines, component callbacks may be asynchronously invoked from outside the execution engine. Likewise, applications are free to host instances of the execution engine within their own processes, instantiating and calling component instances from their own threads, which also results in external invocation. Because of these possibilities and because the SSCLI implementation mixes execution state of both managed and PAL threads, the concurrency model is quite complex.

Transitions between managed and unmanaged code can be created in many different ways, and it is important to understand every one of them since the execution engine must account for each to maintain control and integrity. Significant transitions are not limited to boundaries with external code; even within managed code, isolation needs to be maintained as application domain boundaries or remoting contexts are crossed, as security permissions change, or as exceptions are thrown.

Setting Up a Managed Thread

The easiest transition to understand is the initial transition from unmanaged to managed code, when a PAL thread prepares to run managed code. The linkage between the PAL thread and the managed thread is accomplished in SetupThread, defined in *clr/src/vm/threads.cpp*; the code in Example 6-1 is edited from *threads.cpp* and shows this process.

Example 6-1. Threads are associated with an underlying PAL thread (simplified from clr/src/vm/threads.cpp)

```
Thread* SetupThread( )
{
  Thread* pThread;

  // No-op if managed thread already exists
  if ((pThread = GetThread( )) != NULL)
    return pThread;

  // Thread object may already exist
  if (g_pThreadStore->m_PendingThreadCount != 0) {
    DWORD  ourThreadId = ::GetCurrentThreadId( );

    ThreadStore::LockThreadStore( );
    while ((pThread = g_pThreadStore->GetAllThreadList(pThread,
                      Thread::TS_Unstarted, Thread::TS_Unstarted)) != NULL) {
      if (pThread->GetThreadId( ) == ourThreadId)
        break;
    }
    ThreadStore::UnlockThreadStore( );

    if (pThread)
      return (pThread->HasStarted( ) ? pThread : NULL);
  }

  // Otherwise, this is the first time we've seen this thread in the runtime
  // Create a new managed thread on behalf of underlying PAL thread
  pThread = new Thread( );
  if (!pThread)
    return NULL;

  if (!pThread->InitThread( ))
    goto fail;

  // Store managed thread pointer into thread local store, along with domain
  TlsSetValue(gThreadTLSIndex, (VOID*)pThread);
  TlsSetValue(gAppDomainTLSIndex, (VOID*)pThread->GetDomain( ));

  // Set initial state
  FastInterlockAnd((ULONG *) &pThread->m_State, ~Thread::TS_Unstarted);
  FastInterlockOr((ULONG *) &pThread->m_State, Thread::TS_LegalToJoin);
  ThreadStore::AddThread(pThread);
  pThread->SetBackground(TRUE);
  return pThread;

fail:
  delete pThread;
  return NULL;
}
```

There are two checks made to ensure that the thread being set up does not already have a corresponding instance of Thread. First, a call to GetThread is made via a function pointer established in InitThreadManager. GetThread looks for a cached Thread instance in the TLS for the calling PAL thread. If an instance is found, the calling thread is already known to the execution engine.

If there is no cached thread instance, SetupThread ensures that the call is not coming from a different thread than the thread being initialized. To check this, the ThreadStore (which is exactly what it sounds like—a container for all known Threads) is queried for a matching identifier. If one is found, SetupThread can return, since the thread is known to the execution engine. If the PAL thread is truly unknown to the execution engine, a new Thread object is created, installed on its TLS, and marked as started. The call to Thread::HasStarted completes the initialization of the Thread instance.

In addition to acting as a home for managed execution bookkeeping info associated with the underlying PAL thread, the new Thread instance will be added by the execution engine to the ThreadStore's list of all the threads ever seen. This bookkeeping information is used during thread suspension, during shutdown, and for thread enumeration. Of these threads, those that wander into the execution engine without being known to it become *background threads*, which cannot keep the execution engine alive by themselves. *Foreground threads* have the opposite effect and will keep the CLI execution engine alive as long as they are running. (The thread that calls the main .entrypoint for a managed program, for example, is a foreground thread.) The foreground/background state of a Thread is exposed through its API and can be changed from managed code.

Traversing the Execution Engine Stack

Once a Thread instance has been associated with an underlying PAL thread, managed code can be executed on it. One sequence that will kick off the execution of managed code can be found in MethodDesc::Call, which we discussed in Chapter 5 (and which can be found in *sscli/clr/src/vm/method.cpp*). The implementation of Call relies on the fact that two important tracking structures will be on the stack before JIT-compiled code is executed: an exception handler that will wrap the managed code (which we will see in great detail later in the "Handling Exceptions" section of this chapter), and a chain of *execution engine frames* ("frames," for short—see the sidebar "Frames, Frames, Frames") that will be used to annotate portions of the stack with runtime information produced by the execution engine.

Execution engine frames do not exist in the regions of the stack that are generated by the JIT compiler, since the execution engine already has intimate knowledge about how this code will use the stack and can read the resulting stack data directly, without using frames as markers. But the multiple calling conventions, exception paths, and other nasty details that must be understood when interpreting stack layouts for code not produced by the JIT compiler, or for JIT helper code, are what make frames a necessary part of the SSCLI execution strategy. The intricacies of tracing the stack, as well as the tight requirements placed on stack layout by security, result in a runtime service called the code manager, which knows how to join the managed and unmanaged portions of a stack together into a single coherent view.

Frames, Frames, Frames

Unfortunately, the word "frame" is used within the execution engine in three ways, each of which is different. The most familiar to programmers is the notion of a *stack frame*, which is a region of stack memory that is allocated for a single procedure call, used to hold parameter values, local variables, a return value, and anything else needed by the calling convention in effect. To reduce ambiguity, we will refer to this as an *activation record* in this book, which is a commonly used alternate term.

The second use of "frame" is in the context of exception handling. An *exception handler frame* is a region of the stack that is covered by a particular structured exception handler. Exception handler frames are begun by the use of the try keyword in C# or C++, and conclude at the point following the last corresponding exception handler. Here, we will always refer to this kind of frame in a fully qualified way.

The third kind of frame is unique to the SSCLI execution engine. *Execution engine frames* are bookkeeping structures that are stored on the stack by the execution engine for the purpose of marking significant boundaries. These frames are discussed extensively in the accompanying text, and because of this, we will refer to them as nothing more than frames.

The existence of execution engine frames and the code manager highlight an important aspect of the SSCLI implementation: its stacks contain much more than method invocation state. In fact, the stack for each thread forms a complete record of currently executing code and is an ideal place to put control information needed by the execution engine, since it manages the execution of that code. The execution engine uses the information in the stack to:

- Track and update stack-stored object references for garbage collection
- Hold state for security checks

- Recognize transitions, such as cross-domain or managed-to-unmanaged calls
- Find the correct handler and unwind the stack during an exception
- Generate human-readable call traces for debugger and exception support
- Keep track of exception resources

When needed, this information is accessed via *stackwalking*, which, as the name implies, is the process of traversing interesting spots in the stack's call chain to extract current execution state.

Annotating the Stack with Frames

Frame instances are used polymorphically by the code manager, which relies on virtual method dispatching to produce specialized behaviors. A linked list of execution engine frames is associated with every Thread object, all of which are instances of the Frame class or one of its subclasses, and all of which can be found in *sscli/clr/src/vm/frames.h*. The C++ classes are provided to let the code within the execution engine manipulate existing frames, but frame construction is often done by assembler stubs, from JIT helpers, or by other implementation-specific tricks within the execution engine. Because of this, the class declarations in *frames.h* are tightly coupled with the architecture-specific stub generation code, which makes it important to keep these stubs in sync when changing the frame code in any way. In particular, programmers should avoid attempting to use constructors or destructors on these objects without first examining any related stubs, since many of the frames are not meant to be instantiated in this way (and most constructors are private for this reason).

Frames are often linked to exception handling; there is a frame type for every situation in which protection or special action is needed when crossing a boundary in the context of an exception. Interop calls, context-crossing calls, and internal calls into the execution engine all generate special frames. Any crossing from unmanaged or managed compiled code back into the execution engine is also marked by a frame of some sort. Figure 6-2 contains some of the more interesting types of frames that are used in the SSCLI.

As seen in Figure 6-2, the following types of frames are shown:

DebuggerClassInitMarkFrame
> This frame is used as the very first frame in a given thread's linked list.

GCFrame
> This frame is used to alert the garbage collector to object references that should be tracked within unmanaged execution engine code.

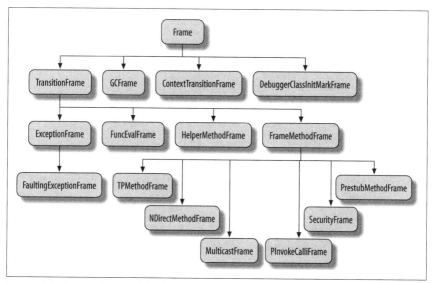

Figure 6-2. A partial view of the frame type hierarchy in the SSCLI

ContextTransitionFrame
This frame marks a transition across an application domain or a context.

TransitionFrame
This frame represents the transition from JIT-compiled code into either an execution engine function or a framed method.

ExceptionFrame
This frame is used to mark an activation record that has caused an exception.

FaultingExceptionFrame
This frame has taken a PAL exception during the execution of JIT-compiled code.

FuncEvalFrame
The debugger "borrows" the stack to do evaluation, and the point at which the stack is borrowed is marked by this frame.

HelperMethodFrame
This frame is used to include JIT helper functions and FCalls in the stackwalk.

FramedMethodFrame
This frame is an abstract superclass for all kinds of method calls that will use a Frame.

TPMethodFrame

This frame marks transitions into the remoting machinery via a transparent proxy.

NDirectMethodFrame

This frame marks a transition into native code via the P/Invoke mechanism.

NDirectMethodFrameEx

A P/Invoke transition, with additional cleanup.

MulticastFrame

This frame is used by multicast delegates to protect arguments from the garbage collector during iteration over its targets.

PInvokeCalliFrame

This frame marks a transition into native code via an indirect P/Invoke call. (The indirection is caused by the IL calli instruction with a P/Invoke target.)

SecurityFrame

This frame is used during security stackwalks and acts as a holder for the security object of an activation record on the stack.

InterceptorFrame

This frame is a SecurityFrame that also protects the arguments of the function from garbage collection.

PrestubMethodFrame

This frame marks a call to the method prestub.

UnmanagedToManagedFrame

This frame is used to mark a transition into managed code from unmanaged code.

UnmanagedToManagedCallFrame

This frame is used to mark a transition from unmanaged code to a managed method, which registers the method arguments with the garbage collector.

UMThkCallFrame

This frame is used to mark a transition into managed code from unmanaged code via a UMThunk, which is a delegate that encapsulates an unmanaged target function.

As you can see, frames come in many flavors, not all of which correspond to method calls in a one-to-one way. The SSCLI stack is a complex mixture of execution engine frames, exception-handling frames, and activation records.

Categorizing Frames

To help make sense of this mixture, we will divide execution engine frames into two categories: data annotations and transition markers. Data annotations are used by the execution engine to track data items of interest in the stack, while transition markers help the execution engine track context.

Annotating data

As an example of a frame that is purely an annotation, consider GCFrame. The only purpose of a GCFrame is to protect one or more object references from being garbage collected while they are manipulated by execution engine code. The execution engine uses GCFrame instances to guarantee stable pointers while allocating objects or doing any other operation that could trigger a GC.

As we will see in the next chapter, garbage collectors spend their life moving objects around in memory and updating references so that they correctly reflect the move. If the garbage collector doesn't know that a reference exists, or if the object is in flux, it can't update its tracking information correctly. This is why "protection" is needed for variables that hold references that are unstable in some way. Without protection, garbage collection holes can result, which often causes serious problems.

The use of GCFrame within the SSCLI code may not be entirely obvious; this operation is hidden under the GCPROTECT_BEGIN macro, which is defined as follows in *frames.h*:

```
#define GCPROTECT_BEGIN(ObjRefStruct)              do {         \
            GCFrame __gcframe((OBJECTREF*)&(ObjRefStruct),       \
            sizeof(ObjRefStruct)/sizeof(OBJECTREF),              \
            FALSE);                                              \
            _ASSERTE(!GetThread()->GCForbidden());               \
            DEBUG_ASSURE_NO_RETURN_IN_THIS_BLOCK
```

Calls to GCPROTECT_BEGIN must be bracketed by a corresponding GCPROTECT_END, which pops the GCFrame back off of the stack. There are other related macros for special cases, such as protecting interior object references or arrays. All of these are used extensively in the source code for the execution engine, and all use instances of GCFrame to get their jobs done. The following method of the Thread class (which can be found in *sscli/clr/src/vm/threads.cpp*) uses a GCFrame to inform the garbage collector that its CultureObj variable is volatile:

```
void Thread::SetCultureId(LCID lcid, BOOL bUICulture)
{
    OBJECTREF CultureObj = NULL;
    GCPROTECT_BEGIN(CultureObj)
```

```
        {
            // Convert the LCID into a CultureInfo.
            GetCultureInfoForLCID(lcid, &CultureObj);

            // Set the newly created culture as the thread's culture.
            SetCulture(CultureObj, bUICulture);
        }
        GCPROTECT_END( );
    }
```

Like GCFrames, debugger frames also annotate data located on the stack. For
example, an instance of DebuggerClassInitMarkFrame is the root for the chain
of frames formed by executing the main entry point for an application. (An
instance of this was laid down in the stack during the trace through *clix* to
ClassLoader::ExecuteMainMethod in Chapter 4.)

Marking transitions

Other frames correspond one-to-one with method or function calls. The
entire family of frames derived from the TransitionFrame class, for example,
is used to capture and store state about the stubs inserted into method bodies by the JIT compilation process.

Recall from Chapter 5 that a component that has not yet been JIT-compiled
has a method table that is entirely fleshed out with thunks. The worker code
in these thunks knows how to use prefabricated sections of code, called
stubs, which can be strung together to do pre- and post-processing for
method calls. As part of its analysis, the compilation process recognizes situations that can be satisfied by the use of these prefabricated templates (such
as unboxing) and produces customized snippets of code tailored to fit both
its method signature and the semantic demands of the situation.

What does this have to do with frames? Since multiple stubs are often mixed
into a single method (to inject security checks or to create proxy code for
remoting, for example), transition frames are important indicators to the
execution engine. Each individually crafted stub in the chain pushes a frame
onto the thread's chain of frames when it is run, and these frames mark the
stubs' passage. The frames also act as a place to store state will be restored
on return, which will be used when unwinding exceptions, or that will be
needed when the stack is walked for purposes such as debugging or
remoting.

Several other frames mark transitions for other purposes. As mentioned
earlier, P/Invoke is a way of making calls from managed code into unmanaged code automatically, based on programmer-provided descriptions of
unmanaged functions. (This facility was called NDirect originally, and you
will see this word widely used in SSCLI comments and function names.

Think of P/Invoke and NDirect as synonyms.) In order for this mechanism to successfully bridge the managed call to the unmanaged call, the calling convention used by the JIT compiler must be matched to the calling convention of the external function, and the managed arguments and return value (if present) must be converted into their unmanaged counterparts. This is done using marshaling frames.

To illustrate what descriptions look like, Example 6-2 shows a P/Invoke declaration that matches an external __cdecl function named foo (found in *mylibrary.dll*) to the static C# method ExternalFooImplementation of the WrapperClass type.

Example 6-2. P/Invoke uses a programmer-provided description to do marshaling

```
public class WrapperClass {

    [DllImport("mylibrary.dll",
                EntryPoint="foo",
                CallingConvention=CallingConvention.Cdecl)]
    public static extern int ExternalFooImplementation(int hWnd, String text,
                    String caption, uint type);
}
```

The execution engine uses a special kind of MethodDesc, called a NDirectMethodDesc, to represent P/Invoke methods of types (in this case, the ExternalFooImplementation method). This NDirectMethodDesc locates the address of the external function foo (loading a shared library, if necessary), and creates a stub on the fly that will call this function, as well as reorder arguments on the stack and/or do data type conversion if necessary. The implementation also caches stubs once they are built, although you can examining this level of detail on your own. The marshaling process is an intricate and delicate piece of engineering that has been revisited many times to improve performance; it is interesting, but not easy, to browse.

Stackwalking

A stackwalk will typically traverse both managed and unmanaged regions of the stack. The managed regions (somewhat perversely referred to as "frame-less frames") consist of a series of activation records for managed code. There is no reason to add the extra overhead of frames to these regions of the stack, since the execution engine knows all about the structure of JIT-produced code. The engine can walk these regions directly, decoding them as necessary by using thread context and code manager information.

In unmanaged regions, a stackwalk must be performed by using Frame objects, which are embedded directly in the stack as navigational aids. To walk the frame chain, either the `Thread::StackWalkFramesEx` method call or the `StackWalkFunctions` macro is used within the execution engine. `StackWalkFramesEx` takes a callback function as a parameter and invokes this function on every frame in the chain that matches its filtering criteria. For each frame, the callback receives a pointer to a `CrawlFrame`, which is a simple wrapper that exposes the `GetFrame` function, which in turn returns the underlying `Frame` pointer if one exists. The wrapper also exposes `GetFunction`, which returns a `MethodDesc` if the frame represents a method call. `StackWalkFunctions` is a simpler variant of `StackWalkFramesEx`, which walks only "true" function calls. (It is used, for example, to generate the stack trace shown whenever an `Exception` is created.)

Figure 6-3 shows how a region of the stack that contains both managed and unmanaged activation records can be walked, combining `Frame` objects with execution engine knowledge of the activation record structure of JIT-compiled methods.

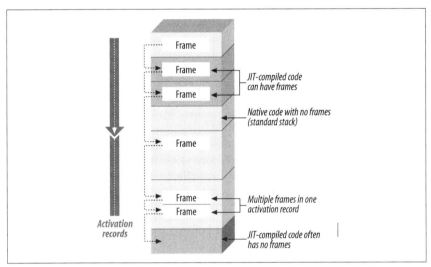

Figure 6-3. Stackwalking uses a combination of Frames and the execution engine's knowledge of the JIT calling convention

Walking the stack is an inherently thread-based activity. Since any given callback is very intimately tied to the state of the thread, stackwalking can be done only on the current thread or on a thread that is suspended. Not surprisingly, `StackWalkFramesEx` is a method of the `Thread` class, which can be found in *clr/src/vm/stackwalk.cpp*. Example 6-3 contains a shortened version of this method.

Example 6-3. Stackwalking using StackWalkFramesEx (simplified from clr/src/vm/stackwalk.cpp)

```
StackWalkAction Thread::StackWalkFramesEx(
                    PREGDISPLAY pRD,         // virtual register set at
                                             // crawl start
                    PSTACKWALKFRAMESCALLBACK pCallback,
                    VOID *pData,
                    unsigned flags,
                    Frame *pStartFrame
                )
{
  CrawlFrame cf;
  StackWalkAction retVal = SWA_FAILED;
  Frame * pInlinedFrame = NULL;

  if (pStartFrame)
    cf.pFrame = pStartFrame;
  else
    cf.pFrame = this->GetFrame();

  cf.isFirst = true;
  cf.isInterrupted = false;
  cf.hasFaulted = false;
  cf.isIPadjusted = false;
  unsigned unwindFlags = (flags & QUICKUNWIND) ? 0 : UpdateAllRegs;

  IJitManager* pEEJM = ExecutionManager::FindJitMan((PBYTE)GetControlPC(pRD));
  cf.JitManagerInstance = pEEJM;
  cf.codeMgrInstance = NULL;
  if ((cf.isFrameless = (pEEJM != NULL)) == true)
    cf.codeMgrInstance = pEEJM->GetCodeManager();
  cf.pRD = pRD;
  cf.pAppDomain = GetDomain();
```

The CrawlFrame class is used to hide the distinctions between managed frames and unmanaged frames, and is used as a cursor for this iterator function. The first task is to initialize this cursor; the iterator starts either at an intermediate frame passed in as a parameter or at the innermost active frame on the Thread. The CrawlFrame also tracks the current application domain, as well as exception and hardware status. (pRD is a pointer to a *register display*, which indirectly holds the captured values of selected microprocessor registers.)

The CrawlFrame also contains references to both the JIT manager and the code manager, since these services will often be needed during a stackwalk. We will now examine the code that is used with "frameless" CrawlFrames, which are the parts of the managed stack that are directly accessed by the execution engine. Since the code being walked is JIT-compiled, this part of StackWalkFramesEx uses the JIT manager to extract information:

```
// Can the debugger handle skipped frames?
BOOL fHandleSkippedFrames = !(flags & HANDLESKIPPEDFRAMES);
```

```
IJitManager::ScanFlag fJitManagerScanFlags = IJitManager::GetScanFlags();

// Begin the actual walk
while (cf.isFrameless || (cf.pFrame != FRAME_TOP)) {
  retVal = SWA_DONE;
  cf.codeManState.dwIsSet = 0;

  // If this is a simple JIT-produced frame, use the JIT manager's
  // services
  if (cf.isFrameless) {
    pEEJM->JitCode2MethodTokenAndOffset((PBYTE)GetControlPC(pRD),
            &(cf.methodToken),(DWORD*)&(cf.relOffset),
            ifJitManagerScanFlags);
    cf.pFunc = pEEJM->JitTokenToMethodDesc(cf.methodToken,
                                      fJitManagerScanFlags);
    EECodeInfo codeInfo(cf.methodToken, pEEJM, cf.pFunc);

    // If a thunk, bracket against beeing freed during code-pitching
    pEEJM->ProtectThunk( *(cf.pRD->pPC), true );
    if (SWA_ABORT == pCallback(&cf, (VOID*)pData)) {
      pEEJM->ProtectThunk( *(cf.pRD->pPC), false );
      return SWA_ABORT;
    }
    pEEJM->ProtectThunk( *(cf.pRD->pPC), false ); // End of protect
```

While the CrawlFrame is iterating through a segment of managed code, the
execution engine uses the JIT manager to turn the address of the code into a
method token and an offset. The token is then used to extract information
about the JIT-compiled code and place it into the CrawlFrame, where it can
be used by the callback function. After setting up the CrawlFrame, the callback function is called with the CrawlFrame as an argument, as well as its
multipurpose data argument pData, through which frame-specific data can
be returned. When the callback returns, it has the option of terminating the
stackwalk, which has the effect of unwinding the stack.

We will skip rest of this long function for now. It continues with special-case
handling and exception-handling details that we will see later in this chapter.

Stackwalking Example: Enforcing Code Access Security

The SSCLI's Code Access Security (CAS) implementation is a good example
of a control mechanism that uses stackwalking. As we saw in Chapter 4, it is
aimed at providing a component-oriented style of security. It relies on the
execution engine to assert and enforce policy in the face of evidence and permissions, based on component demands and behavior.

No single component is responsible for identifying whether a particular permission check succeeds or fails. Instead, all of the components cooperate in such a way that each contributes what it knows (its own evidence and annotations) to the broader context, from which the all-encompassing security engine can draw conclusions. The execution stack provides a wonderful mechanism for both collecting this data and enforcing its use, since context is nested on the stack as components call each other, and the stack is what these components rely on for communication. By intervening in method call processing, the security engine can ensure that a component has permission to do the things that it is attempting to do. And a stackwalk, of course, is the mechanism that the security engine will use during this intervention to check permission grants against permissions that are being demanded.

Permission demands propagate up the stack. When a method call demands a particular type of permission, the security engine must affirm that every component on the stack (prior to the point of the permission demand) has appropriate permissions. If any component does not, the permission demand fails and an exception is thrown to signify this failure. Each frame of the stack can modify the effective set of permissions by calling Assert, Deny, or PermitOnly before making calls, and there are also calls to Revert changes made earlier. Taken together, this mechanism results in aggregate behavior that is constrained by the least privileged component that is participating in a given stack region.

The initial set of permission grants for a stack comes from the application domain that is current when the stack is created, which allows programmers to control security at application domain granularity, which can be very useful. At every frame in the stack where execution shifts from one application domain to another (called a ContextTransition frame), the effective permissions change.

A component's own permission grants, which were loaded as part of the component-loading process described in Chapter 4, are added to the aggregate context as needed. The activation record for every JIT-compiled method call on the stack contains a spot for a security object, which is used to check permissions as the stack is walked. These security objects are created only when needed; if a method makes no changes and doesn't need the services of the security engine, it remains uninstantiated and appears in the stack as a null reference.

As you might well imagine, a complete stackwalk can be an extremely time-consuming and expensive operation, particularly when you stop to consider the frequency in which security checks are called for in the CLI framework code. In today's security-conscious environment, programmers are encouraged to pay more attention to security. Since the CLI was designed from the ground up with modern security requirements in mind, many of its libraries and supporting code rely on security checks. As a practical result, security stackwalks can take a significant amount of time in a managed program, and programmers may find themselves caught in the familiar conundrum of sacrificing performance for the sake of secure operations.

This situation gets even more interesting when you consider interthread dependencies. A thread spawned within the CLI for use by managed code must not only track its own security information, but must also be annotated with the security information of the thread that spawned it. The reason for this is fairly simple and can be illustrated with an example: consider an assembly that wishes to delete a file on the local hard drive. It is easy to check and enforce permissions for this assembly using a stackwalk, but what if the assembly had spun off a thread to perform the delete? The security manager must somehow associate the entire security context that is in effect when the new thread is created with this thread. Not only will a security check on the new thread need to walk its own stack, but it will also need to check the stack of the thread that spawned it.

This is implemented in the SSCLI in a way that satisfies both security and performance requirements. When performing a security stackwalk, it is often the case that only a few of the total number of frames contain information that is actually relevant to the security context. In addition, although activation frames are the structure used to gather the relevant context, the evidence and permissions that make up this context can be cached since they take the form of immutable data. The SSCLI uses a data structure called a CompressedStack to cache the relevant security information obtained from a stackwalk whenever it needs to store this data for calls that cross thread boundaries or calls that are deferred as delegates. CompressedStack is defined in *clr/src/vm/threads.h* and is obtained via a static call to the Security class in *clr/src/vm/security.h*.

Threading and Concurrency

Reading to this point in this chapter, one might think that threads serve as little more than a place to do frame bookkeeping. While this aspect of threads is certainly important, the primary role of threads has always been to organize programming tasks into understandable units of concurrency and synchronization. We will now turn our attention to this more familiar facet of threading, and examine how programmers can use managed threads to build concurrent applications.

Threads are the primary abstraction for execution and concurrency in the CLI. Because the CLI includes support for concurrent execution, it must also allow independently executing parts of a program to communicate and to synchronize their state, as well as provide programmers with the ability to impact the scheduling of concurrent activity.

The execution engine provides mechanisms for all of these:

- Programmers can communicate between component references that have been marshaled between threads using method calls.

- Programmers can synchronize access to instance and static methods, instance fields, and arbitrary regions of their components, either automatically or manually.

- Programmers can control thread scheduling by manipulating instances of the Thread component or by using the CLI *threadpool*, which is an efficient runtime service that simplifies worker thread creation and scheduling.

We will visit each of these mechanisms in turn; but first, we will examine how managed threads are implemented.

Managing Threads

Managed code offers several distinct ways for programmers to use threads, which we will cover in detail in the next few sections. All of these techniques use the Thread type to access the execution state of their managed threads. The Thread type provides a number of properties and methods, and is built as a hybrid component; it is exposed and used as a managed component, but much of its implementation is actually written in C++ and is internal to the execution engine. This is done by marking methods that are implemented natively with the MethodImplOptions.InternalCall method attribute and by using the FCall calling convention described in Chapter 5. The C++ class used to represent managed instances can be found in *comsynchronizable.cpp*.

We've already seen an incoming PAL thread being "taken over" by the execution engine in SetupThread, but threads can also be created directly from managed code. In this case, programmers create a Thread and pass it a ThreadStart delegate via the constructor. Execution can be started at any point after this by calling the Start method of the Thread.

Here is what the managed thread constructor, found in *thread.cs* in the *sscli/clr/src/bcl/system/threading* directory, looks like:

```
public Thread(ThreadStart start) {
    if (start == null) {
        throw new ArgumentNullException("start");
```

```
        }
    SetStart(start);
}
```

Recall that ThreadStart is a delegate type (also declared in *thread.cs*) used to indicate the method that the new Thread should execute. This delegate is passed to SetStart, whose C# representation is:

```
[MethodImplAttribute(MethodImplOptions.InternalCall)]
private extern void SetStart(ThreadStart start);
```

The InternalCall attribute causes any calls on this method to become calls on the corresponding native FCall method in *comsynchronizable.cpp*:

```
void ThreadNative::SetStart(ThreadBaseObject* pThisUNSAFE, Object*
pDelegateUNSAFE)
{
  THREADBASEREF    pThis       = (THREADBASEREF) pThisUNSAFE;
  OBJECTREF        pDelegate   = (OBJECTREF     ) pDelegateUNSAFE;

  HELPER_METHOD_FRAME_BEGIN_2(pThis, pDelegate);

  if (pThis->m_InternalThread == NULL) {
    // If we don't have an internal Thread object associated with this
    // exposed object, now is our first opportunity to create one.
    Thread *unstarted = SetupUnstartedThread();

    pThis->SetInternal(unstarted);
    unstarted->SetExposedObject(pThis);
  }
  // Save the delegate used as starter
  pThis->SetDelegate(pDelegate);

  HELPER_METHOD_FRAME_END();
}
```

Note the use of a helper frame in this function. The HELPER_METHOD_FRAME_ BEGIN_2 wraps around a HelperMethodFrame, which in turn registers two object references (pThis and pDelegate, in the previous example) with the garbage collector. Assuming that the thread is new and has no internal thread, the next call is to SetupUnstartedThread, which can be found in *threads.cpp*:

```
Thread* SetupUnstartedThread()
{
  Thread* pThread = new Thread();

  if (pThread) {
    FastInterlockOr((ULONG *) &pThread->m_State,
                    (Thread::TS_Unstarted | Thread::TS_WeOwn));

    ThreadStore::AddThread(pThread);
  }
  return pThread;
}
```

You can see that care needs to be taken with synchronized access to variables. Also, this is the point at which an internal thread is created and placed into the ThreadStore. The managed thread now has one CLI object instance and two native instances behind it (the CLI Thread instance, the execution engine's C++ Thread, and the entity behind the PAL HANDLE) and is ready to roll.

Thread states

Once a thread is running, its execution can be started and stopped in several ways. Programmers can use the Sleep method directly to yield control momentarily (by yielding its current timeslice) or pause for a minimum amount of time (after which it will be rescheduled). Programmers can also call Suspend, which has the effect of blocking execution of the target thread until Resume is called, or SpinWait, which kills time without yielding control. Finally, a programmer can call Abort, which will cause a ThreadAbortException to be thrown. (This exception may cause the underlying PAL thread to be killed, associated resources to be released, and the Thread instance to be dissociated from the execution engine. The Thread may also survive this exception, however, if it is caught, or if the thread is a worker in a ThreadPool.)

A thread moves through a definitive lifecycle: it is born, it can be paused and resumed, and it will eventually die, either of natural causes (it returns from the ThreadStart delegate passed to it) or by outright murder (Abort). Managed threads have a read-only property named ThreadState that reflects their current states; for example, newly created threads are initially in the Unstarted state and remain in this state until a transition is initiated by a call to Thread.Start. Likewise, external threads that wander into the execution engine are already in the Running state.

When viewed from the perspective of a Thread instance, state transitions seem orderly and straightforward. Once running, there are a number of actions that can cause the thread to change states, and these trigger conditions are uncomplicated. Viewed from the execution engine, however, a thread's lifecycle is anything but simple. Since a thread's execution state transitions must be coordinated for concurrent use by both unmanaged and managed code, these state transitions must be carefully navigated to preserve the integrity of the execution engine. Because of the complexity that this incurs, the internal representation of state uses a bit mask, shown in Example 6-4, rather than an enumerated value to maintain current state. As you can infer from the structure of this masked value, the transitions visible to managed code are considerably simplified.

An example helps show how something that looks simple in managed code can be quite complex beneath the surface. It also helps show how the three elements of execution engine frames, managed threads, and exceptions are tied together. In the CLI, the Thread type supports a number of methods that can be used to control thread lifetimes and scheduling. One of these methods is Abort, which causes the special ThreadAbortException to be raised on any thread on which it is called. This exception will kill the thread, except if that the thread has an exception handler in place to catch it, in which case ResetAbort can be called from within this handler to keep the thread alive, or if the ThreadAbortException is propagated beyond the last managed handler on the stack and into unmanaged code, in which case an implicit ResetAbort occurs. Handling a ThreadAbortException is demonstrated in the simple program shown in Example 6-4.

Example 6-4. Threads can be scheduled and manipulated from managed code

```
using System;
using System.Threading;

public class WorkerClass {
  public static void StartMethod( )
  {
backToStart:
  try {
    for(int i=0; i<10; i++)
    {
      Console.WriteLine("Worker state: {0}.", Thread.CurrentThread.ThreadState);
      Thread.Sleep(100);
    }
    Console.WriteLine("OK, worker finished.");
    return;
  } catch(ThreadAbortException e) {
    Console.WriteLine("Worker caught ThreadAbortException.");
    Console.WriteLine(" Worker state: {0}.", Thread.CurrentThread.ThreadState);
    Console.WriteLine(" Exception message: {0}", e.Message);
    Thread.Sleep(1000);
    Thread.ResetAbort( );
  }
  Console.WriteLine("Worker not dead yet.");
  Console.WriteLine(" Worker state after reset: {0}.",
                      Thread.CurrentThread.ThreadState);
  // how's this? seen a goto lately?
  goto backToStart;
  }
}

class ThreadAbortExample
{
public static void Main( )
  {
```

Example 6-4. Threads can be scheduled and manipulated from managed code (continued)

```
    ThreadStart td = new ThreadStart(WorkerClass.StartMethod);
    Thread worker = new Thread(td);
    worker.Start();
    Thread.Sleep(100);
    Console.WriteLine("Main thread aborting worker.");
    worker.Abort();
    worker.Join();
    Console.WriteLine("Main done.");
    }
}
```

When the program in Example 6-4 is run, the main thread attempts to kill its worker, but the worker is both tireless and prepared, having put an exception handler in place that calls ResetAbort. The Main method of ThreadAbortExample creates and starts a new worker Thread. This Thread goes into a simple loop, writing out its thread state during each iteration and then sleeping. Meanwhile, the Main method continues by sleeping for a brief period and then calling Abort on the worker, followed directly by Join. Since the worker has an exception handler in place for the ThreadAbortException caused by the call to Abort, and since it is running at a high enough permission level to reset rather than die, the worker calls ResetAbort and then runs to completion.

At the point at which Main calls Abort, the worker thread is really in more than one internal state; it is likely to be blocked on a call to Sleep when the other thread calls Abort, and so from the perspective of its two threads, it is in both the WaitSleepJoin and the AbortRequested states at the same time. When the thread receives the ThreadAbortException, this dichotomy will be resolved, but until this point, the thread's state must be carefully maintained. As we will see, the maintenance involved is a nontrivial task that falls to the execution engine. One of the primary design goals for the CLI is to hide complexity, such as these transitional states from higher-level managed code, when possible. Example 6-5 shows the flags used to coordinate transitions.

Example 6-5. Combining flags to represent thread execution state

```
enum ThreadState
{
    TS_Unknown              = 0x00000000,   // starting state

    TS_StopRequested        = 0x00000001,   // stop at next opportunity
    TS_GCSuspendPending     = 0x00000002,   // waiting to get to safe spot for
                                            // GC
    TS_UserSuspendPending   = 0x00000004,   // user suspension at next
                                            // opportunity
```

Example 6-5. Combining flags to represent thread execution state (continued)

```
TS_DebugSuspendPending    = 0x00000008,    // debugger is suspending threads
TS_GCOnTransitions        = 0x00000010,    // Force a GC on stub transitions
                                           // (GCStress only)

TS_LegalToJoin            = 0x00000020,    // now legal to attempt a Join

TS_Background             = 0x00000200,    // Thread is a background thread
TS_Unstarted              = 0x00000400,    // Thread has never been started
TS_Dead                   = 0x00000800,    // Thread is dead

TS_WeOwn                  = 0x00001000,    // this object initiated this thread

// Some bits that only have meaning for reporting the state to clients.
TS_ReportDead             = 0x00010000,    // in WaitForOtherThreads

TS_SyncSuspended          = 0x00080000,    // suspended via WaitSuspendEvent
TS_DebugWillSync          = 0x00100000,    // debugger will wait for sync
TS_RedirectingEntryPoint  = 0x00200000,    // redirecting entrypoint
                                           // (don't call entrypoint when set)

TS_SuspendUnstarted       = 0x00400000,    // latch a user suspension on an
                                           // unstarted thread

TS_ThreadPoolThread       = 0x00800000,    // is this a threadpool thread?
TS_TPWorkerThread         = 0x01000000,    // is this a threadpool worker
// thread?

TS_Interruptible          = 0x02000000,    // sitting in a Sleep, Wait, or Join
TS_Interrupted            = 0x04000000,    // was awakened by an interrupt APC

TS_AbortRequested         = 0x08000000,    // same as TS_StopRequested
                                           // (in order to trip the thread)
TS_AbortInitiated         = 0x10000000,    // set when abort is begun
TS_UserStopRequested      = 0x20000000,    // set when a user stop is requested
TS_Detached               = 0x80000000,    // Thread was detached by DllMain

// We require (and assert) that the following bits are less than 0x100.
TS_CatchAtSafePoint = (TS_UserSuspendPending | TS_StopRequested |
                       TS_GCSuspendPending | TS_DebugSuspendPending |
                       TS_GCOnTransitions),
};
```

In our example, Sleep causes the thread to yield immediately, using the threading facilities of the PAL. This puts it into the TS_Interruptible state. (Suspend has an interesting difference: the execution engine will mark the thread as TS_UserSuspendPending, and bring the thread to a "safe place" before halting its execution and placing it into a blocked state by changing to TS_SyncSuspended.) When Abort is called by the main thread (assuming that the worker is sleeping), an exception is thrown. Because aborting a thread is an exceptional activity that should be undertaken only when normal scheduling solutions are unusable, design tradeoffs have been applied. The codepath is longer and less direct, since it is seldom exercised, and the logic involves careful audit and cleanup of internal structures, since it is meant to work in unanticipated and tenuous situations.

The execution engine first requires that any caller that wishes to call the Abort method have appropriate security permission; it does this by placing SecurityPermissionAttribute on the method declaration for Abort. This can be seen in the declaration in *sscli/clr/src/bcl/system/threading/thread.cs*, as shown in Example 6-6.

Example 6-6. The Abort method is protected using declarative security

```
[SecurityPermissionAttribute(SecurityAction.Demand, ControlThread=true)]
public void Abort() { AbortInternal(); }
```

This declarative demand for a permission check ensures that Abort will be called only if the current security context has the ControlThread permission. The JIT compiler will place a call to the security engine into the code that it produces to check this demand at runtime.

AbortInternal uses an FCall to call into the native implementation, ThreadNative::Abort. This function is shown in Example 6-7.

Example 6-7. The Abort method is actually implemented as an FCall (defined in clr/src/ vm/comsynchronizable.cpp)

```
FCIMPL1(void, ThreadNative::Abort, ThreadBaseObject* pThis)
{
  THROWSCOMPLUSEXCEPTION();
  if (pThis == NULL)
    FCThrowVoid(kNullReferenceException);

  THREADBASEREF thisRef(pThis);
  HELPER_METHOD_FRAME_BEGIN_NOPOLL();
  Thread *thread = thisRef->GetInternal();
  if (thread == NULL)
    COMPlusThrow(kThreadStateException, IDS_EE_THREAD_CANNOT_GET);
  thread->UserAbort(thisRef);

  HELPER_METHOD_FRAME_END_POLL();
}
FCIMPLEND
```

For the first time in this book, we've left all of the ugly SSCLI-specific macros in place in this example. (See Appendix D for details.) We now have enough information about execution engine internals to talk about what they do, and you should be aware of what the code in the distribution actually looks like. These macros are commonplace in the SSCLI code, and you should expect to encounter them routinely. They track various kinds of state on behalf of the execution engine. The first shown here, FCIMPL1, is one of a series of macros used to declare FCalls. It declares that ThreadNative::Abort is an FCall that returns a void and has a single argument, which is a ThreadBaseObject*. After this, THROWSCOMPLUSEXCEPTION is a declaration that indicates that the function may throw a managed exception (and indeed, from what we know about Abort, its main job in this case is to throw an exception, although usually from a different thread). THREADBASEREF is simply a typedef for a ThreadBaseObject* and will be used to obtain a pointer to the internal thread. HELPER_METHOD_FRAME_BEGIN_NOPOLL causes a helper frame to be created for the FCall. (The matching macro at the end of the function causes it to be popped before the function returns. Remember that a helper frame marks FCalls so that they will be visible during a managed stackwalk.) Finally, the real work begins with the call to UserAbort. As we break it down in Example 6-8, notice that the entirety of this large method is dedicated to coordinating a graceful state machine transition.

Example 6-8. The beginning of the internal method that implements Thread::Abort (defined in clr/src/vm/threads.cpp)

```
void Thread::UserAbort(THREADBASEREF orThreadBase)
{
    // We must set this before we start flipping thread bits to avoid races where
    // trap returning threads is already high due to other reasons.
    ThreadStore::TrapReturningThreads(TRUE);

    // continues after Example 6-9
```

Because the call to Thread::Abort could come as other threads are asking the thread to change its state, while overall thread state is being manipulated or during exception processing, reentrancy protection is necessary. However it is not sufficient to take a lock and exclude all other threads, because those threads may have code running in an unmanaged section of the stack that is acting as part of the execution engine. The important work of coordinating, for example, cannot be arbitrarily stopped. Because of this, unmanaged code needs to run unimpeded, because it often holds locks or resources that are needed to continue execution. This makes synchronization harder.

The call to ThreadStore::TrapReturningThreads, which requests that other managed-thread activity be trapped during the processing of this method, shows a typical mechanism of the sort used by the execution engine to maintain control in lieu of a simple lock. The global variable g_TrapReturningThreads is set within this call to detect reentries into managed code by threads currently executing unmanaged code. As threads reenter, they can be safely suspended using the same mechanism that the garbage collector uses to suspend all managed threads. As we will see in Chapter 7, the garbage collector uses code emitted by the JIT compiler to regularly check whether it needs to run. This polling activity is used not only for GC activation, but also to rendezvous with thread state changes, such as the Abort method through which we are browsing. In fact, a quick glance at CommonTripThread, which is the function called during polling, reveals a call to HandleThreadAbort. Its implementation is shown in Example 6-9.

Example 6-9. HandleThreadAbort is actually raises the ThreadAbortException

```
void Thread::HandleThreadAbort ( )
{
  if ((m_State & TS_AbortRequested) &&
      !(m_State & TS_AbortInitiated) &&
      (! IsExceptionInProgress() || m_handlerInfo.IsInUnmanagedHandler( ))) {
    // Generate a ThreadAbort exception
    SetAbortInitiated( );
    ResetStopRequest( );
    // If an abort and interrupt happen at the same time
    //   (e.g. on a sleeping thread), the abort is favored.
    // But we do need to reset the interrupt bits, regardless.
    FastInterlockAnd((ULONG *) &m_State, ~(TS_Interruptible | TS_Interrupted));
    IsUserInterrupted(TRUE /*=reset*/);
    COMPlusThrow(kThreadAbortException);
  }
}
```

The ThreadAbortException that is thrown at the end of the HandleThreadAbort function does the dirty work of polishing off the thread (unless it is caught). As we will see later in this chapter, this is a special type of exception that is used to kill threads. In order for it to be raised during a poll, no exception can be in progress, and the thread state has to be set to TS_AbortRequested. Let's return to tracing through the UserAbort method to understand how TS_AbortRequested is set, as shown in Example 6-10.

Example 6-10. Initiating the abort sequence

```
// If thread was already marked for abort, we are done
if (!MarkThreadForAbort( )) {
  ThreadStore::TrapReturningThreads(FALSE);
  return;
}
// Otherwise, we are the first one to abort and there are no pending exceptions
if (this == GetThread( )) {
  SetAbortInitiated( );
  COMPlusThrow(kThreadAbortException);
}
FastInterlockOr((ULONG *) &m_State, TS_StopRequested);
```

The call to MarkThreadForAbort both sets the thread state to TS_AbortRequested and checks to see whether it has already been set. If it has, there is nothing more to do but wait for a poll to happen and the exception to be thrown. If it has not been set, but the calling thread is simply trying to abort itself, then the simplest thing to do is throw ThreadAbortException directly.

This fast-track approach works because the exception is being thrown on the thread's own stack. There is no need to wait for a poll; the suicide can be accomplished cleanly and efficiently. If the abort is being initiated from a different thread, however, things get more complex. First, the state is set to TS_StopRequested, which will cause the target thread to be stopped at the first opportunity; the CLI specifies that a thread being aborted will be in a Stopped state and can be resurrected from within an exception handler. After this housekeeping is done, the loop is begun, as shown in Example 6-11.

Example 6-11. Synchronization converges within a loop

```
for (;;) {
  // Lock the thread store
  ThreadStore::LockThreadStore();

  // Get the PAL thread handle
  HANDLE hThread = GetThreadHandle();
  if (hThread == INVALID_HANDLE_VALUE) {
    // Take a lock, try again (necessary to sync with the startup code)
    orThreadBase->EnterObjMonitor();
    hThread = GetThreadHandle();
    DWORD state = m_State;
    orThreadBase->LeaveObjMonitor();

    // Could be unstarted, in which case, we just leave.
    if (hThread == INVALID_HANDLE_VALUE) {
      if (state & TS_Unstarted) {
        // This thread is not yet started.
        // Leave the thread marked for abort, making sure to reset the trap
        ThreadStore::TrapReturningThreads(FALSE);
        break;
      } else {
        // Must be dead, or about to die.
        if (state & TS_AbortRequested)
          ThreadStore::TrapReturningThreads(FALSE);
        break;
      }
    }
  }

  // Still in for loop at this point
```

The first thing to be done is to take the lock on the ThreadStore so that only one coordination operation will occur at any time, and races will be avoided. This is followed by a logging call for thread debugging. LOG is a common macro within SSCLI code; it results in a log record being produced, but only when the appropriate build switches and runtime flags have been set by the programmer. In a production environment, LOG is equivalent to a no-op, and does not impact performance.

Each of the conditional statements within this long loop tests for various combinations of state. Because threads are a constantly-moving target, there is always the possibility that the target thread is in a condition that is unsafe to abort. (Remember, code in other threads might be waiting for or holding locks, or consuming resources related to the thread being aborted in other ways. The execution engine must anticipate these dependencies.) This loop is executed until a "safe place" is found to kill the target thread.

The first thing that needs to be done before proceeding is to obtain the handle to the underlying PAL thread for the target. If this handle is set to INVALID_HANDLE_VALUE, which signals a problem, then either the managed thread does not yet have a PAL thread associated with it or it has died. In either case, there is nothing else to do, and the loop can be skipped.

Next, the underlying thread is suspended, as shown in Example 6-12.

Example 6-12. Suspend the underlying thread

```
// Use the PAL to suspend the thread, so it isn't moving under us
::SuspendThread(hThread);   // returns -1 on failure.

// It is possible that the thread has completed the abort already
if (!(m_State & TS_AbortRequested)) {
  ::ResumeThread(hThread);
  break;
}

// If a thread is Dead or Detached, abort is a no-op
if (m_State & (TS_Dead | TS_Detached)) {
  ThreadStore::TrapReturningThreads(FALSE);
  ::ResumeThread(hThread);
    break;
}

// If the thread has already started its abort, we're done
// If the thread is unstarted, it will abort when we start it
if (m_State & (TS_AbortInitiated | TS_Unstarted)) {
  ::ResumeThread(hThread);
  break;
}

// Still in for loop at this point
```

If the thread has an AbortRequested or a Dead or Detached state, the thread can be resumed, to run until its suicide. Likewise, even a thread that is unstarted may be aborted; suicide in this case will be the thread's first and only act. When Start is called, the pending abort will happen.

As shown in Example 6-13, the next conditional is more interesting, because a thread that has been suspended by managed code cannot be aborted without making sure that it drops its locks.

Example 6-13. Drop a thread's locks

```
// If the thread is user suspended (SyncSuspended) we're out of luck
//   (Set the bit and hope for the best on resume)
if (m_State & TS_SyncSuspended) {
  ThreadStore::TrapReturningThreads(FALSE);
  ThreadStore::UnlockThreadStore();
  COMPlusThrow(kThreadStateException, IDS_EE_THREAD_ABORT_WHILE_SUSPEND);
}

// Still in for loop at this point
```

The presence of TS_SyncSuspended means that the thread is waiting for a synchronized resource, and this is why the ThreadStore must be unlocked before the special exception can be thrown.

The SSCLI doesn't cover all possible state changes. Note in this example that suspended threads cannot be cleanly aborted (which is a well-known limitation of the current implementation). This is likely to be fixed in the future.

After this come a series of cases, as shown in Example 6-14.

Example 6-14. Look for special case states

```
// If the thread has no managed code on the call stack, abort is a no-op
if (m_pFrame == FRAME_TOP
    && GetFirstCOMPlusSEHRecord(this) == EXCEPTION_CHAIN_END) {
  FastInterlockAnd((ULONG *)&m_State,
      ((~TS_AbortRequested) & (~TS_AbortInitiated) & /
      (~TS_StopRequested)));
  ThreadStore::TrapReturningThreads(FALSE);
  ::ResumeThread(hThread);
  break;
}

// If an exception is currently being thrown, one of two things will happen.
// Either, we'll catch, and notice the abort request in our end-catch,
// or we'll not catch [in which case we're leaving managed code anyway).
// The top-most handler is responsible for resetting the bit.
if (GetThrowable() != NULL) {
```

Example 6-14. Look for special case states (continued)

```
    ::ResumeThread(hThread);
    break;
}

// If the thread is in sleep, wait, or join interrupt it.
// However, we do NOT want to interrupt if the thread is already
// processing an exception
if (m_State & TS_Interruptible) {
    UserInterrupt();
    ::ResumeThread(hThread);
    break;
}

if (!m_fPreemptiveGCDisabled) {
    // If the thread is running outside the EE, and stub will catch...
    if (m_pFrame != FRAME_TOP && m_pFrame->IsTransitionToNativeFrame() &&
        ((size_t)GetFirstCOMPlusSEHRecord(this) > ((size_t)m_pFrame) - 20)) {
        ::ResumeThread(hThread);
        break;
    }
}
```

```
// Still in for loop at this point
```

The first conditional checks to see whether someone is trying to abort a thread that has no managed code in it. This is checked by looking for a special exception frame that is used only around managed code. If it is not present, all of the state flags are reset, and the thread is resumed. This is followed by a check to see whether an exception is in progress. If it is, the thread is resumed so that the exception handlers can be invoked. If the thread is blocked in a wait operation, it is interrupted so that next time around the loop, the right thing can happen.

If unmanaged code is running (which is checked by examining the garbage collector mode), and there is an execution engine frame in place that signals that a stub exists to capture reentry, the thread is resumed. Once the stub code is run, the polling function that we saw in Example 6-9 will cause exception handling to commence.

Finally, the end of the loop is reached. At this point, the PAL thread is resumed and the ThreadStore is unlocked to allow access before another iteration occurs, as shown in Example 6-15.

Example 6-15. How to finish loop iteration

```
// Ok. It's not in managed code, nor safely out behind a stub that's
// going to catch it on the way in. We have to poll.

::ResumeThread(hThread);
ThreadStore::UnlockThreadStore();
```

Example 6-15. How to finish loop iteration (continued)

```
    Thread *pCurThread = GetThread();  // not the thread we are aborting!
    HANDLE  h = pCurThread->GetThreadHandle();
    pCurThread->DoAppropriateWait(1, &h, FALSE, ABORT_POLL_TIMEOUT, TRUE, NULL);
  } // End of the for(;;) loop
  ThreadStore::UnlockThreadStore();
}
```

If you haven't handled the call by this point, it means that the thread is in a position where you can't really do anything to it. It is most likely running within execution engine code (for example, within an FCall or a stub), and you just need to loop around until the thread comes back to a point where you can deal with it. Of course, in order for a polling strategy like this to work, the execution engine's internal code must be crafted to avoid monopolizing the thread's timeslice while running.

As promised, this is a pretty hefty chunk of code. Similar code exists for suspending and resuming threads; it is a very typical example of coordination-type routines. They are complex because they need to handle every possible state transition and permit code to continue its execution while carefully avoiding race conditions.

Scheduling Execution Using the Threadpool

While it is possible to use the methods of either the managed or unmanaged thread object to manually create, manipulate, and destroy threads, the CLI also includes a pooling mechanism that not only makes concurrent operations much simpler, but in many cases also improves efficiency. Besides being available for general-purpose programming use, this thread pool is used internally by the SSCLI in the following implementations:

- Timer callbacks
- Remoting channels
- Lease management
- Security policy
- The Context type

Threads that spend a great deal of time waiting for an event to occur or for periodic polls in which they update state are candidates for thread pool use. Pooling enables applications to share worker threads that are managed by the execution engine. A single thread monitors the status of all wait operations queued to the thread pool, and when conditions change, dispatches a worker thread from the pool (using the correct application domain) to execute a stored callback function.

There is a single managed thread pool per process, and the Base Class Library (BCL) System.Threading.ThreadPool class is used to mediate access to it. Using the thread pool, you can post work items using either QueueUserWorkItem from managed code or CorQueueUserWorkItem from unmanaged code in the execution engine. These functions use delegates in the managed case (and callbacks in the unmanaged case) that are called by a thread selected and scheduled by the thread pool. The snippet in Example 6-16 demonstrates how to queue up a thread pool task from within managed code.

Example 6-16. Using the ThreadPool

```
using System;
using System.Threading;

class ThreadPoolExample {
  static void Main(string[] args)
  {
    ThreadPool.QueueUserWorkItem(new WaitCallback(Foo));
    Thread.Sleep(5 * 1000); // sleep for five seconds
  }

  static void Foo(object state)
  {
    Console.WriteLine("Inside Foo");
  }
}
```

As would be expected, this program writes "Inside Foo" to the console while the thread spun out from Main blocks for five seconds.

The thread pool itself is created on the first call to QueueUserWorkItem, when a timer or other client queues a callback function. The number of threads in the thread pool is based on a heuristic that takes into account the number of CPUs, how many items are in the work item queue, and how many idle threads are in the thread pool, although the number of threads that can ultimately be created is limited only by available memory.

Most of the CLI's runtime services involve heuristics. You can study the heuristics that thread pool logic uses to decide when to create a new thread and when to reduce the number of threads that it contains by looking in *clr/src/vm/win32threadpool.h* and *clr/src/vm/win32threadpool.cpp*. Certainly there is room for improvement; it is not too hard to imagine some enterprising Computer Science student forming a thesis around ways to adaptively decide how many threads should be alive here, for example. By doing a little code base archeology, you can see that other approaches have already been tried in the past. The execution engine provides many opportunities to tune heuristics or invent new ones.

When the QueueUserWorkItem managed call is called, it eventually routes its way into ThreadpoolMgr::QueueUserWorkItem, as shown in Example 6-17.

Example 6-17. QueueUserWorkItem dynamically creates worker threads as needed (defined in clr/src/vm/win32threadpool.cpp)

```
BOOL ThreadpoolMgr::QueueUserWorkItem(LPTHREAD_START_ROUTINE Function,
                                      PVOID Context,
                                      DWORD Flags)
{
  EnsureInitialized();

  BOOL status;

  EnterCriticalSection (&WorkerCriticalSection) ;
  status = EnqueueWorkRequest(Function, Context);
  if (status) {
    // Grow the worker thread pool, but don't bother if GC in progress.
    if (ShouldGrowWorkerThreadPool() && !(g_pGCHeap->IsGCInProgress())) {
      status = CreateWorkerThread();
    } else {
      // We did not grow the worker pool, so make sure there is a gate thread
      // that monitors the WorkRequest queue to spawn new threads when needed
      if (!GateThreadCreated)
        CreateGateThread();
      MonitorWorkRequestsQueue = 1;
    }
  }
  LeaveCriticalSection (&WorkerCriticalSection) ;
  return status;
}
```

Essentially, ThreadpoolMgr consists of two parts: a list of enqueued work items to execute and a collection of threads at which to throw these work items. The first call, EnsureInitialized, is simply a check to an internal field to see if it's nonzero. If it isn't, you've not yet initialized, and Initialize needs to be called. After initialization is confirmed, QueueUserWorkItem consists of two steps:

1. First, the work request is placed into a queue using EnqueueWorkRequest.

2. Second, the function checks to see whether there needs to be a new thread to handle the queue.

The simple decision-making process is part of ShouldGrowWorkerThreadPool, as shown in Example 6-18. (This is quite a bit different than Microsoft's commercial CLR, which uses a complex heuristic.)

Example 6-18. The logic for creating new worker threads (defined in clr/src/vm/ win32threadpool.cpp)

```
BOOL ThreadpoolMgr::ShouldGrowWorkerThreadPool( )
{
  return (NumRunningWorkerThreads < MinLimitTotalWorkerThreads &&
          NumIdleWorkerThreads < NumQueuedWorkRequests &&
          NumWorkerThreads < MaxLimitTotalWorkerThreads);
}
```

MaxLimitTotalWorkerThreads is simply a constant, defined in the Initialize method mentioned earlier as NumberOfProcessors * MaxLimitCPThreadsPerCPU. This number is a simple, but workable, way to decide whether to increase the size of the thread pool.

Synchronizing Concurrent Access to Components

The sharing of resources between components that are using multiple threads is notoriously difficult. It is a subtle proposition to get right, and whole forests have been sacrificed to the topic. People continue to investigate and experiment with new deadlock detection and avoidance algorithms.

Access to shared resources must always be synchronized or carefully coordinated in some manner. Component programmers can use protection mechanisms that exist in the execution engine specifically for this purpose, choosing to use its primitives manually, or else use higher-level constructs and leave the details to the execution engine. Just as the thread pool makes working with threads easier for some common cases, automatic features, such as synchronized regions of code and synchronized access to component member types, can make programming easier and less bug-prone. As always, the tradeoff is one of complexity and control.

When using execution engine primitives directly, implementers can use a broad palette of managed classes that expose them, including the Interlocked type, the Monitor type, the ReaderWriterLock type, and both the ManualResetEvent and AutoResetEvent types. In addition to these types, WaitHandle is used to represent all synchronization objects in the runtime that allow multiple wait semantics, such as mutex and event handles. WaitHandle encapsulates PAL synchronization handles and uses the thread pool to make callbacks.

The CLI combines operating system synchronization with CLI-specific synchronization constructs (such as the thread pool, which is a collection of threads that are available for communal use) into a single coherent service for programmers. By default, both the instance and static members of a component are not synchronized, and any thread can access any member at any time. Compilers, of course, can implement whatever locking semantics their language requires with the aid of the execution engine primitives. The CLI supports automatic use of *syncblocks* (locks associated with types) for both instances and classes; the CLI will generate code to synchronize on the instance syncblock for instance methods (or on the class syncblock for statics) if it finds the synchronized flag in their metadata.

CLI synchronization is interesting in its use of loosely associated instance data for storing syncblocks. Syncblocks are exposed to the programmer via the managed Monitor object, and can be used to protect global, static, and instance fields and/or methods. Monitors cannot be instantiated by themselves; they are associated on-demand with object or class instances. They expose the ability to take and release the syncblock lock on an object via the static methods Enter, TryEnter, and Exit. It is necessary to be in a synchronized region on an object before calling Wait or Pulse on that object. Wait releases the lock and waits to be notified, at which point it returns, having been granted the lock again. Pulse signals the next thread in the wait queue to proceed.

In the syncblock, the monitor is implemented using the C++ class AwareLock, which can be found in *clr/src/vm/syncblk.h*. As we saw in Chapter 5, each object has a syncblock index associated with it, which begins empty, and is populated only when needed. When an instance is used as part of a synchronization operation, a syncblock is retrieved from the syncblock cache, and it is associated with the object by updating the index. Syncblocks themselves are sparsely allocated data structures, and when they are being used for synchronization purposes, they will contain the AwareLock used to implement synchronized methods and synchronized blocks of code, as well as a list of waiting threads for Monitor.Wait, Monitor.Pulse, and Monitor.PulseAll.

On occasion, a programmer has to break a Thread out of a blocking operation, such as waiting for a syncblock or Sleep call. To do this, Thread provides the Interrupt method, which essentially releases the Thread out of the Wait without having acquired the syncblock.

Handling Component Exceptions

Microsoft's earlier component model, COM, used a fragile and failure-prone mechanism for dealing with violations of component contracts. Most component methods in COM returned an integer status code called an HRESULT. (Why HRESULT? Originally, it was designed to be a handle to a result and only late in the game was its definition simplified.) When COM components are deeply nested, they are supposed to check the HRESULT being returned by their subordinate components and pass errors up the stack either directly or by mapping them into new HRESULTs. As might well be imagined, this discipline is tedious, error-prone, and leads to numerous problems, including inconsistent or erroneous HRESULT checking and bloated code. It also results in lost error information, which makes debugging harder.

From the perspective of the designers of the CLI component model, *structured exception handling* (SEH) seemed to be at least a partial answer to many of these problems. SEH is familiar to programmers from languages such as Java and C++; what is less known is that it is also a standard part of Windows systems programming. It provides two very important capabilities for components: the ability to always execute local cleanup code declared within a finally block, and the ability to alert components further up the food chain about violations of behavioral contracts (whether malicious or innocent), providing those components with the opportunity to recover without necessitating cooperative error-passing. SEH provides a level playing field for components, as well as an opportunity for arms-length cooperation. Exception handling is an easier and safer alternative to HRESULTs. It can also be more efficient than HRESULTs when it is used for exceptional cases only, guaranteeing that the exception path is rarely followed.

One of the strengths of HRESULTs was that their DWORD values needed neither allocation nor cleanup after use; the discipline for creating and destroying HRESULTs was simple and fast, and resulted in good interoperability between languages. In addition, DWORD values can easily be sent between processes or machines, and because of this, HRESULTs worked well for remoting operations across processes or machines. Because the CLI provides support for garbage collection, serialization, and is designed to be language-agnostic from the ground up, both of these original design points look dated. The CLI uses full-fledged objects rather than DWORDs as its error indicators, and instantiation and cleanup are dealt with inside the execution engine. A reference type, System.Exception, is used as the basis for C# exceptions, but any object can be thrown by languages that do not wish to conform to the CTS. (Of course, the Exception type was designed for this purpose. Instances of Exception marshal by value, taking advantage of the CLI's built-in support for serialization. Because of this, they can be simply propagated across application domain, process, or machine boundaries. On unmarshalling they are simply objects that are garbage collected like any other type and need no special cooperative ownership protocol.)

CLI Exception Model

Many programmers think of exception handling as try, catch, and finally blocks in a higher-level language, along with corresponding throw statements, such as those we saw in the Echo component in earlier chapters. The CLI, however, is designed to serve the needs of programming languages with various syntactic models and uses a general approach.

The ECMA specification has a detailed discussion of this abstract model for managed exceptions. There are four distinct kinds of blocks (filter, catch, fault, and finally), several opcodes dedicated to ensuring verifiable control flow (shown in Table 6-1), and a large tree of exception types. It is possible, using these building blocks, to construct many different kinds of high-level exception syntax; since they share underlying plumbing, they can still interoperate safely despite their differences.

Table 6-1. CIL opcodes specific to exception handlers

Opcode	Usage
throw	Throws an exception, using object on stacks
rethrow	Reissues an exception from within a catch handler block.
leave	Used within a section of guarded code to jump out to a specific point. This jump will cause execution of any required termination handlers.
endfinally (alias endfault)	Used at the end of a termination handler to return control back to the execution engine.
endfilter	Used at the end of a filter function to return the handler status back to the execution engine.

In the CLI model, a block of code can be protected by one or more exception handlers. A block so protected is called a *guarded block* (or just a block). There can be multiple guarded blocks in a single stack frame. It is common for C# code to have multiple handlers for a single block, with each handler covering a subset of the possible exceptions, but this is built on top of the simpler CLI model, in which try blocks have a single handler. Handlers themselves may contain catch and/or finally blocks, and catch blocks may have filters associated with them that provide code to determine whether the catch block is eligible for handling a given exception. Catch blocks, filters, a fault block, and a finally block together constitute a single exception handler for a given try block.

Recall that the worker thread's StartMethod in Example 6-4 used exception handling to catch the ThreadAbortException. This method is turned into the CIL found in Example 6-19 by Rotor's C# compiler.

Example 6-19. CIL for the StartMethod in Example 6-4

```
.method public hidebysig static void  StartMethod( ) cil managed
{
  // Code size       167 (0xa7)
  .maxstack  3
  .locals init (int32 V_0,
          class [mscorlib]System.Threading.ThreadAbortException V_1)
  .try
  {
  // bunch of worker code omitted

    IL_002d:  ldstr      "OK, worker finished."
    IL_0032:  call       void [mscorlib]System.Console::WriteLine(string)
    IL_0037:  leave.s    IL_00a6
  }  // end .try
  catch [mscorlib]System.Threading.ThreadAbortException
  {
  // bunch of catch code omitted
    IL_007c:  leave.s    IL_007e
  }  // end handler

  // method continues
```

Notice the block structure that is created, the use of the leave opcode, and the local variable that is created to hold the ThreadAbortException object. Although not shown here, there can be many exception handlers in a single method, and exception handlers can be nested.

Exception handlers are grouped together into an Exception Information Table (EIT). Assemblies contain a compressed precursor for the EIT within the CIL headers that describe methods. This compressed table contains offsets into the CIL code, and is translated by the JIT into the runtime EIT, which is located in memory immediately above the compiled native code for the method.

 finally and fault blocks are not just redundant siblings of the catch block, since they can't be emulated using a catch that rethrows the exception. This approach would cause changes in the order in which filters and handlers are executed due to the two-pass nature of exception handling. Some languages that target the CLI depend on exact ordering of filters and handlers.

Using the EIT that corresponds to the method for each activation record on the managed stack, the execution engine can determine which handlers are in effect at any point during execution. When an exception is raised, all of the eligible catch handlers are visited in turn. Each must either handle the exception or pass it on. After the exception is caught and handled, but before returning control, finally and fault handlers are given the chance to clean up; finally handlers are always called, and fault handlers are called only if an exception has occurred in the block that they guard (see Example 6-20).

Example 6-20. The EIT within an executable image (Defined in clr/src/inc/corhdr.h)

```c
typedef struct IMAGE_COR_ILMETHOD_SECT_FAT
{
    unsigned Kind : 8;
    unsigned DataSize : 24;
} IMAGE_COR_ILMETHOD_SECT_FAT;

typedef enum CorExceptionFlag
{
    COR_ILEXCEPTION_CLAUSE_NONE,                  // This is a typed handler
    COR_ILEXCEPTION_CLAUSE_OFFSETLEN = 0x0000,    // Deprecated
    COR_ILEXCEPTION_CLAUSE_DEPRECATED = 0x0000,   // Deprecated
    COR_ILEXCEPTION_CLAUSE_FILTER  = 0x0001,      // A filter
    COR_ILEXCEPTION_CLAUSE_FINALLY = 0x0002,      // A finally clause
    COR_ILEXCEPTION_CLAUSE_FAULT = 0x0004,        // A fault clause
} CorExceptionFlag;

typedef struct IMAGE_COR_ILMETHOD_SECT_EH_CLAUSE_FAT
{
    CorExceptionFlag    Flags;
    DWORD               TryOffset;
    DWORD               TryLength;      // relative to start of try block
    DWORD               HandlerOffset;
    DWORD               HandlerLength;  // relative to start of handler
    union {
        DWORD           ClassToken;     // use for type-based exception handlers
        DWORD           FilterOffset;   // use for filter-based exception
handlers
    } u;
} IMAGE_COR_ILMETHOD_SECT_EH_CLAUSE_FAT;

typedef struct IMAGE_COR_ILMETHOD_SECT_EH_FAT
{
    IMAGE_COR_ILMETHOD_SECT_FAT    SectFat;
    IMAGE_COR_ILMETHOD_SECT_EH_CLAUSE_FAT Clauses[1];    // variable size
} IMAGE_COR_ILMETHOD_SECT_EH_FAT;
```

These tables can exist for every method. Using the Clauses array, a variable number of handlers can exist for a given method. Each entry in the table will have a guarded block, represented by TryOffset and TryLength, followed by a handler block, represented by HandlerOffset and HandlerLength. (Note that it can take more than one record to store a single compound handler.)

On Windows, interoperability with native SEH was a desirable feature, since managed and unmanaged code share the same execution stack, as shown in Figure 6-4. Even without this requirement, since the CLI exception model is intended for use by components running in managed code, it is important for the execution engine itself to participate in raising and handling exceptions, since it actually controls and manages many of the resources that components depend on. Because of the need for interoperability between native code and managed code, providing portable SEH was an implementation challenge for the SSCLI team. Consistent system-level support for SEH doesn't exist on some of the operating systems for which the SSCLI was created, and so a portable implementation was made part of the PAL using the Win32 SEH APIs as its interface.

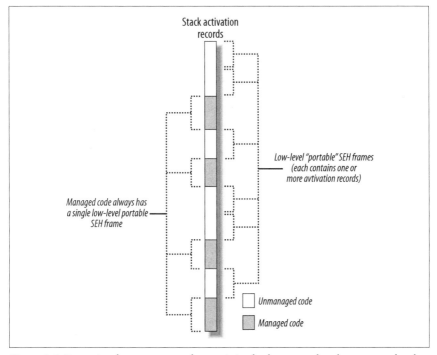

Figure 6-4. Exception frames on a stack containing both managed and unmanaged code

The CLI exception model piggybacks on the lower-level portable implementation, and meshes with it seamlessly. Exceptions can be thrown and caught between the two implementations without restriction, but they are not identical mechanisms; the CLI mechanism is "nested" within the portable SEH mechanism. A CLI exception is not a portable SEH exception, but it may cause one to be raised if it is not handled within a single stack segment of managed code. Likewise, an exception thrown at the lower level, if not consumed by the execution engine for special purposes, may flow into the higher-level CLI system, with the execution engine mapping into the hierarchy of exceptions.

Interestingly, in the SSCLI, the PAL's SEH facility is also used to build the parts of the debugging service. The portable implementation tinkers extensively with the low-level execution context of the microprocessor, which is also what debuggers need to do. Because of this shared need, the exception-handling mechanism was used to implement single-stepping and breakpoints within the SSCLI.

Throwing Exceptions

Exactly how exceptions come into being and are processed is dependent on where they originate. Hardware or software exceptions can originate from user code that has been JIT-compiled or from within the execution engine itself, and yet all cases must be dealt with in such a way as to give the appearance of seamless uniformity to the managed-code programmer. To accomplish this, every exception thrown, whether by hardware or by software, is routed through the PAL's portable SEH layer. This approach ensures consistency and helps simplify interoperability.

There are three distinct ways that exceptions can be raised during the execution of managed code, produced by the JIT compiler:

- Programmatically, from managed code that is throwing an exception
- Programmatically, from the C++ code that implements the execution engine
- From the hardware directly, not initiated by software

If managed code is the source, an object instance is created and the JIT_ Throw function is called, which packs the exception into a form compatible with the portable SEH and throws an exception from within that lower level, as shown in Example 6-21.

Example 6-21. JIT_Throw (extracted from clr/src/vm/jitinterface.cpp)

```
void JIT_Throw(Object* obj)
{
  ResetCurrentContext( );

  HELPER_METHOD_FRAME_BEGIN_ATTRIB_NOPOLL(Frame::FRAME_ATTR_EXCEPTION);

  if (obj == 0)
    COMPlusThrow(kNullReferenceException);
  else
    RaiseTheException(ObjectToOBJECTREF(obj), FALSE);

  HELPER_METHOD_FRAME_END( );
}
```

The call to ResetCurrentContext resets the hardware, taking care of things like resetting the FPU and mask values. After this, a helper frame is pushed to mark the transition from JIT-compiled code to execution engine code. This frame will ensure that the security engine and the garbage collector know about the transition. After this, RaiseTheException (Example 6-22) is called, which is a routine shared by all exception paths.

Example 6-22. RaiseTheException is shared by all types of exception (simplified from clr/src/vm/excep.cpp)

```
VOID RaiseTheException(OBJECTREF throwable, BOOL rethrow)
{
  Thread *pThread = GetThread( );
  ExInfo *pExInfo = pThread->GetHandlerInfo( );

  ULONG_PTR *args;
  ULONG argCount;
  ULONG flags;
  ULONG code;

  // Always save the current object in the handle so on rethrow we can reuse it.
  // This is important as it contains stack trace info.
  pThread->SetLastThrownObject(throwable);

  if (!rethrow
        || pExInfo->m_ExceptionCode == EXCEPTION_COMPLUS
        || pExInfo->m_ExceptionCode == STATUS_STACK_OVERFLOW) {
    args = NULL;
    argCount = 0;
    flags = EXCEPTION_NONCONTINUABLE;
    code = EXCEPTION_COMPLUS;
  } else {
    args = pExInfo->m_pExceptionRecord->ExceptionInformation;
    argCount = pExInfo->m_pExceptionRecord->NumberParameters;
    flags = pExInfo->m_pExceptionRecord->ExceptionFlags;
    code = pExInfo->m_pExceptionRecord->ExceptionCode;
  }
  // Tell GC that scheduling is preemptive before call into OS
  pThread->EnablePreemptiveGC( );

  RaiseException(code, flags, argCount, args);
  SafeExitProcess(0);
}
```

Note the involvement of the Thread object. Exception handling is a stack-intensive activity, and since the Thread object is the "owner" of the stack for the purposes of the execution engine, it is also the logical place to keep the information needed for exception handling. The ExInfo struct is used to store exactly this data and can be found in *sscli/clr/src/vm/excep.h*.

In the function shown in Example 6-14, if a rethrow is in process, information about the original exception will be pulled from the thread's ExInfo and passed along to the PAL's RaiseException function. A reference to the Exception object is also placed into the current managed Thead object, which has a spot reserved for this purpose. The last act before a noncontinuable EXCEPTION_COMPLUS exception is raised (using RaiseException) is to turn off cooperative garbage collection, since system code, being unaware of the execution engine, doesn't take pains to interact safely with the garbage collector. Of course, noncontinuable exceptions are not supposed to return, which explains the call to SafeExitProcess.

Typically, when the exception is thrown from within the execution engine's code directly, one of many different exception-throwing functions that are defined in *sscli/clr/src/vm/excep.h* is used to do the actual raising of the exception. Most of the time, COMPlusThrow is used, which is a macro that wraps RealCOMPlusThrow, and which eventually bottoms out in RealCOMPlusThrowWorker. Atypically, other wrapper functions are used but only in special circumstances, and these additional wrappers usually bottom out in RealCOMPlusThrowWorker themselves, as well. RealCOMPlusThrowWorker is shown in Example 6-23.

Example 6-23. First part of a worker function for throwing exceptions (extracted and simplified from clr/src/vm/excep.cpp)

```
static VOID RealCOMPlusThrowWorker(RuntimeExceptionKind reKind,
                                   BOOL                  fMessage,
                                   BOOL                  fHasResourceID,
                                   UINT                  resID,
                                   HRESULT               hr,
                                   LPCWSTR               wszArg1,
                                   LPCWSTR               wszArg2,
                                   LPCWSTR               wszArg3,
                                   ExceptionData*        pED)
{
  Thread *pThread = GetThread( );

  // Running in managed code, need to be cooperative mode
  if (!pThread->PreemptiveGCDisabled( ))
    pThread->DisablePreemptiveGC( );

  // Is enough of the execution engine in place to run exception code?
  if (!g_fExceptionsOK)
    COMPlusThrowBoot(hr);

  // Out of memory is a special case
  if (reKind == kOutOfMemoryException && hr == S_OK)
    RealCOMPlusThrow(ObjectFromHandle(g_pPreallocatedOutOfMemoryException));

  // Execution engine failure is a special case
  if (reKind == kExecutionEngineException && hr == S_OK && (!fMessage))
```

Example 6-23. First part of a worker function for throwing exceptions (extracted and simplified from clr/src/vm/excep.cpp) (continued)

```
RealCOMPlusThrow(ObjectFromHandle(g_pPreallocatedExecutionEngineException));

// Go ahead now and gather exception data to throw
FieldDesc *pFD;
MethodTable *pMT;
LPWSTR wszExceptionMessage = NULL;

pMT = g_Mscorlib.GetException(reKind);
if (fMessage) {
  wszExceptionMessage =
      CreateExceptionMessage(fHasResourceID, resID,
        wszArg1, wszArg2, wszArg3);
}

// The rest of this very long function omitted for brevity
```

This function first ensures that the garbage collector mode is in the correct state. There is no need to push a transition frame in this case, since the exception is coming directly from within the code of the execution engine, and transition frames will already be in place. The function checks to see that the execution engine has bootstrapped far enough to run managed code; if not, it will not attempt to throw a managed exception, as there is no engine to support this. (This check is also used for teardown. If the execution engine is in the process of shutting down, and is unable to throw a managed exception, it will not attempt it.) If the error is the result of running out of memory or an execution engine failure, preallocated exceptions that were prepared for this eventuality are thrown. Otherwise, an instance of the appropriate managed exception type is created, and the hunt for the appropriate user-readable message begins.

The rest of the function is not shown due to its tedious length and niggling specificity. It spends a good deal of effort on setting up the exception object by ferreting out failure information. If there was no message passed from the caller, the code looks for a message to place into the exception object, sets the source and the HRESULT if available, and ultimately throws the exception using RaiseTheException, as seen previously in Example 6-14. (The HRESULT in this code is purely a result of backwards compatibility and interop, and shouldn't cause consternation.) Much of the work done in the execution engine has to do with mapping the different kinds of errors into the higher-level exception hierarchy, copying appropriate information into the exception objects, and making sure that the execution engine itself is in a safe state. For example, the first-pass exception handler will take lower-level status codes and map them to types that will fit into some part of the exception hierarchy using the function in Example 6-24.

Example 6-24. Mapping from a lower-level exception domain to a higher-level domain (defined in clr/src/vm/excep.cpp)

```
DWORD MapWin32FaultToCOMPlusException(DWORD Code)
{
    switch (Code)
    {
        case STATUS_FLOAT_INEXACT_RESULT:
        case STATUS_FLOAT_INVALID_OPERATION:
        case STATUS_FLOAT_STACK_CHECK:
        case STATUS_FLOAT_UNDERFLOW:
            return (DWORD) kArithmeticException;
        case STATUS_FLOAT_OVERFLOW:
        case STATUS_INTEGER_OVERFLOW:
            return (DWORD) kOverflowException;

        case STATUS_FLOAT_DIVIDE_BY_ZERO:
        case STATUS_INTEGER_DIVIDE_BY_ZERO:
            return (DWORD) kDivideByZeroException;

        case STATUS_FLOAT_DENORMAL_OPERAND:
            return (DWORD) kFormatException;

        case STATUS_ACCESS_VIOLATION:
            return (DWORD) kNullReferenceException;

        case STATUS_ARRAY_BOUNDS_EXCEEDED:
            return (DWORD) kIndexOutOfRangeException;

        case STATUS_NO_MEMORY:
            return (DWORD) kOutOfMemoryException;

        case STATUS_STACK_OVERFLOW:
            return (DWORD) kStackOverflowException;

        default:
            return kSEHException;
    }
}
```

The status codes in this function are defined as part of the PAL, where yet another layer of mapping is clearly taking place, depending on the operating system being used. See the details in Chapter 9 on PAL exceptions to understand this mapping.

In software exceptions from managed code and software exceptions from the execution engine, exceptions are packaged under the EXCEPTION_COMPLUS status code at the level of PAL SEH. In a hardware exception, other status codes will be used, but, in all cases, the portable SEH mechanism is used to find handlers. This is important because the execution engine causes exception handlers to run. By leveraging the portable SEH mechanism, the execution engine locates and executes appropriate handler code in a single, uniform way.

Handling Exceptions

Exception handling within the execution engine is a two-pass process, which is illustrated in Figure 6-5. On the first pass, a stackwalk checks every activation record on the stack until an appropriate filter is found. Then, on the second pass, the stack is "unwound," meaning that any `finally` blocks in the region of the stack about to be discarded are called before execution resumes further up the stack.

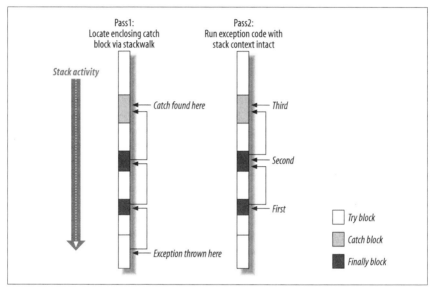

Figure 6-5. Locating exception handlers using a two-pass stackwalk

To initiate stackwalks of the managed regions that are needed for this two-pass algorithm, the execution engine prepares for it by using the portable SEH mechanism to install a standard exception frame around regions of managed code. In this way, regardless of an exception's source (a hardware exception, a soft exception in code produced by the JIT compiler, or an execution engine exception), this SEH filter kicks off the processing. By right of its low-level position, this handler, named `COMPlusFrameHandler`, has the first opportunity at any exception. This potentially platform-specific code is shown in Example 6-25 (although the PowerPC version of the SSCLI uses the same code as the x86 in this case). This example is defined in *clr/src/vm/i386/excepx86.cpp*.

Example 6-25. The normal exception filter

```
EXCEPTION_HANDLER_IMPL(COMPlusFrameHandler)
{
```

Example 6-25. The normal exception filter (continued)

```
  if (g_fNoExceptions)
    return ExceptionContinueSearch; // No EH during EE shutdown.

  if (pExceptionRecord->ExceptionFlags & (EXCEPTION_UNWINDING |
                                          EXCEPTION_EXIT_UNWIND)) {
    return CPFH_UnwindHandler(pExceptionRecord,
                             pEstablisherFrame,
                             pContext,
                             pDispatcherContext);
  } else {
    ResetCurrentContext( );
    pEstablisherFrame->dwFlags &= ~PAL_EXCEPTION_FLAGS_All;
    return CPFH_FirstPassHandler(pExceptionRecord,
                                pEstablisherFrame,
                                pContext,
                                pDispatcherContext);
  }
}
```

The first thing the COMPlusFrameHandler does is verify that the exception engine is in a state in which it can actually handle exceptions. If not, control is passed on to other handlers for the thread, which will more than likely trigger a shutdown. If the exception is already on its second pass, CPFH_UnwindHandler is called; otherwise, the hardware is reset, and the exception-handling process is begun with a call to CPFH_FirstPassHandler.

The first pass handler, found in *sscli/clr/src/vm/i386/excepx86.cpp*, is responsible for detecting nested exceptions and setting up the bookkeeping that surrounds their use. The first pass handler also sorts trhough a myriad of special-purpose exceptions before dispatching any "real" exceptions to the correct handler. To do this, it first ensures that the garbage collector is in the right state. After this preliminary step, the first-pass handler filters out exceptions that are used in special ways by the execution engine: access violations may indicate the need to adjust the garbage collector's write barrier, stack overflows can be remedied by expanding the stack, thread aborts get special treatment, and so on. The call to CPFH_HandleManagedFault continues this winnowing activity, looking specifically at exceptions that occur within JIT-compiled code. The function calls ExecutionManager::FindCodeMan to determine whether the current instruction pointer is executing within JIT-compiled code; if it is, it filters for special cases, which include things like debugger single-step and breakpoints.

You may be curious as to why we keep mentioning garbage collector state during all this discussion of the exception-handling mechanism.youders are interested in modifying or exploring the exception mechanisms within Rotor, we recommend you step with extreme care. As you can probably tell by now, a garbage collection that occurs at the wrong moment during exception processing (or any other deeply integrated service) can make things really ugly really fast, due to monkeying with the thread stack, processor registers, and other sharp objects. Managed handlers in code that was JIT-compiled must execute with the state set to cooperative mode, while PAL handlers must use pre-emptive mode.

If by this point the exception still qualifies as "real," the exception record and machine context are saved into the thread, a FaultingExceptionFrame is pushed to mark this special transition, the PAL_EXCEPTION_FLAGS_ LaunchThrowHelper flag is set on the frame, and finally, a global exception lock is taken. The LaunchThrowHelper will be used to trigger the rethrow of the specific managed exception when the time comes; at this point, you are only preparing for this call and passing control back to the exception engine.

The code used by the first pass handler to locate an existing managed handler is contained in *sscli/clr/src/vm/excep.cpp*. This function uses a stack walk to search the managed stack, as shown in Example 6-26.

Example 6-26. Stackwalking for managed handlers

```
LFH LookForHandler(const EXCEPTION_POINTERS *pExceptionPointers,
                   Thread *pThread, ThrowCallbackType *tct)
{
  if (pExceptionPointers->ExceptionRecord->ExceptionCode == EXCEPTION_COMPLUS &&
            GetIP(pExceptionPointers->ContextRecord) != /
            GetIPgpRaiseExceptionIP) {
    // This check relies on the fact that we record the IP of managed code
    // into m_OSContext. Check to see that the IP in the context record matches.
    if ((pThread->m_OSContext == NULL)  ||
        (GetIP(pThread->m_OSContext) != GetIP(pExceptionPointers->
ContextRecord)))
       return LFH_NOT_FOUND; // Return value will cause continue_search
  }

  // Find if anyone handles the exception
  StackWalkAction action =
        pThread->StackWalkFrames((PSTACKWALKFRAMESCALLBACK)COMPlusThrowCallback,
                             tct,
                             0,
                             tct->pBottomFrame);
  // If there is a handler, the action will be SWA_ABORT with pFunc and dHandler
  // indicating the function and handler to use when handling the exception.
```

Example 6-26. Stackwalking for managed handlers (continued)

```
if (action == SWA_ABORT && tct->pFunc != NULL)
  return LFH_FOUND;

// nobody is handling it
return LFH_NOT_FOUND;
}
```

Each frame is examined using the COMPlusThrowCallback function. This complex function, found in *sslcli/clr/src/vm/i386/excepx86.cpp* (or equivalent, for other architectures), is where the exception stack trace is built and where handler identification takes place. When a handler match is found, the location is recorded in the tct argument, and the stackwalk is aborted. The callback function uses the frame's GetFunction method to procure a metadata token for the method whose activation state it represents. This token is then used to ask the code manager to procure the EIT. (Remember, the JIT compiler produces a header at the beginning of a compiled method in the code heap that includes garbage collection information as well as the EIT.) The flags and offsets of the EIT, along with the current instruction pointer, are used to search outward until an overlapping handler that meets all criteria is found. The exception filter will remember which handler needs to be run, and then return, causing second-pass unwinding to take place.

At this point, if no matching managed handler has been found, the lower-level SEH mechanism continues along its merry way, searching in unmanaged code until a handler is found or the default handler is encountered. If a handler was located, it seems as though starting the managed second pass would be the right thing to do; for the purposes of interoperability, this can't be done until the lower-level SEH has also moved on to its second pass. The first pass handler, to perform this hand-off, sets the PAL_EXCEPTION_FLAGS_ UnwindCallback in the frame where the handler is located and returns ExceptionStackUnwind, which will cause the lower level machinery to stop searching and begin its second pass. The state needed to begin unwinding has been safely stored in the exception record.

Unwinding the Stack

Execution begins with the CPFH_UnwindHandler, already seen in Example 6-17. Two flags may have been set during the first pass: one that designates exceptions coming from unmanaged code that's subordinate to a region of managed code (PAL_EXCEPTION_FLAGS_LaunchThrowHelper) and one that designates that a managed handler was located for the exception (PAL_EXCEPTION_FLAGS_ UnwindCallback). If the latter is set, the execution engine needs to fire any finally or fault blocks and then give the managed code a chance to handle the exception, which requires another walk of the managed stack.

To call a managed handler, `COMPlusAfterUnwind` is invoked, which causes another stackwalk to happen via the `UnwindFrames` function. The callback for this second pass is `COMPlusUnwindCallback`. Once again, the code manager is queried for EIT information, and this information, along with the program counter, is used to find handlers. This time through, the code manager is also used to execute any `finally` or `fault` blocks with `IJitManager::CallJitEHFinally`, and if a handler exists, the handler is jumped to using `IJitManager::ResumeAtJitEH`. Once called, the handler filter itself may decline to handle the exception, in which case control will pass back to the SEH handler chain. By passing through the dispatch phase, the managed blocks have been executed—both portable SEH and managed SEH remain well-synchronized and correct.

Unmanaged faults that occur while running managed code, if unhandled, are rethrown after a `FaultingExceptionFrame` is injected into the stack. The unwind helper calls `LaunchNakedThrowHelper`, which results in a call to `LinkFrameAndThrow` within the execution engine, which sets the threadstate to reflect the managed exception, releases the global exception lock, and calls `RaiseException` anew, using the exception state gathered during the first pass. This second `RaiseException` can be baffling. It was put in the code to enable possible future compatibility and interop with exception resumption.

 It is very important that stackwalks within exception processing be "correct" with regards to security invariants. This is especially tricky for filters because the stack is not yet unwound when filters are called, and because of this, the arbitrary code in them may be called between the time that the exception is thrown and its matching `finally` is called. This has interesting implications for writing secure managed exception handlers and handling reentrancy in managed libraries. To understand more about these issues, see Microsoft's recommendations concerning building secure managed libraries in the .NET Framework SDK.

Summary

The careful checking and rechecking of format, metadata invariants, and typesafety is not worth much without the presence of an execution engine that can enforce policies and keep control over the managed code that is run within it. To maintain control, the SSCLI carefully orchestrates the behavior of threads and exceptions, inserting control structures and bookkeeping information directly into their in-memory data for this purpose.

Threads are appropriated as soon as they are detected by the execution engine, by associating managed-thread instances with them. These managed threads actually share their runtime stacks with any unmanaged code running within them. To keep transitions between managed and unmanaged regions straight, the execution engine uses a control structure called an execution engine frame. Execution engine frames are small chunks of bookkeeping info that are tucked into the stack amidst the activation records that populate it. They are used to both mark transitions and annotate stack usage.

Of course, one of the primary roles of a thread is to provide a home for the runtime stack that contains its nested execution state. We saw in Chapter 5 that the stack in the execution engine is used for traditional language purposes such as parameter passing, but the execution engine also uses it to control security and to track exception-handler boundaries. Code access security walks the stack to find permissions, grants, and demands. Exceptions are used to handle nonlocal transfer of control and keep boundaries around managed regions of code that are interspersed with unmanaged code.

Since multiple threads can share the services of a single execution engine instance, the CLI provides concurrency and synchronization primitives that match its specialized threading implementation. This traditional threading facility has a number of built-in conveniences, such as a thread pool, and synchronization components, such as monitors.

CHAPTER 7

Managing Memory Within the Execution Engine

Component-based applications, viewed as the vast graphs of interconnected type instances that they are, are notorious for their complex internal pointer manipulation, and as a result, their profligate thrashing of memory allocators. One of the longest standing feuds in the world of programming language design has centered on best practices for memory management in this kind of demanding environment. For some, it is even a long-standing joke: it's said that C programmers have long understood that memory management is so critical, it can't be left up to the system, and Lisp programmers have long understood that memory management is so critical, it can't be left up to the programmers.

Since its introduction in the 1950s, garbage collection has received something of a nefarious reputation with many programmers. Garbage collection (GC) was for programmers who couldn't keep track of their own resources; GC was slothful; GC would force an application to hang for nontrivial portions of time while it was running internal bookkeeping; or GC was simply for wimps. But now, it is clear that garbage collection is enjoying something of a renaissance. Why?

For starters, GC implementations have improved. Not only are they running on faster hardware than before, but the algorithms and approaches to managing garbage have gotten more accurate and faster. The pauses during program execution simply aren't there anymore. More importantly, however, programmers have come to realize that a price comes attached to the power of explicit memory management: programmers have to explicitly manage memory. Some project surveys have revealed that a C++ project spends over 50% of its development lifecycle in the practice of memory management: ensuring allocated objects are freed, taking care not to make use of pointers after they've been deallocated, and tracking down bugs that emerge from dangling pointers. To avoid spending this much time on a task that most would consider to be purely plumbing, many programmers now willingly surrender some control and take advantage of automated memory management.

Memory Management Matters

For a real-world look at how much effort can go into memory management, look carefully at the many different allocation and reclamation mechanisms in Rotor. An object instance and its associated type information, for example, commonly occupy memory from five or more distinct heaps. Instance memory is found on the garbage collector heap, except for the instance's SyncBlock record, which is allocated within the execution engine itself. The MethodTable for the object is located in the *high-frequency heap* of its application domain, while the EEClass and associated FieldDescs and MethodDescs are located in its *low-frequency heap*. (The names attached to these heaps refer to frequency of access.) Native code produced by the JIT compiler is found in a *code heap*, which is shared by all application domains. Finally, related items such as stubs are allocated from within a separate region of execution engine memory.

Each memory manager or heap exists for good reason, but keeping track of this level of minutiae can be quite burdensome. Even harder is tracking down bugs that result from incorrect usage; it is not always obvious who should free memory that has been passed from consumer to consumer, for example. Eliminating these concerns by relying on the automated memory management service that is a built-in feature of the CLI is one great reason to use garbage-collected languages.

Is it possible for a general-purpose garbage collection mechanism to serve the decidedly nongeneral patterns of memory usage that algorithms dish out in an efficient enough way to be practical? For the early designers of the CLI, the answer to this question was obvious. Fresh from the nightmare of COM reference counting, which relies to this day on programmers' good behavior for correctness, it was clear that a system-mediated, automatic mechanism was not only desirable, it was an absolute requirement. Garbage collection is not just about programmer convenience—it also has excellent reliability benefits and recovery characteristics in the presence of bugs or malicious code. Security plays into this, as well, since the decision to relieve programmers of the burden of memory management also relieves them of the necessity to deal with memory locations directly (except under tightly controlled circumstances, such as interop). Because of all of these factors, the decision to use automatically managed memory was one of the first decisions made when specifying the CLI.

Memory and Resource Management

C or C++ programmers are already very familiar with the three different types of memory allocation that are commonly used by programming languages, and probably don't give them much thought. *Static allocation, stack-based allocation*, and *dynamic allocation* each represent a slightly different approach to allocating and manipulating values, and all three are available to those using the computational model exposed by the CLI.

Static allocation was the first form of memory allocation used by venerable programming languages such as FORTRAN. It is a simple mechanism, by which a name is bound to a region of memory for the entire lifetime of a program (or in the case of the CLI, for the entire lifetime of a type within an application domain). Regardless of where in the code a static variable is referenced, its location in the local address space will remain the same. In the CLI, static memory is associated with types and referenced by using metadata tokens, as shown in Example 7-1. Rotor also supports per-thread static memory, but this is not a part of the CLI specification.

Example 7-1. Static allocation in CIL is associated with types.

```
.class private auto ansi beforefieldinit StaticExample
      extends [mscorlib]System.Object
{
  .field public static int32 aStatic
}

// CIL can access the value stored in the static variable
IL_0006: ldsfld    int32 StaticExample::aStatic

// store the value 8 into the static memory location
IL_0000: ldc.i4.8
IL_0001: stsfld    int32 StaticExample::aStatic
```

The concept of stack-based allocation appeared with the introduction of stack-based procedural programming languages, in which variable lifetimes are tied to their lexical scope on an *execution stack*. Local variables are automatically allocated on this stack when a call takes place, and automatically deallocated when control returns. The advantage of stack-based allocation is also its disadvantage: the lifetime of storage locations is tied directly to lexical scope, which restricts the expressive possibilities presented to programmers by the computer language. The execution stack is heavily used by languages that target the CLI, and memory is allocated from it in the form of method arguments and local variables. (In addition, stack memory can be allocated using the localloc CIL instruction, although this results in unverifiable code.) Example 7-2 shows instructions that access stack memory for argument values and local variable values.

Example 7-2. Stack-based allocation is used for parameters and local variables

```
ExampleMethod(int32& Param1, int32  Param2)
{
  // This method has two parameters allocated on the stack
  // Two locals are also allocated on the stack, and accessed by position
  .locals init (int32 V_0, int32 V_1)

  // Load argument 0 from the stack
  IL_0000:  ldarg.0
  IL_0001:  ldind.i4
  // Load argument 1 from the stack
  IL_0002:  ldarg.1
  IL_0003:  add
  // Store the result of addition into local 0
  IL_0004:  stloc.0

  // Code skipped here

  // Later, load local 1 and return
  IL_000c:  ldloc.1
  IL_000d:  ret
}
```

Static and stack-based allocation, while useful, did not fully satisfy engineers designing programming languages and the hardware on which these languages were to run. To fully round out their repertoire, language designers introduced dynamic memory models, in which programmers could manipulate variable-sized chunks of memory directly through the use of one or more heaps. In many popular implementations of this approach, dynamic allocation and deallocation are completely under the control of the programmer, and memory is accessed using either handles or pointers. Because programmers are mere mortals, opportunities for mistakes, mischief, and mayhem abound, and yet the power and efficiency that results from the use of pointers and dynamically allocated memory far outweighs its inconveniences. Because of this, the CLI also rounds out its memory model by permitting languages to use pointers and manipulate them, either in a typesafe way with *typed references*, or else directly using unverifiable memory access operators. Example 7-3 shows the CIL involved in dynamic allocation.

Example 7-3. Types can be dynamically allocated on the heap

```
ExampleAllocator([out] object& o)
{
  // This method will return a newly allocated object in argument 0
  IL_0000:  ldarg.0

  // Allocate a new object from the heap
  IL_0001:  newobj     instance void [mscorlib]System.Object::.ctor()
```

Example 7-3. Types can be dynamically allocated on the heap (continued)

```
  IL_0006:  stind.ref
  IL_001c:  ret
}
```

In the context of the CLI, the lifetimes of all three types of memory can be automatically managed. The CLI provides a garbage collector for this purpose, which enables programmers to shed the task of pointer management, while still using dynamic allocation to structure memory. When using a garbage collector, the programmer requests memory, the execution engine tracks its use, and the garbage collector reclaims it when it is time to recycle. This simple technique is a boon for programmers.

Of course, programs written to leverage components not only use memory, but also share and manage resources that are beyond the influence of the execution engine, such as files, window handles, and sockets. Many programming scenarios demand that rigorous walls be in place between components, and in these situations, the rules of sharing or transfer of control can be complex. Garbage collection can ease the details of managing memory, but it doesn't ease the task of managing these resources, since their lifecycles are "owned" by some other entity, usually the operating system.

From a programmer's perspective, any type defined to represent or wrap an external resource must be able to both acquire and release that resource. In the case of a file, for example, a type depending on an external file resource must explicitly obtain an open file handle by calling the operating system and close that handle when its work is complete. The acquisition of the file is simple, but releasing it at the right time can be more difficult, especially when depending on a garbage collector. Since the programmer no longer has the responsibility (or the ability) to release the object instance, the system needs to provide that capability somehow. Within the CLI, this can be done through one of several mechanisms. The simplest to understand and most frequently used is actually built into the CLI garbage collection mechanism and is called *finalization*.

During finalization, the garbage collector calls the Finalize method on any object that chooses to take advantage of this service. By defining a Finalize method, taking no parameters and returning no value, an object declares its interest in cleaning up after itself. In the SSCLI implementation, at some point after an object is classified as recyclable by the garbage collector, but before its underlying memory has been released, the object will be placed into a data structure called the *finalization queue*. This queue is then emptied by a background thread called the *finalization thread*, each object awaiting finalization being called in turn. (Finalization is built directly into the C# language as destructors, which implement the Finalize method automatically.)

Finalization is necessary only when managing external resources. Because all garbage-collected objects fall under the allocator's jurisdiction, a type needs to implement a finalizer only when it needs to release external resources as part of its cleanup. Note that finalization is by no means a complete solution; in many cases explicit programmatic attention, such as calling a dispose method when finished, continues to be necessary to ensure good resource management.

Organizing and Allocating Dynamic Memory

The choice of a discipline for component memory allocation is deeply tied to component lifetimes. Control structures, such as the CLI's threads and application domains, offer simple and efficient disciplines for managing component lifetimes and memory and, as we have seen, are used by the CLI as locations for storing both static and stack-based information. As already pointed out, however, storage strategies based on these mechanisms will work onlywhen the lifetimes of the components and resources being allocated are in sync with the lifetimes of the control structures. There are many cases when this is not the case. There are also many times when storing large amounts of data in runtime control structures might cause resource exhaustion problems or bad locality of reference.

Heaps, of course, solve these problems by using regions of memory that are managed by allocating subblocks to clients and tracking these so that the clients can later release their subblocks in arbitrary order, at any time. When used manually, a programmer "checks out" subblocks of heap memory with a function like malloc, holds them as long as necessary, and then frees them explicitly, which makes the memory available for recycling. Heaps that are managed using garbage collection, on the other hand, permit clients to release their subblocks by simply abandoning references to them. When quantities of heap memory run low, the garbage collection service can take care of locating memory that has been abandoned and recycling it, as shown in Figure 7-1.

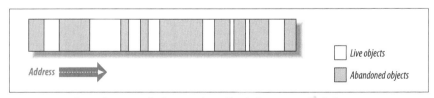

Figure 7-1. A heap that is ready for recycling (dead objects are shaded).

The heap in the SSCLI is periodically renewed by identifying dead objects and then fusing contiguous runs of dead objects into blocks of memory to be reallocated. The approach used for locating dead objects is called *tracing*; by following and recording all live references to heap memory, the garbage collector can easily deduce that the leftover memory is available for reclamation. Live objects are found by looking for heap pointers on all of the stacks, in all statically allocated memory, within all object instances, and in a few other well-known execution engine data structures. Whenever a live pointer is found, the memory that it refers to is itself examined for more pointers, and if more are found, they are likewise followed until the entire set of live objects is known. This procedure is called *tracing the roots*, and results in the transitive closure over the set of live objects, as shown in Figure 7-2.

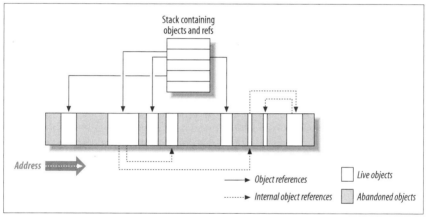

Figure 7-2. Recursively following live object references ("tracing the roots") in preparation for garbage collection

Often, all that is needed when recycling memory is to replenish the heap by locating blocks of memory that are ready for reuse, as outlined in the previous paragraph. This simple approach to replenishment is called *mark-and-sweep collection*—during the trace, live objects are marked, after which unused memory is "swept" into a free list. Mark and sweep collection, while simple and effective, can result in a fragmented heap over time, which can lead to heap exhaustion. To cure this tendency, *compacting collection* was invented. During the simplest kind of compacting collection, the heap is compacted by removing dead objects and pockets of unused memory by sliding live objects down towards the low-address end of each heap segment, or moving them elsewhere, and then repairing any dangling pointers with corrected values. As shown in Figure 7-3, compacting the heap in this way collects available memory together into contiguous stretches and can have the additional positive side effect of maintaining object creation order in memory, which can improve locality of reference; by grouping all live objects close to each other, less virtual memory needs to be paged into the system as those objects are used.

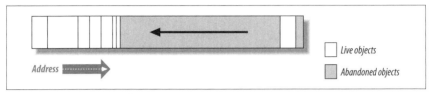

Figure 7-3. Compacting a heap

Simple compacting collection is not used in the SSCLI implementation. Instead, a variation of the compacting mechanism is used, called *copying collection*, in which live objects are periodically moved into an entirely new heap, after which the old heap is discarded or recycled. This technique has several advantages over futzing with object placement within a single heap: because every object is copied into a new heap, the very simple allocation algorithm can be based on a high-water mark, and no elaborate fit-finding tactics are needed. In addition, by compacting into a new heap, good virtual memory locality should result. The main drawback to compacting-and-copying collection strategies is the expense of copying objects and then fixing up references to the objects that have been moved (as well as the need for twice as much raw heap space).

Actually, the expenses of copying can be reduced drastically (or at least amortized) by using an enhancement of the technique called *generational collection*, in which objects are divided into "generations" marked by the passage of time. Generational collection is more complex than simple mark-and-sweep or compacting collection, but it has become the technique of choice for most systems, since the partitioning involved results in shorter interruptions than using other techniques. Generational collection exploits the fact that objects have different lifetime characteristics—some live very short lives, some live very long lives—depending on what they are and how they are used. Objects also vary in size. By dividing the heap into zones that are designated to house objects that exhibit matching lifetime characteristics, and by then collecting these zones using frequencies or algorithms that minimize the cost of collection by exploiting the specificity of the zones, more efficient use of both processor and memory can result. Zones are collected at differen times and at different frequencies, and thus the entire heap does not need to be scanned, nor all objects need be copied.

When a pure generational approach is taken, objects are initially allocated in the youngest generation (which is called this because it houses the youngest objects). If they survive past a collection cycle, then they are promoted to an elder generation by copying them. The refinement of this technique over compacting collection is that objects in the youngest generation have a low survival rate, while objects in the oldest generation have a high survival rate. Because the objects are split into two distinct locations, different techniques can be used to scavenge for free memory. A noncopying, noncompacting collector works best for the elder generation because copying the survivors would be a lot of work for little gain. (Many objects survive in this generation, and fragmentation is low.) However, in the youngest generation, a compacting or copying approach is often the right choice.

The Shared Source CLI uses exactly this approach to collection. It has a simple, two-generation collector, with added support for large object segregation. The younger generation is copy-collected, while the elder generation (and the large object heap that is conceptually part of the elder generation) is collected using a mark-and-sweep algorithm. Garbage collection is triggered by allocation volume or memory scarcity; when heap resources run low, the roots are traced, and either one or both generations are scavenged for memory.

 There is actually an entirely separate second garbage collector in the SSCLI distribution, which manages the lifetimes of components being used for cross-domain computation and distributed computing. These components are managed by a service that is part of the SSCLI remoting library. (The objects within this subsystem are also, of course, managed by the execution engine's regular garbage collector as well, once they have been released by the remoting layer.) A deep discussion of the algorithms used by the remoting library is beyond the scope of this book, but they use leases and a service that implements lease management. The code for both leases and the lease manager can be found in *sscli/clr/src/bcl/ system/runtime/remoting*.

Garbage collection is well worth the complexity and the effort—it pays off handsomely in both program reliability and programmer productivity. However, since maintaining good application performance while using fully automatic memory management is complex, the design of the SSCLI's memory manager pervades nearly every aspect of the execution engine, from its runtime data structures to its JIT compiler. These mechanisms are the subject of the rest of this chapter.

Object Allocation by Generation

In the SSCLI, the garbage collector's heap is made up of one or more *heap segments*, which are blocks of memory procured from system virtual memory. Heap segments themselves are divided into various regions, whose layout is dynamically determined by demand for memory and the kinds of allocations being done. As memory is needed, the heap is expanded by either adding memory from reserves within the current heap segment or by adding entirely new segments. Initially, a single heap segment serves all needs. It is laid out as shown in Figure 7-4.

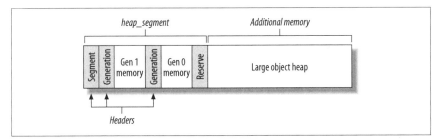

Figure 7-4. The heap is initially subdivided into two generations, reserved additional memory, and a large object area

Heap segments begin with a heap_segment header, shown in Example 7-4. This header occupies the first region of the segment and is used to keep track of subregion boundaries, as well as additional segments created during execution. Both the initial heap_segment and the large object heap are created back-to-back in a single allocation of virtual memory; note that the large object heap is not tracked as part of the heap_segment structure.

Example 7-4. The heap_segment class (defined in clr/src/vm/gcsmppriv.h)

```
class heap_segment
{
public:
    BYTE*           allocated;
    BYTE*           committed;
    BYTE*           reserved;
    BYTE*           used;
    BYTE*           mem;
    heap_segment*   next;
    BYTE*           plan_allocated;
    BYTE*           padx;

    BYTE*           pad0;
#if ((SIZEOF_OBJHEADER+ALIGNFIXUP) % 8) != 0
    BYTE            pad1[8 - ((SIZEOF_OBJHEADER+ALIGNFIXUP) % 8)];
#endif
    plug            mPlug;
};
```

Heap segments can be chained together, and each has an instance of the heap_segment class, followed directly by the actual heap, aligned appropriately for the local processor. The heap_segment header is utilized throughout the CLI code via inlined accessor functions; to obtain the memory being used for object storage in a segment, for example, the following function is used:

```
inline
BYTE*& heap_segment_mem (heap_segment* inst)
{
    return inst->mem;
}
```

These accessor functions are all declared along with their backing classes in *gcsmppriv.h*. A segment contains various, self-explanatory pointers to allocated memory, and it also has a field named used which points to the end of the currently initialized portion of the segment. (This is significant because the memory lying beyond the used pointer is known to be zero initialized and hence does not need to be zeroed when first used.) The other fields in heap_segment are used for calculating padding and offsets. Since the garbage collector views objects as nothing more than chunks of memory, there is a fair amount of pointer arithmetic required during access to the heap. To make this arithmetic efficient, quad-word alignment is used.

As already discussed, live objects are partitioned into two generations. Objects allocated within the quantum between two passes of the garbage collector are defined as being the same age, and once an object has survived for the length of this quantum without becoming garbage, it is *promoted* to elder status. Generational collectors operate on the assumption that elders do not need to be checked for liveness as often as their younger counterparts. Because of this, the younger generation is referred to as the *ephemeral* generation, since the younger the object, the more likely it is to become garbage. Although the SSCLI is configured to have just two generations, the code is written to be very general, and can easily be changed to accommodate more generations, as shown in Example 7-5.

Example 7-5. The generation class (defined in clr/src/vm/gcsmppriv.h)

```
class generation
{
public:
    // Don't move these first two fields without adjusting the references
    // from the __asm in jitinterface.cpp.
    alloc_context    allocation_context;
    heap_segment*    allocation_segment;
    BYTE*            free_list;
    heap_segment*    start_segment;
    BYTE*            allocation_start;
    BYTE*            plan_allocation_start;
    BYTE*            last_gap;
    size_t           free_list_space;
    size_t           allocation_size;
```

Example 7-5. The generation class (defined in clr/src/vm/gcsmppriv.h) (continued)

```
};
```

An object's generation can be determined simply by comparing its address to the addresses of the ephemeral generation boundaries. Not surprisingly, the member fields of generation include a segment pointer and an allocation context, which is a small, zeroed out region of the segment from which objects are allocated. When the allocation context pointer exceeds its internal limit, the allocator will make a call to get another chunk of zeroed memory, which may trigger a collection. Also in the class are a free list and bookkeeping fields, the use of which will become more obvious when we talk about reclamation later in this chapter.

As demand for memory grows, the boundaries of both generations change. The growth of the ephemeral generation is limited, since in the SSCLI this generation never spans more than one segment. However, if there is not enough space for new objects within the original heap_segment, the heap is expanded by adding additional segments to the elder generation. Because of expansion, the elder generation can eventually consist of many heap segments chained together. Within any of these additional heap segments, the oldest objects can usually be found at the lowest addresses, but the order may be scrambled because of the effects of mark-and-sweep garbage collection or because of the presence of *pinned objects*, which are objects that cannot be moved due to the existence of external pointers to their contents.

To avoid polluting the ephemeral generation with pinned objects, generation zero is always created afresh after every collection. The memory that had belonged to the previous incarnation is either recycled into the segment's reserved memory or else is added to the memory already used by the elder generation. Understanding this detail should help understand why the generations are laid out in reverse order in the initial heap segment: generation zero follows generation one in memory to simplify the expansion of the generation one and reallocate generation zero from the reserve simple.

Large Object Allocation

Although it is convenient to think in terms of the garbage collector as a single heap partitioned into generations, the actual implementation of the SSCLI is not this simple. The performance impact of garbage collection can be huge, and it was important for implementers to capture opportunities to improve performance, when possible. The performance characteristics of the garbage collector and the execution engine are tightly interwoven, and because of this, the Shared Source CLI implementation employs a few specialized strategies, the first of which is to treat very large objects differently than objects of more "normal" size.

As previously explained, the garbage collector slices and dices its heap into multiple regions, reserving the large object heap for objects over a certain size. The large object heap itself is further subdivided into an area for objects that contain pointers to other objects and an area for objects that contain no pointers. Any object that doesn't contain internal pointers does not need to be scanned recursively when the roots are traced at collection time. Since in large objects the act of scanning for pointers can be very expensive, this segregation makes sense. The two heaps that result can be seen in the gc_heap class, which is shown in Example 7-6.

Example 7-6. Large object features of the gc_heap class (excerpted from clr/src/vm/ gcsmppriv.h)

```
class gc_heap
{
public:
    static l_heap* make_large_heap (BYTE* new_pages, size_t size, BOOL managed);
    static CObjectHeader* allocate_large_object (size_t size,
                                BOOL pointerp, alloc_context* acontext);
protected:
    static BYTE* allocate_in_older_generation (size_t size);
    static l_heap* lheap;
    static gmallocHeap* gheap;
    static large_object_block* large_p_objects;
    static large_object_block** last_large_p_object;
    static large_object_block* large_np_objects;
    static size_t large_objects_size;
    static size_t large_blocks_size;

    // many other fields and methods omitted
```

A singleton instance of the gc_heap class manages both the large object heap and the heap segments used by the generational collector. To keep these separate, it implements two distinct methods for doing allocation: allocate and allocate_large_object. Beside the two lists of large objects—lheap, gheap, large_p_objects with internal pointers and large_np_objects without internal pointers—this class has other members that relate to special-casing large object allocation, including the threshold large_objects_size (defined in gc.h as 85,000 bytes) used to determine whether an object should be allocated in the large-object heap.

The large-object heap itself is implemented using an open source malloc-style heap implementation, which can be found in *gmheap.hpp*. Since this heap does not implement compaction, a long-running process that has many large objects might experience some performance degradation from fragmentation of the heap.

How does the allocator know whether the large object being created contains internal pointers? Objects are allocated based on their types, which are partially represented by a MethodTable at runtime (see Chapter 5). When the MethodTable for a type is created from metadata, the metadata is examined for references to other types, and this is noted (along with whether the type qualifies for "large object" status) in its flag bits. Metadata comes to the rescue once again.

The Write Barrier

It is not uncommon that the only live reference to an object is found in an object that lives in a different generation, a so-called *cross-generational reference*. By tracking which objects contain cross-generational references, and by visiting these objects when performing a trace, the collector can scan the heap for these root pointers very efficiently. The SSCLI's write barrier exists to facilitate exactly this approach.

A write barrier, as the name implies, is an entity that detects writes into memory when they occur. Such a mechanism can be (and is) used for many different system-level purposes, including cache management and virtual memory features. When used in the SSCLI, the write barrier is used to watch for any writes into the heap of object references so that these heap-based roots can be located and so that pointers that refer to them can be updated easily when their locations change. The write barrier narrows the amount of heap to be scanned during garbage collection. Without a write barrier, the entire heap would need to be scanned to correctly ferret out objects kept alive in the younger generation by intergenerational pointers, which would be very expensive.

Since the CLI is a strongly typed execution environment with a carefully designed set of opcodes, all pointer manipulations done by a piece of CIL code can be caught during compilation and made to use the write barrier. Whenever the JIT compiler encounters an operation that stores a reference, it emits code not only to perform the store, but also code to update a carefully maintained bitmap called a *card table*, which reflects the pointer contents of the GC heap, as shown in Figure 7-5. (The origin of "card table" might be colorful, but alas, it is unknown to the authors.)

Card tables use 1 bit to represent 128 bytes of heap; the code in the SSCLI that implements the write barrier actually works at a coarser grain than this, updating 1 byte at a time, which means that in actuality the minimum unit tracked by the card table is a 1 KB region of the heap (128 bytes times 8 bits). The x86 assembly code used for this can be found as OrMaskUP in *clr/src/vm/i386/asmhelpers.asm* and is implemented as a simple or instruction:

```
or   dword ptr [ecx], edx
```

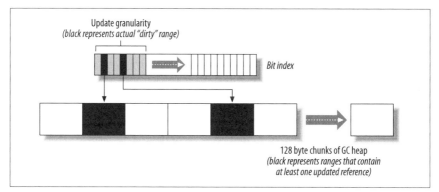

Figure 7-5. A card table is a bit index for the GC heap

Each processor demands a different approach, of course. Here is the sequence of instructions used in the PowerPC version of the same macro (from *clr/src/vm/ppc/asmhelpers.s*):

```
lwarx   t0, 0, a0
or      t0, t0, a1
stwcx.  t0, 0, a0
bne     _OrMaskGN
sync
```

These various processor-specific versions of the logical or operation are hidden behind a single function named FastInterlockOr.

In subdirectories such as *sscli/clr/src/vm/i386* and *clr/src/vm/ ppc*, you'll find assembler files that contain processor-specific implementations. For x86 code, there are duplicate files, one with a *.s* file extension and the other with an *.asm* extension. These files must be manually kept in sync by developers making modifications. They exist because the SSCLI uses different toolchains on different platforms; on Windows, the Microsoft MASM assembler is used, while on FreeBSD and Mac OS X, the GNU assembler is used. There is unfortunately no easy way to automatically eliminate this redundant code, and so if you modify it, be sure to replicate your work to both files.

The FastInterlockOr function is used to update the card table, as shown in Example 7-7.

Example 7-7. Updating the write barrier (defined in clr/src/vm/gcsmp.cpp)

```
void setCardTableEntryInterlocked(BYTE* location, BYTE* ref)
{
  if(ref >= g_ephemeral_low && ref < g_ephemeral_high) {
    size_t card = gcard_of(location);
#ifdef BIGENDIAN
    FastInterlockOr(&(g_card_table [card / sizeof(LONG)]),
```

```
                    0xFF000000 >> (8 * (card % sizeof(LONG)))));
#else
    FastInterlockOr(&(g_card_table [card / sizeof(LONG)]),
                    0xFF << (8 * (card % sizeof(LONG)))));
#endif
  }
}
```

If the pointer value being written refers to an object in the ephemeral generation (which is the only generation from which objects are copied), then the
card table must be updated to reflect the location of this pointer. The bit
location to be updated is obtained using the gcard_of function, and 0xFF is
masked into it. Of course, this masking operation must correctly reflect the
endian-ness of the processor.

The JIT compiler emits a helper function whenever memory containing a
reference to an object in the ephemeral generation is updated. This simple
helper function, shown in simplified form in Example 7-8, first updates the
pointer and then calls FastInterlockOr.

*Example 7-8. The JIT helper function that implements the write barrier (simplified from
clr/src/vm/gcee.cpp)*

```
void JIT_WriteBarrier(Object **dst, Object *ref)
{
  *dst = ref;
  setCardTableEntryInterlocked(*(BYTE**)&dst, *(BYTE**)&ref);
}
```

There are several flavors of this helper function, but all are used in the same
way. With the card table in place and being updated, the garbage collector
uses it during collection to search for object references that are embedded in
objects in the heap. For example, the function copy_through_cards_for_
segments (which we will revisit shortly) uses this technique. The function,
that scans every object in the elder generation designated by the write barrier as possibly updated, takes a single parameter which is a callback function. This callback is invoked for each object found. Not every object found
will qualify (or will even have *contained pointers*), but overscanning is a safe
strategy to use, and the card table helps narrow the search. There is a corresponding function for large objects, named copy_through_cards_for_large_
objects.

A *brick table* is somewhat related to the card table; it is another interesting
indexing structure and is maintained alongside the card table in *gcsmp.cpp*.
Brick tables are arrays of 16-bit signed integers that cover the entire GC
heap, much like a card table. Unlike the card table, which is a bitmap, each

entry in a brick table can be one of three things: a 16-bit positive offset, a negative displacement within the brick table itself, or a special reserved value that is used as a flag. When the heap isn't being collected, a positive entry means that there is an object at that offset in the 2 KB range that the entry describes. A negative number, on the other hand, means that there is no object, but if you use the entry as a displacement in the brick table, backing up as many slots as specified, you will find an object in that position. The flag value is simply a marker that is used for initialization and large-object designation. Brick tables are used by the collector to locate objects on the heap, given a range of addresses. For example, during a scan of the elder generation using `copy_through_cards_for_segments`, the brick table is used to locate the first valid object in a region marked as updated in the write barrier via the `find_first_object` function.

Both brick tables and card tables are kept up to date on the fly; much like a cache, they are not guaranteed to be completely consistent.

Reclaiming Memory

Reclamation in the SSCLI consists of two principal steps: the copying of promoted ephemeral objects into the elder generation, followed optionally by a sweep of the elder generation for dead objects. A copy collection performed without a sweep is called an *ephemeral collection* to contrast it to a *full collection*. For either kind of collection, an initial liveness trace is used to distinguish live from dead objects within the generations that have been *condemned* (designated for collection); generation zero is traced alone for ephemeral collection, while both generations are traced for full collection.

The SSCLI garbage collector, like many of the runtime services, is heavily instrumented in logging. Not only does this help find and fix bugs, but it can also be very useful for understanding how it works. Try setting the COMPlus_LogLevel environment variable to 9 and the COMPlus_LogFacility environment variable to 0x80001 (which is a combination of the flag for logging the roots found and the flag for logging collection itself) and both COMPlus_LogToConsole and COMPlus_LogEnable to 1, to watch the garbage collector in action when running your programs. If you really want to go crazy, set COMPlus_GCtraceStart to 1, and you will see a live play-by-play trace of every action. See *sscli/docs/techinfo/logging.html* for detailed documentation on logging.

To quickly and safely visit all objects during the trace, all threads running managed code are suspended (except, of course, for the thread performing the GC). Each thread is brought to a "GC safe" place before being stopped by the execution engine and scanned for object references, as shown by the code in Example 7-5. Of course, suspending all threads is a very expensive operation and shouldn't be done lightly. Many of the important implementation choices in building a garbage collector have to do with deciding when and how to interrupt the flow of the running program's execution, and the mechanism that the SSCLI uses to do this will be covered in more detail later in this chapter.

Promoting Ephemeral Survivors

The first step in any collection, after suspending all managed threads, is to promote all surviving live objects from the ephemeral generation into the elder generation by copying them. The promotion algorithm is straightforward: live objects are located using a recursive scan, copied into the elder generation, and finally, any references to these copied objects are then updated to reflect their new locations. The code for promoting objects to the elder generation can be found in the first half of the copy_phase method, shown in Example 7-9.

Example 7-9. The first step in garbage collection is to promote the live objects in generation zero to the elder generation (extracted from gc_heap::copy_phase in clr/src/vm/gcsmp.cpp)

```
// Promote any objects referred to by cross-generational pointers
copy_through_cards_for_segments (copy_object_simple_const);
copy_through_cards_for_large_objects (copy_object_simple_const);

// Promote any objects found on the stack or in the handle table
CNameSpace::GcScanRoots(GCHeap::Promote, condemned_gen_number,
                        max_generation, &sc, 0);
CNameSpace::GcScanHandles(GCHeap::Promote, condemned_gen_number,
                          max_generation, &sc);

// Promote any object referred to from the finalization queue
finalize_queue->GcScanRoots(GCHeap::Promote, heap_number, 0);
```

First, the elder generation and the large-object heap are scanned references in the ephemeral generation. If such roots are found, each object containing references is marked as live (for use by later mark-and-sweep scans), and then the object(s) to which they refer are copied, using the copy_object_ simple_const callback function. After this, GCScanRoots walks the stack for each managed thread, calling GCHeap::Promote for ephemeral object references that it finds.

The function GCScanHandles demands more explanation. Besides the heap and the stacks, there is an additional control structure called the *handle table* that needs to be traced in the SSCLI. The execution engine and other unmanaged code carefully track the differences between memory that is part of the garbage-collected heap and memory that came from other sources. To do this, they use *object handles* to hold references to managed component instances.

To facilitate the tracing of these handles, they are kept in tables associated with the application domain in which the referenced object resides. (Handles are implemented in *ObjectHandle.cpp* in the *sscli/clr/src/vm* directory.) Since these tables contain pointers to heap-allocated memory, they are traced as part of the garbage collector's search for the roots. However, since code that knows nothing about the semantics of garbage collection may be using the memory referred to in these handles, the handles themselves come in different flavors, each named after the client behavior that they have been designed to accommodate. They are listed in Example 7-10, along with the macros that unmanaged code uses to manipulate them.

Example 7-10. Common handle types and macros for manipulating them (ObjectHandle. h in sscli/clr/src/vm)

```
#define ObjectFromHandle(handle)                          HndFetchHandle(handle)
#define StoreObjectInHandle(handle, object)               HndAssignHandle(handle,
object)
#define InterlockedCompareExchangeObjectInHandle(handle, object, oldObj) \
            HndInterlockedCompareExchangeHandle(handle, object, oldObj)
#define StoreFirstObjectInHandle(handle, object)   HndFirstAssignHandle(handle,
object)
#define ObjectHandleIsNull(handle)                        HndIsNull(handle)
#define IsHandleNullUnchecked(pHandle)
HndCheckForNullUnchecked(pHandle)


#define HNDTYPE_DEFAULT                  HNDTYPE_STRONG
#define HNDTYPE_WEAK_DEFAULT             HNDTYPE_WEAK_LONG
#define HNDTYPE_WEAK_SHORT              (0)
#define HNDTYPE_WEAK_LONG              (1)
#define HNDTYPE_STRONG                 (2)
#define HNDTYPE_PINNED                 (3)
```

In the same way that managed code shares the stack with unmanaged code, managed-heap memory must be capable of holding pointers to unmanaged memory and resources, and unmanaged memory should be able to hold pointers into the managed heap. The different handle types defined by these macros represent different usage scenarios.

Strong references are "normal" object references—they represent a pointer to memory, this pointer can be moved as part of a compacting operation, and the pointer will always be traced. *Pinned references*, on the other hand, are strong references that would be unsafe to move for some reason. In particular, pinned references are often used to interoperate with code that is unaware of the conventions of the execution engine; a pinned reference being used in this way will always need to stay in the same place so that the external code can safely access the memory location directly. This, of course, prevents the memory from being available for relocation; an object in this state can prevent compaction from consolidating unused areas in a heap segment into a single range. Fortunately, pinning is relatively infrequent. *Weak references* are object references that track, but do not keep an object alive. They are useful when implementing finalization and other runtime services, and there are actually two different types of weak reference: *weak short* and *weak long*. (We will talk more about the specifics of these in the "Finalization" section of this chapter. They are exposed through the System.WeakReference type in the Base Class Libraries, which can be found in *clr/src/BCL/System/WeakReference.cs*.)

Returning once again to the promotion algorithm, the final place that is searched for ephemeral roots is the finalization queue. Any objects that are referred to from objects awaiting finalization must be kept alive. Even if the finalization queue is the only valid reference, they cannot be eliminated until finalization has occurred.

Relocation Fix-Up

After ephemeral objects have been copied, outstanding references to them must be updated. The code that does this is shown in Example 7-11.

Example 7-11. After ephemeral objects have been copied, references to them must be updated (extracted from gc_heap::copy_phase in clr/src/vm/gcsmp.cpp)

```
// Fix up cross-generational pointers
copy_through_cards_for_segments (get_copied_object);
copy_through_cards_for_large_objects (get_copied_object);

// Fix up references on the stack and in the handle table
CNameSpace::GcScanRoots(GCHeap::Relocate, condemned_gen_number,
                        max_generation, &sc);
CNameSpace::GcScanHandles(GCHeap::Relocate,condemned_gen_number,
                        max_generation, &sc);

// Fix up references in objects awaiting finalization
finalize_queue->RelocateFinalizationData (condemned_gen_number, __this);
```

The same root locations that were visited during the trace are now visited to update references that were found. During the original trace, when objects were being copied from the ephemeral generation into the elder generation, the object instances being moved were updated so that their abandoned syncblock indexes no longer contained valid integers but rather forwarding addresses for the new copies. (Note that this implementation choice introduces a hard requirement: the syncblock index must be able to contain a pointer.) As the relocation phase unfolds in Example 7-9, each of the original references is found once again, and as they are found, a call to CObjectHeader::GetRelocated is used to update their contents with the forwarding value from the old, now-invalid object:

```
if (!IsPinned( ))
  return (BYTE*)*(((DWORD**)this)-1);
else
  return (BYTE*)this;
```

After each reference is visited and updated with a forwarding address, all references will refer to object locations in the elder generation. At this point, the ephemeral generation can be recycled or added to the elder generation if pinned objects are found. With the exception of those pinned objects (which do not move and hence need no updating), all ephemeral objects have been moved.

Marking the Elder Generation

The SSCLI garbage collector uses a mark-and-sweep algorithm as its reclamation strategy for the elder generation. The tracing of live objects follows a similar path as did the ephemeral generation, although cross-generational references does not need to be visited, since the objects containing these references will have had their mark bits set as part of the preceding copying collection. Example 7-12 is a simplified version of the code that performs the elder generation trace.

Example 7-12. Marking the elder generation (extracted from gc_heap::mark_phase in clr/src/vm/gcsmp.cpp)

```
// Set up accumulator structure
reset_mark_stack( );

// Mark objects referred to from the stacks or the handle tables
CNameSpace::GcScanRoots(GCHeap::Promote, condemned_gen_number,
                    max_generation, &sc, 0);
CNameSpace::GcScanHandles(GCHeap::Promote, condemned_gen_number,
                    max_generation, &sc);

// Mark objects referred to from the finalization queue
finalize_queue->GcScanRoots(GCHeap::Promote, heap_number, 0);
```

This code is nearly identical to what we saw for the ephemeral generation. Note that the trace uses the same GCHeap::Promote callback function that was used during copying. Rather than using copy_object_simple_const to do the work, however, during the mark phase, this callback uses mark_object_simple to recursively set the mark bit on live objects. The call to reset_mark_stack sets up a simple stack structure that is used as an accumulator during this recursive visit. Stacks, handle tables, and the finalization queue are all marked, just as they were for the ephemeral generation.

After a number of calls that perform bookkeeping (which we will examine at the end of this chapter), the sweeping phase is begun with a call to sweep_large_objects, which removes any dead large objects from the two linked lists containing large objects. At the conclusion of this function, all live objects in the elder generation, whether newly copied, in the large object heap, or already resident, will have their mark bit set for use during reclamation.

Reclaiming Memory by Sweeping

The gc_heap::sweep_phase function performs the actual reclamation of memory, during which dead objects are converted into free list entries, ready to be used for the allocation of new objects in the elder generation. The ephemeral generation, since it is created anew after every garbage collection, can use a simple and fast allocation technique: new objects are appended from space at the end of its heap. The elder generation, however, does not move the objects that it contains and, because of this, must use a more complicated allocation algorithm. In this case, fragmentation is avoided by coalescing dead objects together when possible (when they are contiguous), and then linking these dead zones together into a freelist, which is used for first-fit allocation.

The SSCLI uses a nonobvious strategy for constructing this freelist. Since objects lie tightly packed in the heap, and since the garbage collector uses knowledge of this to traverse the heap, it is desirable for dead zones to appear to contain valid objects, even when these regions have been constructed through the coalescence of multiple instances. To do this, the garbage collector converts the instances found in these dead zones into a single instance of a reserved type used specifically to represent entries in the freelist. This type is held in the global variable g_pFreeObjectMethodTable. Since each instance can be a different length, the type is a subtype of System.Array. You can see how this type is constructed in InitializeGarbageCollector, part of which is shown in Example 7-13.

Example 7-13. Constructing the special freelist MethodTable (excerpt from InitializeGarbageCollector in clr/src/vm/ceemain.cpp)

```
// Build the special Free Object used by the Generational GC
g_pFreeObjectMethodTable =
    (MethodTable *) new (nothrow) BYTE[sizeof(MethodTable) - sizeof(SLOT)];

if (g_pFreeObjectMethodTable == NULL)
  return (E_OUTOFMEMORY);

// As the flags in the method table indicate there are no internal references
// in this filler object, which means that there is no gc descriptor, which in
// turn means that there is no need to adjust GCDesc.

// Since the instances need to vary in size, they should be Arrays
g_pFreeObjectMethodTable->m_BaseSize = ObjSizeOf (ArrayBase);

// This MethodTable needs no metadata - it is internal to the execution engine
g_pFreeObjectMethodTable->m_pEEClass = NULL;

g_pFreeObjectMethodTable->m_wFlags = MethodTable::enum_flag_Array | 1;
```

Using the g_pFreeObjectMethodTable to identify dead zones, and the array size field that occupies the first word of instance data to hold the length of each zone, the heap remains tightly packed and traversable. The second word of instance data is then used by the gc_heap::scavenge_phase function (called from copy_phase) to link freelist objects together. All of this is shown schematically in Figure 7-6.

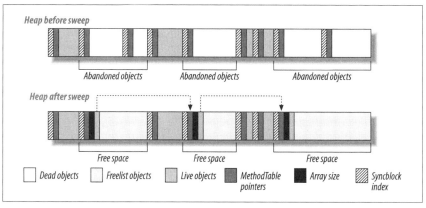

Figure 7-6. Dead objects in the elder generation are coalesced and threaded together to make up the freelist

The code that performs the final sweep, and sets up the pointers that link the freelist objects together, is shown in Example 7-14 and is abridged from *clr/src/vm/gcsmp.cpp*.

Example 7-14. Sweeping the elder generation

```
void gc_heap::sweep_phase (int condemned_gen_number)
{
  generation*  condemned_gen = generation_of (condemned_gen_number);

  // Reset the free list
  generation_free_list (condemned_gen) = 0;
  generation_free_list_space (condemned_gen) = 0;

  // Elder generation can have multiple heap segments, which are swept in order.
  heap_segment*  seg = generation_start_segment (condemned_gen);
  BYTE*  end = heap_segment_allocated (seg);
  BYTE*  first_condemned_address = generation_allocation_start (condemned_gen);

  // Start with the first object on the heap
  BYTE*  x = first_condemned_address;

  // The "plug" is a contiguous ranges of live objects. The "end of the plug"
  // refers to the start of a dead zone. When starting the traversal,
  // the only safe hypothesis is that the first object is garbage, making
  // the end of the plug equal to the current object. Plug_end will normally
  // point to the last live object in the last run of live objects.
  BYTE*  plug_end = x;

  while (1) {
    // Whenever the end of the plug coincides with the end of the segment,
    // move to the next segment, if there is one.
    if (x >= end) {
      assert (x == end);
      heap_segment_allocated (seg) = plug_end;
      if (heap_segment_next (seg)) {
        seg = heap_segment_next (seg);
        end = heap_segment_allocated (seg);
        plug_end = x = heap_segment_mem (seg);
        continue;
      } else {
        break;
      }
    }

    if (marked (x)) {
      // Whenever a live (marked) object is found, start a new "plug"
      BYTE*  plug_start = x;

      // Thread_gap builds the freelist to reflect the space between the end
      // of the last plug and the newly found live object. It also resets the
      // brick table. This, and clearing the marked and pinned bits, is the
      // real work of the sweep phase.
      thread_gap (plug_end, plug_start - plug_end);

      // Now build up the new plug, starting from first marked object.
      BYTE*  x1 = x;
```

Example 7-14. Sweeping the elder generation (continued)

```
    while (marked (x1) && (x1 < end)) {
      // While building the plug, clear the mark and pin bits, since this is
      // the last time that they are used during this collection cycle.
      clear_marked_pinned (x1);
      x1 = x1 + Align (size (x1));
    }

    // Reset x and plug_end for next iteration before leaving
    x = x1;
    plug_end = x;

  } else {
    // Skip over objects that are not marked (which make up the free list)
    // There should normally be only one, of type g_pFreeObjectMethodTable.
    BYTE* x1 = x;
    while ((x1 < end) && !marked (x1)) {
      x1 = x1 + Align (size (x1));
    }
    // Reset x to be last dead object in run of dead objects.
    x = x1;
  }
  // Continue the traversal
  }
}
```

The sweep_phase function does three important things: it clears the mark and pin bits for live objects, it threads the freelist together, and finally, it cleans up the brick table to reflect the disappearance of dead objects that were converted into free space.

At the conclusion of the scan, the mark and pin bits, set during the trace, must be cleared, since they are masked into the same memory location that holds an object's MethodTable pointer during normal execution. Because these bits take up space in a value that is normally interpreted directly as a pointer, it is critical that the bits be zeroed so that the address is not corrupted.

It is also important for the elder generation allocator to be able to walk the freelist, looking for blocks of memory when new objects are allocated. This scan is enabled by writing a pointer value into the instance data of freelist objects that points to the next entry. This pointer value follows the array size and occupies the second word of instance data, and is used to find the next available block of memory. The freelist is reconstructed after every mark-and-sweep cycle, to fold newly created gaps into the list.

By this point, it should be obvious that a tracing garbage collector needs to be able to find the complete set of root objects to perform its trace. As you can see from the previous code, the roots for the SSCLI can be found in the process stacks, the heaps, the handle table, and the finalization queue.

We've also seen the code that handles intergenerational references, which are references that emanate from fields within reference-typed objects. There is a final form of reference that is also a source of roots: *interior pointers*. The SSCLI can handle stack-based interior pointers; it cannot refer to locations on the heap. Compilers can pass references to these interior pointers as *byref* parameters in the same places that object references to heap-allocated types can be passed.

Structuring Metadata for Collection

We have already touched on object layout in other chapters, but we should now look at it again in more detail. All object instances begin with a pointer to their method table; as we have seen, the space allocated for this pointer is overloaded during garbage collection to contain two critical bit flags, one for marking the object as live and the other for marking the object as pinned. It is guaranteed that the normal activity of the execution engine will be suspended during a collection, leaving the collector free to monkey around with memory. Because of this, the garbage collector can get away with overlaying bit flags directly; the pointer itself will always contain zeros in the necessary locations because of the way that memory is laid out, and the execution engine will not try to redirect through the pointer during collection.

The MethodTable, as we saw in Chapter 5, contains more than just a table of method pointers. It is also a useful place to store additional information related to garbage collection that is per-type rather than per-instance. As an example of this kind of per-type information, a set of flag bits for MethodTable can be seen in Example 7-15.

Example 7-15. MethodTable flags include garbage collection information (defined in clr/src/vm/class.h)

```
enum
{
    enum_flag_Array             =   0x10000,
    enum_flag_large_Object      =   0x20000,
    enum_flag_ContainsPointers  =   0x40000,
    enum_flag_ClassInited       =   0x80000,
    enum_flag_HasFinalizer      =   0x100000,
    enum_flag_Sparse            =   0x200000,
    enum_flag_Shared            =   0x400000,
    enum_flag_Unrestored        =   0x800000,

    enum_TransparentProxy       =   0x1000000,
    enum_flag_SharedAssembly    =   0x2000000,
    enum_flag_NotTightlyPacked  =   0x4000000,
```

```
        enum_CtxProxyMask               = 0x10000000,
        enum_InterfaceMask              = 0x80000000,
};
```

Both the flag for finalization and the flag used to designate objects with contained object references are checked during collection. The large object flag is used by the SSCLI only for debugging; the large object allocator uses a value that is defined in *gc.h* to determine membership in this set. The information about proxies is also used during some collection phases, since proxies do not have instance data.

MethodTable can also contain data that is located at a negative offset to its this pointer, in the same way that object instances were shown to store their syncblock index at a negative offset in Chapter 5. The variable-length data associated with MethodTable, if present, consists of an instance of the GCDescSeries class, seen in Example 7-16, which describes the location of object references within instances of the type. (This information is per-type rather than per-instance.)

Example 7-16. The GCDesc structure (defined in clr/src/vm/gcdesc.h)

```
struct val_serie_item
{
    HALF_SIZE_T nptrs;
    HALF_SIZE_T skip;
    void set_val_serie_item (HALF_SIZE_T nptrs, HALF_SIZE_T skip)
    {
        this->nptrs = nptrs;
        this->skip = skip;
    }
};

class CGCDescSeries
{
public:
    union
    {
        size_t seriessize;              // adjusted length of series
        val_serie_item val_serie[1];    // coded serie for value class array
    };

    size_t startoffset;

    // class continues
```

The garbage collector relies on the information in the CGCDesc to locate object references that are stored in instance variables and arrays. To see how it is used, consider the go_through_object macro in Example 7-17.

Example 7-17. go_through_object uses CGCDesc to find contained pointers (defined in clr/ src/vm/gcsmp.cpp)

```
#define go_through_object(mt,o,size,parm,exp)                               \
{                                                                           \
    CGCDesc* map = CGCDesc::GetCGCDescFromMT((MethodTable*)(mt));           \
    CGCDescSeries* cur = map->GetHighestSeries();                          \
    CGCDescSeries* last = map->GetLowestSeries();                          \
                                                                            \
    if (cur >= last)                                                        \
    {                                                                       \
        do                                                                  \
        {                                                                   \
            BYTE** parm = (BYTE**)((o) + cur->GetSeriesOffset());           \
            BYTE** ppstop =                                                 \
                (BYTE**)((BYTE*)parm + cur->GetSeriesSize() + (size));      \
            while (parm < ppstop)                                           \
            {                                                               \
                {exp}                                                       \
                parm++;                                                     \
            }                                                               \
            cur--;                                                          \
                                                                            \
        } while (cur >= last);                                              \
    }                                                                       \
    else                                                                    \
    {                                                                       \
        SSIZE_T cnt = (SSIZE_T)map->GetNumSeries();                         \
        BYTE** parm = (BYTE**)((o) + cur->startoffset);                     \
        while ((BYTE*)parm < ((o)+(size)-plug_skew))                        \
        {                                                                   \
            for (SSIZE_T __i = 0; __i > cnt; __i--)                         \
            {                                                               \
                HALF_SIZE_T skip = cur->val_serie[__i].skip;               \
                HALF_SIZE_T nptrs = cur->val_serie[__i].nptrs;             \
                BYTE** ppstop = parm + nptrs;                               \
                do                                                          \
                {                                                           \
                    {exp}                                                   \
                    parm++;                                                 \
                } while (parm < ppstop);                                    \
                parm = (BYTE**)((BYTE*)parm + skip);                        \
            }                                                               \
        }                                                                   \
    }                                                                       \
}
```

This macro walks through the pointer series contained in the CGCDesc instance to locate contained object references and is used when tracing roots that emanate from cross-generational pointers. The CGCDesc is also used when tracing the stack; when a value type or an array is encountered, the stackwalk uses it to find any interior references that need to be added to the mark set. The CGCDesc runtime structure is filled in when the MethodTable is initially populated; see the BuildMethodTable method of EEClass in *class.cpp* for the gory details.

Scheduling Collection

We've already seen the JIT compiler's role in maintaining the write barrier on behalf of the garbage collector. The compiler has another equally important role to play with regard to garbage collection scheduling in the SSCLI. Garbage collection, although it is triggered by the allocator running out of space, can occur only when all threads are at safe points in their execution and yield control to the collector. In Rotor, your thread will trigger a GC only when it asks for a collection explicitly, when it performs an object allocation, or else when it is running JIT-compiled code that *polls*. The last case involves generating calls from within the JIT compiler that offer to yield the thread if necessary. The helper function that the JIT inserts to implement polling is shown in Example 7-18.

Example 7-18. The JIT compiler marks good places to perform a collection (summarized from clr/src/vm/jitinterface.cpp)

```
void JIT_PollGC( )
{
    Thread  *thread = GetThread( );
    if (thread->CatchAtSafePoint( ))    // Does someone wants this thread stopped?
    {
        CommonTripThread( );            // Indicate we are at a GC safe point
    }
}
```

The JIT emits calls to this trap in places that might cause a piece of code to take a long time to complete. It uses one simple rule to place these calls: trap at all backward branches in the execution path (conditional branches, jumps with negative offsets, or leave operations). CommonTripThread indicates to the thread-scheduling machinery that it would be safe to suspend the thread and perform a collection. For example, consider the following simple C# application:

```
class MainApp {
  public static void Main( ) {
    int i = 0;
```

```
    do {
      i++;
    } while (i < 1000);
  }
}
```

When compiled using the JIT compiler in the SSCLI, the x86 code for the loop portion (extracted using the SOS debugger extension that ships as part of the SSCLI distribution) is as follows:

```
02d42d3b e2fc           loop    02d42d39
02d42d3d 33c0           xor     eax,eax
02d42d3f 8945f0         mov     [ebp-0x10],eax
02d42d42 8b45f0         mov     eax,[ebp-0x10]
02d42d45 50             push    eax
02d42d46 b801000000     mov     eax,0x1
02d42d4b 59             pop     ecx
02d42d4c 03c1           add     eax,ecx
02d42d4e 8945f0         mov     [ebp-0x10],eax
02d42d51 8b45f0         mov     eax,[ebp-0x10]
02d42d54 50             push    eax
02d42d55 b8e8030000     mov     eax,0x3e8
02d42d5a 50             push    eax
02d42d5b b8dbd43779     mov     eax,0x7937d4db
02d42d60 ffd0           call    eax (sscoree!JIT_PollGC)
02d42d62 58             pop     eax
02d42d63 59             pop     ecx
02d42d64 3bc8           cmp     ecx,eax
02d42d66 0f8cd6ffffff   jl      02d42d42
```

Don't fret if you don't know x86 assembler. Because the do loop had a backwards branch at the while keyword, the compiler emitted this polling operation into the instruction stream to ensure timely garbage collection.

When the JIT compiler emits traps, it is asserting that the code is at a safe point, and that it has made sure that the scratch registers do not contain any object references. In addition, if collection is triggered immediately after a method return instruction that returns an object reference, it must be sure to protect the exposed object reference from being incorrectly scavenged.

The JIT compiler does more than generate code that lives by the rules. When compilation occurs, the compiler provides a map of what the evaluation stack will look like at safe points to the portion of the execution engine called the code manager so that the stack can be correctly and completely scavenged. (Among other things, the code manager constructs the GCDesc structures already discussed.) The map is used by the code manager in *fjit_ eetwain.cpp*. To see it in action, examine the portions of the code that do stack encoding.

Finalization

There is an obvious problem with using automatic memory management in conjunction with pointers to unmanaged resources: when components hold references to nonmanaged resources that need to be explicitly disposed of, it is necessary to make sure that the resource is disposed of before the object is collected. The CLI supports a concept called finalization to solve this problem. Finalizable objects are placed on a special weak reference list when created. The collector monitors this list and when all strong references to a finalizable object are released, moves the reference from the weak list to the finalization queue, which continues to keep the object alive. (We saw the finalization queue appear in numerous scan examples earlier in this chapter.) The finalization thread will go though the list of objects in a lazy fashion and call the finalization method on each object. If an object does not become reachable again as a result of being finalized (remember, arbitrary code is being run within the finalization method that can reestablish references!), the finalization reference will be released, and the object will be collected in a normal fashion.

One interesting issue for programmers is that garbage collection happens at unpredictable times, depending on the algorithm and the load. Because of this, it is sometimes desirable to go beyond finalization and revert to an old-fashioned disposal pattern, in which programmers are required to explicitly "close" resources by calling a Dispose method directly. The code for the Base Class Libraries that is contained in *sscli/clr/src/bcl* uses this convention in many places, and it is well documented in the .NET SDK documentation.

To make a component eligible for finalization, it should override the Object. Finalize method, as in Example 7-19. (In C#, finalization is done using the object destructor syntax, which produces code that overrides Finalize.) The Finalize method can have a negative impact on performance, however, since there is extra bookkeeping involved. Because of this, the mechanism should be used only when necessary.

Example 7-19. Adding a destructor to the echo component will trigger its finalization

```
~ Echo {
    System.Console.WriteLine("Echo component is finalizing!");
    // if any external resources were being held, release here
}
```

The C# compiler turns the destructor body into a method named Finalize that has the correct signature. But how is this method called at the correct time? The heart of the finalization thread, which watches for objects that are ready for finalization, is shown in Example 7-20.

Example 7-20. The SSCLI finalization loop (excerpt from clr/src/vm/gcee.cpp)

```
FinalizerThread->SetBackground(TRUE);
BOOL noUnloadedObjectsRegistered = FALSE;

while (!fQuitFinalizer) {
  // Wait for work to do...
  FinalizerThread->EnablePreemptiveGC();
  WaitForFinalizerEvent (GCHeap::hEventFinalizer);

  // The finalizer thread is a good place to do small work items
  if (FinalizerThread->HaveExtraWorkForFinalizer()) {
    FinalizerThread->DoExtraWorkForFinalizer();
  }

  FinalizeAllObjects(NULL, 0);

  // Schedule any objects from an unloading app domain for finalization
  // on the next pass, even if they are reachable. It may take several passes
  // to complete the unload, if new objects are created during finalization.
```

Example 7-20. The SSCLI finalization loop (excerpt from clr/src/vm/gcee.cpp) (continued)

```
if (GCHeap::UnloadingAppDomain != NULL) {
    if (!FinalizeAppDomain(GCHeap::UnloadingAppDomain,
                           GCHeap::fRunFinalizersOnUnload)) {
        if (!noUnloadedObjectsRegistered) {
            // There is nothing left to schedule.  However, there are
            // possibly still objects left in the finalization queue.
            // We might be done after the next pass, assuming
            // we don't see any new finalizable objects in the domain.
            noUnloadedObjectsRegistered = TRUE;
        } else {
            // We've had 2 passes seeing no objects - we're done.
            GCHeap::UnloadingAppDomain = NULL;
            noUnloadedObjectsRegistered = FALSE;
        }
    } else {
        noUnloadedObjectsRegistered = FALSE;
    }

    // Anyone waiting to drain the queue can now wake up.  Note that there is a
    // race in that another thread starting a drain, as we leave a drain, may
    // consider itself satisfied by the drain that just completed.  This is
    // acceptable.
    SetEvent(GCHeap::hEventFinalizerDone);
}
```

Note that reclamation will require at least two garbage collection cycles. On the first pass, objects from the finalization queue that are ready for finalization are detected and marked as ready for finalization. In the interim, the finalization thread becomes active and calls `FinalizeAllObjects`, which ultimately results in a call to the `CallFinalizer` method on the `MethodTable` class. This, in turn, will cause the object's `Finalize` method to be called from the context of the finalizer thread, as shown in Example 7-21. At this point, a future garbage collection will find the dead finalized objects, since all references, both weak and strong, have been eliminated. (The object is no longer in the queues, nor anywhere else in the GC root set.)

Example 7-21. Constructing the call to the finalizer (defined in clr/src/vm/class.cpp)

```
void MethodTable::CallFinalizer(Object *obj)
{
    ARG_SLOT arg = (ARG_SLOT)obj;
    s_FinalizerMD->Call(&arg);
}
```

Since the finalization method is standard, its `MethodDesc` can be shared, and it is stored in a static variable. After many marks and moves, the object is told to eviscerate itself, and life goes on.

There is one final wrinkle to finalization, which has to do with object handles. Objects that are being tracked using weak handles have two options with regard to their finalization behavior. In particular, since there is latency involved with objects resting in the finalization queue, it is possible to resurrect objects that had been eligible for collection. Of course, these objects may or may not have had their Finalize methods called. To give programmers control over this, there are two different flavors of weak handles—*weak short* and *weak long*. Weak long handles are designed to track resurrection, while weak short do not.

In Example 7-22, we revisit the copy_phase method one last time to see how handles are checked (there is similar code in mark_phase). After objects have been left for dead, weak short handles can be cleaned up, and the dead objects must be added to the finalization queue if necessary. This code shows where these bookkeeping activities are performed.

Example 7-22. Finalization housekeeping (extracted from gc_heap::copy_phase in clr/src/vm/gcsmp.cpp)

```
// After promotion check to see whether short weak pointers can be eliminated
CNameSpace::GcShortWeakPtrScan(condemned_gen_number, max_generation, &sc);

// After promotion, check for objects that can now be finalized
finalize_queue->ScanForFinalization (condemned_gen_number, 1, FALSE, __this);
```

Summary

We've seen many ways in which Rotor provides automatic memory management on behalf of managed code. The JIT compiler colludes with the code manager (for stack walking) and the metadata system to track every object reference that exists in code being managed by the execution engine. Any object instance that is in use will have at least one outstanding reference to it; because of this, instances that are no longer needed can be detected by recursively "tracing the roots," or walking all known live references. The difference between the complete set of object references and the set of live references yields garbage, or memory that can be reclaimed.

Rotor uses a hybrid generational copying strategy for memory reclamation. When an object is allocated, the new instance is classified as either a normal object or a large object. Large objects are allocated from a special pool of memory and are managed as a simple linked list. Normal objects are allocated first within the ephemeral generation, a compact heap that uses a fast and simple allocation scheme. Instances with short lifecycles can come and go in this generation during the span of a single collection cycle; since the heap that backs the generation is fully reallocated on every cycle, their memory is reclaimed as old instances are overwritten. To avoid clobbering live objects, any object in the ephemeral generation that is found to be live when collection occurs has new space allocated for it in the elder generation and is relocated. Elder objects are never again moved; objects in this generation that are no longer needed are discovered during tracing and moved onto a freelist, from which their space can be recycled.

The process of finding root references and tracing from them is complex but fascinating. The runtime stack, since it holds variables and parameters (as well as internal object instances such as the security object), is a fertile source of roots. The JIT compiler, as it computes the layout of method activation records, notes where object references will occur in a method's activation record. This information, along with similar information provided by frames on the stack, is used by the garbage collector when it is seeking live objects. The objects themselves can also contain subreferences. When type metadata is loaded and memory layout is computed, the class loader doing the work builds descriptions of the locations at which object references will be found within the type being loaded. This information is used by the garbage collector as it searches for live objects.

The heap used by the garbage collector is also a source of roots. The collector keeps several indexing structures, known as brick tables and card tables, to accelerate the process of scanning the heap for live objects. These indexes are maintained not only during garbage collection, but also at runtime. The JIT compiler assists in this process by emitting code that maintains a write barrier: every time an object reference is assigned a new value from managed code, the emitted code records this fact in the card table on behalf of the garbage collector. Using cards and bricks, the heap can be scanned efficiently.

Other sources of roots are the handle tables that belong to application domains and the finalization queue. During collection, these are visited and scanned for live objects, just as the stack and heap are scanned.

The garbage collector is triggered by resource scarcity (or by programmatic invocation) and begins its search for root objects by suspending the execution of all managed threads. Once all roots have been traced, the garbage collector promotes any surviving ephemeral objects to elder status, updates object references to reflect these relocations, executes finalization code as necessary, and prepares its freelist for further use by the allocator by sweeping any dead objects in the elder generation into it. At this point, execution can be resumed until another collection cycle is triggered.

CHAPTER 8

Interlude: Enabling Component Integration with Metadata

We've now met all of the major actors in the CLI component model. Types, which are programmers' specifications about component structure and behavior, are the core around which the CLI is built. Transforming these types into processor-specific values and weaving these values into the native instruction stream is the runtime task of the CLI's execution engine, and is done using a combination of loaders, runtime services, and the JIT compiler.

In the data-driven world of the CLI, the representation of types constantly unfolds during the process of loading and execution. There is an incremental, but constant, build-up of data associated with types. This build-up is caused by the collaboration between the facilities of the execution engine as type metadata is poked, prodded, transformed, augmented, and annotated. While the CLI lays out data and creates code, and ushers types and their instances through their lifecycles, the execution engine not only consumes metadata, but also produces large volumes of it.

Altering Metadata Representation

Consider the process of moving type information into and out of assemblies. If you carefully examine the code that makes up the metadata implementation, you will discover that there are two completely different codepaths: one for creating and modifying editable metadata, and another for mapping read-only metadata into memory. Programmers know that the existence of two implementations often implies conflicting requirements. In this case, easily editable metadata must take on a radically different runtime shape than the compact, fast-loading, and efficiently searchable metadata that is loaded from disk with assemblies. For editable metadata, the data structures are connected using pointers, since they are frequently altered and rearranged. For read-only metadata, the data is carefully arranged using optimized layouts in advance, since speed and size make all the difference. It makes sense to have multiple views.

As metadata is used throughout the CLI execution engine, additional specialized views are built that augment what is already there. Remember from Chapter 5 that a separation exists between "hot" data that is used constantly at runtime versus "cold" data that is used when compiling methods or reflecting. The organization of metadata within the execution engine, since it is most often used to provide efficient runtime access to type information, bears little resemblance to the assembly metadata from which it is derived. Within an assembly, metadata is structured to be ready to scan and efficient to map from secondary storage directly into memory, while within the execution engine, the same data is factored into a pointer-based graph that facilitates traversal by various execution engine services. The metadata contained in the EEClass and the MethodTable, although derived directly from assembly metadata, has been *transformed*.

Likewise, when a type is loaded, the data that represents its structure is moved from abstract, passive form into a processor-specific form. In this case, the assembly metadata is also actually augmented by the execution engine's built-in knowledge of the local execution environment. For example, native byte order and processor word length are pieces of knowledge that the execution engine implementation adds to the original processor-independent metadata to give more specific context.

Transforming Metadata in the CLI

The sequence of annotation, transformation, and continuous refinement results in constant production of metadata and interpretation of that metadata. As we mentioned in Chapter 1, this sequence defines a data-driven architecture, onto which it is easy to graft new services. The integration costs of a data-driven architecture for extensibility are low compared to one based on API definitions, and since component integration is the most important feature enabled by the CLI specification, a data-driven architecture is the right choice for the task. Using this approach, one subsystem's data becomes another subsystem's executable code. (The programming community has known this since the fifties, and it is as good an idea now as it was then.)

Figure 8-1 shows some of the transformations and augmentations that occur in the SSCLI. Starting from the left, an abstract type, written as code in a high-level programming language, is transformed by a high-level compiler into CIL and type metadata, which is bundled into an assembly. After this, file loaders, module loaders, and class loaders sequentially transform an on-disk PE file to an in-memory structure that is optimized for the JIT compiler and the execution engine. With these structures in place, the JIT compiler can produce native code from the intermediate representation.

Unlike traditional compilers, a JIT compiler makes decisions in the context of the current execution environment; as it generates native code it also verifies for typesafety and makes layout decisions. It enriches already present in-memory data structures with new information for the code access security engine, the garbage collector, and the exception-handling mechanism.

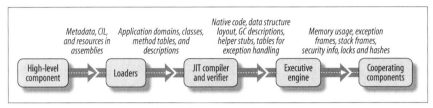

Figure 8-1. The CLI's sequential transformation and augmentation of types.

Once native code has been produced, this code is executed under the control of the execution engine. The execution engine continues to annotate the type, maintaining information about its memory use and injecting frames and exception handlers into the runtime stack. The runtime bookkeeping, of course, is based on information that was originally provided by the high-level language compiler, the loaders, and the JIT compiler. The execution engine simply builds on what was available. As components are created and referenced by other components, the execution engine allocates and tracks resources for their use, cleans up after their demise (whether clean or exceptional), and protects them from one another.

The chain of metadata augmentation and annotation does not need to stop at this point. In fact, two of the most useful runtime services in the CLI, serialization and remoting, extend it even further.

Serializing Components by Using Metadata

To many programmers, the task of serializing component state is numbingly familiar. Every time that a component needs to be "saved," whether for preservation in a database, for transmission via XML, or for the purposes of copying the component into another process, its state needs to be squirreled away. In the past, this was often a manual process, despite the repetitive nature and highly structured characteristics of the task. Each component needed custom (and bug-prone) code to move its state from memory into a stream or a file; this code was typically matched to a separate routine that could read the saved state back into a new object during the process of reconstituting the original object.

The act of transforming a component's data so that it can be transferred or saved is often called *externalization*. In the CLI, thanks to the presence of metadata, externalization has become considerably easier. To convert a component instance (or graph of instances) into some storage-oriented format, an automatic serialization service only needs to examine the member types of the component and apply a set of generic *pickling* routines to these members to move their values in and out of storage. When pickling values in this way, moving state from a component instance into storage is typically called *serialization*, and when moving state from storage back into an instance, *deserialization*. The service that performs both serialization and deserialization in the SSCLI is implemented in the System.Runtime. Serialization namespace, and features a set of types that have been engineered to provide pickling via Formatter objects and serialization via the ISerialize interface and the Serializable custom attribute.

Creating Proxies Using Metadata

Besides having the information needed to externalize component state, the execution engine also has enough metadata to create proxy objects, which mimic other objects by conforming to the type signature of the object that they mimic. Instead of implementing type-specific behavior, proxies generically forward any and all operations to other objects, as shown in Figure 8-2.

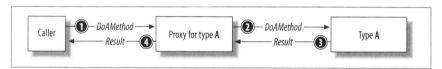

Figure 8-2. Forwarding proxy objects can be created automatically using metadata.

In Figure 8-2, a proxy object forwards operations to a "real" instance of its underlying type. By doing this, the proxy appears to behave exactly as though it were an instance of the underlying type. Proxy objects such as this are frequently used in distributed computing to provide location transparency. The proxies stand in for remote object instances that cannot or should not be moved, giving the impression that local instances exist. The SSCLI has a complete remoting subsystem, including support for this kind of transparency. The code is complicated but worth examining; generic behavior can be automatically provided by using metadata to create fields and methods that stand in for their remote counterparts.

Even when running in a single process, proxies are used to provide isolation between application domains in the SSCLI. The implementation of a proxy lives in code implemented as part of the execution engine, and because of this, the SSCLI can rely on it to stand between instances that reside in different domains and enforce safe separation.

Types are always loaded in the context of an application domain, and that application domain serves to isolate type implementations from one another. Isolation itself is implemented by using frames on the stack to mark transitions, by enforcing code access security, and by automatically emitting special code that creates and uses proxy-based communication. With remoting barriers in place, components can communicate safely without leaving themselves vulnerable to faults or malicious behavior.

Metadata in Action

The thing that programmers spend the most time doing today is jiggering and adapting code for the purposes of integration: moving from format to format, from place to place, from API to API, or from operating system to operating system. Programming was once largely about algorithms and clever performance tricks, but in today's connected world in which programs are built by combining third-party components, it is much more about mapping, copying, integrating, and communicating intelligibly.

Rich, runtime-available metadata makes it possible to do such operations automatically, by "rule." On the surface, this would seem to be a statement about programmer productivity, but it is actually deeper, since metadata standards enable meaningful communications in an extensible way. By providing standard ways to refer to types and behaviors across processor types and across time (i.e., across versions), the CLI enables stable interoperability, and once stable interoperability is available, large component ecosystems can and will form.

CHAPTER 9

The Platform Adaptation Layer

Portability is a key design goal for Rotor. To achieve portability, all of the code in the distribution is written against an API layer, called the Platform Adaptation Layer (PAL), which hides the differences between underlying operating systems and provides consistent operating semantics. Since Rotor started life as a large Win32 application, it should come as no surprise that the PAL mimics a subset of the Win32 API. Only the subset absolutely required by the SSCLI and its supporting tools is implemented, however, which means that there is does not need to be any support for graphics, most of COM, the Windows registry, Active Directory, or other features commonly used by Windows programmers.

This chapter, rather than act as a comprehensive catalog of the PAL's nooks and crannies, will instead visit the areas most crucial to understanding the CLI mechanisms described in earlier chapters, since Rotor's runtime infrastructure heavily depends on the operating systems constructs provided by the PAL. In Chapter 6, for example, the sections "Threads," "Synchronizing Concurrent Access to Components," and "Handling Component Exceptions" referred repeatedly to the PAL's threading and synchronization model, as well as its structured exception-handling facilities. Chapter 7, in its discussion of "Organizing and Allocating Dynamic Memory," highlighted the reliance of Rotor's heaps on virtual memory (and how different uses of virtual memory features can impact application performance). By examining the PAL implementation from an internal perspective, the implications of design choices made in higher-level code should become clearer.

PAL Overview

The PAL is actually two things: a specification and an implementation of that specification. The specification, located in *docs/techinfo/pal_guide.html*, describes the minimum subset of the Win32 API that a PAL implementation must provide. (Writing a richer PAL would be fine, but the code in Rotor wouldn't care.) It also specifies, on a per-API basis, which features of a function need to be implemented.

Those who need to understand the PAL specification in detail will need to read it with a copy of Microsoft's MSDN documentation near at hand. The PAL specification is written to call out differences in behavior from the baseline Win32 API rather than as a standalone description of correct behaviors.

In addition to the PAL, Rotor includes the code for a dynamically loadable library referred to as the *PAL runtime*, which implements a number of additional Win32 APIs. These implementations do not depend on the hosting operating system; they are completely implemented within their library and do not need to interact with external resources. Since they are self-contained, they do not need to be reimplemented for each new PAL; they are essentially internal support functions for the SSCLI implementation.

The Rotor distribution provides two PAL implementations: one for Win32 (XP and Windows 2000) and one for Unix operating systems that has been ported and tested on FreeBSD (Versions 4.5–4.7) and Mac OS X (Version 10.2).

Could another Win32 API layer or emulator be used to support Rotor? The PAL specification calls out the Win32 APIs that must be implemented in order for Rotor to run correctly, and the existence of two distinct implementations in the code has proven that this approach works. In theory, other Win32 layers could be linked against Rotor to replace the PAL, although it is highly likely that many bugs and subtle compatibility problems would have to be fixed to make this work. PAL-specific functions would also have to be implemented, and the Rotor build process modified, to accommodate this change. Nonetheless, another new PAL implementation could certainly be created by adapting code from other sources.

One might question why a PAL is provided for Win32, since the API is literally a subset of the Win32 API plus a small number of additional functions. There are four reasons:

PAL-specific APIs

There are 20 APIs in the PAL that are not in Win32 at all. These APIs can be identified by the PAL_ prefix to their names. Good examples of these APIs are the `PAL_Initialize` and `PAL_Terminate` APIs, located in *pal/win32/win32.c.* These APIs are called by the program hosting the PAL before the first and after the last PAL API is used, and encapsulate startup and termination tasks.

More portable abstractions

In several cases, Win32 does not provide a distinct and separable set of APIs for a given task, although the task is needed within the CLI implementation. For this small number of cases, it made sense to construct new abstractions in the PAL layer. `PAL_Random` and `PAL_GetUserConfigurationDirectory` are two examples of this approach.

Development conveniences

During the development of the SSCLI, having a PAL allowed the development team to catch cases in which code was inadvertently using functionality that was outside the PAL specification, through the use of parameter validation in the checked build. The code to do this was left in the Win32 PAL so that anyone making future modifications to the SSCLI could do the same kinds of validation on their own modifications.

Event logging

One extremely powerful debugging technique for a complex system, such as the SSCLI, is to log important events that occur during execution to narrow down the source of a problem. The development team implemented a logging mechanism in both the Win32 and the Unix PALs to assist in debugging failures.

An important design point for the PAL was that, with the exception of C runtime calls, calls from the SSCLI should flow through the PAL before using operating system resources, making it a place where impedance-matching code could be placed. The thickness of this impedance-matching code varies, depending on the services offered by an underlying operating system and how closely they match the semantics specified by the PAL. Not surprisingly, the Win32 PAL is quite thin, while the Unix PAL is much more substantial. Unless otherwise noted, the remaining sections of this chapter refer to the Unix PAL.

Common Infrastructure

Before going through the sections of the PAL that support the subsystems already discussed in this book, two areas need to be explored that are important plumbing details but not directly seen by PAL consumers: *shared memory* and the *handle manager*. Remember that although the PAL is represented by an API, the API has code behind it that manages operating system resources on behalf of the programmer. In the case of the Unix PAL, the visibility of Windows resources is very different than the visibility of resources within the Unix process hierarchy. To implement the looser Windows semantics, shared memory is used by the Unix PAL to make data available to any Unix process that is using the services of the CLI execution engine. A set of one or more processes that share a shared memory segment in the Unix PAL are referred to collectively as a *PAL process group*.

> The term "process group" can be confusing, since a process group does not always need to consist of multiple Unix processes. In fact, it is normal for a single Rotor PAL process to live within a single Unix process. Even when this is the case, we will refer to this singleton process as a process group in an effort to differentiate PAL processes, Unix processes, and shared process groups.

Many of the Win32 resources within a PAL process group are represented to programmers using opaque handles. Handles are used as parameters to the calls that manipulate them, such as `WriteFile` or `SuspendThread`. (Not all APIs use handles. The WinSock API, for example, exposes and manages its own opaque token, called a *socket*.) The handle manager tracks the handles that are in use, and maintains the associations between internal data structures and their handles.

Sharing Memory Between Unix Processes

A PAL process group uses a segment of shared memory to share its state between Unix processes. A debugger, for example, might need to share operating system state with the managed processes under its control. The PAL would use its shared memory as a shared database of system resources to support this scenario. (There is also a small amount of shared configuration information that can be computed directly and does not need to occupy shared memory.) Figure 9-1 shows how sharing is implemented for a single PAL process group.

There are a number of structures that are stored in the shared memory:

SHMPROCESS
> Defined in *pal/unix/thread/process.h*, this is used to keep track of PAL processes that are members of a process group.

SHM_NAMED_OBJECTS
> This is a list of named objects associated with a given PAL process group. (See the later section "The Handle Manager" in this chapter for a discussion.)

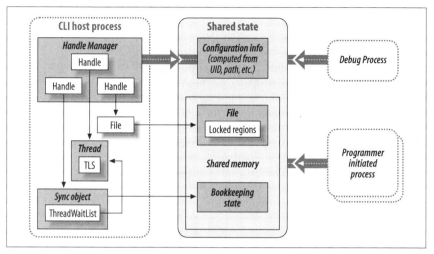

Figure 9-1. Many operating system processes may share a single PAL process group and its shared memory segment.

SHMFILELOCKS
> Defined in *pal/unix/include/pal/file.h*, this is used to keep track of access rights to open files associated with a PAL process group.

HREMOTEOBJSTRUCT
> This is used by the handle manager and can be found in *pal/unix/handlemgr/handle.c*.

GLOBAL_FILE_MAPPING_OBJECT
> Found in *pal/unix/map/map.c*, this enables other processes to access memory-mapped objects.

GLOBAL_EVENT_SYSTEM_OBJECT
> This is used when working with events to access named events from other processes. It can be found in *pal/unix/sync/event.h*.

GLOBAL_MUTEX_SYSTEM_OBJECT
> Defined in *pal/unix/include/pal/mutex.h*, this is used to make mutexes accessible to other processes.

The implementation of shared memory can be found in *pal/unix/shmemory/shemory.c*. It is based on the Unix mmap system call. Access to shared memory is controlled by a *lockfile* (see SHMInitialize) and a *spinlock* mechanism (see SHMLock and SHMRelease). Each PAL process that joins a process group is responsible for determining whether shared memory has been initialized.

Processes hosting the Unix PAL will share the same memory segment if they are run using the same dynamically loaded library and a matching user ID. The uid at the time that the process was launched, along with the inode of *librotor_pal.so* on FreeBSD, or librotor_pal.dylib on Mac OS X, determine this. PAL processes don't need to have an ancestor/child relationship to share their state. As long as the same uid is used to launch them and the same *librotor_pal* runs both, they use the same shared-memory region.

How Much to Share?

The criteria that determine when a PAL is shared, the user ID and the library's *inode*, may not be appropriate for all situations. The current settings keep different implementations of the PAL and their users quite isolated, which is good for experimentation during development. Security settings are also scoped to user identity (as can be seen in the code for the *caspol* utility), which is an important factor.

If the SSCLI were to be used in other settings, it might make sense to make its PAL more shared, perhaps by dropping its user ID partitioning.

A file to back the shared-memory region is created from within the SHMInitialize call, which uses PALGetPalConfigDir to find the directory in which to place this file. The config directory itself comes from INIT_ InitPalConfigDir in *pal/unix/init/pal.c*, which creates directories that follow a */tmp/.rotor-pal-<uid>-<inode>* convention.

Once a PAL process has been initialized, SHMLock enters a critical section (discussed in "Synchronizing Processes and Threads") to ensure that only one of the process' threads is attempting to obtain the lock. Having obtained the critical section, it then calls InterlockedCompareExchange (defined in *pal/unix/ arch/<architecture>/interlock.c*) on a spinlock located in the shared-memory header. If the spinlock is set to 0, no one holds it; otherwise, it will contain the process ID of the lock holder. If some other process holds the lock, SHMLock will loop, testing the value until the lock is released. To enable other threads and processes to run without waiting, the code makes calls to the operating system to yield its time to other processes. SHMRelease simply resets the spinlock to 0 and releases the critical section obtained in the SHMLock code.

The use of a spinlock might seem like an odd choice; why not use a SysV mutex instead? Originally, this was the design choice, but on FreeBSD 4.5, the mutex implementation is not pthread-friendly. When any thread in the process blocked on a SysV mutex, the kernel would stop scheduling the entire process until the mutex was unblocked. The spinlock code works correctly on all platforms, but there is a good efficiency argument to be made for looking for better mechanisms on other platforms.

The PAL's shared memory segment is structured as a series of segments, as shown in Figure 9-2, to which pointers can be found in shm_segment_bases in *shmemory.c*.

Each segment contains a SHM_SEGMENT_HEADER, which contains the name of the next segment and an array of pointers that reflect the beginnings and ends of memory pools within the segment. There are four different memory pools in each segment, one each for 16-, 32-, 64-, and 520-byte objects. (520 is twice the value of Windows' MAX_PATH, so long Unicode strings used for pathnames will fit in a buffer of this size. The mismatch between Unix and Windows maximum path lengths might cause problems; this is something to be aware of.) The total size of each of these pools is determined when the segment is added to the shared memory region; initially, the calculation in SHMInitialize divides the available memory in the segment evenly between each of the pools. Subsequent additions in SHMAddSegment allocate memory to each pool in a new segment using the ratio of memory currently in use by all pools in all other segments that contain the same-sized objects. Once allocated, the pool size in a segment cannot be changed. Since each pool contains fixed-sized objects, once the pool size is set and the end pointer is established, the memory manager can treat the pool as an array of fixed-size elements.

The first segment is distinguished from any that follow, because it contains three additional pieces of information in memory after its SHM_SEGMENT_ HEADER. The first of these is the location where the segment's spinlock can be found. After this, for each of the pools, an array header points to the size-specific free block lists. Finally, there is an array of pointers to linked lists containing the three classes of data stored in shared memory: SHMPROCESS, SHM_NAMED_OBJECTS, and SHMFILELOCKS.

The free lists are created initially when pools are reserved for each segment. If a block is free, it contains a next pointer to another free block (which is initially the next item in the pool). When subsequent segments are allocated, the additional pools that they contain are added to this list. A count

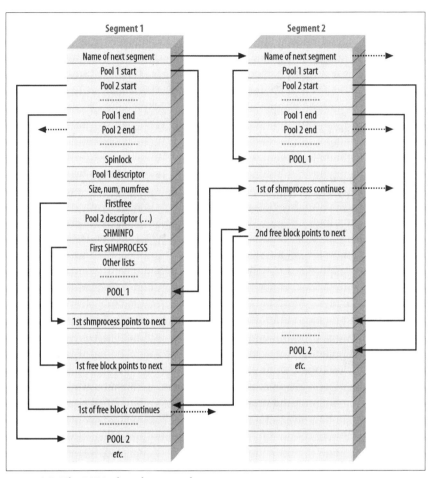

Figure 9-2. The PAL's shared-memory layout.

of free items in each pool across all segments is also maintained as part of the SHM_POOL_INFO structure in the first segment, which is shown in Example 9-1.

Example 9-1. The structure of a shared-memory pool (defined in pal/unix/shmemory/ shmemory.c)

```
typedef struct
{
 int item_size;    /* size of 1 block, in bytes */
 int num_items;    /* total number of blocks in the pool */
 int free_items;   /* number of unused items in the pool */
 SHMPTR first_free; /* location of first available block in the pool */
} SHM_POOL_INFO;
```

When an allocation is requested, SHMalloc determines which pool's item_ size will be large enough to contain the allocation and then consults the number of free_items in that pool. If free blocks exist, the block at the head of the list is returned and the number of free blocks is decreased. Otherwise a new segment is allocated. (It is important to note that the SHMPTR that is returned actually contains two pieces of data: the segment ID from which the allocation came and the offset into the segment. Thus, the pointer cannot be used directly, but instead must be dereferenced through the macro SHMPTR_TO_PTR.)

For SHMFree, the SHMPTR is first decomposed to recover the segment to which the allocation belongs. After this, a series of sanity checks are performed on the SHMPTR's offset to ensure that the block was actually handed out by the shared-memory allocator and to identify the pool to which it belongs. The block is inserted as the first free block in the free block list, the current head pointer is injected into the freed block as a next pointer, and the head pointer is updated. Finally, the number of free blocks is increased by 1.

The linked lists of SMHPROCESS, SHM_NAMED_OBJECTS, and SHMFILELOCKS are each built by the respective portions of the PAL that store these data structures. The array in the first segment is provided for their use—no other portion of the shared memory keeps track of those lists.

The Handle Manager

The PAL makes extensive use of handles to identify the resources that the PAL creates, operates on, and destroys. The HANDLE data type is defined in *pal/rotor_pal.h* as a void*, to be opaque. The consumer of a HANDLE does not need to understand what backing data structure the HANDLE refers to—but only that it is an identifier for the object in question. The PAL itself can internally disambiguate the type of a handle by examining the type field in the handle header, as shown in Example 9-2.

Example 9-2. The HOBJSTRUCT used to represent PAL handles, along with their valid types (defined in pal/unix/include/pal/handle.h)

```
typedef enum
{
  HOBJ_PROCESS,
  HOBJ_THREAD,
  HOBJ_FILE,
  HOBJ_MAP,
  HOBJ_SEMAPHORE,
  HOBJ_EVENT,
  HOBJ_MUTEX,
  HOBJ_LAST,      // this is not a type, it is a convenience value
```

Example 9-2. The HOBJSTRUCT used to represent PAL handles, along with their valid types (defined in pal/unix/include/pal/handle.h) (continued)

```
} HOBJTYPE;

struct _HOBJSTRUCT
{
 HOBJTYPE type;
 /* callback functions for type-specific work */
 DUPHANDLEFUNC  dup_handle;
 CLOSEHANDLEFUNC close_handle;
};
```

The handle manager, located in *pal/unix/handlemgr/handle.c*, is responsible for tracking handles and their backing data. At the core of the handle manager is an array, handle_table, of HANDLE_SLOT structures. Each HANDLE_SLOT contains three fields: a pointer to the HOBJSTRUCT shown in Example 9-2, a lockcount used to track the number of times that the handle has been locked so that it is not incorrectly deleted or modified, and a field named closing used to signal when the handle is being closed.

To generate the value for a handle, the index into handle_table is offset by 1 and multiplied by 4, duplicating the Win32 semantics in which all handles are multiples of 4, and 0 represents a null handle. Using this scheme, the handle code can easily convert a handle into an index in handle_table. The macros HANDLE_TO_INDEX and INDEX_TO_HANDLE perform this conversion.

The HOBJSTRUCT structure has a type field of HOBJTYPE, which enumerates all possible resource types: PROCESS, THREAD, FILE, MAP, SEMAPHORE, EVENT, and MUTEX. For each handle type, there is a corresponding structure defined in the portion of the PAL that deals with that type, such as the MUTEX_HANDLE_OBJECT. Each of these data structures defines an HOBJSTRUCT as its first field. By doing this, any of these structures may be cast to an HOBJSTRUCT, and the handle code does not need to know anything about their details.

The two additional fields in HOBJSTRUCT, close_handle and dup_handle, contain function pointers used to close the resource and duplicate the handle. These functions are supplied by the subsystem in the PAL that defines the type-specific handle. Again, code does not need to understand the details of each handle type to close or duplicate handles. It simply defers to a PAL subsystem using the helper functions provided. (This is good, old-fashioned ANSI C object-oriented code. Perhaps C++ is good for something after all.)

Handles are allocated in a way that helps catch bugs that arise from handle recycling (which are characterized by code that frees a handle, allocates another, and depends on the second to be the same as the first). The allocator maintains a singly linked list of free handles in the handle table; the head is in free_handle_list and free_handle_list_tail is the final element. These values hold indexes in the handle_table array. Handles on the free list use the object field to hold the index in the next free element in the list.

Initially, all handles are on the free list. When a handle is allocated, the handle at the head of the list is used, and the object field points to a resource-specific handle data structure. When a handle is released, it is placed at the tail of the linked list. The allocation and freeing of the resource-specific handle data structure is the responsibility of the PAL subsystem responsible for the resource in question.

As with Win32, the opening or creation of a handle occurs during a resource-specific API, such as OpenFile. Duplication and closing, as we have seen, are general routines. (Not every handle can be duplicated. The PAL specification calls out those that can be.) Handles are closed when their lock_count, maintained by HMGRLockHandle/HMGRUnlockHandle, reaches 0 and their closing flag is set. The actual call to the handle-specific close_handle routine is made by HMGRUnlockHandle. If there are any handles still open when HMGRStopHandleManager is called during PAL shutdown, the corresponding close_handle calls are made unconditionally.

Processes and Threads

The SSCLI provides a rich set of threading features to the developer, and because of this, it makes some heavy demands on the operating system beneath its PAL. The PAL specification requires support for:

- Process creation
- Process termination
- Process exit code access
- Interprocess memory access
- Interprocess communication using memory mapping
- Interprocess communication using events
- Inheritance of standard handles through process creation

Between the C runtime, POSIX system calls, and *pthreads* (the POSIX threads package), the Unix PAL has most of what it needs to implement these features on Mac OS X and FreeBSD.

PAL Processes

The model for process isolation in the PAL is simple: each process created is mapped to an underlying operating system process. The first process is created by a program that wishes to host the PAL, which can then create additional subordinate processes by calling CreateProcess. (CreateProcess, as with many Win32 APIs, comes in two related flavors: CreateProcessA for use with ANSI string arguments and CreateProcessW for use with Unicode string arguments.) The API ensures that the executable file being used is either a valid CLI PE file or else a native executable. If it is a CLI executable, the name of the application launcher, clix, is prepended to the command line. From there, the Unix PAL uses fork to create the new process and execve to launch it, inheriting standard filehandles if requested.

Information about processes is divided between two important data structures defined in *pal/unix/thread/process.h*: the PROCESS and the SHMPROCESS. Processes also contain an additional structure, INITIALPROCINFO, which contains the command line and current directory used to launch the process. One PROCESS structure is allocated for the initial process, as well as for each Win32 process that is created via a call to CreateProcess or OpenProcess. The SHMPROCESS structure is shared across the PAL process, primarily for the use of debuggers, and so it is allocated in shared memory and reference-counted. (It is deleted by the closeProcessHandle helper when all outstanding references are removed.) Each PROCESS structure contains a pointer to its corresponding SHMPROCESS structure.

All of these relationships are demonstrated in Figure 9-3, which shows two Unix processes, one subordinate to the other, sharing a single PAL process group. Process 1 belongs to the program hosting the PAL, while Process 2 was created with a call to CreateProcess. Within Process 2, there are two process handles pointing to the same PROCESS, implying a call to DuplicateHandle.

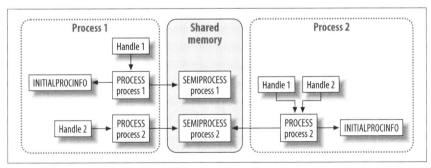

Figure 9-3. The relationship of PROCESS, INITIALPROCINFO, and SHMPROCESS.

The first PROCESS within a program hosting the PAL is created by a call to PAL_Initialize, which in turn calls PROCCreateInitialProcess to set up necessary scaffolding within a hosting process. Initialization can be performed automatically on Unix by including the header file *clr/src/inc/palstartup.h*. Using simple macrology, this header file redefines the main entrypoint as PAL_startup_main and then interposes its own main function, shown in Example 9-3, which takes care of initialization and that the PAL_Terminate function will be called when the process exits. Lastly, this function does is chain to the "real" main from within a call to exit, which executes the hosting program transparently.

Example 9-3. The PAL is initialized by hooking a hosting program's main entrypoint (defined in clr/src/inc/palstartup.h)

```
int __cdecl main(int argc, char **argv) {
 if (PAL_Initialize(argc, argv)) {
  return 1;
 }
 atexit((void (__cdecl *)(void)) PAL_Terminate);
 exit(PAL_startup_main(argc, argv));
 return 0;
}
```

Looking at the PROCESS structure itself, which is reproduced in Example 9-4, notice how the HOBJSTRUCT header for this handle is embedded as the first element of the structure. This layout technique of beginning with the handle header, which enables easy access via casting and was discussed in the section entitled "The Handle Manager," is used throughout the PAL for entities represented by handles.

Example 9-4. The PROCESS structure is used to track Unix processes associated with the PAL (defined in pal/unix/thread/process.h)

```
typedef struct _PROCESS
{
 HOBJSTRUCT  objHeader;
 HANDLE      hProcess;
 DWORD       dwMagic;
 DWORD       processId;
 DWORD       refCount;
 CRITICAL_SECTION critSection;
 INITIALPROCINFO *lpInitProcInfo;

 SHMPROCESS *shmprocess;
 PROCESS_STATE state;
 DWORD       exit_code;
} PROCESS;
```

Within the PROCESS structure, the handle's type will always be HOBJ_PROCESS, and its type-specific close and duplicate helper routines will be closeProcessHandle and dupProcessHandle, which can be found in *pal/unix/thread/process.c*. The handle manager is called to assign the actual handle value found in hProcess, as follows:

```
lpProcess->hProcess = HMGRGetHandle((HOBJSTRUCT *) lpProcess);
```

To track the underlying process, the processID field contains the value returned by getpid. Calls to the PAL API GetCurrentProcessID return this field directly. The refCount field is used to keep track of the number of references to a process, and is increased by calls to dupProcessHandle and decremented by closeProcessHandle. Once the refCount goes to 0, the underlying process is freed.

The exit_code and state fields are used to implement the routine GetExitCodeProcess. The PAL uses the system routine waitpid to obtain the exit code of a child process. The catch is that once a process has exited, waitpid may only be called once. If the data is needed at some later time, it must be stored. Since Win32 allows a PAL consumer to call GetExitCodeProcess on a process handle as often as it likes, the implementation of this API first checks the state field, which it uses to determine whether an exit code has been cached in the exit_code field. If the state is set to PS_DONE, the exit_code field already contains the exit code for the process. Otherwise, exit_code is filled by calling waitpid in nonblocking mode, as shown in Example 9-5.

Example 9-5. Retrieving a process exit code (Extracted from pal/unix/thread/process.c)

```
wait_retval = waitpid(process->processId, &status, WNOHANG);

if ( wait_retval == process->processId ) {
 /* success; get the exit code */
 if ( WIFEXITED( status ) ) {
  *exit_code = WEXITSTATUS(status);
 } else {
  *exit_code = EXIT_FAILURE;
 }
 *state = PS_DONE;
}
```

Finally, the dwMagic field within the PROCESS structure deserves some explanation. A field of this name is used to perform validity checking, not only for processes, but also for threads, semaphores, and events. Each has a dwMagic field following its HOBJSTRUCT header and each sets the dwMagic field to a known value that is unique for its type—PROCESS_MAGIC in the case of a process object. When the Unix system entity that they track is no longer valid, their dwMagic field will be set to NULL.

The dwMagic field is checked by type-specific routines named isValid*systype*Object. These routines check that the dwMagic field is non-NULL and that it matches the known value for the type, and are called before operations that depend on the underlying system object being valid.

Controlling PAL Processes

Once a PAL process has been created, it can be further manipulated using the Win32 process APIs that are implemented as part of the PAL. These include GetCurrentProcess, OpenProcess, ExitProcess, and TerminateProcess.

GetCurrentProcess returns the handle of the current process. Following the definition of this API in the PAL specification, the handle that is returned is a special handle that the PAL recognizes as the current process. The handle's value is taken from the variable hPseudoCurrentProcess and has the value 0xFFFFFF01.

In the PAL API subset, OpenProcess is used only to support debuggers or other development tools. (If you are not building tools, you will probably never need to call it.) Given a processID, OpenProcess will return a process handle that can then be used with other APIs. Only PAL processes within the same process group may be opened in this way. The SHMPROCESS structures for a process group are searched, and if a matching process is found, a new PROCESS structure is created, the refcount is incremented, and the process handle is returned.

ExitProcess is the main PAL function for shutting down a process cleanly and is shown in Example 9-6.

Example 9-6. ExitProcess is the main PAL shutdown function (summarized from pal/unix/threads/process.c)

```
ExitProcess(IN UINT uExitCode)
{
 DWORD old_terminator;
 old_terminator = InterlockedCompareExchange(&terminator,
                      GetCurrentThreadId( ),0);

 if(GetCurrentThreadId( ) == old_terminator) {
  if (!PALIsInitialized( )) {
   exit(uExitCode);
  } else {
   PROCEndProcess(GetCurrentProcess( ), uExitCode, FALSE);
  }
 } else if(0 != old_terminator) {
  // If another thread ending process, sleep for a really long time
  poll(NULL,0,INFTIM);
 }

 if ( PALInitLock() && PALIsInitialized( ) ) {
  PROCQueueDllMainCalls( );
  LOADCallDllMain(DLL_THREAD_DETACH);
  PROCEndProcess(GetCurrentProcess( ), uExitCode, FALSE);
 } else {
  exit(uExitCode);
```

Example 9-6. ExitProcess is the main PAL shutdown function (summarized from pal/unix/ threads/process.c) (continued)

```
}

/* this should never get executed */
PALInitUnlock( );
}
```

A normal exit begins with the highlighted call to PROCQueueDllMainCalls, which ensures that DLL_THREAD_DETACH events are posted to each dynamically loaded library. (Note that there is no guarantee that these events will actually be received by the libraries on any thread besides the calling thread, as the PAL specification makes clear.) After this, the DllMain entry point for each library is called directly with DLL_PROCESS_DETACH as a parameter. Finally, TerminateProcess is called from within PROCEndProcess.

TerminateProcess is a simple routine, whose real work is done in a call to PROCCleanupProcess, which first corrals other threads in the process by suspending them (discussed later in "Suspending and Resuming PAL Threads"). After the process' threads are under control, any libraries loaded through LoadLibrary and still resident are unloaded, all mutexes are abandoned, and PALShutdown is called. Having successfully shut down the PAL, HMGRStopHandleManager is invoked to stop the handle manager and close any currently open handles, and finally SHMCleanup is called to shut down access to shared memory and remove the current process from the list of client processes that make up the PAL process group.

TerminateProcess is a lower-level entry point and should be used by PAL consumers only in extreme situations where immediate exit with no cleanup is required. Internally, TerminateProcess is used when a critical error occurs for which the only solution is to kill off the process.

Threads

Rotor's C# frameworks depend on the CLI's threaded execution model for concurrency, and the Rotor implementation itself makes heavy internal use of threads within the execution engine and within its build tools. The semantics of threading, however, vary widely from operating system to operating system. The PAL takes care of hiding these differences beneath a single set of APIs.

Like PAL processes, PAL threads have a one-to-one correspondence with an underlying thread. The Unix PAL uses the pthreads library for this purpose, backing each PAL thread with a matching pthread. Although the pthreads library provides a solid basis, there are a number of areas in which the PAL's threading requirements differ from the features provided by the pthreads package, including interthread synchronization. There are also Win32 features for which there are no pthread equivalents, such as queued Asynchronous Procedure Calls (APCs). To support the additional features demanded by the PAL specification, a fairly thick layer of code wraps and extends the pthreads package within the Unix PAL.

The representation of PAL threads within the PAL is very similar to the representation of PAL processes. The thread itself has a THREAD structure that contains its state and that begins with an HOBJSTRUCT followed by a handle and a dwMagic field. Also contained in this struct is a field named dwThreadID, which is used to store the pthread's thread identity number, and a field to contain the thread's current THREAD_STATE, named thread_state. Valid thread states are defined as follows:

TS_STARTING
A thread with this state is being created. It is used for debugging purposes.

TS_RUNNING
A thread with this state is in the normal running state.

TS_FAILED
This state is used to indicate that a thread has failed initialization. It is used as an internal signal between CreateThread and the worker function THREADEntry (whose use is described shortly, in the discussion of CreateThread).

TS_DONE
A thread with this state has finished executing and is either being destroyed or has been destroyed. It is used to prevent reentrancy problems that would result from other threads accessing its state during destruction and to keep the THREAD structure alive after the destruction of its underlying pthread so that its exit code can be retrieved.

TS_DUMMY
This special state indicates that the THREAD represents a process as a whole rather than a pthread. The PAL uses this type of thread when creating a process that starts in a suspended state.

Much like GetCurrentProcess, the PAL reserves a special handle to represent the current thread, which has a value of 0xFFFFFF03 and is stored in the variable hPseudoCurrentThread. This handle is returned by the GetCurrentThread API.

Threads are created using the CreateThread API, which is actually implemented as two mutually dependent, but distinct, functions:

THREADCreateThread and THREADEntry. The first of these is called directly, allocating and initializing a THREAD structure and handle and requesting that a platform-specific thread be created on its behalf. The second function, however, is not called directly. Instead, it is called from the new thread once it has been spawned. THREADEntry allocates and initializes any runtime resources that must be associated with the context of the new thread.

There are three reasons for creating threads using this two-step mechanism:

Thread-specific initialization
> Some of the thread initialization sequence needs to occur prior to a new pthread being created, while other parts must occur in the new thread's context, such as the initial setup for structured exception handling.

Initially suspended threads
> The pthread_create function does not support creating threads in a suspended state. To implement this feature for the PAL, there needs to be point at which control can be suspended before any client code is run.

Graceful failure
> While some of the code in THREADCreateThread could migrate to THREADEntry, the general strategy is to do work that might need to be undone prior to creating the actual pthread. In this way, backing out of THREADCreateThread remains as simple as possible.

Once a thread has been created, it is scheduled based on its priority. Mapping the PAL's concept of thread priority to the POSIX thread priority scheme takes a little work. PAL thread priorities run from THREAD_PRIORITY_IDLE to THREAD_PRIORITY_TIME_CRITICAL (which correspond to the integer range −15 to 15). In the POSIX world, however, there are no fixed minimum and maximum thread priorities. Instead, a thread runs with a scheduling policy that has its own concept of minimum and maximum priority. To map the Win32 approach onto the POSIX approach, SetThreadPriority retrieves the underlying pthread's scheduling policy as well as its minimum and maximum limits. The requested PAL priority is then normalized against the reported range and added to the minimum pthread priority. The underlying pthread is updated with the normalized number, while the originally requested (nonnormalized) thread priority is stored in the threadPriority field in the THREAD.

PAL threads, like PAL processes, can either exit gracefully (via ExitThread) or be terminated abruptly (via TerminateCurrentThread). ExitThread calls DllMain for each loaded library with a parameter value of DLL_THREAD_DETACH and cleans up other runtime structures, such as the thread's hostent structure (used by the networking code). As with processes, most of the real work of ExitThread is performed by the lower-level termination function. In

TerminateCurrentThread, outstanding mutexes are abandoned, support buffers are freed, and threads that are waiting on the thread being terminated are removed from the waiting thread list and are awakened. After these tasks have been performed, the number of remaining threads in the process is checked, and if the thread being terminated is the final thread, TerminateCurrentProcess is called. Otherwise, the thread is removed from the list of threads in the process, and the thread-specific data that remains is cleaned up. As with all handle-based objects, the thread data structure does not disappear automatically—if there are outstanding references to the object, it remains allocated until the final reference is released (or until the process closes).

Thread Local Storage

Thread Local Storage (TLS) is a useful feature that allows a PAL consumer to associate data with a particular thread, so it can be retrieved later in that thread's context. To use TLS, a programmer requests a slot by calling TlsAlloc. If a slot is available, an LPVOID-sized piece of memory is allocated in each thread in the process, which can have its value set using TlsSetValue and be retrieved with TlsGetValue. The PAL implements TLS as a process-wide 64-bit bitmask, sTlsSlotFields, which is used to keep track of slot reservations, and a per-thread array, tlsSlots, which is a member of the THREAD structure.

The pthreads package has an API named pthread_key that could have been used to implement TLS slots, but this approach was rejected in favor of the simple, array-based mechanism described here. In particular, the SSCLI implementation depends on having zeroed memory in TLS slots, and bugs on some flavors of Unix prevented this from always being true.

Synchronizing Processes and Threads

The CLI was designed to provide programmers with numerous design alternatives when creating components and when grouping components together into collaborative systems. Many of these have to do with using boundaries, such as processes, threads, and application domains, to package and protect component instances. To enable collaboration between components protected in this way, the PAL must not only support creating the boundaries, but also communicating across them. To complement the several kinds of isolation provided by the PAL to component implementers, the PAL also provides a rich set of synchronization primitives.

The Win32 synchronization mechanisms provided by the PAL are:

Critical sections
> Critical sections are regions of code that are protected in such a way that only one thread at a time may enter the region and execute code.

Mutexes (mutual exclusion objects)
> Mutexes are locks used to protect resources that guarantee ownership by a single thread at a time. A mutex can be used by multiple processes simultaneously; one thread from one process will be given ownership at a time.

Events
> Events allow the programmer to send a message from one thread to another. Events can be used to communicate between threads in different processes.

Semaphores
> Semaphores act as a gate and allow a limited number of threads (up to a programmable maximum) to enter. Rotor's PAL limits the use semaphores to a single process.

Processes and threads
> The PAL has the ability to wait for the termination of a process or a thread, which is a form of synchronization.

To implement these mechanisms in the PAL, a bewildering number of mapping choices were available in the form of Unix synchronization primitives. After evaluation, the venerable Unix pipe, a workhorse that is portable, works both cross-thread and cross-process, and has the blocking granularity of a single thread, was selected as the basis for all of the PAL's synchronization mechanisms, save critical sections, which are implemented using the pthread package's own mutex mechanism. We will discuss both approaches in turn.

Critical Sections

A critical section (often referred to in the code as a *critsec*) is a programming device used to enforce mutual exclusion between threads. A thread that is running code protected by a critical section is guaranteed that no other thread in its process can be running the same code at the same time. Once a critsec is released, there is no guarantee as to which pending thread will be granted ownership. In addition, there is no mechanism for detecting when a critsec has been abandoned by a thread that has exited, which means that deadlocks can occur when threads unexpectedly terminate. The structure used to represent a critical section in the PAL is shown in Example 9-7.

Example 9-7. Critical sections are widely used in the PAL's multithreaded code (defined in pal/rotor_pal.h)

```
typedef struct _CRITICAL_SECTION {
  PVOID   DebugInfo;
  LONG    RecursionCount;
  HANDLE  OwningThread;
  HANDLE  LockSemaphore;
} CRITICAL_SECTION, *PCRITICAL_SECTION, *LPCRITICAL_SECTION;
```

Calls to EnterCriticalSection and LeaveCriticalSection are used to bracket sections of code to be protected. They can be acquired recursively by a single thread (typically in nested calls), and the RecursionCount field is used to record the number of times the critical section has been acquired in this way. A critsec that has been acquired multiple times on a thread must be released the same number of times. The OwningThread field contains a handle to the thread that currently owns the critical section, with NULL being used to indicate no owner.

While the LockSemaphore field looks as though it might be a handle to a PAL object, it is actually a pointer to a pthread_mutex_t, which is a type defined by the POSIX threading library. Each PAL critical section has a corresponding pthread mutex. The pthreads implementation maps quite well to the Win32 critical section APIs: pthread_mutex_lock corresponds to EnterCriticalSection, pthread_mutext_unlock corresponds to LeaveCriticalSection, and pthread_mutex_trylock corresponds to TryEnterCriticalSection.

> The pthreads mutex implementation is very different from the Win32-style mutex implementation found in the PAL. The PAL's implementation is described in the later section "Mutexes."

The routines EnterCriticalSection and LeaveCriticalSection are wrappers over the PAL's SYNCEnterCriticalSection and SYNCLeaveCriticalSection routines. These two functions are used internally within the PAL, and each take an additional parameter that is used to indicate when a call is being made from within the PAL. This distinction is important for the implementation of thread suspension and resumption, which is discussed in the "Suspending and Resuming PAL Threads" section of this chapter.

The BlockingPipe and the ThreadWaitingList

Every THREAD has a single pipe associated with it, called its *blocking pipe*. The file for this pipe, created by createBlockingPipe, can be found in the configuration directory for the PAL process group, and the filename is a combination of the process ID, the thread ID, and the string .rotor_pal_ threadpipe. For example, a thread with a PID of 1064 and a TID of 657840 might have the name */tmp/.rotor-pal-503-1067299/.rotor_pal_threadpipe-1064-657840*. Using canonical names like this, it is easy for one PAL process to locate the thread pipe for a thread in another process using only information that it has in its handles.

Threads signal one another in various communication patterns by using synchronization objects as notification channels. When a thread wishes to be signaled by a synchronization object—for example, in response to a call to WaitForSingleObject—a thread adds itself to a structure called a *thread waiting list*, which is associated with the object in question. This is done using an object-specific routine, such as MutexAddThreadToList. After adding itself to this list, the thread then blocks by calling poll on its blocking pipe. Eventually, when the object wishes to wake up the thread by signaling from a different thread, the signaling object opens the blocking pipe and writes a wakeup code, which brings the thread back from the poll call. At this point, the original thread can remove itself from the object's thread waiting list, again using an object-specific routine such as MutexRemoveWaitingThread.

As you can see from this discussion, waiting on the blocking pipe is central to the operation of almost all of the PAL's synchronization mechanisms. The data structure ThreadWaitingList, shown in Example 9-8, is used to represent the outstanding synchronization requests within the PAL. It is used by synchronization objects to keep track of the blocking pipes for its clients.

Example 9-8. The ThreadWaitingList data structure is used to implement synchronization objects (defined in pal/unix/include/pal/thread.h)

```
typedef struct _ThreadWaitingList {
  DWORD threadId;
  DWORD processId;
  int  blockingPipe;
  union
  {
    SHMPTR shmNext;
    struct _ThreadWaitingList *Next;
  }ptr;
  union
  {
    SHMPTR shmAwakened;
    LPBOOL pAwakened;
  }state;
} ThreadWaitingList;
```

The threadId and processId fields of ThreadWaitingList contain the thread and process IDs associated with a synchronization object, and the blockingPipe field contains the file descriptor of the pipe used for synchronization on the thread wishing to be signaled. The blockingPipe is used to wake up a thread when it is being signaled, but the value in this field, since it is a file descriptor, is only valid within the process that initialized the list. When the process being signaled is not the same as the process in which the synchronization object resides, the threadId and processId are used to locate the pipe to be used, and the blockingPipe field is not referenced.

ThreadWaitingList structures are strung together into a singly linked list whose root can be found in the synchronization object with which they are associated. Depending on the nature of the synchronization object, this structure can reside in process memory (the case for threads and semaphores) or in shared memory (the case for mutexes and events). Thus the ptr field is a union of a SHMPTR and pointer to the ThreadWaitingList structure.

There is a potential race condition in the window between the return from poll and the thread's removal from the thread waiting list during which the thread could be resignaled, which would interfere with completion of the wakeup procedure already underway. The solution for this is to store a pointer to the thread's waitAwakened field in the list entry. This field can be used to track the thread's execution state and to check it during signaling (see THREADInterlockedAwaken in *pal/unix/thread/thread.c* for more details). Since this pointer may need to reference threads that live in other processes, a union of a shared-memory pointer and process pointer is once again used.

Semaphores

A *semaphore* object maintains a count between 0 and a specified maximum value. This value is incremented each time a thread releases the semaphore and is decremented each time a thread completes a wait on the semaphore. The initial value of the count can be specified at creation time.

The Semaphore structure, shown in Example 9-9, contains the usual fields for a PAL entity, the objHeader, dwMagic, and refCount fields. The critSection field is used internally to guarantee atomic updating of the structure. Since this is a *waitable* entity, the waitingThread field acts as a head pointer for its thread waiting thread list. The waiting list is maintained as a FIFO (first-in, first out) queue by the semaphore implementation, and only allows references to threads that reside in the same process as the Semaphore.

Example 9-9. The Semaphore structure (described in pal/unix/sync/semaphore.h)

```
typedef struct _Semaphore
{
  HOBJSTRUCT        objHeader;
  DWORD             dwMagic;
  INT               refCount;

  LONG              semCount;
  LONG              maximumCount;

  CRITICAL_SECTION  critSection;
  ThreadWaitingList *waitingThreads;
} Semaphore;
```

The PAL has several wait functions (although all are implemented using WaitForMultipleObjectsEx). When a wait function is called on a semaphore, the semCount, if greater then 0, is decremented and the function returns immediately, indicating that the semaphore was acquired. If semCount is 0, the thread is put on the semaphore's thread waiting list, and the thread blocks.

To increment the semCount, ReleaseSemaphore is called. As long as the value remains less then maximumCount, the value is increased and the semaphore is released. If the value is at its maximum, the first waiting thread in the thread waiting list is signaled. Since the thread waiting list is maintained as a FIFO, threads are awakened in the order in which they acquired the semaphore.

Due to the limited definition of semaphores in the PAL, their implementation is fairly straightforward. When compared with the Win32 implementation, which requires cross-process capabilities and the OpenSemaphore API, the PAL version appears trivial. The simpler requirements of the SSCLI allowed the Rotor team to keep the design simple.

Events

Events are signaled using the SetEvent and ResetEvent APIs. These APIs enable one thread to signal another thread directly, as a message. Events come in two flavors: the *manual-reset event* and the *auto-reset event*. A manual-reset event is like an on/off switch; when SetEvent is called, it signals all threads waiting on it to proceed and continues to do so until ResetEvent is called. An auto-reset event is very different; when SetEvent is called, the event signals a single thread from its thread waiting list and then immediately returns to an unsignaled state.

Events may be shared between processes, which makes them trickier to implement then semaphores. (By default, an event that is named is accessible to other processes.) Events are represented within the PAL as two related data structures: the Event, which is the in-process portion, and the GLOBAL_ EVENT_SYSTEM_OBJECT, which is the shared-memory portion. Both are shown in Example 9-10.

Example 9-10. The paired data structures for events (defined in pal/unix/sync/event.h)

```
typedef struct _Event
{
  HOBJSTRUCT   objHeader;
  DWORD        dwMagic;
  SHMPTR       info;
  INT          refCount;
} Event;

typedef struct _GESO
{
  SHM_NAMED_OBJECTS  ShmHeader;

  INT                refCount;
  BOOL               state;
  BOOL               manualReset;
  SHMPTR             waitingThreads;
  SHMPTR             next;
}GLOBAL_EVENT_SYSTEM_OBJECT, * PGLOBAL_EVENT_SYSTEM_OBJECT;
```

The Event structure itself is minimal, including the same objHeader, dwMagic, and refCount fields described in the discussion of PAL processes earlier in this chapter. Its only real purpose, besides enabling handle management for the event itself, is to provide a place to put a pointer to an associated GLOBAL_ EVENT_SYSTEM_OBJECT structure that is stored in shared memory.

Important fields in GLOBAL_EVENT_SYSTEM_OBJECT are the state field, which indicates whether the event is signaled and the manualReset field, which indicates the event's type. The object name is stored in the SHM_NAMED_OBJECTS structure. When threads are waiting to be signaled, they occupy a thread waiting list, whose head can be found in the waitingThreads field.

Events are created using CreateEvent, although this API defers first to OpenEvent to ensure that the name has not already been used. If the event does not already exist, a paired set is created consisting of a GLOBAL_EVENT_ SYSTEM_OBJECT in shared memory and an Event in local memory. Events may be created without a name, in which case the handle must be passed among all parties wishing to use the event.

Mutexes

A *mutex* is a PAL entity that is used as a lock when accessing resources. The name is a contracted form of "mutual exclusion," which is the principle that a mutex enforces: only one thread can own the mutex at a time. Mutexes implement a simple toggle; they are unsignaled when no thread owns them and signaled when owned by a thread. (When unsignaled, they can be acquired without waiting. When signaled, a thread must wait for access.)

Like critical sections, mutexes are used to coordinate access between multiple threads. Unlike critical sections, mutexes can be used by multiple processes, and because of this, mutexes share implementation similarities with events. Mutexes also differ from critical sections in that they have a well-defined order in which clients are granted access. (Critical sections do not guarantee wake order.)

Like events, a mutex may be created with or without a name. Unlike events, the name does not govern the cross-process visibility of the mutex: all mutexes are available in shared memory to other PAL processes within a process group. This is done to support the PAL_LocalHandleToRemote API, which can be used to pass a mutex handle to another process. (This is used when debugging. An unnamed mutex is created and then duplicated using this API for the debugger to use.) The pair of structures used to represent a mutex is shown in Example 9-11.

Example 9-11. The paired data structures that represent mutexes (defined in pal/unix/include/pal/mutex.h)

```
typedef struct _MHO
{
  HOBJSTRUCT      HandleHeader;
  UINT            Ref_Count;
  SHMPTR          ShmKernelObject;

  struct _MHO *  pNext;
  struct _MHO *  pPrev;

} MUTEX_HANDLE_OBJECT, * PMUTEX_HANDLE_OBJECT;

typedef struct _GMSO
{
  SHM_NAMED_OBJECTS  ShmHeader;
  SHMPTR             ShmWaitingForThreadList;
  UINT               Ref_Count;
  UINT               Mutex_Count;
  BOOL               abandoned;
  struct {
    DWORD ProcessId;
    DWORD ThreadId;
  } Owner;
} GLOBAL_MUTEX_SYSTEM_OBJECT, * PGLOBAL_MUTEX_SYSTEM_OBJECT;
```

MUTEX_HANDLE_OBJECT is the in-process data structure that acts as a local proxy for the GLOBAL_MUTEX_SYSTEM_OBJECT. It contains the usual HOBJSTRUCT and Ref_Count found in all objects and described in the section on PAL processes in this chapter. Its ShmKernelObject field is the pointer to shared memory in which the actual mutex object resides.

GLOBAL_MUTEX_SYSTEM_OBJECT is used to represent the mutex in shared memory. Its Ref_Count field holds a count of all outstanding references, its ShmHeader field contains the mutex' name, and its ShmWaitingForThreadList field contains the head of the thread waiting list for the mutex. This list is managed as a FIFO queue, in the same way that semaphores managed their waiting threads, guaranteeing that threads are granted access to the mutex in the order they initiate waiting.

The Mutex_Count field deserves explanation. After all, if only one thread can gain ownership of the mutex at a time, why have a count? The reason is that the specification requires that a thread be able to acquire the mutex multiple times. Mutex_Count keeps track of these references. Each call to acquire the mutex must have a matching call to ReleaseMutex, which decrements this counter.

There are two other fields that are unique among synchronization entities: the pNext and pPrev fields of the MUTEX_HANDLE_OBJECT. In addition to being held in the handle table, in-process mutex objects are joined as a doubly-linked list that is rooted in the process global pMutexHandle. This list is used when a thread exits while holding a mutex, a process known as *abandonment*. Abandoning a mutex is the equivalent of calling RelaseMutex until the mutex's Mutex_Count reaches 0. To abandon the mutexes held by a thread, the routine MutexReleaseMutexes traverses the list, examining each ProcessId and ThreadId looking for a match with the current process and thread. The abandoned field in the GLOBAL_MUTEX_SYSTEM_OBJECT is also set when the mutex is abandoned, and is reset only when a new thread takes ownership.

Implementing Signaling

The PAL provides a number of waiting functions for threads. All of these (WaitForSingleObject, WaitForMultipleObjects, Sleep, and SleepEx) are implemented using WaitForMultipleObjectsEx. Because of this, this section will step through only WaitForMultipleObjectsEx. You will understand how signal waiting is done in the PAL if you understand how this function, defined in *pal/unix/sync/wait.c*, works.

 The code for WaitForMultipleObjectsEx can be tricky to trace at runtime, due to its use of indirect recursion, as well as its use of a worker thread when waiting for a process to terminate.

Here is the function prototype for WaitForMultipleObjectsEx:

```
WaitForMultipleObjectsEx(
        IN DWORD nCount,
        IN CONST HANDLE *lpHandles,
        IN BOOL bWaitAll,
        IN DWORD dwMilliseconds,
        IN BOOL bAlertable)
```

The arguments lpHandles and nCount combine to specify an array containing the handles of all objects to wait on. If all objects must signal before the function returns, bWaitAll is set to true; otherwise, the first object to signal will cause the function to return. The dwMilliseconds argument is used to indicate how long a timeout to use before returning, regardless of success. This argument may be INFINITE, in which case the wait will return only when all wait conditions have been met. Finally, bAlertable indicates that the wait may be terminated by a queued APC, which is discussed in the later section "Asynchronous Procedure Calls."

The first thing done in WaitForMultipleObjectsEx is to validate the handles passed in the lpHandles argument and lock them. A check is made that the handles are waitable, which means that they are of type PROCESS, EVENT, SEMAPHORE, MUTEX, or THREAD, but not FILE or MAP. A check is also made to make sure that there is at most one process object in the list to wait on. (The one-process limitation was specified because the SSCLI never needs to wait on more then one process, and this limitation greatly simplifies the implementation.) The code looks like this:

```
for (i = 0; i < nCount; i++) {
  // Create a local copy of lpHandles before locking, since
  //  caller might change out from under us.
  hHandles[i] = lpHandles[i];
  hObjs[i] = HMGRLockHandle(hHandles[i]);

  if (hObjs[i] == NULL) {
    SetLastError(ERROR_INVALID_PARAMETER);
    goto WaitFMOExit;
  }

  handles_locked++;

  if ((hObjs[i]->type != HOBJ_PROCESS)  &&
      (hObjs[i]->type != HOBJ_EVENT)  &&
      (hObjs[i]->type != HOBJ_SEMAPHORE)  &&
      (hObjs[i]->type != HOBJ_MUTEX)  &&
      (hObjs[i]->type != HOBJ_THREAD)) {
    SetLastError(ERROR_INVALID_HANDLE);
    goto WaitFMOExit;
  }

  // Remember index of process handle
```

```
      if(HOBJ_PROCESS == hObjs[i]->type) {
        if (-1 == process_index) {
          process_index = i;
        } else if(!bWaitAll) {
          // There must never be more than 1 process handle
          ASSERT("found more than 1 process handle in the array!\n");
        }
      }
    }
  }
```

After this, a check is made to see whether the wait is alertable and if there are any queued APCs. If these conditions are met, the queued APCs are called, any handles are unlocked and the wait returns with STATUS_USER_APC. Notice that if an APC is queued to a thread while the thread is waiting on other objects, the wait will be cut short and the APC called:

```
if (bAlertable) {
  NumAPCCalled = THREADCallThreadAPCs();
  if (NumAPCCalled == -1) {
    ERROR("Failed in calling APCs for the current thread\n");
    goto WaitFMOExit;
  } else if (NumAPCCalled > 0) {
    retValue = STATUS_USER_APC;
    goto WaitFMOExit;
  }
}
```

The code then classifies the wait into one of three cases:

1. There is one object to wait for (nCount == 1), the object is a process, and the wait is nonalertable (bAlertable is false).

2. There is more then one object to wait on (nCount > 1), and the programmer has requested waiting for all of them (bWaitAll is true).

3. All other waits.

The first two cases are clearly subsets of the third case. What is useful about these two subsets is that they can be implemented more optimally than the general case. For the first case, WFMO_WaitForProcess is called with appropriate parameters. The routine calls GetExitCodeProcess inside an infinite loop, which breaks out when either the timeout has expired or the process exits. (GetExitCodeProcess does not wait for the process to end. It returns immediately, either with an exit code or with STILL_ACTIVE to indicate that the process is alive.) We will skip the code for this case, since it is straightforward.

Here is the start of the code that implements the second case, which can be found in the WFMO_WaitForAllObjects function:

```
// Save current time, so that we can know when the timeout is elapsed
old_time = GetTickCount();

// Step 1 : wait for processes and threads.
```

```
for(i=0;i<nCount;i++) {
  if ( HOBJ_PROCESS == hObjs[i]->type || HOBJ_THREAD  == hObjs[i]->type ) {
    ret = WaitForSingleObject(lpHandles[i], dwMilliseconds);
    if (WAIT_TIMEOUT == ret) {
      return WAIT_TIMEOUT;
    }
  } else {
    // Build arrays of "resettable" handles (mutexes, events, semaphores)
    resetables[resetable_count] = lpHandles[i];
    resetable_objs[resetable_count] = hObjs[i];
    resetable_count++;
  }

  // If we have a timeout value, adjust it
  if ( 0 != dwMilliseconds && INFINITE != dwMilliseconds ) {
    WFMO_update_timeout(&old_time, &dwMilliseconds);
    if (0 == dwMilliseconds) {
      return WAIT_TIMEOUT;
    }
  }
}

// If only process and thread objects were given, we can stop here
if( 0 == resetable_count) {
  return WAIT_OBJECT_0;
}
```

The list of valid object types for case 1 can be divided into two groups: handles that can have their signal state reset, which are events, semaphores, and mutexes, and handles that cannot have their signal reset, which are threads and processes. (The signal is the exit code in these cases.) Since the termination criterion for this particular case is that every handle must signal, there is no point in worrying about handles that might set and reset their signals (perhaps multiple times) until the handles that cannot reset their signals have signaled.

WFMO_WaitForAllObjects calls WaitForSingleObject on any process or thread that is in its list. In a not-entirely-unexpected display of recursion, WaitForSingleObject bottoms out in a call to WaitForMultipleObjectsEx, but with a single handle and with bWaitAll and bAlertable both set to False. For the purpose of this discussion, it is important to know that calls to WaitForSingleObject with a thread or a process handle are synchronized, and so each call will wait for its thread or process to actually terminate before the next object is checked. Before proceeding, the timeout value is updated to account for the time spent waiting on nonresettable objects.

Now that process and thread handles have signaled, the code drops into a large loop to wait on the remaining objects. First, there is a call to WaitForSingleObject on the current blocking_object, which is initialized as the index of the first item in the list of resettable handles.

(WaitForSingleObject will recursively make a synchronized call to WaitForMultipleObjectsEx.)

```
blocking_object = 0;
while(1) {
  ret = WaitForSingleObject( resetables[blocking_object], dwMilliseconds);
  if (WAIT_TIMEOUT == ret) {
    return WAIT_TIMEOUT;
  }
  got_abandoned = was_abandoned[blocking_object] = WAIT_ABANDONED==ret;

  // function continues
```

The list of resettable handles is then walked, and WaitForSingleObject is called on each with a timeout of 0 (skipping the blocking_object). The objective is to check for handles that have already signaled. If none of the waits return WAIT_TIMEOUT, then all handles have signaled, and the routine returns successfully. Otherwise, the wait that returns WAIT_TIMEOUT causes the walk to halt, and the handle that caused this return is marked as the blocking object:

```
for(i=0; i<resetable_count;i++) {
  // Skip the first object we waited on, it's already signalled
  if (i == blocking_object) {
    continue;
  }
  // Wait on all others without blocking, to see if they're signaled
  ret = WaitForSingleObject(resetables[i], 0);

  if (WAIT_TIMEOUT == ret) {
    resetables[i]);
    break;
  }

  was_abandoned[i] = WAIT_ABANDONED == ret;
  if (was_abandoned[i]) {
    got_abandoned = TRUE;
  }
}

  // function continues
```

The list of resettable objects is now walked backwards from the handle before the blocking_object to the start of the list. Since all of these handles have already signaled, they are released so that other waiting threads may be unblocked.

Mutexes that were acquired due to abandonment are released with WTC_ ABANDON as their wakeup code for the next thread waiting. Other mutexes and semaphores are released normally, and events are placed into a signaled state by calling SetEvent:

```
  // If the for loop completed normally, all object were signal
  if (i == resetable_count) {
    if (got_abandoned) {
      return WAIT_ABANDONED;
    }
    return WAIT_OBJECT_0;
  }

  // We'll wait on object that wasn't signalled next pass.
  blocking_object = i;

  // Give up ownership or re-signal all events we succesfully waited on
  for(; i>=0;i--) {
    switch(resetable_objs[i]->type) {
      case HOBJ_MUTEX:
        if (was_abandoned[i]) {
          // Re-flag as abandoned if that's how it was
          MutexReleaseMutex((MUTEX_HANDLE_OBJECT *)resetable_objs[i],
                                                  WUTC_ABANDONED, FALSE);
        } else {
          ReleaseMutex(resetables[i]);
        }
        break;

      case HOBJ_SEMAPHORE:
        ReleaseSemaphore(resetables[i], 1, NULL);
        break;
      case HOBJ_EVENT:
        SetEvent(resetables[i]);
        break;
      default:
        break;
    }
  }

  // If we have a timeout value (not infinite), update
  if ( 0 != dwMilliseconds && INFINITE != dwMilliseconds ) {
    WFMO_update_timeout(&old_time, &dwMilliseconds);
    if (0 == dwMilliseconds) {
      return WAIT_TIMEOUT;
    }
  }
}
```

Finally, the timeout value is updated by subtracting the time spent on this pass. The loop continues until all handles have signaled or the timeout is reached.

Broadly speaking, the PAL's implementation of signal waiting can be divided into two types of code, the first of which, as we have just seen, involves process waiting by polling, and the second deals with the general case. The code for the first, with its polling loops, is more complicated than the general case, but there is a good reason to break it out.

There is an impedance mismatch between the Unix process model and the PAL process model. In Win32, a wait on a process is the same as a wait on another handle, and any handle can terminate a call to WaitForMultipleObjectsEx. In the Unix PAL, process terminations must be treated very differently than other handles, and catching them requires heavy software machinery in the form of a new thread. The expense of creating a new thread is why the PAL attempts to avoid the general-case solution.

The code for the general case will make the differences clear. At its start, the list of handles to wait on is checked for the presence of a process. If one is included, a set of expensive resources is created (if they do not already exist) that will be used to enable the wait on the process, as follows (error handling has been removed for readability):

```
// If there is a process handle, get ready to use a worker thread
if ( -1 != process_index) {
  if (NULL == worker_handle) {
    // First-time initialization : create worker thread and event
    DWORD tid;
    keep_going = TRUE;
    process_handle = NULL;
    worker_event = CreateEventW(NULL, FALSE, FALSE, NULL);
  }

  // Create event used to indicate worker thread is going to standby mode
  standby_event = CreateEventW(NULL, FALSE, FALSE, NULL);
  // Create event used by worker thread to signal process termination
  process_event = CreateEventW(NULL, FALSE, FALSE, NULL);
  // Create the worker thread itself
  worker_handle = CreateThread(NULL, 0, &WFMO_workerthread, NULL, 0, &tid);
}

// Tell worker thread which process to wait on, and how long
process_handle = hHandles[process_index];
worker_timeout = dwMilliseconds;

// Housekeeping code to set up wait state deleted

for (i = 0; i < handles_locked; i++) {
  if (i == process_index) {
    // Reached the index of the process handle. Tell worker thread to wait,
    //   and wait on event as proxy.
    ret = WaitOn(HOBJ_EVENT, process_event, shmThreadWaitState);
    SetEvent(worker_event);
  } else {
    ret = WaitOn(hObjs[i]->type, *(hHandles+i), shmThreadWaitState);
  }

  if (WOC_SIGNALED == ret || WOC_ABANDONED == ret) {
    // One object was signaled, we are done
    if (WOC_SIGNALED == ret) {
```

```
    retValue = WAIT_OBJECT_0 + i;
} else {
    retValue = WAIT_ABANDONED_0 + i;
}

StopWaitingOnObjects(hObjs, hHandles, i, process_index);

// Rest of function not shown
```

Two events and a thread are needed to properly catch process termination in a nonsynchronized fashion. A thread (worker_thread) acts as the proxy for the process while waiting, the standby_event is used to signal from the worker thread to the waiting thread that the process has terminated and is entering "standby" mode, and the process_event is used by the waiting thread to signal the worker thread to begin waiting on the process. The standby_event becomes a proxy handle for the process that can be waited on like other PAL handles. This is an expensive solution indeed, but once it is in place, the rest of WaitForMultipleObjectsEx is straightforward.

With the process proxy in place, the list of handles to wait on is walked, and WaitOn is called on each. WaitOn is a dispatcher function that defers to handle-specific routines to set up the wait. If there are no errors and no objects have already signaled, ThreadWait is called which in turn calls PollBlockingPipe to enter a polling loop, waiting for a wakeup code to be written to the thread's blocking pipe.

Once WaitOn returns, StopWaitingOnObjects is called to clear the pending waits. The wait may have stopped due to an object signaling, an APC being queued (since this is an alertable wait), the time limit being exceeded, or a mutex being abandoned. Each case is converted to an appropriate exit code, and if the object that signaled was the worker_event, this signal is mapped back to the original process object. At this point, control is returned to the caller, as WaitForMultipleObjectsEx returns.

Suspending and Resuming PAL Threads

Now that we have discussed synchronization and signaling within the Unix PAL, we can see them in action in the way that PAL threads are suspended and resumed. Although the POSIX threads package meets most of the PAL's requirements, the pthread API does not contain a standard way to suspend or resume a thread. To further complicate matters, PAL threads must be able to suspend themselves, and they should be capable of tracking and recovering from multiple requests for suspension by maintaining a suspend count. (Nonstandardized extensions to pthreads certainly exist, such as

FreeBSD's pthread_suspend_np and pthread_resume_np functions, but none of these fully capture the PAL's Win32 semantics.)

To implement self-suspension, the code in SuspendThread waits on the thread's blocking pipe until another thread calls ResumeThread, which resumes the thread by writing to the pipe. Since this use of the blocking pipe (an expensive resource to allocate on a per-thread basis) is shared with the signaling mechanism described in "Implementing Signaling," the SuspendedWithPipeFlag in the THREAD structure is used to indicate when the pipe is being utilized for suspension rather than for waiting.

When suspending another thread, platform-specific approaches are used. On FreeBSD, SuspendThread utilizes the pthread_suspend_np routine, keeping a suspension count in the field dwSuspendCount. On Mac OS X, the pthread_t is converted to a Mach thread ID, and thread_suspend is called. (These calls, conditionally compiled, can be seen in Example 9-7.)

The code in the Unix implementations of SuspendThread and ResumeThread is very susceptible to deadlocks, due to the PAL's internal use of critical sections to serialize access to its data structures when using and updating them. The danger arises when a thread is suspended while it holds a PAL-internal critical section; subsequent threads attempting to access the same structure will block until the first thread is resumed. Under the worst case scenario, for example, a thread might hold a critical section on a structure required to resume execution, resulting in deadlock. (The Win32 PAL does not share this problem, since it defers to the Windows implementation of SuspendThread and ResumeThread, which are written without the use of critical sections.)

To avoid the deadlock problem, each thread maintains a count of the number of PAL-internal critical sections it has entered. By keeping this count, the PAL can implement a conservative strategy through which a thread will not be suspended until its critical section count has gone to 0. When SuspendThread is called, the code immediately enters spin lock, as follows:

```
while(0 != InterlockedCompareExchange(&lpThread->suspend_spinlock,1,0))
    sched_yield();
```

The lock guarantees that only one thread will gain access to the code following the spinlock. Normally, you would use a critical section to ensure this restricted access, but since you are trying to avoid using critical sections, the more conservative (and expensive, because of its processor usage) spinlock approach makes sense.

After acquiring the spinlock, the critical section count must go to 0. The code that accomplishes this is shown in Example 9-12.

Example 9-12. SuspendThread must reduce the target thread's critical section count to zero before suspending (extracted from pal/unix/thread/thread.c)

```
if(0 != lpThread->critsec_count) {
  pthread_mutex_lock(&lpThread->suspension_mutex);
  pthread_mutex_lock(&lpThread->cond_mutex);
  lpThread->suspend_intent = TRUE;

  // Let the thread run until it releases all its critical sections
#if HAVE_PTHREAD_NP
  pthread_resume_np((pthread_t)lpThread->dwThreadId);
#elif HAVE_MACH_THREADS
  thread_resume(pthread_mach_thread_np((pthread_t) lpThread->dwThreadId));
#endif

  // Wait for signal
  pthread_cond_wait(&lpThread->suspender_cond,
                    &lpThread->cond_mutex);

  // Once mutex is tripped, it is safe to suspend
#if HAVE_PTHREAD_NP
  pthread_suspend_np((pthread_t)lpThread->dwThreadId);
#elif HAVE_MACH_THREADS
  thread_suspend(pthread_mach_thread_np((pthread_t) lpThread->dwThreadId));
#endif

  lpThread->suspend_intent = FALSE;
  // Allow target thread to acquire the mutex and continue when resumed
  pthread_mutex_unlock(&lpThread->cond_mutex);
  pthread_mutex_unlock(&lpThread->suspension_mutex);
}
```

The pthread_mutex_lock API is used to lock the suspension_mutex and cond_mutex mutexes, both of which are fields of the THREAD structure. Once both mutexes have been acquired, the suspend_intent field in the target thread is set to true and the target thread is resumed using pthread_resume_np on FreeBSD and thread_resume on Mac OS X. The calling thread then blocks until the outstanding critical sections are released.

Having been resumed, the target thread is now running. Every time the routine SYNCLeaveCriticalSection (the code used to exit a critical section) is executed, the critsec_count is decremented and checked to see whether it is zero. When this constraint is met, the code sequence in Example 9-13 is executed.

Example 9-13. The handshake used to protect SuspendThread from deadlock (extracted from pal/unix/sync/critsect.c)

```
// Wait until the suspender thread is calling pthread_cond_wait
pthread_mutex_lock(&pCurrentThread->cond_mutex);
pthread_mutex_unlock(&pCurrentThread->cond_mutex);
```

Example 9-13. The handshake used to protect SuspendThread from deadlock (extracted from pal/unix/sync/critsect.c) (continued)

```
// Let suspender thread suspend this thread
pthread_cond_signal(&pCurrentThread->suspender_cond);

// Wait for the suspender to unlock AND for the resumer to resume
pthread_mutex_lock(&pCurrentThread->suspension_mutex);

// We have been resumed; release the mutex.
pthread_mutex_unlock(&pCurrentThread->suspension_mutex);
```

The two mutexes are being used as a handshake mechanism between the thread wishing to suspend and the thread that will be suspended. The target thread signals the suspender via pthread_cond_signal, and then attempts to lock the suspension_mutex where it will remain until the ResumeThread is called. Once the suspender thread is signaled, SuspendThread resumes. Using pthread_suspend_np, it once again suspends the target thread and then unlocks the two mutexes. (Unlocking the mutexes has no effect on the target thread because it is now suspended.) After incrementing dwSuspendCount and releasing the spinlock, SuspendThread returns.

Asynchronous Procedure Calls

Asynchronous Procedure Calls (APCs), which provide a way to execute code within the context of a specific thread, are used by Rotor's threading implementation. (Specifically, they provide a way to politely interrupt threads that are busily beavering away at something else.) They are implemented as callback functions, which always have the signature:

```
VOID CALLBACK APCProc(ULONG_PTR dwParam);
```

An APC is queued to a thread, where it is scheduled for execution. While not strictly a synchronization mechanism, the queuing of an APC has an effect similar to synchronization.

The QueueUserAPC API adds the APC passed as a parameter to a per-thread queue of functions to be called. A thread will call its APCs only when it is alertable, which is defined to be after it uses WaitForMultipleObjectsEx or SleepEx with the alertable parameter set to True. APCs are called in FIFO order.

In the Unix PAL, the thread maintains its queue as a singly linked list of APC_ TRACKER structures:

```
typedef struct _APC_TRACKER
{
    PAPCFUNC        pfnAPC;
    ULONG_PTR       pAPCData;
```

```
    struct _APC_TRACKER *pNext;
} APC_TRACKER, *LPAPC_TRACKER;
```

The root of this list can be found in the lpAPCTracker field of THREAD.

Since each APCProc takes a ULONG_PTR argument, each element of the APC
tracker list must hold onto the function argument in addition to the function pointer. The routine THREADCallThreadAPCs handles the calling of the
APC functions and is called in three places: before the thread starts actually
waiting on handles in WaitForMultipleObjectsEx, before the DLL_THREAD_
ATTACH call in THREADEntry, and after the blocking pipe has been released in
ThreadWait.

Handling Exceptions in the PAL

The SSCLI implementation uses Win32 Structured Exception Handling
(SEH) heavily, and because of this, the PAL must provide an implementation of this feature for its use.

Before launching into the details of how the PAL implements SEH portably,
a quick review is in order. SEH takes the following form in Win32 code:

```
__try {
  <guarded code>
}
__except (<filter>) {
  <exception handler>
}
__finally {
  <termination handler>
}
```

The filter and its exception handler are executed if an exception occurs during the execution of the guarded code; if an exception occurs within the try
block, the filter is used to determine whether the except block should be
run. The termination handler is an optional piece of code that is executed
whenever control moves out of the guarded section; as control moves out of
the *try* block for any reason, the finally block is executed. Any code blocks
may themselves contain *try* blocks, except blocks, or finally blocks (or call
functions that contain such blocks), and because of this, handlers may be,
and often are, nested to an arbitrary depth.

The algorithm for exception handling is as follows:

1. An exception is raised.

2. The system looks at the hierarchy of active exception handlers and executes the filter of the handler with highest precedence. This is the exception handler most recently installed and most deeply nested.

3. If the filter passes control by returning EXCEPTION_CONTINUE_SEARCH, execution returns to step 1 but at the next highest precedence exception handler.

4. If the filter returns EXCEPTION_CONTINUE_EXECUTION, execution continues where the exception was raised

5. If the filter returns EXCEPTION_EXECUTE_HANDLER, then:

    a. Each termination handler on the stack is executed in order of precedence, up to the scope of the current exception handler.

    b. The stack is unwound, clearing all stack frames between the currently executing code (in which the exception was raised), and the stack frame that contains the exception handler gaining control.

    c. The exception handler is executed.

    d. Control passes to the line of code that follows the end of the exception handler.

The act of traversing the exception handlers and running the filter functions is commonly referred to as the *first pass* of exception handling. The act of executing the termination handlers, unwinding the stack, and executing the exception handler is commonly called the *second pass* of exception handling. (This is the same terminology used in Chapter 6 when discussing exception handling in the execution engine.)

Win32 SEH is not available on non-Windows platforms, although C/C++ exception handling is. One seemingly obvious implementation alternative for the PAL would be to use C++ exception handling to implement Win32 SEH. Unfortunately, C/C++ exception handling lacks several of the features of Win32 SEH, which renders this choice untenable. The missing features are:

Two-pass semantics
> The two-pass semantics of Win32 SEH are hard to emulate using single-pass C/C++ exception handling.

Very low-level hooks
> Special hooks are necessary to handle exceptions in JIT-compiled code. These hooks must provide a level of control comparable to x86 Windows, in which the chain of exception handlers can be manipulated directly.

Order of execution
> The Rotor execution engine depends on subtle details such as the fact that a termination handler is executed before the stack is unwound. These details are hard to guarantee using generic C/C++ exception handling.

Because of this, the Rotor team decided to implement SEH as part of the PAL. It is exposed as a set of macros to use as though they were the Win32 constructs. The complete set of macros and their differences from the Win32 SEH constructs are documented in the PAL specification and in Appendix D, and the macro definitions can be found in rotor_pal.h. For a quick taste of the use of these macros, Example 9-14 contains pseudocode for both Win32 SEH code and corresponding PAL SEH code.

Example 9-14. Win32 SEH and PAL SEH compared

```
// Win32-style exception handling

// local variable declarations
__try {
  // code which references locals from above
} __except ( ExceptionFilter(GetExceptionInformation( ), pData) ) {
  // code which references locals from above
}

// PAL-style exception handling

// local variable declarations
PAL_TRY {
  // code which references locals from above
} PAL_EXCEPT_FILTER(ExceptionFilter, pData) {
  // code which references locals from above
} PAL_ENDTRY
```

To implement SEH, the PAL defines five new routines:

- PAL_TryHelper
- PAL_EndTryHelper
- PAL_SetBottommostRegistration
- PAL_GetBottommostRegistration
- PAL_GetBottommostRegistrationPtr

The PAL specification describes signatures for all of these functions.

Handling Signals with Exception Handlers

On Windows, SEH provides a unified way to handle exceptions arising from hardware faults, the operating system, and user code. The PAL provides the same unification on Unix by mapping synchronous Unix signals into exceptions.

During PAL startup, PAL_Initialize calls SEHInitialize, which in turn calls SEHInitializeSignals to set up signal handlers. The handle_signal function is called to install signal handlers for every signal that a user process is permitted to handle. Signal handlers are installed for both signals that are transformed into exceptions, such as SIGKILL, SIGTRAP, SIGFPE, SIGBUS, and SIGSEGV, and for events that are transformed into application termination by the PAL, such as SIGINT and SIGQUIT. All signals that the PAL handles have the SA_RESTART flag set, which tells the operating system to automatically restart any restartable system call that is interrupted by a signal.

On Mac OS X, the PAL uses a worker thread to listen on a task's Mach exception port. When a message arrives, the worker thread manipulates the contents of the faulting thread's registers to perform a nonlocal goto to PAL_DispatchException and to set up an EXCEPTION_POINTERS structure on the faulting thread's stack. While this is a lower-level interception mechanism than signals, it is used because Mac OS X signal handlers don't receive the full processor context of the faulting thread, but Mach exception handlers do.

When a signal that is being mapped to an exception is raised, the signal handler initializes an exception record and converts the signal's siginfo and context into an exception code using the routine CONTEXTGetExceptionCodeForSignal. The exception address and CONTEXT record, which are architecture- and operating system–specific, are then associated with the exception and filled in from the context that is passed to the signal handler.

The last task to be performed before an exception is actually raised is to check the thread's safe_state flag to determine whether a signal is already being processed. If one is, the PAL assumes that this is a major problem and the code in common_signal_handler will call ExitProcess to halt execution. If no signal is being processed, safe_state is set to false, and the exception is raised by calling the routine SEHRaiseException.

Managing Exception State

Before diving into the code for SEHRaiseException, you need to understand the data structures used to represent exceptions and how they are managed. The PAL's SEH implementation uses a per-thread linked list of exception handlers. The root of this list is the SEH_TLS_INFO structure, shown in Example 9-15.

Example 9-15. There is one SEH_TLS_INFO structure per thread in the PAL

```
typedef struct
{
  PPAL_EXCEPTION_REGISTRATION  bottom_frame;
  EXCEPTION_RECORD             current_exception;
  BOOL                         safe_state;
  int                          signal_code;
} SEH_TLS_INFO;
```

There is one instance of this structure for each PAL thread, and a pointer to it is stored in each thread-local storage. The `bottom_frame` field points to the bottom-most registration frame for this thread, while `current_exception` contains a copy of the current exception record and `signal_code` contains a copy of the code from the Unix signal (or 0 for user mode exceptions). Both values are copied into the `SEH_TLS_INFO` structure, because the original record is typically created on the stack, where it quickly becomes invalid as the stack is unwound. As discussed in the discussion on signal handling, `safe_state` is used as a flag to indicate whether a signal is currently being processed.

A registration frame, shown in Example 9-16, is a structure that holds data about handlers. Registration frames are arranged in a singly linked list, with the head pointer stored in the `bottom_frame` field of the `SEH_TLS_INFO` for a thread.

Example 9-16. The PAL_EXCEPTION_REGISTRATION structure holds data about exception handlers

```
typedef struct _PAL_EXCEPTION_REGISTRATION {
  // pointer to next exception record up the stack
  struct _PAL_EXCEPTION_REGISTRATION *Next;

  // pointer to the exception filter expression
  EXCEPTION_REGISTRATION_RECORD PFN_PAL_EXCEPTION_FILTER Handler;

  // parameter to pass verbatim to the filter function
  PVOID pvFilterParameter;

  // PAL_EXCEPTION_FLAGS_* constants
  DWORD dwFlags;

  // reserved for the PAL (typically a CRT jmp_buf or sigjmp_buf struct)
  char ReservedForPAL[PAL_TRY_LOCAL_SIZE];
} PAL_EXCEPTION_REGISTRATION, *PPAL_EXCEPTION_REGISTRATION;
```

The first parameter in the registration frame is a `Next` pointer, which is used to build up the linked list of handlers. After this is an optional exception filter function, `Handler`, and the parameter to this function, `pvFilterParameter`. The `dwFlags` that follows is treated as a 2-bit bitfield. The least significant bit, `PAL_EXCEPTION_FLAGS_UNWINDTARGET`, is used to mark the frame that is handling an exception. The other bit, `PAL_EXCEPTION_FLAGS_UNWINDONLY`, marks frames that need special stack unwinding and are used by JIT-compiled code. The final field, `ReservedForPAL` is where data that enables a jump to the handler using `setjmp` is stored.

New registration frames are added to the list when `PAL_TryHelper` is called and removed when `PAL_EndTryHelper` is called. This can occur in the macros defined for PAL SEH, where `PAL_TRY` allocates space for a `PAL_EXCEPTION_`

REGISTRATION structure by declaring a local variable of that type named PalSEHRecord, thus adding it to the current stack activation record. (This is safe to do; the try block's lifetime is linked to the lifetime of the routine it is being run in.)

The PAL macros in *pal/rotor_pal.h* have an interesting structure created by using two nested do loops. Their pseudocode skeleton, created by laying the macros back-to-back, is shown in Example 9-17. (Macro boundaries are shown as comments in this pseudocode and are highlighted.)

Example 9-17. How the PAL exception-handling macros fit together

```
// PAL_TRY                                                              \

PAL_SEH_DISPATCHER_STATE PalSEHDispatcherState = SetUpForSEH;
PAL_EXCEPTION_REGISTRATION PalSEHRecord;
volatile int PalSEHExceptionCode = 0;
int alloca; alloca = 0;

do {
  do {
    if (PalSEHDispatcherState == InTryBlock) {

// END OF PAL_TRY
// PAL_EXCEPT_FINALLY_COMMON(__pfnFilter, __pvFilterParameter)

      break; // break out of do loop
    } else if (PalSEHDispatcherState == SetUpForSEH) {
      PalSEHRecord.Handler = (__pfnFilter);
      PalSEHRecord.pvFilterParameter = (__pvFilterParameter);
      PalSEHRecord.dwFlags = 0;
      PAL_TryHelper(&PalSEHRecord);
      PalSEHExceptionCode = PAL_setjmp(PalSEHRecord.ReservedForPAL);
      if (PalSEHExceptionCode == 0) {

// setjmp returned 0 - ready to run the "try" block

        PalSEHDispatcherState = InTryBlock;
      } else {

// setjmp returned nonzero - unwind in progress, so run the handler

        PalSEHDispatcherState = InExceptFinallyBlock;
        break; // break out of do loop
      }
    }
  } while(1);
  if(PalSEHDispatcherState == InExceptFinallyBlock) {

// run the handler block
```

Example 9-17. How the PAL exception-handling macros fit together

```
// END OF PAL_EXCEPT_FINALLY_COMMON
// PAL_ENDTRY

  }
  PalSEHDispatcherState = (PAL_SEH_DISPATCHER_STATE)
  PAL_EndTryHelper(&PalSEHRecord, PalSEHExceptionCode);
} while (PalSEHDispatcherState != DoneWithSEH);

// END OF PAL_ENDTRY
```

Within the PAL SEH loops, PAL_EXCEPT_FINALLY_COMMON is used to do the bulk of the work. It first sets up the filter and filter parameter if they exist. After this, the dwFlags word is zeroed, and PAL_TryHelper is called to add the registration frame to the chain for the thread. Then the ReservedForPAL field is populated by a call to PAL_setjmp, which will return 0 during normal execution and a nonzero value when the stack is being unwound. This call is made after PAL_TryHelper, because the stack unwind during the second pass will pop stack frames off the stack, executing a siglongjmp for each unmanaged frame being removed that has a termination handler (the data for which is stored in registration frame). When execution resumes at the longjmp, it will fall through to the termination code. If PAL_TryHelper were called after PAL_setjump, control flow would be incorrect.

Bracketing the termination handler code in Example 9-17 is the PAL_ENDTRY macro, with its call to PAL_EndTryHelper that removes the registration frame originally put in place by PAL_EXCEPT_FINALLY_COMMON. PAL_ENTRY will return with a value of 0 (DoneWithSEH) if the exception handler has been reached (dwFlags is PAL_EXCEPTION_FLAGS_UNWINDTARGET), in which case the while loop will be exited. Otherwise, it will call SEHUnwind, which will cause the next frame to be removed, and execution will never return to this point in the code.

The SEH routines are also called before entering and after leaving JIT-compiled code. As discussed in Chapter 6, all managed regions of the stack have an enclosing try block. To add the registration frame, helper code calls the PAL_TryHelper function, setting dwFlags to PAL_EXCEPTION_FLAGS_UNWINDONLY and supplying a special filter function that is used during stack unwinding.

Raising Exceptions and Unwinding the Stack

We've now seen how guarded regions of code can be set up using the PAL's exception macros, as well as the runtime code that is produced by those macros. We've also seen how Unix signals are converted into exceptions. Only one important detail remains to be seen: how the exceptions themselves are raised and propagated, and how the stack is unwound as a part of this process, when SEHRaiseException is called.

SEHRaiseException and SEHUnwind correspond to the first and second pass of Win32 SEH. SEHRaiseException uses a while loop to walk the frames for its thread, starting with the frame returned by PAL_GetBottommostRegistration. As it walks up the chain of registration frames, it calls the filter function for each frame that has one. This loop is shown in Example 9-18.

Example 9-18. Registration frames are walked to find exception handlers (extracted from SEHRaiseException in pal/unix/exception/exception.c)

```
// code to initialize walk omitted

while( frame ) {

// code to locate appropriate frames omitted

handler_retval =
            frame->Handler(lpExceptionPointers, frame->pvFilterParameter);

// more code omitted

  switch(handler_retval) {
    case EXCEPTION_EXECUTE_HANDLER:
      frame->dwFlags |= PAL_EXCEPTION_FLAGS_UNWINDTARGET;
      break;
    case EXCEPTION_CONTINUE_SEARCH:
      frame->dwFlags &= ~PAL_EXCEPTION_FLAGS_UNWINDTARGET;
      break;
    case EXCEPTION_CONTINUE_EXECUTION:
      TRACE("Filter returned EXCEPTION_CONTINUE_EXECUTION");
      return;
    default:
      ASSERT("Filter for frame %p returned an invalid value!\n", frame);
      break;
  }

  if ( frame->dwFlags & PAL_EXCEPTION_FLAGS_UNWINDONLY) {
    memcpy(frame->ReservedForPAL, lpExceptionPointers->ExceptionRecord,
           min(sizeof(EXCEPTION_RECORD), PAL_TRY_LOCAL_SIZE));
  }

  if ( frame->dwFlags & PAL_EXCEPTION_FLAGS_UNWINDTARGET) {
    break;
  }
  frame = frame->Next;
}

// Allow signal handling to resume
SEHSetSafeState(TRUE);

// If a handler was found, frame will hold the registration frame that was
```

Example 9-18. Registration frames are walked to find exception handlers (extracted from SEHRaiseException in pal/unix/exception/exception.c) (continued)

```
// being examined when break caused us to fall through from the walk
if ( frame ) {
  SEHUnwind();
}

// function continues with default handling
```

A filter that returns EXCEPTION_CONTINUE_EXECUTION wishes to continue the execution. Execution continues from the spot where the exception was thrown, possibly using a modified machine context if the context passed as a parameter is modified by the filter. In this case, SEHRaiseException returns immediately so that execution can continue; it is up to the calling function to determine what happens next. If SEHRaiseException was called from common_signal_handler in response to a signal, this routine will uninstall the signal handler and execute a sigreturn, thereby allowing default operating system behavior to occur. If, on the other hand, the source of the exception was a call to RaiseException, SEHRaiseException simply returns.

A filter that returns EXCEPTION_CONTINUE_SEARCH wishes the search for an appropriate handler to continue. In this case, the value of the PAL_EXCEPTION_FLAGS_UNWINDTARGET bit is preserved, the rest of the bitfield is cleared, and the walk continues.

A filter that returns EXCEPTION_EXECUTE_HANDLER wishes to schedule execution of the handler block found in frame->Handler. To do this, the PAL_EXCEPTION_FLAGS_UNWINDTARGET bit of the dwFlags bitfield is set to record the fact that this handler should be called during the second pass. The frame thus becomes the *target* of the stack unwind process that is about to occur. With the target located, execution of the loop is terminated (after the exception record is stored into the ReservedForPAL field, if necessary).

Assuming a target was found, SEHUnwind is called to start the second pass. SEHUnwind revisits the bottom-most registration frame and walks up the chain of frames in order, as shown in Example 9-19.

Example 9-19. The second-pass walk of a thread's registration frames (extracted from pal/unix/exception/exception.c)

```
jmp_frame = PAL_GetBottommostRegistration();

// loop until a frame to execute is found
while (NULL != jmp_frame) {
  if ( jmp_frame->Handler == NULL ) {
    // finally blocks have no filter entry
    // if this is a finally block, break out of loop and longjmp
    break;
```

```
    }

    // this case for JIT compiled (or special) code
    if( jmp_frame->dwFlags & PAL_EXCEPTION_FLAGS_UNWINDONLY) {
        // code for exceptions from JIT-compiled code omitted
        jmp_frame->dwFlags &= ~PAL_EXCEPTION_FLAGS_UNWINDTARGET;

        PAL_SetBottommostRegistration(jmp_frame);

        ep.ExceptionRecord = (PEXCEPTION_RECORD) jmp_frame->ReservedForPAL;
        ep.ExceptionRecord->ExceptionFlags |= EXCEPTION_UNWINDING;
        ep.ContextRecord = NULL;

        retval = jmp_frame->Handler(&ep, jmp_frame->pvFilterParameter);

    // this case for "normal" exception handling
    } else if ( jmp_frame->dwFlags & PAL_EXCEPTION_FLAGS_UNWINDTARGET ) {
        break;
    }

    jmp_frame = jmp_frame->Next;
}

// when loop is terminated using "break", execute the frame's handler
if (jmp_frame) {
    // get set for second pass to continue
    PAL_SetBottommostRegistration(jmp_frame->Next);
    siglongjmp((LPVOID)jmp_frame->ReservedForPAL,1);
}
```

The unwinding of the stack involves non-local transfers of control, which is accomplished by using Unix' *longjmp* mechanism. When the target frame is found, or when the Handler field is NULL (which indicates that the frame is a termination handler that must be executed), the walk of registration frames is terminated using break, and siglongjmp is called with the contents of the ReservedForPAL field. The jump transfers execution directly to the frame's exception or termination handler. Before doing this, the bottom-most handler in the chain of registration frames is reset to point to the Next registration frame in the chain. If the handler that is the target of the jump is a termination handler, it will continue the unwinding process; every termination handler will be called up the chain until the target frame is reached. The code in the target frame's handler will be run at that point, after which normal execution can resume.

Careful examination of Example 9-19 will reveal an alternative unwinding strategy used by registration frames that have their PAL_EXCEPTION_FLAGS_UNWINDONLY flag set. The filter function in this case is an execution engine helper routine, and rather than jumping nonlocally, control is transferred using a function call on the handler directly. Note that an EXCEPTION_RECORD is set up for this function, and that the exception record has its EXCEPTION_UNWINDING flag set. By checking this value, the helper can continue unwinding the chain of registration frames through managed regions of the stack.

Frames marked as "unwind only" in this way are used to handle exceptions that occur in JIT-compiled code. Every entry into JIT-compiled code is protected by the execution engine helper function, which will dispatch exceptions to managed handlers as appropriate. If a regular PAL_TRY/PAL_EXCEPT were used to protect JIT-compiled code, it would not be able to execute second-pass handlers, since their activation records would have been eliminated from the stack by the call to longjmp. "Unwind only" frames are also much faster to set up than regular PAL_TRY frames, because they do not capture CPU state using setjmp. Because of this, they are used internally by some execution engine functions. (See Object::Validate in *clr/src/vm/object.cpp* for an example of this use.)

If no frame is found to handle an exception after two passes over the chain of registration frames, the process is terminated by a call to TerminateProcess, unless the exception was raised by a signal. In this case, the signal handler is removed and SEHRaiseException returns, allowing the signal to be raised again, just as if EXCEPTION_CONTINUE_EXECUTION had been encountered. The advantage to this approach is that unhandled PAL exceptions turn into Unix core dumps.

Managing Memory with the PAL

Memory is a fundamental computational resource, and not surprisingly, the PAL provides memory allocation as a service to the SSCLI. The four Win32 routines, VirtualAlloc, VirtualFree, VirtualProtect, and VirtualQuery, form the basis for this service and are what lie beneath the intricate memory management mechanisms that we examined in Chapter 7. In the Unix PAL, the logical implementation choice would seem to be to use the mmap functions as a basis for these APIs. This is, in fact, ultimately the choice, although a few problems had to be solved along the way to get the code to work, mostly having to do with the lower-level nature of mmap.

While mmap has the ability to allocate memory in a way that maps nicely to VirtualAlloc, there is no standard equivalent to VirtualQuery. What is ore problematical is that some implementations of mmap are unable to provide memory at a specific virtual address and, instead, assign the address unilaterally. (The hint parameter, which is provided in the API for this purpose, is honored by most implementations but not all.) VirtualAlloc, of course, has a nearly opposite usage: allocation either happens at the location specified or the request fails.

The SSCLI depends on the `VirtualAlloc` approach, since several of its algorithms use structures that have known starting addresses to simplify address calculations. Because of this, and because of the lack of `VirtualQuery` functionality, the PAL implements extra infrastructure to keep track of the state of memory, and additionally defines several platform-specific macros: `MMAP_IGNORES_HINT` and `HAVE_VM_ALLOCATE` (for use with Mac OS X). The use of these flags causes the file *pal/unix/map/virtual.c* to be a slightly gnarly combination of several solutions under `#ifdef`.

Working Around Inconsistencies

FreeBSD doesn't ignore `mmap`'s address hint, but other Unix implementations do. To ensure portable behavior, the general solution selected was to map a file into memory—the PAL uses its own on-disk image for this purpose, since it is reasonably certain to exist—and to reserve a 1 GB chunk of address space within that map. Memory can then be suballocated from the resulting address range by using a local allocator and a free list to replace `mmap` allocation. `VirtualQuery` and `VirtualProtect` can remain unchanged within this scheme, but `VIRTUALReserve` and `VirtualCommit` must use the PAL routines in place of calls to `mmap`. `VirtualFree` also needs to have a slightly different codepath.

Mac OS X ignores the address hint. On this operating system, however, there is an alternative workaround. Rather then reimplement the allocator, the OS X PAL handles this case by calling Mach's `vm_allocate` to allocate the memory at the requested address and, if successful, then calls `mmap` at the same address. Not pretty, but it seems to work. (Of course, one good reason to use an adaptation layer is to isolate such less-than-pretty bits from the main code base.)

There is only one data structure of note, the CMI list, which is used by the virtual-memory management code. This list is a doubly linked list of CMI structures, shown in Example 9-20, which is rooted in the global variable pVirtualMemory. Notice the use of `HAVE_VM_ALLOCATE` in this structure definition.

Example 9-20. CMI structures

```
typedef struct _CMI {
  struct _CMI * pNext;    /* Link to the next entry. */
  struct _CMI * pLast;    /* Link to the previous entry. */
```

Example 9-20. CMI structures (continued)

```
UINT        startBoundary;       // Start of page-aligned region.
UINT        memSize;             // Size of the region

#if !HAVE_VM_ALLOCATE
  DWORD         accessProtection; // Initial access protection
  DWORD         allocationType;   // Initial allocation type
  BYTE        * pAllocState;      // Per-page protection tracking
  BYTE        * pProtectionState; // Per-page allocation type tracking #endif //
!HAVE_VM_ALLOCATE
}CMI, * PCMI;
```

The CMI list represents all virtual memory managed by the PAL. Each startBoundary field contains the page-aligned starting location of the memory region for an entry, and memSize is its page-aligned size. allocationType is used for the initial allocation type of the region, and is recorded directly from the arguments to VirtualAlloc, and is one or more of the following: MEM_COMMIT, MEM_RESERVE, or MEM_TOP_DOWN (which is ignored by the PAL). The initial allocation type for the region can be found in the allocationType field, whose value is recorded directly from the call to VirtualAlloc.

There is a single critical section, virtual_critsec, to protect access to the CMI list. Locking is designed to minimize lock contention.

Protecting Memory

The PAL provides memory protection to help minimize the chances of corrupting the contents of memory. The accessProtection field of the CMI structure contains the initial access protection setting for a range of memory, while the pProtectionState field points to an array of bytes, each of which represents the protection state of a corresponding page of memory in the region. In the PAL, protection setting can combine: PAGE_NOACCESS, PAGE_READONLY, PAGE_READWRITE, PAGE_EXECUTE, PAGE_EXECUTE_READ, and PAGE_EXECUTE_READWRITE. The values stored in the pProtectionState array are converted from these PAL-specified values to internal values defined in the enum VIRTUAL_CONSTANTS.

The implementation of the VirtualProtect API is fairly straightforward. After protection flags are checked for valid combinations, the requested starting address and size is page-aligned, and the CMI list is consulted to see whether the starting address is known. If it is, the code ensures that all of the pages that are covered by the request have been committed, and mprotect is called on the pages with new protection flag values. Finally, the list's byte array is updated with the new protection values.

Reserving Versus Committing Memory

VirtualAlloc is actually a simple wrapper over two distinct functions: VIRTUALReserveMemory and VIRTUALCommitMemory. In the Win32 model, pages of virtual memory are classified as *free*, *reserved*, or *committed*. PAL programmers can reserve a range of addresses, using VIRTUALReserveMemory, without actually requiring committed pages for those addresses until they are needed, at which point VIRTUALCommitMemory can be called. Address reservation is separated from page commitment in this way since contiguous ranges of addresses are often useful for algorithmic efficiency, and yet the system resources required to back large ranges with physical memory can be prohibitively expensive. Since the pages in a range are typically not needed all at one time, incremental commitment is a good solution.

VIRTUALReserveMemory takes the same arguments as VirtualAlloc. After aligning to the nearest 64 KB boundary and adjusting the allocation size to be page-aligned (and increasing the size if necessary to make up for starting alignment), this function calls mmap using MAP_ANON | MAP_PRIVATE. There is a catch here, since mmap both reserves and commits memory in the same action, and most Unix memory managers can overcommit memory. (Overcommitment means that the first time an application touches some page, the memory manager may discover that it can't find a free physical page and is forced to segfault!) In an attempt to mitigate this situation, VIRTUALCommitMemory writes a 0 to each page, verifying that the physical page is available. (If it is not, the PAL fails, which is the desired behavior, since the SSCLI is not built to expect segfaults that result from committing memory.)

VIRTUALCommitMemory uses the pAllocState field in Example 9-20 to track the status of the pages being managed by the PAL. pAllocState contains a pointer to an array of bytes that represents a bitmap over all of the pages in the region. This bitmap is used to implement the separate actions of page reservation and page commitment; it records whether a page is committed.

VirtualFree also supports the separation between memory reservation and memory commitment. Decommitting memory (bringing the memory back to the reserved state) and releasing memory (releasing the reserve back to the operating system) are both possible. In fact, the two operations cannot be done at one time; if this is attempted, an error occurs. This is a good example of a PAL-only simplification; on Windows, recommitting and releasing memory may be combined into a single operation under some, but not all, circumstances.

When releasing memory, the starting address supplied to the function must match the base address of a CMI region, and the size parameter must be 0. VirtualFree calls munmap with the region's base address and size, which is obtained from the CMI list. The region is removed from the CMI list via VIRTUALReleaseMemory.

Updating Memory with Interlocked Instructions

The PAL includes a family of routines that is extremely valuable for implementing runtime infrastructure in a multithreaded environment. Each of these routines guarantees that the action it performs, such as incrementing or decrementing a memory location, is done atomically. Even if two threads in different processes were to access a shared memory location, atomic operations guarantee that only one will be able to read or write at a time, and no interleaving will occur.

Other mechanisms in the PAL, such as critical sections, achieve the same effect, but the routines in this family are typically much more lightweight in terms of processor overhead. Their limitation is that they can update only a single memory location, and exchange only two memory locations. Critical sections or mutexes must be used for anything larger.

The interlocked routines must typically be implemented in assembler, and almost always leverage unique processor characteristics. Consider one of the routines used in several places in the PAL: InterlockedCompareExchange. The code for the Intel x86 version of this function can be found in *pal/unix/arch/i386/interlock.c*:

```
__asm__ __volatile__(
    "lock; cmpxchgl %2,(%1)"
    : "=a" (result)
    : "r" (Destination), "r" (Exchange), "0" (Comperand)
    : "memory"
    );
```

Note that the cmpxchgl instruction is being used, which performs the compare and exchange in a single operation, in combination with the lock prefix, which is required to cause an atomic update in a multiprocessor environment. Now consider what this routine looks like in *pal/unix/arch/ppc/interlock.s*, which is an implementation for the Motorola PowerPC chip:

```
InterlockedCompareExchange
    lwarx r6, 0, r2
    cmpw r6,r5
    bne ContW
    stwcx. r4,0,r2
    bne _InterlockedCompareExchange
ContW:
    sync
    mr r2,r6
    blr
```

The PowerPC has no single instruction equivalent to cmpxchgl, and so the compare and exchange is implemented using *load* and *store with reservation* operations.

Exploring the Rest of the PAL

The rest of the PAL's implementation has much less impact on the algorithms and operation of the execution engine than the topics already discussed in this chapter. It does, however, bear marks left by higher-level design choices, and perusing the code looking for these marks can be a very interesting exercise.

The code that provides network and file I/O, for example, is straightforward until the point where it hits semantic differences between Unix and the programming model of the CLI's frameworks. As a final source-code expedition, we will briefly outline two areas in which these semantic mismatches require the PAL to install expensive impedance-matching code.

Locking File Regions in Multiple Processes

Unlike most flavors of Unix, Win32 supports region locking within opened files. Even so, implementing this feature in the PAL would be straightforward, were it not for the locked regions of opened files that must be accessible to all PAL processes. Because the feature is exposed by the Lock and Unlock methods of System.IO.FileStream in the base class library, locking must be valid across process group boundaries, and the data used to represent opened files must be stored in shared memory. As discussed in the previous section "Sharing Memory Between Unix Processes," shared memory is a potential bottleneck to system throughput due to its region locking. Because of this, the data needed to implement file I/O, like all of the other handle-based implementations in the PAL, is divided between local- and shared-memory structures.

The file structure, with its now-familiar initial HOBJSTRUCT, holds file data local to a process, while the SHMFILELOCKS and SHMFILELOCKRGNS structures combine to represent region-locking data that must be available in shared memory. All of these structures are defined in *pal/unix/include/pal/file.h*, and all are shown in Example 9-21.

Example 9-21. The structures used to represent region locking in files (defined in pal/unix/ /include/pal/file.h)

```
typedef struct _file
{
  HOBJSTRUCT        handle_data;
  struct _file      *self_addr;
  int               unix_fd;
  // Windows can open a file for writing only, so this must exist here
  DWORD             dwDesiredAccess;
  int               open_flags;
```

```
  BOOL            open_flags_deviceaccessonly;
  char            *unix_filename;
  SHMPTR          shmFileLocks;
  BOOL            inheritable;
} file;

typedef struct
{
  SHMPTR          unix_filename;
  SHMPTR          fileLockedRgns;
  UINT            refCount;
  SHMPTR          next;
  SHMPTR          prev;
  DWORD           share_mode;
  int             nbReadAccess;
  int             nbWriteAccess;
} SHMFILELOCKS;

typedef struct
{
  DWORD           processId;
  file            *fileStructPtr;
  UINT64          lockRgnStart;
  UINT64          nbBytesLocked;
  int             lockType;
  SHMPTR next;
} SHMFILELOCKRGNS;
```

The self_addr field in file is set to point to the head of the _file structure and is used strictly for PAL debugging. Unsurprisingly, unix_fd contains the handle of the underlying Unix file descriptor, valid only while the underlying file is open (and otherwise set to -1). The dwDesiredAccess field contains a copy of the parameter value of the same name passed to the CreateFile functions, while open_flags are the flags that were actually used to open the Unix file. The value of the open_flags field is ultimately a combination of the dwDesiredAccess and dwCreationDisposition arguments to CreateFile, and since it is used for a number of file code operations, it makes sense to calculate it and then cache the resulting value, which is exactly what is done. The open_flags_deviceaccessonly field is used when a file is opened with dwDesiredAccess equal to 0, which indicates that the call is intended to allow queries about file or device attributes, and not to access the file or device. The inheritable field is used to indicate whether the file can be inherited by spawned processes, and finally, shmFileLocks contains a pointer to the shared memory information that details the lock structures associated with a file.

The two data structures used to implement file locking for PAL processes within a process group are SHMFILELOCKS and SHMFILELOCKRGNS. In SHMFILELOCKS, the unix_filename field is a pointer to shared memory that is used to uniquely identify the file with which a locked region is associated. (To see this field in action, examine the function FILEGetSHMFileLocks in *pal/unix/file/file.c*.)

The fileLockedRgns field contains a pointer to a linked list of SHMFILELOCKRGNS that define individual locked regions of a file. Like other shared memory structures, SHMFILELOCKS structures are placed in a doubly linked list; hence the next and prev pointers. Each region stores the dwShareMode argument from calls to CreateFile into its share_mode field the first time that a file is opened. Subsequent opens, whether within a process or from another process in the PAL process group, will consult this field to check for sharing flags.

Both nbReadAccess and nbWriteAccess are used as reference counts to track the count of open file handles with, respectively, GENERIC_READ and GENERIC_WRITE access. When CreateFile is called to open a file, the file's nbReadAccess and nbWriteAccess counts will be consulted if the file is open within the process group. For each reference count that is nonzero, dwShareMode must have the appropriate bit set (FILE_SHARE_READ and/or FILE_SHARE_WRITE) to open the file. The value of the lockType field may contain one of two values: either USER_LOCK_RGN for normal locks that come from a call to LockFile, or RDWR_LOCK_RGN for locks that are used internally by the PAL to implement ReadFile and WriteFile.

Finally, the linked list of SHMFILELOCKRGNS is sorted by the value of the lockRgnStart field, which represents the start of the locking region. Both lockRgnStart and nbBytesLocked (which holds the number of bytes to lock in the region) are UINT64 values so that they can be used with very large files.

As you can see, by requiring that region locking be visible across process boundaries, a simple task was made much more complex!

Asynchronous Socket Operations

The PAL supports both the Winsock 1 and Winsock 2 APIs. Most of Winsock 1 is provided by a very light layer over the BSD socket API, since the functionality is nearly identical. Winsock 2, however, is more difficult to map, since its model for asynchronous I/O is different.

The basic approach used by the PAL to implement asynchronous sockets is to employ a worker thread for handling socket operations in the background. Commands to this thread are one-way, and are sent using a pipe.

The thread is created, along with its pipe, the first time WSAStartup is called. It is destroyed in WSACleanup when the SOCK_startup_count goes to 0. (See *pal/unix/socket/socket2.c* for details.) There is never more than one worker thread at a time in a given process.

The heart of the worker is the function SOCKWorkerThreadMain, which can be found in *pal/unix/socket/async.c*. It is a large while loop in which a list of sockets is repeatedly checked using poll for:

- Pending data that is ready to be received
- Sockets that are ready to accept outgoing data
- Sockets that have completed connecting
- Pending connections that are ready to be accepted
- Sockets that have been closed remotely
- Errors

When the worker thread calls poll to wait for its next activity, it includes the descriptor for its communication pipe in the list of file descriptors. Doing so allows the worker thread to wake up when either an interesting event occurs on a socket being monitored, or when a new command has been issued by another thread in the system via a call to WSARecv, WSASend, WSARecvFrom, WSASendTo, or WSAEventSelect.

Commands are represented by the ws2_op structure, which is shown in Example 9-22.

Example 9-22. The ws2_op structure is used to control asynchronous socket operations

```
typedef struct _ws2_op
{
  struct _ws2_op * self_addr;
  PAL_SOCKET       s;
  enum ws2_opcode  opcode;
  HANDLE           event;
} ws2_op;
```

Commands, when they are sent, set the socket value s on which the operation will be performed. The field opcode in sw2_op can take on any of the following values:

WS2_OP_SENDTO
    Queues data to be sent on the socket

WS2_OP_RECVFROM
    Queues a buffer into which data will be received from the socket

WS2_OP_EVENTSELECT
    Informs the worker thread which network events to monitor

`WS2_OP_CLOSESOCKET`
  Closes the socket, when overlapped operations have concluded

`WS2_OP_STOP_THREAD`
  Terminates the worker thread

Wrapping up our discussion of the mechanism, the event in Example 9-22 named, somewhat ambiguously, event, is used for close notifications, since the `WS2_OP_CLOSESOCKET` command cannot take place immediately if overlapped operations are pending.

Once again, what could have been a very thin wrapper on preexisting Unix functionality became a more heavyweight and more complicated solution, due to an impedance mismatch between the semantics of the higher-level programming API and the systems-level service. The PAL may abstract platform differences away for the purposes of Rotor's source code, but those differences are very real from the perspective of resource consumption and processor cycles.

Joining Components to the OS

The PAL contains important lessons for students of high-level abstractions such as the CLI. Structure and behavior represented as CLI types must eventually become code that runs within the boundaries imposed by the APIs of some operating system. This code must accommodate the processor instruction set and device drivers of the system unequivocally; there is no give-and-take. Because of this, the options presented by an operating system API profoundly affect all abstractions built above them, including virtualized execution.

One could imagine the opposite also being true: the CLI's integration model could be so valuable that it could affect the capabilities and abstractions of underlying operating systems. Boundaries that enhance the safety of collaboration, such as those that accompany the concepts of component, of application domain, of typesafe code, of automatic memory management, and of generalized chained protection frames, characterize the CLI integration model. One of the main purposes of operating systems is to enable the integration of code from many sources with concepts such as device drivers, applications, and system libraries—so the design of OS boundary abstractions is also very important.

There is currently overlap between the mechanisms invented to support CLI components and those that support operating systems, such as the use of threads and structured exceptions, but this overlap is surprisingly small. The successful joining of component-based software to operating systems and hardware design seems to be a page yet to be written.

A Quick Tour of Rotor

Expanding the Rotor tarball reveals a bewildering collection of scripts, license files, specifications, and subdirectories full of mysterious source code. The prospective Rotor enthusiast may wonder where best to begin poking around. This appendix provides a "view from the top," and will help you find your way around.

There are four interesting "districts" in the Rotor code:

- The CLI runtime execution engine
- Programming frameworks that expose the services of this execution engine
- Compilers and other tools that target the execution engine
- A platform adaptation layer (PAL), its tests, and related build utilities

These four areas are spread across the source tree. As with any large software project, both history and build dependencies have conspired to make navigation less than perfect. However, the documentation will help: whether you want to learn about, tinker with, or experiment with Rotor's infrastructure, you are likely to find that the files in the *docs* directory are a valuable first stop (along with the file named *readfirst.html* found in the root of the distribution).

Execution engine (the clr/src directory and environs)
Conceptually, the execution engine is the heart and soul of the CLI runtime, and as such, it contains a large quantity of fascinating code. Compilers and tools that target this engine, including the C# and JScript compilers that come as a part of Rotor, create and manipulate executable files that contain metadata tables, resource blobs, and code in the form of abstract CIL opcodes.

The loading of a managed program is a miracle of self-assembly, during which those inert blobs of metadata, resources, and CIL are transformed into instructions that execute directly on the microprocessor. The *vm* subdirectory contains the main core of the life-support system for managed components that accomplishes this transformation, including the CLI's sophisticated automatic heap and stack management, its object-capable type system, and its mechanisms for dynamically loading code safely. The *fusion* and *md* (metadata) subdirectories are also important; they comprise important parts of the data-driven process and have code for resolving references to external types, and metadata manipulation and validation code, respectively.

Frameworks (fx, managedlibraries, bcl, and classlibnative)
In addition to the exotic machinery of managed code, you'll also find more familiar programming support infrastructure in the Rotor CLI, wrapped up as a set of class frameworks. The specification for these frameworks is part of ECMA-335, and includes the BCL, runtime infrastructure and reflection classes, networking and XML classes, and floating-point and extended array libraries. All of these are in Rotor, in source-code form. There are also a few additional libraries included in this distribution, most notably support for regular expressions and an extensive framework for type serialization, object remoting, and automatic type marshaling.

Compilers and tools (jscript and clr/src/csharp)
The JScript compiler, found in the *jscript* directory, is completely written in C#. The language itself is quite interesting from the perspective of a compiler writer, since it supports dynamic reshaping of classes, as well as the runtime evaluation of arbitrary fragments of code. For those who would like to implement dynamic languages, such as Python or Scheme, on top of the CLI runtime, or understand how this could be done, this code will prove instructive. In particular, note the heavy use of runtime reflection and the dynamic emission of metadata.

In order to build the sources for the JScript compiler, there must be a C# compiler in the Rotor distribution. Not surprisingly, there is, and it can be found in the *clr/src/csharp* directory. The Rotor C# implementation should be a useful guide to anyone building their own C# compiler and/or frameworks.

Besides the C# compiler, the sources to a managed code debugger, an assembler and disassembler (*ilasm* and *ildasm*), an assembly linker, and a stand-alone verification tool reside in subdirectories of *clr/src*. These tools will be indispensable as you look through Rotor and work with the code; they will serve as both implementation examples and everyday programming tools.

The final compiler to point out during this leg of the tour is the combination JIT compiler and verifier that live in the *clr/src/fjit* directory. Large parts of Rotor are written in C#, and because the Rotor C# compiler outputs CIL opcodes rather than native code, this means that large parts of Rotor are compiled by the JIT compiler when the types are loaded, at the last possible moment.

The Platform Adaptation Layer and build (pal, palrt, tests, and tools)
Rotor's PAL, tests, and build tools enables the moving of this distribution to alternate platforms. The code for the Unix PAL, which is found in the *pal/unix* directory, is well worth a peek. This code was written to conform to a subset of the Win32 API, outlined in *docs/techinfo/pal_guide.html* and implemented in *pal/rotor_pal.h*. By mimicking Win32's semantics for structured exception handling, threading, synchronization primitives, file and network I/O, debugger support, and other similar system-level services, porting the Rotor code base became more of an exercise in finding PAL bugs than in reimplementing existing code.

The bootstrap sequence for the Rotor build process is interesting and shows that the PAL is important for more than just the CLI runtime itself. The first thing to build on any platform is the PAL itself; obviously, this must be done using native libraries and tools. After the PAL has been successfully built, Rotor's own build tools are then compiled against the PAL, after which the CLI C# compiler can be built. At this point, you have a working C# compiler, and so the large number of C# files that are a part of this distribution can be compiled. And since C# uses the managed execution environment, the last step of the build process actually occurs when you run any of the programs that contain managed code—the JIT compiler is invoked on your behalf!

The build tools used in this bootstrap sequence can be found in the tools directory and are documented in the *docs/buildtools* directory. Once the build has been successfully executed and you are making modifications, you should to pay a visit to the tests directory, in order to take advantage of its PAL suite, as well as the general Rotor quality suites, which currently contain base IL tests, base verification tests, and some JIT verification tests.

There is no better way to learn about the CLI and C# standards than by browsing and building the Rotor sources. These sources are included on the accompanying CD-ROM in the file *sscli.tgz*. See Appendix B for instructions on how to extract and compile the source code in this archive. In addition to the Rotor sources, the CD-ROM includes the following directories:

archives
Rotor source code and reference documentation, in separate compressed file archives

ecma

Standards and support documentation for ECMA-334 (The C# Language Specification) and ECMA-335 (The Common Language Infrastructure)

presentations

Various presentations on Rotor

refdocs

Extensive programming documentation for Rotor's Base Class Library frameworks

samples

C# sample code from this book

sscli

Uncompressed Rotor sources

Building Rotor

Rotor 1.0 can be built on Windows XP, FreeBSD 4.7, and Mac OS X 10.2 (Jaguar). It should also build on Windows 2000 and earlier versions of FreeBSD (as far back as 4.5), but your mileage may vary on these platforms. You will need about 80 MB of disk space to extract the Rotor source code. However, Rotor will end up using much more when its compilation is complete (about a gigabyte on FreeBSD and half that on Windows). You should set aside a bit more to account for temporary files and swap file growth.

The build process may take several hours on a low-end machine, especially if you are running with less than the suggested amount of memory. For Windows, we suggest 256 MB of RAM. For Mac OS X and FreeBSD, 512 MB of RAM is ideal, but you can get by with less.

Before you install Rotor, you'll need to download the source code from *http://msdn.microsoft.com/net/sscli* or copy the archive from the CD-ROM. Later sections ("Building Rotor on Windows" and "Building Rotor on Unix") list instructions on how to extract the source code.

 Whether you are on Windows or Unix, you must not extract Rotor into a directory whose path contains spaces. (Some tools used during the build process do not work correctly on paths that contain spaces.) For example, *C:\Documents and Settings\dstutz\My Documents* would be a bad choice on Windows, as would */Users/dstutz/Source Code* on Mac OS X.

Build Mode

Rotor supports three build modes. To select a build mode, pass one of the following arguments (checked, fastchecked, or free) to the *env.bat*, *env.sh*, or *env.csh* script.

checked

> Turns off optimizations, enables debug code, and generates debugging symbols

free

> Turns on optimizations, disables debug code, and generates debugging symbols

fastchecked

> Turns on some optimizations, enables debug code, and generates debugging symbols

Windows Prerequisites

Under Windows, you'll need Visual Studio .NET, Perl 5.6 (we suggest ActivePerl, available at *http://www.activestate.com*), and an archiving utility that can handle tar files compressed with gzip. We suggest the command-line *gzip* and *tar* utilities, available from *ftp://ftp.gnu.org/pub/gnu/windows/emacs/utilities/i386/*.

FreeBSD Prerequisites

Under FreeBSD, FreeBSD Version 4.7 is recommended for building Rotor. You should use the standard install CD-ROM rather than the minimal boot install. To be sure that you have all the tools you need, select the Developer install when the FreeBSD installer prompts you to choose an installation type.

Mac OS X Prerequisites

To build Rotor on Mac OS X, you will need Mac OS X 10.2 (Jaguar) and the Developer Tools from Apple. If you bought the boxed version of Mac OS X, the Developer Tools should be included on a separate CD-ROM. If you bought a new Macintosh that came with Mac OS X preinstalled, the Developer Tools installer will probably be in */Applications/Installers*. If either of these fail, or if you'd like to get the latest version of the tools, they are available to Apple Developer Connection (ADC) members at *http://connect.apple.com/*.

Building Rotor on Windows

First, extract the archiving using *gzip* and *tar*. If you use the *gzip* and *tar* utilities from *ftp.gnu.org*, you will need to pipe *gzip*'s output to *tar*, since this version of *tar* does not support the z option for reading compressed

---

archives. (You could also use WinZip to extract the archive, but if you do, make sure that "smart" CR/LF conversion is turned off in the *miscellaneous options* tab).

```
>gzip -dc sscli_20021101.tgz | tar xvf -
sscli/
sscli/buildall
sscli/buildall.cmd
sscli/clr/
sscli/clr/bin/
... output truncated ...
```

If you see an error message that states "couldn't change access and modification times of sscli," don't worry. This error occurs with the version of *tar* available from the *ftp.gnu.org* site and is harmless. When the file is completely extracted, change directory to *sscli* and run the environment settings batch file:

```
>cd sscli

>env.bat
Setting environment for using Microsoft Visual Studio .NET 2003 tools.
(If you have another version of Visual Studio or Visual C++ installed and wish
to use its tools from the command line, run vcvars32.bat for that version.)
CLR environment (C:\sscli\clr\bin\rotorenv.bat)
Building for Operating System - NT32
              Processor Family - x86
                     Processor - i386
             Build Environment = C:\sscli\rotorenv
                    Build Type - fastchecked
```

env.bat accepts an optional argument, which can be one of free, fastchecked, or checked. (See "Build Mode," earlier in this appendix.) Next, run *buildall.cmd*. This will build the Shared Source CLI.

```
>buildall.cmd

--- Building the PAL ---
... output truncated ...
```

 On either Windows or Unix, you can invoke *buildall* (or *buildall.cmd*) with the -c option to force a clean build. This deletes all intermediate object files before building.

Building Rotor on Unix

First, extract the archive using *tar* (under Mac OS X, you should use the *gnutar* utility instead of the older Unix *tar*):

```
% tar xvfz sscli_20021101.tgz
sscli/
```

```
sscli/buildall
sscli/buildall.cmd
sscli/clr/
sscli/clr/bin/
... output truncated ...
```

When *tar* is finished, change directory to the *sscli* directory and load the environment settings. Use *env.csh* if you are using the *csh* or *tcsh* shell:

```
% cd sscli
% source env.csh
Fastchecked Environment
%
```

If you are using *bash*, *ksh*, or *sh*, use *env.sh*:

```
$ cd sscli
$ . env.sh
Fastchecked Environment
$
```

The *env.csh* and *env.sh* scripts accept an optional argument, which can be one of free, fastchecked, or checked. (See "Build Mode," earlier in this appendix.) Next, run the *buildall* script. It will start by running a configuration script and then will proceed to compile the Shared Source CLI (SSCLI):

```
% ./buildall
Running configure...
Building the PAL...
... output truncated ...
```

After you've built the SSCLI, you may need to run the rehash command (use hash under the *bash* shell) so that the newly created binaries appear in your PATH:

```
% clix
clix: Command not found.
% rehash
% clix
Managed application launcher.

Usage: clix managed_exe [optional arguments to the exe]
```

Tests

The tests in the SSCLI are broken into two large sections, with each section broken into several smaller subsections. The large sections are:

PAL test suite
> This test suite and driver were developed to act as a quality suite for the PAL, which is used to implement the SSCLI on multiple platforms.

SSCLI quality suites
> These suites and the associated driver test everything else in the system.

PAL Test Suite

The PAL test suite is designed to validate the quality of the PAL. You can run this test suite before anything else in the SSCLI runs; therefore, it has no dependencies on anything running other than the PAL itself. The driver script for the PAL test suite is called *pvtrun.pl*. After you build the PAL, change directory to *%ROTOR_DIR%/tests* and execute the tests by running this script; it will execute around 1,200 tests from the *palsuite* directory.

The PAL test harness is located in the *%ROTOR_DIR%/tests/harness/test_harness* directory. The test harness uses several environment variables that indicate where to find its test list, where to store results, and where to find its helper driver *xrun*. These environment variables are usually set in a wrapper script, such as *pvtrun.pl*, but they can also be set individually in the environment for manual execution.

Additional tests are not run by default from the driver script. See the PAL test *%ROTOR_DIR%/tests/palsuite/readme.txt* for more details on running the remaining suites.

SSCLI Quality Suites

The SSCLI quality suites are the tests for everything other than the PAL. The main test driver is implemented in *%ROTOR_DIR%/tests/rrun.pl*. The *rrun* driver traverses the directory tree starting with the working directory of the process that invoked the driver and working down the directory structure collecting the test information. All tests that match a simple set of criteria are executed and the results reported.

The source comments at the top of the *rrun.pl* file should be consulted for more complete details of driver operation.

To run the entire test inventory, execute the *rrun* driver from within the *%ROTOR_DIR%/tests* directory. To run a subset of tests, simply change to one of the following tests, and then run *../rrun.pl*:

Base verification tests
> The base verification tests (BVTs) are a set of quick tests that can be run after a source modification is made to ensure that basic functionality continues to work correctly. These are sometimes called *smoke tests*. These tests are located in *%ROTOR_DIR%/tests/bvt*.

CIL tests
> The base CIL tests are located in *%ROTOR_DIR%/tests/il_bvt*. These tests provide core coverage of the CIL instructions in the system.

Verifier tests

Verifier tests check the verifier in the JIT-compiler. These tests are located in *%ROTOR_DIR%/tests/security/verifier*. In addition to these tests, many tests throughout the tree require verification to be either off or on; these are marked with the attributes <VERIFIERMUSTBEOFF> and <VERIFIERMUSTBEON> in the appropriate source file.

Base class library tests

You can find tests for the base class libraries in *%ROTOR_DIR%/tests/bcl*.

Miscellaneous tests and support infrastructure

The *%ROTOR_DIR%/tests/utilities* directory contains support functions for other tests. The *%ROTOR_DIR%/tests/dev* directory contains tests that cover specific cases not covered by other tests but discovered during the development process.

Build Scenarios

If you want to modify the SSCLI's source code, you need to know what is built at various stages of the SSCLI's build process, and how to run selected portions of the build.

The SSCLI build process is responsible for building a series of elements:

- Primary bootstrap elements: the PAL and unmanaged bootstrap build tools
- Secondary bootstrap elements: the remaining tools and support infrastructure
- Core elements: The core CLI implementation, base class libraries, the C# compiler, and supporting tools
- The FX class libraries and supporting tools
- Other assemblies
- Managed compilers

If you'd like to modify part of the source tree, you should first build the entire SSCLI using the instructions in this appendix. After you've done that, you can modify the source code and rebuild just the element that you changed.

 All of the environment variables, such as %ROTOR_DIR% or ${ROTOR_DIR}, are defined by the *env.csh*, *env.sh*, or *env.bat* scripts, so you do not need to replace them yourself in the examples that follow.

Primary Bootstrap

The Primary Bootstrap phase builds the PAL and the *nmake*, *binplace*, and *build* utilities.

Building the PAL

Since *build* and other tools depend on the PAL, it must be built first. To build the PAL (*%TARGETCOMPLUS%\rotor_pal.dll*) on Windows:

```
>cd %ROTOR_DIR%\pal\win32
>build
```

To build the PAL (*${TARGETCOMPLUS}/librotor_pal.so or .dylib*) on Unix:

```
% cd ${ROTOR_DIR}/pal/unix
% make
```

Building nmake

The SSCLI expects that *nmake* (program maintenance utility) is already available on Windows, so it uses only its own *nmake* on Unix platforms. To build *nmake* (*${TARGETCOMPLUS}/nmake*) on Unix:

```
% cd ${ROTOR_DIR}/tools/nmake
% make
```

Building binplace

The *binplace* tool collects compiled binaries and places them in the Rotor installation directory. To build *binplace* (*%TARGETCOMPLUS%\binplace.exe*) on Windows:

```
>cd %ROTOR_DIR%\tools\binplace
>make.cmd
```

To build *binplace* (*${TARGETCOMPLUS}/binplace*) on Unix:

```
% cd ${ROTOR_DIR}/tools/binplace
% make
```

Building build

The *build* utility drives the compilation of libraries and executables in the SSCLI. To build *build* (*%TARGETCOMPLUS%\build.exe*) on Windows:

```
>cd %ROTOR_DIR%\tools\build
>make.cmd
```

To build *build* (*${TARGETCOMPLUS}/build*) on Unix:

```
% cd ${ROTOR_DIR}/tools/build
% make
```

Secondary Bootstrap

This phase assumes that the Primary Bootstrap phase is complete and that all the build tools are working. During this phase, the resource compiler and the PAL runtime are built.

Building the resource compiler

This is the Rotor equivalent of the CLR resource compiler (*rc.exe*) on Windows. To build the resource compiler (*%TARGETCOMPLUS%\resourcecompiler.exe*) on Windows:

```
>cd %ROTOR_DIR%\tools\resourcecompiler
>build
```

To build the resource compiler (*${TARGETCOMPLUS}/resourcecompiler.exe*) on Unix:

```
% cd ${ROTOR_DIR}/tools/resourcecompiler
% build
```

Building the PAL runtime

The PAL runtime supports high-level functionality that the SSCLI relies on. To build it (*%TARGETCOMPLUS%\rotor_palrt.dll*) on Windows:

```
>cd %ROTOR_DIR%\palrt\src
>build
```

To build the PAL runtime (*${TARGETCOMPLUS}/librotor_palrt.so* or *.dylib*) on Unix:

```
% cd ${ROTOR_DIR}/palrt/src
% build
```

Core Elements

After the primary and secondary bootstrap elements are built, you can build the core SSCLI implementation, C# compiler, and base class libraries. This section of the build is very complex due to interdependencies between the core CLI code, C#, and the base class libraries. This section includes the following:

%ROTOR_DIR%\clr\src\utilcode
Common shared C++ utility code

%ROTOR_DIR%\clr\src\vm
A large portion of the CLI execution engine

%ROTOR_DIR%\clr\src\fusion
Assembly searching and binding

%ROTOR_DIR%\clr\src\dlls
Unmanaged CLI support libraries

%ROTOR_DIR%\clr\src\ilasm
> The *ilasm* assembler tool

%ROTOR_DIR%\clr\src\ildasm
> The *ildasm* disassembly tool

%ROTOR_DIR%\clr\src\fjit
> The JIT-compiler implementation

%ROTOR_DIR%\clr\src\tools
> Supporting tools and utilities

%ROTOR_DIR%\clr\src\csharp
> The C# compiler

%ROTOR_DIR%\clr\src\bcl
> The base class libraries; these are the most fundamental managed-code assemblies

%ROTOR_DIR%\clr\src\toolbox
> Some additional managed tools

%ROTOR_DIR%\clr\src\md
> The metadata reader and writer

When making changes to any portion of this tree, you should rebuild the entire tree starting at %ROTOR_DIR%\clr\src. To build these core elements on Windows:

```
>cd %ROTOR_DIR%\clr\src
>build
```

To build them on Unix:

```
% cd ${ROTOR_DIR}/clr/src
% build
```

FX Class Libraries

This element includes the *System.dll* and *System.Xml.dll* managed-class libraries. Both DLLs are placed in the *%TARGETCOMPLUS%* directory.

System.dll
> To build *System.dll* (*%TARGETCOMPLUS%\System.dll*) on Windows:
> ```
> >cd %ROTOR_DIR%\fx\src\sys
> >build
> ```
> To build *System.dll* (*${TARGETCOMPLUS}/System.dll*) on Unix:
> ```
> % cd ${ROTOR_DIR}/fx/src/sys
> % build
> ```

System.Xml.dll

To build *System.Xml.dll* (%*TARGETCOMPLUS*%*System.Xml.dll*) on Windows:

```
>cd %ROTOR_DIR%\fx\src\xml
>build
```

To build *System.Xml.dll* (${*TARGETCOMPLUS*}/*System.Xml.dll*) on Unix:

```
% cd ${ROTOR_DIR}/fx/src/xml
% build
```

Managed-Class Libraries

The *System.Runtime.Serialization.Formatters.Soap.dll* and *System.Runtime. Remoting.dll* managed-class libraries are part of this element. Both DLLs are placed in the *%TARGETCOMPLUS%* directory.

System.Runtime.Serialization.Formatters.Soap.dll

To build *System.Runtime.Serialization.Formatters.Soap.dll* on Windows:

```
>cd %ROTOR_DIR%\managedlibraries\soapserializer
>build
```

To build it on Unix:

```
% cd ${ROTOR_DIR}/managedlibraries/soapserializer
% build
```

System.Runtime.Remoting.dll

To build *System.Runtime.Remoting.dll* on Windows:

```
>cd %ROTOR_DIR%\managedlibraries\remoting
>build
```

To build it on Unix:

```
% cd ${ROTOR_DIR}/managedlibraries/remoting
% build
```

Managed Compilers

The SSCLI includes a managed JScript compiler (*jsc.exe*). After it's built, it is placed in the *%TARGETCOMPLUS%* directory. To build *jsc.exe* on Windows:

```
>cd %ROTOR_DIR%\jscript
>build
```

To build it on Unix:

```
% cd ${ROTOR_DIR}/jscript
% build
```

Troubleshooting

This section lists some of the errors you may encounter building the SSCLI, and the corresponding solutions:

"C compiler cannot create executables"

You will encounter this error on Unix systems where the C compiler is not installed or not configured properly. On Mac OS X, you will need the Developer Tools (see "Mac OS X Prerequisites," earlier in this appendix). Under FreeBSD, you should have selected the Developer install when you installed the operating system (see "FreeBSD Prerequisites," earlier in this appendix).

"The type or namespace name 'SR' could not be found"

This indicates that Perl is not installed. For Windows, you can get Perl from *www.activestate.com*. Mac OS X includes Perl, and it will be installed on FreeBSD if you selected the Developer install during installation.

"conflicting types for 'PAL_vfprintf'"

You'll get this error on Mac OS X if you're using the gcc2 compiler instead of gcc3. gcc3 is the default on Mac OS X 10.2 (Jaguar). If you've changed your C compiler by executing the gcc_select 2 command, you must issue the command sudo gcc_select 3 to change it back to the default. To remove any cruft that may have accumulated while you were using the wrong compiler, run the command ./buildall -c from the root level of your *sscli* directory tree to rebuild everything from scratch.

"'mc.exe' is not recognized as an internal or external command"

You'll get this error on Windows if Visual Studio .NET is not installed. The current release of the SSCLI requires the full Visual Studio installation and can't be compiled using only the Framework SDK.

APPENDIX C

Porting Rotor

So, you're thinking of moving the SSCLI code base onto another operating system or targeting a hot new experimental processor. What is involved?

Besides basic portability hygiene, such as using the portability macros found *sscli/clr/src/inc/palclr.h* and the endian and CPU-specific conditional compilation switches, there are several areas of Rotor that present unique challenges. The PAL, the JIT compiler, and the execution engine each have code that must be modified for every port. To help you make these modifications, many of the spots that have platform-specific code have been written to compile correctly when moved to a new CPU platform, using conditionally compiled code that will either assert or issue a warning when run. The PORTABILITY_ASSERT and PORTABILITY_WARNING macros, defined in *clr/src/inc/palclr.h*, are used for this purpose, as follows:

```
#if defined(_X86_)
  _ASSERTE(SOMETHINGTOCHECK > SOMEVALUE);
  // x86 code here
#elif defined(_AMD64_) || defined(_PPC_)
  // other code here
#else
  PORTABILITY_ASSERT("Calling convention not specified for new platform");
#endif
```

Using *grep* or *findstr* to search for "PORTABILITY," "PPC," "UNIX," "APPLE," and other related strings will help find these spots, and indicate the size of the task at hand.

Also important to consider is the toolchain that you will be using: many small incompatibilities and differences exist between compilers (and even versions of the same compiler), and if you propose using a compiler that has never been used to compile Rotor, you may find yourself spending a lot of time fixing small, but infinitely frustrating, nits. Even things like filesystem characteristics are important: how mixed-case filenames, or filenames with unusual characters, are handled can make quite a difference. If your tool-chain or filesystem decisions demand new targets, the Rotor build process will need to be updated to accomodate this. The *rotorenv/bin* directory contains tools that may need to be modified as a part of your work, and the *env* scripts in the root directory, since they are the source of initial build parameters, will also likely need work. (The *env* scripts and the parameters that they set are well-documented in *docs/buildtools/env.html*.)

The PAL is the most conceptually straightforward area to scope when porting. If you intend to run on an operating system that is not yet supported, you'll need to tweak one of the existing PAL implementations or write a new one from scratch. Writing a new PAL is certainly possible, but the presence of a fairly complete test suite is a pretty compelling reason to modify the PAL that currently supports FreeBSD and Mac OS X. There is a specification in the Rotor distribution named *docs/techinfo/pal_guide.html* that should provide helpful clarification of PAL semantics and API subsetting issues.

While the PAL generally insulates Rotor from platform specifics, the one place where this is not accomplished is pathnames. The Unix PAL assumes that paths will be Unix-style, with the one exception that both \ and / are supported as path separators. All other Windows-specific filename and path conventions, including things like drive letters, Universal Naming Convention (UNC) paths, and predefined device names, are not supported. In most cases, the SSCLI and its tools based on the PAL do not process paths, but rather treat them as though they were opaque tokens.

The JIT compiler and execution engine stubs need to be modified and/or replaced when you are targeting a new chip, or when calling convention details due to compiler or operating system changes. The most obvious decisions to be made have to do with code generation, but there are a number of other interesting porting issues that must be considered when thinking about JIT compilation.

Because native calling conventions are used for JIT-compiled code, and because JIT-compiled code calls out to C/C++ code regularly, you must choose a calling convention as the foundation for your JIT implementation that matches a calling convention available to your C++ compiler, or else add substantial new interop code. The JIT compiler implementation uses macros to parameterize the calling convention selected, and these should be defined on a per-platform basis. See *clr/src/fjit/fjitcore.h* for details on this. Also important is the stack architecture: how will a new platform lay out activation records and arguments, and what registers will be used to manage the stack?

The JIT compiler itself was designed to use multiple layers of macros during its code generation, one for platform-specific code sequences and the other for portable, but possibly less efficient, sequences written in C. A quick port can be done by reimplementing a subset of the low-level macros and then incrementally tuning performance by adding more macro redefinitions. The high-level macros can be found in *clr/src/fjit/fjitdef.h*, while the low-level, platform-specific ones are in *clr/src/fjit/i386/x86def.h* and *clr/src/fjit/ppc/ppcdef.h*. High-level macros that have been tuned for the x86 can be found in *clr/src/fjit/i386/x86fjit.h*; the same could be done for the PowerPC or any other processor. The comments and organization of *fjitdef.h* and *fjitcore.h* should be very helpful when working with the existing JIT compiler. Code pitching is accomplished by the compiler using thunks, which need to be ported.

Of course, the JIT compiler also heavily depends on JIT helper functions and execution engine stubs, many of which are platform-dependent and implemented in assembler. Stubs are emitted dynamically at runtime, using a StubLinker. The templates used by the StubLinker, as well as implementations of some JIT helper functions can be found in the *clr/src/vm/i386* or *clr/src/vm/ppc* directories. Besides the obvious work involved in creating new versions of stub templates and helper functions for new processors, these implementations may also be platform-specific. For example, when calling through P/Invoke, the marshaling to be done will be sensitive to alignment conventions. Marshaling, security, delegate implementation, remoting, array operations, and the prestub are all areas where this may be true.

The execution engine uses several register-dependent structures internally, such as the CONTEXT and REGDISPLAY structures discussed in the "Stackwalking" section of Chapter 6. Modifications to these will potentially cause changes in exception handling, threading, and stackwalking (as well as the stubs already mentioned). Tools that involve manipulating these low-level mechanisms directly (particularly *cordbg*, in which single-stepping and breakpoints make extensive use of exceptions and the stack), will also demand significant work.

Given the three major variables that exist within the porting equation—toolchain, operating system, and/or type of processor—how much work will be involved? The amount of time needed to bring a new version online will vary wildly, of course, depending on what is changing, and whether it requires brand new code. A single developer, porting of the PAL to a slightly different x86-based Unix, or building support into the build system for a new compiler, might spend anywhere from a couple of weeks to three months on this task. Bringing up a new chip under the existing JIT compiler could easily take two or three months (and beware: the accompanying changes to the execution engine could easily take twice as long!). Plugging in a new JIT compiler or garbage collector might be slightly more achievable in short order but would demand familiarity with the dynamics of Rotor's runtime subsystems. As usual, when working in a large code base, bounding your work can be difficult!

However, Rotor was created specifically to enable this kind of experimentation. The build system and the tests will make your life easier, not to mention the code already written to support diverse targets. There are active mailing lists and web sites related to Rotor, and others have gone before you (and will be able to help). Have fun, and happy hacking!

Rotor Macrology

The Jargon Dictionary provides the following definition for "macrology":

> **macrology** (mak-rol'*-jee) *n.* 1. Set of usually complex or crufty macros, e.g., as part of a large system written in LISP, TECO, or (less commonly) assembler. 2. The art and science involved in comprehending a macrology in sense. 3. Sometimes studying the macrology of a system is not unlike archeology, ecology, or theology, hence the sound-alike construction. See also *boxology*.

When hacking or browsing Rotor's code, you will encounter a number of exotic (and not-so-exotic) macros sprinkled through the code. What follows is a FAQ-like catalog of some of the more important ones. This list should help you understand what the macros do, where you should use them, and where they can be found in the source code. It is by no means complete; consult the documentation that is part of the source code distribution, as well as the header files themselves, to get more information.

The developer documentation that ships with Microsoft's commercial version of the CLI will also be useful when chasing down API definitions. In particular, the SDK include files, which are documented in the Tool Developer's Guide (which can be found in a subdirectory of the SDK), contain information on the profiling, metadata, error, and debugging APIs that is applicable to Rotor, although it is not completely accurate. (Remember, Rotor was begun using the commercial code base but evolved significantly.) When conflicts in documentation arise, your very best documentation will be the SSCLI source code itself!

General Macros

_ASSERTE
> Defined in *clr/src/inc/debugmacros.h*, this is used to verify that an invariant holds true at runtime in debug-enabled builds.

`C_ASSERT`
`CPP_ASSERT`

These macros are used for language-specific compile-time assertions.

`DEFINE_LOG_FACILITY`

Defined in *clr/src/inc/loglf.h* to produce the list found in *clr/src/inc/loglf. h*, this is used to define facilities called out for individual configurability when tracing.

`GET_UNALIGNED_16`
`GET_UNALIGNED_32`
`GET_UNALIGNED_64`

Defined in *clr/src/inc/palclr.h*, these macros dereference a pointer and fetch a value, even if the pointer is not a naturally-aligned pointer. Natural alignment is defined as `((UINT_PTR)p & (sizeof(p)-1)) == 0`.

For platforms that automatically handle misaligned memory references, these macros expand to a simple dereference. See also `SET_UNALIGNED`.

`IfFailGoto`
`IfFailGo`
`IfFailRet`

Also defined in *clr/src/inc/debugmacros.h*, these are used to branch conditionally on `HRESULT` values.

`LOG`

Defined in *clr/src/inc/log.h*, this is used in debug-enabled builds to issue a logging message. See also `DEFINE_LOG_FACILITY`.

`MAKEDLLNAME_A`
`MAKEDLLNAME_W`

These macros are used to convert a platform-independent basename into a platform-specific loadable library name. They append the operating system-specific prefix and suffix to the generic name. For example, `MAKEDLLNAME_A("foo")` will create *libfoo.dylib* on Mac OS X, *libfoo.so* on FreeBSD, and *foo.dll* on Windows. These macros are defined in *clr/src/ inc/palclr.h*.

`OPDEF`

Use this macro, found in *clr/src/inc/openum.h*, to define CLI opcodes. The file *clr/src/inc/opcode.def* contains all opcode definitions for Rotor, and is shared by the C# compiler, the assembler and disassembler, and the execution engine.

`PORTABILITY_ASSERT`
`PORTABILITY_WARNING`

These are used within regions of code that differ from platform to platform. They are no-ops while working on a port, and once you've finished porting a platform-specific region, its WARNING should be changed to a matching ASSERT. To find regions of code that are platform-specific, use your favorite search or indexing utility to find these macros.

SET_UNALIGNED_16
SET_UNALIGNED_32
SET_UNALIGNED_64

Defined in *clr/src/inc/palclr.h*, these store a value into a pointer, even if the pointer is not naturally aligned. For platforms that automatically handle mis-aligned memory references, these macros expand to a simple dereferenced assignment. See also GET_UNALIGNED.

SwapString
SwapStringLength
SwapGuid

Defined in *clr/src/inc/palclr.h*, these perform an in-place byte swap of a string, counted string, or GUID structure.

VAL16

VAL32

VAL64

Defined in *clr/src/inc/palclr.h*, these are used to simplify writing code to run on both big-endian and little-endian processors. They are no-ops on little-endian platforms, but byte-swapped on big-endian platforms. Given a value composed of 16, 32, or 64 bits in little-endian format, they return the value in the native format.

Execution Engine Macros

BEGIN_FORBID
ENDFORBID

Defined in *clr/src/vm/threads.h*, these macros bracket code in which garbage collection is forbidden. They are activated in debug-enabled builds only.

COMPlusThrow

This macro, defined in *clr/src/vm/exceptmacros.h*, is used to throw exceptions from within execution engine code.

COMPLUS_TRY
COMPLUS_CATCH
COMPLUS_END_CATCH
COMPLUS_FINALLY
COMPLUS_END_FINALLY

These macros wrap the PAL_TRY family of macros with additional code that maintains internal execution engine data structures. In particular, these protect the integrity of the frame chain. They are defined in *clr/src/vm/exceptmacros.h*.

EE_TRY_FOR_FINALLY
EE_FINALLY
EE_END_FINALLY

This is a simplified version of the COMPLUS_TRY macro that supports only finally clauses. (COMPLUS_TRY supports both catch and finally clauses.) It is defined in *clr/src/vm/exceptmacros.h*.

FCDECL*
FCIMPL*

The macros from this large series, defined and documented in *clr/src/vm/fcall.h*, are used to declare and implement FCalls. Platform-to-platform differences in FCall calling conventions are encapsulated inside these macros.

FCThrow

This macro is used to throw exceptions from within FCall implementations when a helper frame is not erected for the FCall. (COMPlusThrow would be used to throw exceptions if a helper frame were erected.) It is defined in *clr/src/vm/frames.h*.

GCPROTECT_BEGIN
GCPROTECT_ARRAY_BEGIN
GCPROTECT_BEGININTERIOR
GCPROTECT_END

This series of macros is used to mark memory locations (usually local variables) that contain object references. Locations that are protected using GC_PROTECT are visible to the garbage collector, and the objects that they reference can be promoted safely. These macros are defined in *clr/src/vm/frames.h*.

GETTHROWABLE
SETTHROWABLE

Defined in *clr/src/vm/exceptmacros.h*, these macros are used to get or set the thrown exception. GETTHROWABLE is usually used inside a COMPLUS_CATCH clause.

HELPER_METHOD_FRAME_*

Defined in *clr/src/vm/fcall.h*, these macros are used to erect a helper frame within an FCall implementation. These helper frames must exist when an FCall wishes to call other parts of the execution engine that might trigger garbage collection or cause nonlocal changes. Simple FCalls do not need helper frames. Some flavors of HELPER_METHOD_FRAME expose a simplified version of GC_PROTECT, to reduce the number of frames pushed in the FCall.

THROWSCOMPLUSEXCEPTION

This macro, defined in *clr/src/vm/exceptmacros.h*, is used to mark code blocks that can throw exceptions. This is used only in debug-enabled builds.

TRIGGERSGC

This macro is used in debug-enabled builds to mark code blocks that can trigger garbage collection. It is defined in *clr/src/vm/threads.h*.

JIT Compiler Macros

The JIT compiler uses a large system of interrelated macros. The following verifier macros can be found in *clr/src/fjit/fjitverifier.h*:

CHECK_STACK
CHECK_STACK_SIZE

When verification is turned on, these macros will verify that the evaluation stack is deep enough to be valid or that it matches an exact depth.

FJIT_FAIL

This macro will cause the current JIT compilation to fail and return an error code.

VALIDITY_CHECK

If verification is turned on, this macro will conditionally terminate a JIT compilation and return an error code that indicates that invalid code was provided.

VERIFICATION_CHECK

If verification is turned on, this macro will conditionally emit code to throw a verification exception. It is used within the JIT compiler.

There is a large series of macros used to emit code, which is contained in *clr/src/fjit/fjitdef.h* and is augmented by platform-specific redefinition files that can be found in subdirectories named after their processor targets:

x86_*

These are low-level, x86-specific macros used by *fjitdef.h*.

---

ppc_*

These are low-level, PowerPC-specific macros used by *fjitdef.h*.

emit_*

These are high-level, macros defined in *fjitdef.h* that can be redefined by platform-specific low-level macros.

emit_<IL OPCODE NAME>_*

These are portable macros that implement opcodes, and are frequently separated by the size of the stack and frame registers.

ARG_*

These definitions represent argument registers.

RETURN_*

These definitions represent return value registers.

The file *clr/src/fjit/fjitdef.h* also contains macros used to emit code for manipulating the stack and calling helper functions:

deregisterTOS
enregisterTOS

These macros are used by the JIT compiler to manage the top of the stack.

emit_arg
emit_reg_arg
emit_tos_arg
emit_tos_fixedsize_arg
emit_tos_indirect_to_arg
emit_reg_to_arg

These simple portable calling convention macros are used by the JIT compiler to set up arguments being passed on the stack.

emit_callhelper_*

These macros represent a portable way to make a call to a helper function.

emit_loadresult_*
emit_pushresult_*

These macros manage return value placement. (The mechanism used to return values is platform-specific.)

Finally, there are a few JIT macros that affect the runtime execution of code:

LABELSTACK

This macro, defined in *clr/src/fjit/fjit.cpp*, saves the a map of the evaluation stack and associates it with the current IL offset so that the garbage collector will be able to find roots on the stack. This macro is used before calls to JIT helper functions that may trigger garbage collection.

```
THROW_FROM_HELPER
THROW_FROM_HELPER_RET
```
These macros define a mechanism by which JIT helper functions can construct an exception context as though the exception occurred within the code of the JIT-compiled function that called them rather than in their own code. They are defined in *clr/src/fjit/fjit.h*.

PAL and Platform Macros

The Unix PAL and the portions of the build that contain non-Windows code use a set of macros to probe for platform configuration. They are defined when a host operating system implements particular features, detailed and described in *pal/unix/configure.in*. These #defines include:

```
_PPC_
```
This is defined when compiling for Motorola PowerPC.

```
_X86_
```
This is defined when compiling for Intel x86.

```
BIGENDIAN
```
This is defined on big-endian platforms, and undefined on little-endian platforms.

```
HAVE_CASE_SENSITIVE_FILESYSTEM
```
This macro is defined to differentiate filesystems that are case-sensitive, such as FreeBSD, from filesystems that are case-insensitive, such as Windows or HFS+, the default and most frequently used Mac OS X filesystem.

```
HAVE_CFSTRING
```
This is defined if Mac OS X CoreFoundation CFString is present.

```
HAVE_COMPATIBLE_ASIN
HAVE_COMPATIBLE_ACOS
HAVE_COMPATIBLE_*
```
This is defined when C runtime math functions produce Windows-compatible results for edge-case values.

```
HAVE_POLL
```
This is defined if the poll( ) system call is implemented.

```
HAVE_STRTOK_R
```
This is defined if the strok_r( ) API is implemented.

```
MMAP_IGNORES_HINT
```
This is set when the mmap( ) system call ignores its hint argument.

```
PAL_TRY
PAL_EXCEPT
PAL_EXCEPT_EX
PAL_EXCEPT_FILTER
PAL_EXCEPT_FILTER_EX
PAL_FINALLY
PAL_FINALLY_EX
PAL_ENDTRY
```

The file *pal/rotor_pal.h* contains the API definitions for the PAL, as well as these macros, which result in calls against the PAL's exception-handling mechanism.

PLATFORM_UNIX

This is defined when building for Unix systems, and is used to control the formatting of things dictated by convention, such as line breaks, path and environment separator characters, and the like.

There are a number of macros used within the Unix PAL implementation:

ASSERT

This macro is different from the Win32 PAL and execution engine ASSERT macros in that it doesn't take an expression as an argument. It is a printf-style logger plus an optional debug breakpoint. This is a no-op in the "free" build.

LOGAPI

This is a printf-style logging call for the PAL. It is a no-ops in the "free" build.

PALASSERT

This macro asserts if its argument is false and is a no-op in the "free" build.

TRACE
WARN
ERROR

These printf-style logging calls are defined in *pal/unix/include/dbgmsg.h* and are no-ops in the "free" build.

Index

We'd like to hear your suggestions for improving our indexes. Send email to *index@oreilly.com*.

About the Authors

David Stutz is currently working on the team that is implementing the Microsoft Shared Source CLI. He is also well-known for his kibitzing on the design of peer-to-peer and distributed computing infrastructure. During his tenure at Microsoft and Microsoft Research, he has participated in designing programming languages, component technologies, operating systems, developer tools, and a whole lot of software plumbing. He is also an accomplished early music performer and a wine grape farmer.

Ted Neward is an independent software development architect and mentor in the Sacramento, California area. He is the author of a number of books, including *Server-Based Java Programming* (Manning) and the forthcoming *Effective Enterprise Java* (Addison-Wesley), and coauthor of *C# in a Nutshell* (O'Reilly) with Peter Drayton and Ben Albahari. He is also an instructor with DevelopMentor, where he teaches and authors both the Java and .NET curriculum. He speaks frequently for technology user groups and writes technical papers for *www.javageeks.com* and *www.cirgeeks.com*. He currently labors on behalf of the University of California, Davis, architecting a rebuild of the Davis Accounting and Financial Information Services software system. Past clients include companies such as Pacific Bell, Edfund, Synergex, and Intuit.

Geoff Shilling is a product unit manager at Microsoft Corporation, currently leading the Shared Source CLI project. During his career at Microsoft, Geoff has been tester, developer, and manager, shipping five versions of C, one version of FORTRAN, and three versions of Visual Basic. When not building development tools, Geoff is frequently found at a loom weaving or in the shop building another boat.

Colophon

Our look is the result of reader comments, our own experimentation, and feedback from distribution channels. Distinctive covers complement our distinctive approach to technical topics, breathing personality and life into potentially dry subjects.

The animal on the cover of *Shared Source CLI Essentials* is an African openbill and is found in Africa, south of the Sahara and Madagascar. When its bill is closed, there is a gap between the two mandibles, and this is thought to be an adaptation for holding the large water snails, which form a major part of their diet.

Sarah Sherman was the production editor and copyeditor for *Shared Source CLI Essentials*. Matt Hutchinson was the proofreader and provided quality control. Mary Anne Weeks Mayo, Darren Kelly, and Claire Cloutier provided quality control. John Bickelhaupt wrote the index.

Emma Colby designed the cover of this book, based on a series design by Edie Freedman. The cover image is a 19th-century engraving from the Dover Pictorial Archive. Emma Colby produced the cover layout with Quark-XPress 4.1 using Adobe's ITC Garamond font. David Futato designed and produced the CD label with QuarkXPress 4.1 using Adobe's ITC Garamond font.

David Futato designed the interior layout. This book was converted by Mike Sierra to FrameMaker 5.5.6 with a format conversion tool created by Erik Ray, Jason McIntosh, Neil Walls, and Mike Sierra that uses Perl and XML technologies. The text font is Linotype Birka; the heading font is Adobe Myriad Condensed; and the code font is LucasFont's TheSans Mono Condensed. The illustrations that appear in the book were produced by Robert Romano and Jessamyn Read using Macromedia FreeHand 9 and Adobe Photoshop 6. The tip and warning icons were drawn by Christopher Bing. This colophon was written by Sarah Sherman.

Other Titles Available from O'Reilly

Microsoft .NET Programming

VB.NET Language in a Nutshell, 2nd Edition

By Steven Roman, Ron Petrusha & Paul Lomax
2nd Edition May 2002
682 pages, ISBN 0-596-00308-0

The documentation that comes with VB typically provides only the bare details for each language element; left out is the valuable inside information that a programmer really needs to know in order to solve programming problems or to use a particular language element effectively. *VB .NET Language in a Nutshell*, 2nd Edition documents the undocumented and presents the kind of wisdom that comes from the authors' many years of experience with the language. Bonus CD ingegrates the book's reference section with Visual Studio .NET.

Programming C#, 2nd Edition

By Jesse Liberty
2nd Edition February 2002
650 pages, ISBN 0-596-00309-9

The first part of *Programming C#*, 2nd Edition introduces C# fundamentals, then goes on to explain the development of desktop and Internet applications, including Windows Forms, ADO.NET, ASP.NET (including Web Forms), and Web Services. Next, this book gets to the heart of the .NET Framework, focusing on attributes and reflection, remoting, threads and synchronization, streams, and finally, it illustrates how to interoperate with COM objects.

Learning Visual Basic .NET

By Jesse Liberty
1st Edition October 2002
320 pages, ISBN 0-596-00386-2

Learning Visual Basic .NET is a complete introduction to VB.NET and object-oriented programming. By using hundreds of examples, this book demonstrates how to develop various kinds of applications—including those that work with databases—and web services. *Learning Visual Basic .NET* will help you build a solid foundation in .NET.

Programming ASP.NET

By Jesse Liberty & Dan Hurwitz
1st Edition February 2002
960 pages, ISBN 0-596-00171-1

The ASP.NET technologies are so complete and flexible; your main difficulty may lie simply in weaving the pieces together for maximum efficiency. *Programming ASP.NET* shows you how to do just that. Jesse Liberty and Dan Hurwitz teach everything you need to know to write web applications and web services using both C# and Visual Basic .NET.

C# in a Nutshell

By Peter Drayton & Ben Albarhari
1st Edition March 2002
856 pages, ISBN 0-596-00181-9

C# is likely to become one of the most widely used languages for building .NET applications. *C# in a Nutshell* contains a concise introduction to the language and its syntax, plus brief tutorials used to accomplish common programming tasks. It also includes O'Reilly's classic-style, quick-reference material for all the types and members in core .NET namespaces, including System, System.Text, System.IO, and System.Collections.

ASP.NET in a Nutshell

By G. Andrew Duthie & Matthew MacDonald
1st Edition June 2002
816 pages, ISBN 0-596-00116-9

As a quick reference and tutorial in one, *ASP.NET in a Nutshell* goes beyond the published documentation to highlight little-known details, stress practical uses for particular features, and provide real-world examples that show how features can be used in a working application. This book covers application and web service development, custom controls, data access, security, deployment, and error handling. There is also an overview of web-related class libraries.

O'REILLY®

To order: 800-998-9938 • order@oreilly.com • www.oreilly.com
Online editions of most O'Reilly titles are available by subscription at safari.oreilly.com
Also available at most retail and online bookstores.

Microsoft .NET Programming

.NET Framework Essentials, 2nd Edition

By Thuan L. Thai & Hoang Lam
2nd Edition February 2002
320 pages, 0-596-00302-1

.NET Framework Essentials, 2nd Edition is a concise and technical overview of the Microsoft .NET Framework. Covered here are all of the most important topics—from the underlying Common Language Runtime (CLR) to its specialized packages for ASP.NET, Web Forms, Windows Forms, XML and data access (ADO.NET). The authors survey each of the major .NET languages, including Visual Basic .NET, C# and Managed C++.

Learning C#

By Jesse Liberty
1st Edition September 2002
368 pages, ISBN 0-596-00376-5

With *Learning C#*, best-selling author Jesse Liberty will help you build a solid foundation in .NET and show how to apply your skills by using dozens of tested examples. You will learn how to develop various kinds of applications—including those that work with databases—and web services. Whether you have a little object-oriented programming experience or you are new to programming altogether, *Learning C#* will set you firmly on your way.

COM and .NET Component Services

By Juval Löwy
1st Edition September 2001
384 pages, 0-596-00103-7

COM & .NET Component Services provides both traditional COM programmers and new .NET component developers with the information they need to begin developing applications that take full advantage of COM+ services. This book focuses on COM+ services, including support for transactions, queued components, events, concurrency management, and security.

VB.NET Core Classes in a Nutshell

By Budi Kurniawan
1st Edition May 2002
576 pages, ISBN 0-596-00257-2

VB.NET Core Classes in a Nutshell, provides a concise and thorough reference to the types found in the core namespaces of the .NET Framework Class Library. A companion to *VB.NET Language in a Nutshell*, this is a reference that VB.NET programmers will turn to repeatedly. Due to a special partnership between O'Reilly and Microsoft, this book also includes a CD that integrates the book's reference into Visual Studio .NET.

Programming .NET Web Services

By Alex Ferrara
& Matthew MacDonald
1st Edition October 2002
414 pages, ISBN 0-596-00250-5

This comprehensive tutorial teaches programmers the skills they need to develop XML web services hosted on the Microsoft .NET platform. *Programming .NET Web Services* also shows you how to consume these services on both Microsoft and non-Windows clients, and how to weave them into well-designed and scalable applications. For those interested in building industrial-strength web services, this book is full of practical information and good old-fashioned advice.

Object-Oriented Programming with Visual Basic .NET

By J.P. Hamilton
1st Edition September 2002
308 pages, ISBN 0-596-00146-0

Visual Basic .NET is a language that facilitates object-oriented programming, but does not guarantee good code. That's where *Object-Oriented Programming with Visual Basic .NET* comes in. It will show you how to think about similarities in your application logic and how to design and create objects that maximize the benefit and power of .NET. Packed with examples that will guide you through every step, *Object-Oriented Programming with Visual Basic .NET* is for those with some programming experience.

O'REILLY®

To order: *800-998-9938* • *order@oreilly.com* • *www.oreilly.com*
Online editions of most O'Reilly titles are available by subscription at *safari.oreilly.com*
Also available at most retail and online bookstores.

How to stay in touch with O'Reilly

1. Visit our award-winning web site

http://www.oreilly.com/

★ "Top 100 Sites on the Web"—PC Magazine
★ CIO Magazine's Web Business 50 Awards

Our web site contains a library of comprehensive product information (including book excerpts and tables of contents), downloadable software, background articles, interviews with technology leaders, links to relevant sites, book cover art, and more. File us in your bookmarks or favorites!

2. Join our email mailing lists

Sign up to get email announcements of new books and conferences, special offers, and O'Reilly Network technology newsletters at:

http://elists.oreilly.com

It's easy to customize your free elists subscription so you'll get exactly the O'Reilly news you want.

3. Get examples from our books

To find example files for a book, go to:

http://www.oreilly.com/catalog

select the book, and follow the "Examples" link.

4. Work with us

Check out our web site for current employment opportunites:

http://jobs.oreilly.com/

5. Register your book

Register your book at:
http://register.oreilly.com

6. Contact us

O'Reilly & Associates, Inc.
1005 Gravenstein Hwy North
Sebastopol, CA 95472 USA
TEL: 707-827-7000 or 800-998-9938
         (6am to 5pm PST)
FAX: 707-829-0104

order@oreilly.com
For answers to problems regarding your order or our products. To place a book order online visit:

http://www.oreilly.com/order_new/

catalog@oreilly.com
To request a copy of our latest catalog.

booktech@oreilly.com
For book content technical questions or corrections.

corporate@oreilly.com
For educational, library, government, and corporate sales.

proposals@oreilly.com
To submit new book proposals to our editors and product managers.

international@oreilly.com
For information about our international distributors or translation queries. For a list of our distributors outside of North America check out:

http://international.oreilly.com/distributors.html

adoption@oreilly.com
For information about academic use of O'Reilly books, visit:

http://academic.oreilly.com

O'REILLY®